Longman Critical Readers

General Editor:
STAN SMITH, Research Professor in Literary Studies, Nottingham Trent University

Modern Genre Theory

Contents

Preface

This anthology evolved slowly, and its contents have been influenced by a number of people whose advice and encouragement I very gratefully acknowledge. My idea for a collection of modern writings on genre originated during my residence in Poland, where I had the good fortune to work in an English department which embodied some of the strongest theoretical traditions of Eastern Europe. My initial debt, then, is to my former colleagues at the University of Gdańsk, in particular Andrzej Zgorzelski and Joanna Kokot, who shared and deepened my interest in genre theory, and alerted me to important Polish contributions in this field. My thanks, too, to David Malcolm, who agreed to translate the essay of Ireneusz Opacki which appears in this volume, and whose career, like mine, has spanned Gdańsk and Aberdeen. My colleagues, and former colleagues, at Aberdeen have been similarly supportive of this project. I am particularly grateful to Paul Coates, whose sophisticated command of theory and intimate knowledge of Polish he generously put at my disposal; to George Rousseau, who commented very perceptively on a draft of the Introduction and, over a series of conversations, answered a host of other queries; to Ian Maclachlan, Michael Syrotinski and other members of the Aberdeen Critical Theory Seminar, who responded enthusiastically to an exploratory paper I gave, and made some valuable suggestions; to Gert Ronberg, who helped me on linguistic matters; and to Frank Krutnik and Liz Mahoney, who gave useful advice on other aspects of my topic. Jean Gregorek, from further afield, performed a similar service; as did Graham Allen, with whom I conversed profitably on the subject of intertextuality. I warmly acknowledge too the personal and intellectual hospitality I received in 1996 during a visit to the University of Regensburg, where I discussed plans for this anthology, and received expert guidance on German genre theory. Thanks also to Ann Shukman, who translated the Tynyanov essay, and shared her knowledge of Russian Formalism; and to the Faculty Research Committee at the University of Aberdeen, who allocated funds which paid for this and the Opacki translation. Stan Smith has been a most responsive general editor, and Liz Mann an equally courteous publisher; my gratitude to them extends to members of the production staff at Longman, and to my excellent copy-editor, Katy Coutts. Finally, I must thank Helen Lynch, whose passion for this subject is not as great as my own, but who occasionally brought to bear her intelligence upon it; and our two lovely daughters, Konstancja and Miriam, both of whom learnt to pronounce the word 'genre' not long after the word 'daddy' – which is no mean achievement.

David Duff
Aberdeen
March 1999

Acknowledgements

We are grateful to the following for permission to reproduce
copyright material:

Cambridge University Press for 'The Origin of Genre' by Tzvetan
Todorov in GENRES IN DISCOURSE, translated by Catherine Porter,
1990; Cornell University Press/Taylor & Francis for 'Magical
Narratives: On the Dialectical Use of Genre Criticism' by Fredric
Jameson in THE POLITICAL UNCONSCIOUS: NARRATIVE AS A
SOCIALLY SYMBOLIC ACT (published by Routledge 1981);
Christopher Busby, the author's agent for 'Transformations of Genre'
by Alastair Fowler in KINDS OF LITERATURE: AN INTRODUCTION
TO THE THEORY OF GENRES AND MODES. Published by Oxford
University Press, 1982. © Alastair Fowler 1982; Johns Hopkins
University Press for 'The Law of Genre' by Jacque Derrida in GLYPH
7 Weber, Gl hVII pp. 202–13. © 1980 Johns Hopkins University Press;
Macmillan Press Ltd/St Martin's Press Inc for an extract from 'Genre
and Gender' by Mary Eagleton in RE-READING THE SHORT STORY
edited by Clare Hanson. Copyright © Clare Hanson; The Editor,
Latislav Matejka for 'Fairy Tale Transformations' by Vladimir Propp
in READINGS IN RUSSIAN POETICS: FORMALIST AND
STRUCTURALIST VIEWS ed. Ladislav Matejka and Krystyna
Pomorska (trans. C. H. Severens); Nauka and the translator,
Ann Shukman for 'The Literary Fact' in POETIKA, ISTORIYA
LITERATURY KINO (1977) by Yury Tynyanov (first published 1924);
Ossolineum, the author, Ireneusz Opacki and translator David
Malcolm for 'Royal Genres' from PROBLEMY TEORII LITERATURY
by Ireneusz Opacki. 2nd edition, ed. H. Markiewicz. First published
in PAMIETNIK LITERACKI, 54:4; Peter Owen Ltd London for an
extract from 'Criticism of the Theory of Artistic and Literary Kinds'
in AESTHETIC AS A SCIENCE OF EXPRESSION AND GENERAL
LINGUISTIC by Benedetto Croce, trans. Douglas Ainslie, 2nd edition
1953; Princeton University Press for 'The Mythos of Summer:
Romance' in ANATOMY OF CRITICISM: FOUR ESSAYS by Northrop
Frye, 1957. Copyright © 1957, renewed 1985 by Princeton University
Press; University of California Press for extracts from 'Genre-Systems
and the Functions of Literature' by Rosalie Colie in THE
RESOURCES OF KIND: GENRE-THEORY IN THE RENAISSANCE
(1973) and 'The Architext' by Gérard Genette from THE ARCHITEXT:
AN INTRODUCTION, trans J. E. Lewin, 1992 © Editions du Seuil

1979; University of Minnesota Press for extracts & notes from 'Theory of Genres & Medieval Literature' in *TOWARD AN AESTHETIC OF RECEPTION* by Hans Robert Jauss, trans. Timothy Bahti (1982); University of Texas Press for extracts from 'Epic Novel: Toward a Methodology for the Study of the Novel' by Michael Bakhtin in *THE DIALOGIC IMAGINATION: FOUR ESSAYS* by M. M. Bakhtin, edited by Michael Holquist. Copyright © 1981 by University of Texas Press; University of Texas Press for extracts from 'The Problem of Speech Genres' in *SPEECH GENRES AND OTHER LATE ESSAYS* by M. M. Bakhtin, translated by Vern W. McGee, edited by Caryl Emerson & Michael Holquist. Copyright © 1986 University of Texas Press.

Key Concepts

ARCHETYPE   A recurrent pattern or motif which derives from ancient myth or ritual, and ultimately from a universal 'grammar' of the human imagination. Although archetypes are not specifically literary phenomena, the concept has featured in several modern theories of genre, most strikingly in the work of Northrop Frye.

ARCHITEXT   Gérard Genette's term for overarching textual categories such as genres and modes. Architextuality is the most abstract and general of the five types of transtextual relationship defined by Genette in his book *Palimpsests* (1998), the four others being **intertextuality**, paratextuality, metatextuality and hypertextuality. For brief explanations of these terms, see headnote to Chapter 12, below.

AUTOMATIZATION (also known as **habitualization**)   The process whereby literary devices or entire genres lose their potency and cease to be perceived as artistic entities as a result of formulaic repetition and over-familiarity. The artistic potency and perceptibility of a genre or device can sometimes be restored through acts of **defamiliarization** such as parody or other kinds of **transformation**.

CANONIZATION   The process whereby a genre acquires cultural recognition or prestige through inclusion within a select list or 'canon' of highly valued genres. In Russian Formalist theory, the 'canonization of the junior branch' is the process whereby a previously marginal genre or subgenre moves up the hierarchy of genres to assume a position of influence or dominance over other genres. For Mikhail Bakhtin, however, the term canonization is normally pejorative, this being another form of **automatization**, and the price of official acceptance being the loss of a genre's subversive potential.

CHRONOTOPE   The distinctive perception of time and space, and of their relation to one another, that is characteristic of a particular genre or historical epoch. A term from theoretical physics adopted and redefined by Mikhail Bakhtin.

CONVENTION   A stylistic or formal device, or element of subject matter, which is characteristic of a particular genre or period. Traditionally, conventions are defined as tacit agreements between author and reader (or audience) that make possible certain types of artistic representation of reality (as, for example, in the Elizabethan theatrical convention of the soliloquy). In Neoclassical poetics, such conventions were usually expressed prescriptively in terms of generic 'rules'. In structuralist genre theory, however, the term is extended to cover the systems of rules or 'codes' that underlie the production of *all* meaning, the assimilation – often unconscious – of these conventions being the basis of what Jonathan Culler calls a reader's **literary competence** (*Structuralist Poetics* (1975), pp. 113–30).

COUNTER-GENRE   A genre or subgenre that develops in implicit or explicit opposition to an existing genre: for example, 'anti-pastoral', or various kinds of novel which defined themselves against romance. The term was coined by Claudio Guillén.

DECORUM   In classical and Neoclassical poetics, the principle that each element of a literary genre, including subject matter, characters, action and style, should match one another in an appropriate way. Implicit in this doctrine is the idea that genres and styles are ordered hierarchically, and that the hierarchy of literary genres should reflect and maintain social hierarchies.

DEFAMILIARIZATION   The process by which literary works challenge and refresh our habitual perceptions of the world – and of language itself – by using words in unfamiliar ways, or by other artistic devices for slowing down and intensifying the reader's perception. Individual genres possess their own repertoire of defamiliarizing devices, but are themselves subject to the same law, and can only retain their artistic potency by constantly transforming or 'evolving', a process sometimes accelerated by means of parody. The opposite of defamiliarization (a term coined by Viktor Shklovsky) is **automatization** or **habitualization.**

DEVICE   Any element of a literary text which has a discrete artistic function (though that function may change in different contexts, and such devices normally work in conjunction rather than isolation). In early Russian Formalist theory, a literary work is defined as the 'sum of its devices', and a genre as a repertoire of more or less standardised devices: the device which 'focuses' a given work or genre by subordinating other elements is assigned the name of the **dominant**.

DISPLACEMENT   Northrop Frye's term for the 'adaptation of myth and metaphor to canons of morality or plausibility' (*Anatomy of Criticism*, p. 365): in Frye's account, part of the process by which ancient myths and rituals evolve into literary genres, and then undergo subsequent shifts towards realism. The term has other, largely unrelated, meanings in psychoanalysis, linguistics and deconstruction.

DOMINANT   The device or constructional principle which serves as 'the focusing component of a work of art: it rules, determines, and transforms the remaining components' (Roman Jakobson, 'The Dominant', in *Language in Literature* (1987), p. 41). Not only individual works, but also entire genres can be seen to possess such a dominant; and, by extension, a dominant genre or (Ireneusz Opacki's synonym) **royal genre** is a genre which performs a similar role within the **genre-system**, colouring and transforming the other genres which surround it. In different periods, one royal genre may be superseded by another, such shifts in the **hierarchy of genres** being a principal mechanism of literary **evolution**.

EVOLUTION   A metaphor widely used in modern genre theory to denote the process by which literary genres (and other elements of literature) change across time. Some theorists extend this biological metaphor by describing the mechanisms of literary evolution in quasi-Darwinian terms: the 'competition' of genres, their 'struggle for survival', their 'fitness' to their environment, the possibility of 'extinction'. Sudden changes are sometimes characterised by the complementary metaphor of revolution.

FORM   Often used synonymously with **genre** to mean simply a type or category of literary work (sonnet, novel, tragedy, etc.); but genre theorists also distinguish between the form and function of a given genre, and – a less reliable distinction – between its form and content (that is, its structural as distinct from thematic characteristics). Another common distinction, central to Romantic theory, is between 'mechanical' and 'organic form', the former being the fixed, pre-established form imposed by generic rules, and the latter the individual form generated by the internal forces within a literary work. Historically, the development of the notion of organic form contributed to the decline of Neoclassical genre theory.

GENERICITY   The condition of belonging to a genre, or the elements of a given text that are modelled by genre. Jean-Marie Shaeffer, who coined the term (by analogy with Jakobson's 'poeticity', meaning that which makes poetry 'poetic'), further distinguishes between analytical and synthetic genericity, the former being a relation to genre which is mediated by explicit rules or prescriptions, the latter a generic relation arising from contact with specific textual models.

GENOLOGY   The branch of literary theory that is concerned with the study of genres. A term coined by Paul Van Tieghem in the 1930s, but now rarely used.

GENRE   A recurring type or category of text, as defined by structural, thematic and/or functional criteria. A term increasingly used in the classification of non-literary (and non-written) as well as literary texts; notably films and media programmes. The linguistic concept of **speech genre** represents a further extension of the term. In a second sense, the term is often used, sometimes pejoratively, to denote types of popular fiction in which a high degree of standardisation is apparent: for instance, detective stories, historical romances, spy thrillers and science fiction. These are collectively known as 'genre fiction', as distinct from more 'serious', highbrow fiction. In a third and unrelated sense, the term 'genre painting' is used in art history to denote a type of painting whose subject matter is drawn from ordinary life rather than from history or mythology.

GENRE-CONSCIOUSNESS   The awareness of genre displayed by a particular author or period: an awareness which has both a conscious component, manifest in the explicit use made of generic categories and terminology by writers, critics, booksellers, publishers, librarians and other cultural institutions; and an unconscious element, suggested by the attempts of many writers, readers and critics, especially in the modern era, to conceal or repress their dependence on genre. The forms which genre-consciousness takes, and the intensity with which it is experienced, are subject to both personal and historical variation.

GENRE-SYSTEM   A set of genres that is understood to form a coherent system of some kind; or a theoretical model that offers a comprehensive list of genres and an explanation of the relations between them. Theories of genre have always tended to have a systematic character (hence one can speak of 'the Aristotelian genre-system', 'the Neoclassical genre-system', etc.), but the metaphor of system has been particularly prominent in modern genre theory, partly through the influence of structural linguistics, which had revolutionised linguistics by conceiving of language as a system of differences. Some theorists refine the metaphor by specifying that genre-systems are *dynamic* rather than *static* systems, since the relations between genres, like genres themselves, are constantly changing; and because the relationship is often one of conflict (i.e. genres compete rather than peacefully co-exist). The metaphor of system is also sometimes applied to individual genres, or to individual works. See also **hierarchy of genres**.

HABITUALIZATION   See **automatization**

HIERARCHY OF GENRES   A set of genres understood as a hierarchy of differently ranked categories. Like other classification systems, most genre theories are explicitly hierarchical, but the criteria by which the hierarchy of genres has been defined have varied widely. Aristotle's *Poetics*, for example, ranked literary genres according to three main criteria: size, formal complexity, and the social rank of the characters represented. Russian Formalism, on the other hand, ranks genres mainly according to the power that they have to influence other genres. In other contexts, very different hierarchies have been established on the basis of, for instance, sales figures or audience ratings. Opinion has also varied as to the degree of stability within the hierarchy of genres: broadly, classical and Neoclassical genre theory assumed that the hierarchy is static, modern genre theory that it is variable. See also **genre-system**.

HISTORICAL/THEORETICAL GENRES   A distinction made by Tzvetan Todorov between genres which have actually existed (or continue to exist), and those which are theoretically possible.

HYBRIDIZATION   The process by which two or more genres combine to form a new genre or subgenre; or by which elements of two or more genres are combined in a single work.

INTERNALIZATION   The process by which, at a certain stage in its historical development, a genre becomes a vehicle for authorial self-reflection: a complex development which, in the case of many genres, occurred in the Romantic period. This concept is associated particularly with the work of Harold Bloom.

INTERTEXTUALITY   The relationship between a given text and other texts which it cites, assimilates or transforms; or the branch of literary studies which examines such relationships. In its broadest and most radical definition (that of Julia Kristeva, who coined the term, having derived the concept from her reading of Mikhail Bakhtin), the term denotes any relationship, implicit or explicit, between two or more texts or 'signifying systems', including relationships constituted by genre. Other theorists, notably Gérard Genette, restrict the term to relationships involving the explicit presence of one discrete text in another, as specified by traditional critical terms like source, echo, allusion, plagiarism. See also **architext**.

KIND   An archaic term for **genre**. Crudely summarised, 'kind' was the standard term in the Renaissance, 'species of composition' in the eighteenth century, and 'genre' in the twentieth century; though Alastair Fowler's *Kinds of Literature* (1982) is a notable attempt to revive the Renaissance term.

LITERARY COMPETENCE   See **convention**

MODE   A term which, confusingly, is used in two almost opposite senses in modern genre theory: to denote the manner of representation or enunciation in a literary work (the three basic modes, in this sense, being the narrative, the dramatic and the lyrical – though the validity of this triad has been questioned); and to denote more strictly literary categories such as the tragic, the comic, or the pastoral, which are thematically specific but *non*-specific as to literary form or mode of representation. In this second sense, a mode is often distinguished from a **genre**, the latter term being reserved for types of literature which are both thematically *and* formally specific: tragedy as distinct from the tragic, comedy as distinct from the comic, etc.

MORPHOLOGICAL GENRE THEORY   A term occasionally applied to the ideas of the Russian Formalists (who sometimes styled themselves 'the Morphological School') and their successors, but more commonly associated with German approaches to genre derived from a combination of two seminal concepts in the work of Johann Wolfgang von Goethe: his notion of 'morphology', the quasi-evolutionary thesis that all forms of life represent transformations of basic 'ur-types'; and the notion of *Naturformen*, the idea that epic, lyric and drama are the three 'natural forms', as distinct from ordinary poetic species (*Dichtarten*) such as the epigram, the ode and the novel.

PRIMARY/SECONDARY GENRES   A distinction made by Mikhail Bakhtin between relatively simple, everyday genres (primary genres) such as letters, diaries, anecdotes and jokes, and more complex and highly developed genres (secondary genres) such as novels, dramas and scientific papers; the latter being formed, in many cases, through an assimilation and transformation of the former. Similar distinctions (simple/complex, minor/major, micro/macro) are often made by other genre theorists.

ROYAL GENRE   See **dominant**

SOCIOLOGY OF GENRE   A critical methodology which examines the social and economic factors affecting the production and reception of literary (or other) genres. A particular concern of such approaches is the ideological character and function of literary genres, a notion sometimes expressed in the phrase 'politics of genre'.

SPEECH GENRE   A type of oral utterance or speech situation which is governed by recognisable conventions or 'codes', such as greetings, interviews, committee meetings, conference speeches, proposals of marriage. The systematic study of 'speech genres' is a very recent development in applied linguistics, but the term was already being used in the 1950s by Mikhail Bakhtin, who made the radical claim that we *always* employ speech genres, that is, *all* our utterances 'have relatively stable typical forms' (below, p. 89).

STREET GENRES   Extra-literary genres such as the pamphlet, the newsbook, the broadside ballad and the playground rhyme, which exist outside the official **hierarchy of genres**, and have often been classified as ephemera.

SUBGENRE   A type or class of text which is identifiable as a subclass or offshoot of a larger category; for instance, the epistolary novel, the *Bildungsroman* and the historical novel are all subgenres of the novel, and the pastoral elegy a subgenre of both pastoral verse and elegy. Less commonly, the term is used to express a value judgement, a subgenre in this sense being a type of text that exists outside a given canon, or low on a **hierarchy of genres**.

TRANSFORMATION   In modern genre theory, a term used in two related but distinct senses: to denote a significant modification of a genre in the course of its historical development; and to denote a particular realisation of a basic generic model. The former is a diachronic concept, the latter synchronic. An example of a diachronic use of the term is Alastair Fowler's essay (Chapter 14), which seeks to identify the main processes of generic change; Vladimir Propp (Chapter 3), on the other hand, uses the term in both a synchronic and a diachronic sense: to enumerate the different forms in which the same narrative motifs or functions can manifest themselves across a range of texts, and to define the types of mutation or substitution which give rise to those differences.

Introduction

> I am a comic writer. You have to submit to the huge power of the
> genre you are in. Genre really does determine outcomes.
>
> Martin Amis[1]

In modern literary theory, few concepts have proved more problematic
and unstable than that of genre. Having functioned since Aristotle as
a basic assumption of Western literary discourse, shaping critical
theory and creative practice for more than two thousand years, the
notion of genre is one whose meaning, validity and purpose have
been repeatedly questioned in the last two hundred. Although Henry
James could still speak in 1908 of the literary 'kinds' as being 'the
very life of literature',[2] the modern period has been more typically
characterised by a steady erosion of the perception of genre, and by
the emergence of aesthetic programmes which have sought to dispense
altogether with the doctrine of literary kinds or genres. If the death
of the author has been a familiar refrain of modern literary theory, so
too has the dissolution of genres, an apparently liberating ambition
that links the otherwise radically opposed poetics of Romanticism
and Modernism, attracting authors, readers and critics alike. To the
modern ear, the word genre – in the sphere of literature at least –
carries unmistakable associations of authority and pedantry. Even
when there is no mention of 'rules' or 'conventions' (its usual corollary),
the term seems almost by definition to deny the autonomy of the author,
deny the uniqueness of the text, deny spontaneity, originality and
self-expression. Most of us have an instinctive or ideological attachment
to one or more of these values, and most of us are therefore at some
level resistant to, or suspicious of, the concept of genre.

As we enter the twenty-first century, however, there are indications
that this resistance is beginning to abate. The anti-generic tendencies
of Romanticism and Modernism have given way to an aesthetic stance
which is more hospitable to notions of genre, and which no longer
sees as incompatible the pursuit of individuality and the espousal of
'generic' identities, of whatever sort. This may have something to do

with the elevation of popular culture which is so conspicuous a
feature of Postmodernism,[3] involving as it does a recognition that a
much more favourable estimate of the value of genre has always
prevailed in the popular sphere, despite the apparent rejection of the
concept by the literary avant-garde. At the same time, the increasing
cultural dominance of the popular genres themselves (in literature,
film and television), and of the labels and labelling systems that
accompany them, have ensured that it is less and less plausible to
portray our own era as one that has, in any decisive sense, moved
'beyond genre'.[4] Indeed, the word genre now seems to have lost most
of its negative charge, and to be operating instead as a valorising
term, signalling not prescription and exclusion but opportunity and
common purpose: genre as the enabling device, the vehicle for the
acquisition of competence. Thus redefined and democratised, not
only is the term enjoying renewed currency in literary discourse;
it also shows signs of becoming a general cultural buzzword,
used in contexts increasingly remote from literary criticism, and
applied to forms of writing and speech that have little or no
relation to literary genres.[5]

This seems an appropriate moment, then, at which to re-examine
the theoretical basis of the notion of genre: to reconsider the arguments
for its abolition and retention, and explore in a systematic way the
advances and setbacks that have marked the modern development
of what we now call genre theory. To facilitate such a revaluation is
one aim of the present anthology, which assembles for the first time a
selection of the most important work in genre theory since the beginning
of the twentieth century. It includes theoretical statements from a
wide range of disciplines and no fewer than ten countries, a diversity
which is indicative not only of the genuinely international nature
of the debate this topic has provoked, but also of the fact that the
problem of genre is always liable to open into larger questions about
the organisation and transmission of knowledge, and the dynamics
of cultural change. In certain of the essays and extracts, these larger
concerns are explicit; in others, the focus is a single genre, or the genre-
system of a particular period. In every case, however, the criterion
for inclusion has been that the piece in question contributes to a
general understanding of the notion of genre, or of the methodological
problems which surround it. This is not intended to be a theoretical
handbook for particular genres, nor an anthology of historical poetics
– though the inclusion of, for instance, Rosalie Colie's work on
Renaissance genre-systems (Chapter 9) makes the point that some of
the best insights in the area of modern genre theory have arisen out
of research into the history of genre-consciousness, or the analysis
of specific textual examples. While the rationale of this collection is

therefore theoretical rather than empirical, the notion of 'theory' is interpreted broadly, and the concept of genre itself explored in relation to a variety of intellectual traditions and concrete examples.

Origins of modern genre theory

The origins of the modern debate on genre lie, as I have already indicated, in the European Romantic movement, especially the tradition of radical aesthetic speculation centred in Germany in the late eighteenth and early nineteenth centuries. It was here, in the work of Herder, Goethe, Schiller, Novalis, Schelling and the Schlegel brothers, that the Aristotelian doctrine of the division of genres – the cornerstone of Renaissance and Neoclassical poetics – was first called seriously into question, and the concept of genre itself came under scrutiny for the first time. 'We already have so many theories about poetic genres', wrote Friedrich Schlegel in his *Critical Fragments* of 1797; 'Why have we no concept of poetic genre? Perhaps then we would have to make do with a single theory of poetic genres.'[6] The quest for such a theory – a *philosophical* theory of genre, as distinct from a purely descriptive account of individual genres – has remained a powerful tradition in Germany to this day,[7] most often expressing itself in the form of philosophic reflections on what Goethe in 1819 called the three *Naturformen* or 'natural forms' of poetry: epic, lyric and drama.[8]

This familiar tripartite division is normally traced back to Aristotle, but Gérard Genette has conclusively demonstrated (see Chapter 12) that the attribution, though ubiquitous, is erroneous, and that the 'seductive triad' is really a conflation of two separate genre theories: that of Plato (which distinguishes between three different modes of literary representation: narrative, dramatic and mixed) and that of Aristotle (which differentiates literary types according to mode *and object* of representation, but reduces to two the number of modal categories). Neither system, it should be noted, assigns a proper place to lyric, which is only incorporated into the supposedly Aristotelian triad by much later acts of substitution and amendment. That such a serious mistake, implying not only a misreading of Aristotle's *Poetics*, but also (in some cases, at least) a confusion about the *basis* of generic classifications, should have remained undetected for so long is a worrying reminder of the sort of difficulties that beset the genre theorist, especially when attempting to construct a systematic taxonomy of genres. Philosophical analysis of the lyric–epic–dramatic triad has, nevertheless, contributed greatly to our understanding of the phenomenon of genre, the most distinguished exponent of this mainly Germanic tradition in the twentieth century being the Swiss phenomenological critic Emil Staiger.[9]

Another major development in genre theory which occurs in the Romantic period is the recognition of the historical character of genres. To the modern reader this seems so obvious and fundamental a point that an effort of imagination is required to recall a time when it was believed that genres were static, universal categories whose character did not alter across time; and that it was therefore feasible to judge a work written in, say, 1750 by rules formulated in the fourth century BC, or to deny the existence of a new genre on the grounds that Aristotle didn't define it. Yet such beliefs and practices were absolutely orthodox before the advent of Romanticism, as almost any example of Neoclassical criticism would illustrate. How they eventually came to be abandoned – in face of the irrefutable fact of the ascendancy of the novel, and the irresistible claims of an 'expressive' poetics – is a remarkable episode in the history of ideas. Its result was a new conception of genres as historically determined, dynamic entities, a view given fullest expression in Hegel's famous lectures on aesthetics.[10]

Hegel's historicist model of genre, based on his dialectical interpretation of the history of consciousness, has continued to exert enormous influence on genre theory, most notably in the work of Lukács.[11] Equally great, if less direct, has been the influence of another masterwork of the nineteenth century, Darwin's *Origin of Species* (1859). Since organic metaphors already dominated Romantic genre theory, and the term 'species' was common to both discourses, it was inevitable that the Darwinian theory of evolution would commend itself as a model for the development of literary forms. By the end of the nineteenth century, most literary historians had adopted the evolutionary paradigm, none more enthusiastically than the French critic Ferdinand Brunetière, whose magnum opus *L'évolution des genres* (1890) carried furthest the evolutionary analogy. Brunetière has often been criticised for his crude application of Darwinian precepts – which implies that genres are autonomous entities rather than culturally constructed categories, and that the process of generic change is not determined by individual agency or creative will – but he provided a point of departure for many subsequent theorists, and has interesting ideas of his own about, for instance, the way literary genres develop out of one another (a theme directly taken up by the Russian Formalists).[12]

The most pervasive legacy of Romanticism, however, was the idea that it was possible to ignore altogether the doctrine of genres. Such notions were not unknown in earlier periods, but it was the literary theorists of Romanticism who formulated this idea explicitly. Again, Friedrich Schlegel was among the pioneers, and it is in his *Fragments on Literature and Poetry* (1797) that we encounter, for the first time in literary history, the proposition – now commonplace, then little short of revolutionary – that 'every poem is a genre unto itself' (*eine Gattung für sich*);[13] and it was Friedrich Schlegel too who proclaimed that the traditional distinctions of genre were 'as primitive and childish as the old pre-Copernican ideas of astronomy'.[14] There are echoes of these statements (coexisting rather uneasily with the attempts we have already noted to *reconstitute* a theory of genre) throughout the writings of the Jena circle and of others who came into contact with their ideas.[15] Opposition to the notion of genre rapidly became one of the battle-cries of the European Romantic movement,[16] and later entered, through a somewhat altered rationale, into the aesthetic manifestos and creative practice of early twentieth-century Modernism.

One of the transitional figures, in the domain of theory, was the Italian philosopher Benedetto Croce, whose enormously influential *Aesthetic* (the *Fundamental Theses* of which were published in 1900) contains the most extreme statement of the anti-generic position (see Chapter 1). For Croce, the whole doctrine of the artistic and literary kinds is nothing more than a 'superstition', of ancient classical origin, which 'survives to contaminate modern literary history' and to deceive us as to the true nature of the aesthetic.[17] Croce's arguments, partly intended as a refutation of Brunetière and the literary evolutionists, marked an escalation of the controversy over genre, and provided much of the impetus for the subsequent debate on the subject. An equally uncompromising stance was later adopted by the French writer and theorist Maurice Blanchot, who aspired to separate the category of the 'book' from the category of genre, arguing that the book arises from literature alone, and refuses all rubrics which attempt to fix its place and determine its form.[18] Blanchot's thesis, or more precisely his creative practice, is in turn taken as the text for Jacques Derrida's influential essay 'The Law of Genre' (1979), which makes the typically ingenious argument that the marks by which a work inscribes itself within a genre paradoxically do not belong to that genre; and hence the generic boundary is dissolved at the very moment when it is established. The most striking feature of the essay, however, is Derrida's characterisation of the authoritarian imperative which, for Derrida as for Blanchot, requires to be resisted or deconstructed – his recognition that 'As soon as the word "genre" is sounded, as soon as it is heard, as soon as one attempts to conceive it, a limit is drawn. And when a limit is established, norms and interdictions are not far behind: "Do", "Do not", says "genre", the word "genre", the figure, the voice, or the law of genre' (below, p. 221).

It is no coincidence that some of the strongest resistance to the 'law of genre' should have come from France and Italy where, at one time, the Neoclassical doctrine of genres was maintained in its most dogmatic form. In beginning his essay on the question of the 'mixing of genres', Derrida indeed seems to be returning to the most heated of all Neoclassical quarrels, an issue over which duels were once fought and blood once spilled – not to mention an exceedingly large quantity of ink. In Britain, the tyranny of Neoclassicism was somewhat milder, and those who would defy it could always appeal to the supreme example of Shakespeare, who mixed genres as freely as most people mix metaphors. By the same token, it is not altogether facetious to observe that English resistance to the law of genre, or non-acceptance of the theory that upholds it, is expressed by the word 'genre' itself, which is virtually unpronounceable in English – which is to say that we are reminded of its alienness every time we utter it. There are of course other words for genre, and English usage of 'genre' to denote a literary category is established only around the beginning of this century; but it is surely significant that this irremediably French word (from the Latin *genus*) should have been adopted in English, as a replacement for the older, Anglo-Saxon word 'kind', at precisely the point at which that concept was being seen throughout Europe as increasingly problematic.[19]

Russian Formalism

The breakthrough, on the problem of genre as in many other areas of literary theory, occurred in eastern Europe, in the remarkable work of the Russian Formalists. Russian Formalist thinking on the question of genre has not achieved anything like the currency, in the West, of notions such as defamiliarisation and the dominant, and there are many lingering misapprehensions about this aspect of Formalism, not least as a result of deliberate distortions which were put into circulation in the mid-1920s in order to discredit the Formalists for essentially political reasons. The most serious of these misapprehensions is the belief that the Russian Formalists were not interested in literary history, and that they always insisted, as did the American New Critics of the 1930s, in isolating the single text as an object of study, and ignoring its historical or generic determinants. This is simply false, though it is a view that has been encouraged by the constant reprinting in Western anthologies of literary theory of a single essay of Viktor Shklovsky's, whose title is usually translated as 'Art as Device' or 'Art as Technique'. This is a highly entertaining piece, and also a kind of manifesto of Formalist methodology, but it belongs to an early phase in the Formalist project (1917), when Shklovsky and others were preoccupied with a theoretical struggle against the Symbolist conception of art as 'thinking in images' (Shklovsky's title itself initiates the polemic). According to Boris Eikhenbaum's 1926 essay 'The Theory of the Formal Method' (which is a systematic, chronological summary of the achievements of the school by one of its leading practitioners, and probably still the best short introduction to their work), it was not until 1921 that the Formalists turned their attention to genre, this interest being reflected in essays such as Shklovsky's on 'Rozanov', and Yury Tynyanov's on 'Dostoevsky and Gogol' (subtitled 'Towards a Theory of Parody'), 'The Ode as a Rhetorical Genre' and 'On Literary Evolution'. The most sustained treatment of the subject is Tynyanov's seminal essay 'The Literary Fact' (1924), which appears below in English translation for the first time (Chapter 2).

What is clear from these essays is that for the Russian Formalists, in their later phase, genre is the central mechanism of literary history, and its proper object of study. From nineteenth-century scholars such as Brunetière and the Russian Alexander Veselovsky, the Formalists inherit the problematic of literary evolution, but they turn that concept on its head by arguing, first of all, that literary evolution is discontinuous, as expressed in Shklovsky's chess metaphor of the knight's move (the title of one of his works), and his claim that in the history of literature the legacy is not transmitted from father to son, but from uncle to nephew.[20] Secondly, they maintain that the evolution of a particular genre cannot be understood from the genre-system as a whole; thirdly, that genre is defined by function as well as form, and that functions as well as forms evolve (so that, for instance, the Russian ode performs a different function in the eighteenth century than in the Romantic period – which is true of the English ode too); fourthly, that, as Shklovsky puts it, 'a new form arises not in order to express a new content [as Veselovsky had maintained], but because the old form has exhausted its possibilities';[21] and fifthly, that there is, as the Neoclassicists believed, a hierarchy of genres, but – here's the difference – *the hierarchy is always changing*. It changes because, in each literary epoch, different literary schools and literary genres are in competition with one another, and what often happens is that a genre which has previously been minor or marginal acquires a new position of dominance – a process sometimes known as 'the canonisation of the junior branch'.[22]

Tynyanov's essay on 'The Literary Fact' will explain and develop most of these points, but it may be worth emphasising here certain general features of this approach: for example, the fact that this is, in essence, a *revolutionary* as well as an *evolutionary* model of genre – not only in that it acknowledges the possibility of radical alterations in the hierarchy of genres, but because it regards the condition of genre itself as something like a state of permanent revolution. Genres 'evolve' because the act of belonging to a genre involves both adoption of and resistance to its conventions; hence the special place of parody in Formalist thinking, because parody explicitly works by exposing and subverting conventions. Hence too the notion that the possibilities of a genre can be exhausted, not least as the result of a ransacking by an able parodist. It is obvious too how this theory of genre can be said to extend the notion of defamiliarisation, which was originally defined (in Shklovsky's 'Art as Technique', for example) in relation to literary language. The underlying principle is aptly summed up in the title which Tynyanov gave to a collection of his essays: *Archaists and Innovators* – his point being that the great artists, in their use of genre, are both of these at once.

Such a theory of genre is, then, far from being ahistorical, but it does incorporate the epistemological stance of structural linguistics, notably in its concept of the 'genre-system'. Russian Formalism, let us remember, was the first sustained application of Saussure's 'synchronic' methodology to the study of literature, yet it also retained a *diachronic* perspective, a particular genre being defined in relation both to the genres that surround it, and to the previous manifestations of that genre. Though this is true, the Formalist theory does, nevertheless, *put in question* the relationship between genre and history by postulating a degree of autonomy in the process of generic change – a process which Eikhenbaum refers to as 'the dialectical self-creation of new forms'.[23] This is probably one of the greatest insights of the Russian Formalists, but it was also one of their most dangerous, for it was precisely because of this apparent devaluation of the role of historical and sociological determinants in literary evolution that the Formalists, in the mid-1920s, fell foul of the political authorities, and the school was eventually suppressed.[24] Eikhenbaum's inclusion of the word 'dialectical' in his description of this process was undoubtedly a calculated political move, as he attempted to summarise and defend the work of the Formalists in the climate of an increasingly rigid Marxist orthodoxy; but it seems that the Formalist theory of literary history was not dialectical enough, or not perceived to be so, to satisfy the political censor. Nor indeed to satisfy certain other critics of Formalism whose objections were not so obviously motivated by political expediency.

Sociologies of genre

It is in this category that I believe the early work of the Bakhtin school should be placed, notably the Bakhtin/Medvedev book *The Formal Method in Literary Scholarship* (1928). Subtitled 'A Critical Introduction to Sociological Poetics', this has been called 'the most extended and scholarly critique of [Russian Formalism] ever undertaken by a Marxist';[25] and it certainly contains some trenchant criticisms of earlier Formalist statements on genre,[26] although some of the criticisms – and indeed some of the proposed adjustments – are anticipated in the essays of Tynyanov, of which the Bakhtin/Medvedev book does not take account.[27] What is interesting, from our perspective, is the book's reaffirmation of the centrality of genre within its vision of a 'sociological poetics', and its foregrounding of the problem of the ideological dimension of genre. Whatever the justice of the critique, we can see in retrospect that this particular quarrel with Formalism is paradigmatic of a long series of debates within Marxism as to the precise nature of what Bakhtin/Medvedev call the 'sociology of genre', or the dialectic of literary change. Modern reformulations of this dialectic include Raymond Williams's influential work on the history of dramatic forms, the theoretical basis of which is made explicit in his book *Marxism and Literature* (1977); Lucien Goldmann's equally penetrating and (in France, at least) comparably influential work on the sociology of the novel; the Italian Marxist critic Franco Moretti's brilliantly suggestive essays on the sociology of literary forms in *Signs Taken for Wonders* (1983); John Frow's illuminating book *Marxism and Literary History* (1986); and Tony Bennett's astute analysis of the sociology of genres in *Outside Literature* (1990).[28] The most subtle version of Marxist genre theory, though, is the one outlined in Fredric Jameson's 'Magical Narratives: On the Dialectical Uses of Genre Criticism', from his book *The Political Unconscious* (1981), an essay which submits the entire enterprise of modern genre theory to a rigorous Marxist critique. A substantial extract is included in this anthology (Chapter 10).

The most fruitful and far-reaching exploration of genre that takes the encounter with Russian Formalism as its starting point, however, is the work of Mikhail Bakhtin himself. Whether or not he wrote the Medvedev book (this is still disputed), Bakhtin went on to produce startlingly original and now increasingly influential ideas about a whole range of matters connected with genre, and above all one particular genre: the novel. David Lodge may be right in imputing to Bakhtin 'an almost messianic view of the novel as a literary form',[29] and I certainly share some of the reservations of other scholars about Bakhtin's downgrading of other genres ('dead languages', he calls them) in order to elevate this one; but it is Bakhtin, more than anyone else, who has appreciated the extent to which traditional genre theory is rendered obsolete by the advent of the novel, or of how – to use his own words – 'Faced with the problem of the novel, genre theory must submit to a radical restructuring' (below, p. 73). That restructuring is a task that, for Bakhtin, begins in his earliest work, notably the 1924 essay 'Content, Material and Form in Verbal Art'[30] (which predates the Medvedev book and contains his first, arguably more profound critique of Russian Formalism), and continues right through to his last writings, the fascinating essays and fragments collected in the volume *Speech Genres and Other Late Essays* (1986).

Gary Morson and Caryl Emerson, two of the leading American translators and scholars of Bakhtin, have recently attributed to him the creation of a 'Prosaics' (a term of their own invention),[31] but this might equally be called a 'poetics of content', for the theoretical reorientation that Bakhtin consistently seeks involves a centralising of the problematic of *content* – which, for Bakhtin, is almost always defined in *ideological* terms. In this respect, Bakhtin's difference of emphasis from Formalism, especially early Formalism, is considerable, which may partly reflect the fact that the Formalist enterprise began as an investigation of *poetic language*. What Bakhtin does is to shift attention from the vexed question of the relationships between literary and ordinary language, and between poetry and prose (issues that were taken up again and developed by the Prague Structuralists), and to concentrate instead on the relationship between what he calls 'primary' and 'secondary genres'. Primary genres include things like letters, diaries, minutes, everyday stories, as well as the so-called 'speech genres', namely the different forms of dialogue; secondary genres are the more complex entities – including the vast majority of literary genres – that are formed by the combination and transformation of primary genres. The novel, for Bakhtin, is unique because of its extreme receptiveness to the primary genres, and because it retains as its structural principle (at least in certain types of novel) the interplay of voices that constitute the materials from which it derives. But all genres, of literature and speech, are not simply sets of devices and conventions, but 'forms of seeing and interpreting particular aspects of the world', ways of 'conceptualising reality' that are stored within the 'genre memory', it being the role of the great artist to awaken the 'semantic possibilities' that lie within a particular genre.

Here I am conflating statements from across the range of Bakhtin's oeuvre,[32] two major samples of which are included below: an extract from his 1941 essay 'Epic and Novel' (Chapter 4), and part of an essay from 1952–3 on 'Speech Genres' (Chapter 5). Like other aspects of Bakhtin's work, his writings on genre are often read out of context. It is necessary to reconstruct that context to see, for example, that many of the ideas that we most readily associate with Bakhtin – 'dialogue', the conflict of genres, the use of sub-literary forms, for example – are foreshadowed in the work of Shklovsky, Eikhenbaum, Tynyanov and other of his Formalist predecessors. Several commentators have noted too the striking parallels between Bakhtin's essay on 'Epic and Novel' and Lukács's early *Theory of the Novel* (subtitled 'A Historio-philosophical Essay on the Forms of Great Epic Literature'), another classic work in the sociology of genres, which Bakhtin began translating in the 1920s.[33] Although space precludes it here, it would be instructive also to set Bakhtin's ideas alongside those of the American cultural historian Walter Ong, whose well-known book *Orality and Literacy* (1982) contains incisive suggestions about the possible impact on genre (particular genres, and the concept of genre itself) of the shift from the predominantly oral culture of the Middle Ages to the book culture of the Renaissance, and the further shifts that have marked the growth of literacy and the development of technology.[34] These are also among the many concerns of Kenneth Burke, whose ideological system elaborated in his early book *Attitudes to History* (1937) adumbrates a theory of genre, involving 'frames of acceptance' and 'frames of rejection', that is not unlike Bakhtin's 'forms of seeing and interpreting', but which insists, as does Burke's later work, on the genuinely original, if slightly obscure, idea of writing as 'symbolic action'.[35]

The present anthology does, however, include the work of a more recent critic who has a more direct connection with Bakhtin, namely the Franco-Bulgarian theorist Tzvetan Todorov, one of Bakhtin's most influential interpreters. Along with his fellow expatriate Julia Kristeva, he was one of the first to bring the work of the Formalists to the attention of French literary theorists in the mid-1960s, which had enormous consequences for the development of French structuralism; and both also performed similar services for Bakhtin. Todorov's essay 'The Origin of Genres' (1976), as well as being an introduction to Bakhtin's later work, written some time before it became available in French or English, is a helpful attempt to clarify the relationship between Bakhtin's notion of 'speech genres' and Anglo-American speech-act theory, with which Bakhtin himself was unfamiliar. It also lays bare for the first time some of Bakhtin's profound debts to German Romantic genre theory.[36]

Structuralism and reception theory

The work of Todorov constitutes only one of the many links between Formalism and structuralism, and the distinction between the two methodologies is especially hard to preserve in the area of genre theory, which almost by definition partakes of both. Few would dispute that the first recognisably structuralist analysis of narrative was performed by Vladimir Propp in his book *The Morphology of the Folktale* (1927) and essay 'Fairy Tale Transformations' (1928), the latter of which is reprinted here (Chapter 3). Though not a member of *Opoyaz*, the Formalist group in his native St Petersburg, Propp was undoubtedly influenced by their work, but he carried further Shklovsky's exploration of the 'laws of plot construction' and Tynyanov's concept of the literary 'function' to uncover what might be called a grammar of genre.[37] The genre in question was the folk tale, or rather its magical subtype the fairy tale, but what Propp proposed was not simply a new definition but a new *kind* of definition, involving the identification of plot 'functions' and 'invariants'. Propp's claim was that all stories of this type, whatever their superficial differences of content, were essentially constructed in the same way, out of a fixed repertoire of actions and character roles. The surface details vary from story to story but these elements or 'functions' remain constant, and always occur in the same order, though certain functions may be omitted or repeated.

Theorists have often remarked on the analogy between Propp's pioneering analysis of the 'grammar' of the fairy tale and Noam Chomsky's theory of transformational generative grammar, which revolutionised many areas of linguistics in the late 1950s and 1960s; and it is probably no coincidence that Western interest in Propp's work dates from around the time of Chomsky's early publications (*The Morphology of the Folktale* was first translated into English in 1958, and came to wide attention with Lévi-Strauss's review in 1960). Without wishing to underestimate the far greater technical complexity of Chomsky's work, it is worth emphasising that Propp's research predates Chomsky's by some 30 years, and that the 'transformational generative' model which distinguishes deep from surface structure, and identifies a system involving 'invariants' and 'transformations' (terms used by Propp), was applied to literary texts long before it was applied to language itself. Both developments may be seen in part as a radical extension (in Chomsky's case, almost an inversion) of the structuralist premises of Saussurean linguistics, but Propp's inspired methodological leap was to combine Saussure's technique of synchronic investigation with two other distinct influences: the ethnographic criticism of the Russian literary historian Alexander Veselovsky, who first proposed the idea of breaking down folk tales and other literary forms into devices and motifs; and, more unexpectedly, the concept of 'morphology' derived from Goethe's scientific writings on the metamorphosis of plants. Propp was not alone in adopting the term 'morphology' – the Russian Formalists sometimes referred to their method as 'morphological' – but he gave new prominence to the term, and expressed his debt to Goethe by choosing as one of the epigraphs to his book Goethe's famous statement that 'the study of forms is the study of transformations'.[38]

Such a conception of the task of genre analysis is now commonplace, and Propp is widely acknowledged as, in effect, the inventor of what is now called narratology, unquestionably one of the most successful branches of literary structuralism. However, Propp himself did not seek to extend his insights about the folk tale to other genres, and others have found that his analytic method seems to work less well when applied to more complex types of literature. This may be because the degree of abstraction to which such texts must be reduced in order to reveal their invariants tends to make the very category of genre disappear. Indeed, this is a tendency of all structuralist analysis. It is symptomatic, for example, that the Czech Structuralism which developed out of Russian Formalism following the emigration to Prague of Roman Jakobson rapidly moved from the problematic of genre, a major item on the agenda drawn up by Jakobson and Tynyanov in their joint statement on the 'Problems in the Study of Language and Literature' (1928),[39] to the question of aesthetic norms in general.[40]

A similar shift of attention – from the category of genre to the literary or cultural system in general – marks the semiotic structuralism of Yury Lotman and the Tartu school, which revived the project of Russian Formalism under the very different intellectual conditions of the postwar Soviet Union.[41] The same tendency can even be observed in the very different kind of structuralism practised by the Canadian critic Northrop Frye. By his own admission, Frye's programme of 'archetypal criticism' involves the attempt to extend 'the kind of comparative and morphological study now made of folk tales and ballads into the rest of literature',[42] but it is his account of *pre-generic* structures – the four primal narrative types or *mythoi* he calls tragedy, comedy, romance and irony – rather than his 'theory of genres' as such (that is, his treatment of literary forms in their *rhetorical* dimension) that proved so influential in Anglo-American criticism of the 1960s and 1970s. As far as genre theory *per se* is concerned, the real value of his work lies in his demonstration of the sheer complexity of the process by which literary forms originate and develop, and his illuminating hypothesis that such structures evolve through different degrees or stages of literariness (Frye identifies five such stages: myth, romance, high mimetic, low mimetic, ironic). To comprehend this process in anything like its full complexity requires an alertness not only to the technical possibilities and constraints of a given literary medium, but also to an enormous range of other psychological, historical and anthropological factors. Frye's ability to move between these different levels of explanation is well illustrated by the celebrated account of romance from his *Anatomy of Criticism* (1957), which appears below (Chapter 6).

13

The concept of genre itself does, however, remain a point of focus in at least two schools of literary thought which ultimately stem from Russian Formalism. The first is the Polish Formalist movement, established in Warsaw and Wilno in the 1930s, and resurrected after the war in Lublin and more recently Gdańsk. The work of the school is still little known outside Poland, and almost none of it has been translated into English, but included here (Chapter 7) is an excerpt from an essay by one of its most distinguished members, Ireneusz Opacki. First published in 1961, and conceived partly as a critique of the theory of literary genres outlined in René Wellek and Austin Warren's influential *Theory of Literature* (1949), Opacki's essay moves from general methodological problems to the question of generic cross-fertilisation or 'hybridisation'. Using a number of case studies, Opacki offers a lucid theoretical description of a process whose exact nature remains unclear in most earlier accounts of literary evolution: namely, the process by which genres modify and combine with one another, producing variant forms and eventually giving rise to new genres in which the different evolutionary layers can still be discerned. As in Russian Formalist theory, generic change is seen to involve competition as well as combination, and any one period tends to be 'dominated' by a particular genre which affects other genres by, ultimately, transforming them into hybrids of itself. Extending the quasi-political metaphor of the hierarchy of genres, Opacki calls these dominant genres the 'royal genres', and suggests how analysis of them can provide the key to the poetics of the given literary trend or period.

Another structuralist/formalist project in which questions of genre remain central is that of Hans Robert Jauss and the Konstanz school, whose work elaborates the insights and techniques of the Czech Structuralists, but reinstates the problematic of genre as defined in the later writings of the Russian Formalists. As is shown by the extract below (Chapter 8) from Jauss's essay on 'The Theory of Genres and Medieval Literature' (1970), where his methodology differs from that of the Formalists is in the transfer of attention from the point of production (the writer, or the 'self-creation of new literary forms') to the point of reception (the reader, and the mechanisms by which works of art are understood and evaluated). Such is the reorientation of interest signalled by Jauss's well-known phrase 'horizon of expectation', though it might be more precisely described as a shift from a *morphology* of genre concerned primarily with *form* to a *sociology* of genre concerned primarily with *function*.

This brings it very close to the contract theory of genre developed, from very different premises, in the semiotic structuralism of Jonathan Culler. Culler has been an influential mediator for English readers of the whole structuralist enterprise, but his own contribution to genre theory is a distinctive one, in that it combines the notion of *contract* – which had been applied to genre at least as far back as Wordsworth's 1800 Preface to *Lyrical Ballads* – with the linguistic concept of *competence* derived from Chomsky's theory of transformational generative grammar. The result is a model of 'literary competence' which defines our ability as readers to recognise and interpret the codes of a given genre, and hence to 'perform' readings of particular examples of the genre.[43] Such an argument finds its logical conclusion in the theory of 'validity of interpretation' expounded in 1967 by the American hermeneutic critic E.D. Hirsch, who invokes Wittgenstein's idea of 'language games' to make the very important claim – also found in Bakhtin, and in speech-act theory – that there is, in effect, a middle term between Saussure's *langue* and *parole*, a term which Hirsch calls the 'type of utterance' as distinct from the individual utterance (*parole*) and the language system itself (*langue*). This quasi-linguistic concept of type forms the basis of Hirsch's definition of genre, which in turn underlies his theory of interpretation; and since the essence of the 'typical' or the 'generic' is their non-unique and non-arbitrary character, Hirsch's model of interpretation is a normative one, governed by criteria of 'validity'.[44]

Recent developments

The notion of literary competence thus begins to look suspiciously like a reassertion (projected onto the reader rather than the writer) of the prescriptive theory of genre that earlier theorists had sought to dismantle. Derrida's deconstruction of the 'law of genre' might therefore very plausibly be viewed as a re-enactment of the Romantic revolt against the Neoclassical conception of genre, a re-enactment rendered necessary by what Derrida plainly saw as the totalising claims of modern structuralist thought. That moment of need has probably now passed, and a degree of consensus is beginning to emerge about both the possibilities and the limitations of the concept of genre. It is revealing, for example, that a recent article by Vincent Leitch purporting to offer a 'post-structuralist conceptualisation of genre'[45] arrives at conclusions not markedly different from those of the Marxist critic Fredric Jameson; and that the word genre, once regarded as so flawed and so archaic a concept as to be on the point of dropping out of the modern critical vocabulary, has recently been described by one reviewer as 'precisely that theoretical term which encapsulates, in the problems that it poses, all the uncertainties, contradictions, and confusions of the post-modern era, whether in the cultural, intellectual, or political domains'.[46]

The defensive tone of earlier genre theory seems indeed to have been replaced by a tone of almost exuberant confidence in the concept, as witnessed by the rousing title of Adena Rosmarin's book *The Power of Genre* (1985)[47] and the wordplay of Betty Rosenberg's title *Genreflecting: A Guide to Reading Interests in Genre Fiction* (1982).[48] In Australia, the group of applied linguists who are exploring the use of genre in education is now admiringly referred to as the 'genre school',[49] and the term 'genre' has now been officially adopted in the English and Scottish National Curriculum. Meanwhile the theory of genre continues to play a central role in film studies, partly reflecting the foundation of that discipline at the height of the structuralist vogue of the 1960s and 1970s, as well as the ubiquitous use of genre concepts in the cinema industry itself. A more recent development is the interest in the category of genre in women's studies, an interest partly inspired by the proximity of the words genre and gender (which are one and the same word – *genre* – in French). As Mary Eagleton's helpful essay explains (Chapter 15), this has resulted in a major rethinking of the history of genres, especially those that appear to be 'gendered' in terms of their authors or readers, or in the case of film and other media genres, their audiences.

Equally striking is the adoption of the concept in disciplines such as political science, history and religious studies. Genre has long been a focus for comparative studies in literature and, more recently, film, as well as for interdisciplinary work within the broad base of cultural studies.[50] Now, it serves as a tool for ever more ambitious interdisciplinary work, which in many cases makes no reference to literary structures of any kind. In fact, genre has become part of the very metalanguage of interdisciplinarity, the merging of disciplines being itself a manifestation of what Clifford Geertz calls the 'blurring of genres'.[51] Bakhtin's notion of 'speech genres' permits a still further expansion of the concept by suggesting that all acts of communication, even gestural ones, can be modelled in terms of genre, insofar as they are partly dependent on codes and conventions.

This decisive upturn in the fortunes of genre may, as I have suggested, be part of a cultural logic of popularisation, or may simply mark the end of the Romantic polemic. But the apparent consensus may be misleading. It is likely that genre theories will always, at some level, compete with author theories, and that authors (or directors) will continue to insist on the uniqueness and autonomy of their work, while also wanting (as my epigraph from Martin Amis illustrates) to exploit the resources – the *power* – of genre. It is probable too that the concept of genre will continue to be put in question by more open-ended models of textuality, both those that stress the instability of all linguistic systems and those that emphasise the potentially unlimited scope of intertextuality (genre is, in effect, a *restrictive* model of intertextuality). Distinctions of genre are, moreover, still liable to be displaced by other analytical categories, as for instance in recent discussion of *'l'écriture féminine'*, or as when Foucault calls upon us to overlook superficial boundaries 'form' and 'genre' in order to perceive the circulation of entire discourses such as medicine, political economy and biology.[52] Foucault's 'archaeology of knowledge' still in effect competes with the 'sociology of genres'.

That the American journal *Genre*, latterly subtitled *Forms of Discourse and Culture*, contrives to combine Foucauldian *and* Bakhtinian keywords in its name[53] does not alter this fact, nor diminish one of the enduring problems of genre theory, namely confusion of terminology. To give just one example, the term *mode* currently carries at least two indispensable but incompatible meanings: one that refers to the manner of representation of a literary work (narrative, dramatic or lyrical, in the pseudo-Aristotelian triad), and one that refers to the extension of notionally fixed genres such as tragedy, comedy or elegy into more plastic categories (tragic, comic, elegiac) that modify and combine with other genres: a meaning of the term employed by Alastair Fowler in Chapter 14. It is hard to see how agreement will ever be reached to differentiate these meanings by separate words, but the need remains pressing. Equally confusing is the distinction between 'form' and 'genre'. Is 'generic form' a tautology, or does it imply a useful distinction between the individual form of a single work and the 'generic form' of a *type* of work? How, similarly, do we distinguish between 'inner' and 'outer' form (an opposition that Wellek and Warren propose[54]), or between 'form' and 'structure'?

Part of the problem is that in 'genology'[55] or genre theory, unlike in botany and zoology, there is no 'species' term to accompany the 'genus' term *genre*. The phrase 'species of composition' was common in the eighteenth century, but this was before the word genre was in use, and the latter has simply replaced, rather than defined itself against, the former. We talk today of 'subgenres' and even 'microgenres',[56] but this assumes a measure of agreement about relative size or stability of the type of entity called 'genre' (or 'macrogenre') that in reality does not exist. No modern language seems to have solved this problem of nomenclature, and, as we have seen, the confusions extend back at least as far as Aristotle. This may serve as a warning to the reader venturing into genre theory for the first time, and perhaps as a stimulus to the more experienced reader who feels able to elucidate these terminological confusions (genre theory still awaits its Linnaeus).

On a less negative note, it should be clear from this anthology that there are many aspects of genre theory which invite further investigation. For instance, the radical restructuring of which Bakhtin spoke is by no means complete, and it needs to involve not only a rethinking of the novel but also a reconsideration of poetry and, above all, drama (which Bakhtin almost totally ignores[57]). We also need to recall, and absorb, and refine, the insights of some of the other eastern European theorists whose work – on genres other than the novel, and on the phenomenon of genre itself – has been temporarily eclipsed by the cult of Bakhtin. And we need to return to Romantic genre theory, the partially acknowledged source of so much modern thinking about genre, and a much under-explored field in its own right (this is especially true of the English Romantics, about whose perceptions of genre much confusion still exists). A better understanding of this whole intellectual tradition will not only lead to a more productive dialogue – already a feature of the most interesting work in the field – between formalist and historicist approaches, but also enable future genre theorists to avoid the impasse reached by, for instance, the Chicago school of the 1950s, where – despite initial breakthroughs – the search for a critical methodology founded on a static, neo-Aristotelian theory of genre degenerated into reductive acts of classification and authoritarian reading practices.[58]

For many readers, though, the main function of this anthology will be the empirical application of the terms and concepts it contains. I will therefore end this introduction by spelling out in more general terms the sort of literary study that a clearer understanding of genre might permit. Without reverting to the Neoclassical delusion of a comprehensive taxonomy of the literary kinds, or succumbing to the structuralist fantasy of a total science of the literary system, it is possible to conceive of a type of literary history that has an accurate perception of the genre spectrum that obtains at any given period; that is able to identify the dominant genre or genres (what Opacki calls the 'royal genres'), and to explain how they attained that position of dominance – as well as how they cross-fertilise, or impoverish, or conflict with, neighbouring genres; that is able to show how the genre spectrum may vary from one period to another, and how the cultural assumptions and aspirations of an era are reflected in its hierarchy of genres; and that is able to illustrate the process of change itself through re-orderings of the generic hierarchy, or the proliferation of new forms, or alterations in the cultural perception of genre. It would be possible, in this context, to speak with some precision about the ideological functions of genre, about the conditions of possibility for the existence of particular genres, and the reasons for their flourishing or decline. It might also enable us to assess the performance of an author across a variety of genres, and determine the significance of his or her choice of certain genres and not others; while at the same time, at the level of the individual text, helping us not only pinpoint innovations in technique, but also locate the generic sources of the 'power' of which Amis speaks (so often a product of the interaction of *different* generic elements, as modern genre theory teaches us). Some of these goals can be, and have been, achieved by other means; but there are, undoubtedly, advances to be made and new insights to be had.

Notes

1. Quoted in JASON COWLEY, 'Portrait: Martin Amis', *Prospect* (Aug.–Sept. 1997).

2. Preface to *The Awkward Age*, in HENRY JAMES, *The Art of Criticism: Henry James on the Theory and Practice of Fiction*, ed. William Veeder and Susan M. Griffin (Chicago: University of Chicago Press, 1986), p. 310.

3. On the role of genre concepts within Postmodernism, see *Postmodern Genres*, ed. Marjorie Perloff (Norman: University of Oklahoma Press, 1988).

4. In this sense, the implications of the title of PAUL HERNADI's *Beyond Genre: New Directions in Literary Classification* (Ithaca, NY: Cornell University Press, 1972) have not been borne out. Hernadi's analysis of tendencies in modern genre theory remains, however, an extremely valuable and informative one.

5. For instance, a recent bibliometric search found evidence of widespread use of the term and concept of genre between 1980 and 1995 in five social science disciplines: education, history, political science, psychology and sociology. The study also showed a marked increase in the use of the term since 1990. See ENRICO TORTELANO, unpublished PgD/MSc thesis in information studies, Robert Gordon University, 1996.

6. *Critical Fragments*, no. 62, in *Friedrich Schlegel's* Lucinde *and the Fragments*, trans. with intro. by Peter Firchow (Minneapolis: University of Minnesota Press, 1971), p. 150.

7. See RENÉ WELLEK, 'Genre Theory, the Lyric and *Erlebnis*', in his *Discriminations: Further Concepts of Criticism* (New Haven, Conn.: Yale University Press, 1970); HERNADI, *Beyond Genre*, chs 1–3; MARGOT E. ZUTSHI, *Literary Theory in Germany: A Study of Genre and Evaluation Theories, 1945–1965* (Berne: Peter Lang, 1981).

8. Goethe's notes to *West-östlicher Divan* (1819), quoted by ERNEST L. STAHL, 'Literary Genres: Some Idiosyncratic Concepts', in *Theories of Literary Genre*, ed. Joseph P. Strelka, Yearbook of Comparative Criticism, vol. 8 (University Park: Pennsylvania State University Press, 1978), p. 86. For more recent discussions of Goethe's contribution to German Romantic genre theory, see CYRUS HAMLIN, 'The Origins of a Philosophical Genre Theory in German Romanticism', *European Romantic Review*, 5:1 (1994), 3–14; and LUBOMÍR DOLOŽEL, *Occidental Poetics: Tradition and Progress* (Lincoln: University of Nebraska Press, 1990), ch. 3.

9. EMIL STAIGER, *Basic Concepts of Poetics*, trans. Janette C. Hudson and Luanne T. Frank (University Park: Pennsylvania State University Press, 1991). First published in German in 1946. The modern tradition in German genre theory, and Staiger's place within it, is analysed by KLAUS WEISSENBERGER, 'A Morphological Genre Theory: An Answer to a Pluralism of Forms', in *Theories of Literary Genre*, ed. Strelka. See also ZUTSHI, *Literary Theory in Germany*.

10. Relevant passages can be found in vol. II of G.W.F. HEGEL, *Aesthetics: Lectures on Fine Arts*, trans. T.M. Knox, 2 vols (Oxford: Clarendon Press, 1975).

11. The influence of Hegel on Lukács's theory of genre is examined by HERNADI, *Beyond Genre*, pp. 114–31.

12. See DAVID FISHELOV, *Metaphors of Genre: The Role of Analogies in Genre Theory* (University Park: Pennsylvania State University Press, 1993); and, for the history of the concept, RENÉ WELLEK, 'The Concept of Evolution in Literary History', in Wellek, *Concepts of Criticism*, ed. Stephen G. Nichols, Jr (New Haven, Conn.: Yale University Press, 1975).

13. *Literary Notebooks 1797–1801*, quoted in PETER SZONDI, 'Friedrich Schlegel's Theory of Poetical Genres: A Reconstruction from the Posthumous Fragments', in SZONDI, *On Textual Understanding and Other Essays*, trans. Harvey Mendelsohn (Manchester: Manchester University Press, 1986), p. 93. Szondi's own distinguished contribution to genre theory is analysed by TIMOTHY BAHTI, 'Fate in the Past: Peter Szondi's Reading of German Romantic Genre Theory', *boundary 2*, 11:3 (1983), 11–25.

14. *Athenaeum Fragments*, no. 434, in *Friedrich Schlegel's* Lucinde *and the Fragments*, p. 237.

15. The formation and influence of the Jena circle are analysed in detail in ERNST BEHLER, *German Romantic Literary Theory* (Cambridge: Cambridge University Press, 1993). For a more comprehensive account of the critical currents of the period, see RENÉ WELLEK, *A History of Modern Criticism: 1750–1950*, vol. 2: *The Romantic Age* (London: Jonathan Cape, 1955).

16. A useful selection of such statements can be found in LILIAN R. FURST, ed., *European Romanticism: Self -Definition* (London: Methuen, 1980), Section 3: 'Romantic Art: Form and Genre'.

17. BENEDETTO CROCE, *Aesthetic as Science of Expression and General Linguistic*, trans. Douglas Ainslie, 2nd edn (London: Peter Owen, 1953), p. 449.

18. MAURICE BLANCHOT, 'The Disappearance of Literature' (1953), in *The Blanchot Reader*, ed. Michael Holland (Oxford: Blackwell, 1995), p. 141.

19. According to the *Oxford English Dictionary*, 2nd edn, the earliest use of the word in English to denote a type of literary work was in 1770; but this was an isolated instance, and it was not until the end of the nineteenth century that its use became widespread. In 1910, IRVING BABBITT in his Preface to *The New Laokoon* (p. vii) remarks that 'The word *genre* seems to be gaining some currency in English'; and it confirms my point that he does so in a book which itself foregrounds the problem of genre (the subtitle is *An Essay on the Confusion of the Arts*). In French, the literary sense of *genre* dates from the mid-seventeenth century, though the word itself, which has many other meanings and applications, originates from the twelfth century.

20. 'Literature without a Plot: Rozanov', in VIKTOR SHKLOVSKY, *Theory of Prose*, trans. Benjamin Sher (Elmwood Park, Illinois: Dalkey Archive Press, 1990), p. 190.

21. 'The Relationship between Devices of Plot Construction and General Devices of Style', in SHKLOVSKY, *Theory of Prose*, p. 20.

22. For a selection of Russian Formalist statements on genre and related concepts, see the invaluable 'Contextual Glossary of Formalist Theory' in *Russian Poetics in Translation*, vol. 4: *Formalist Theory*, ed. L.M. O'Toole and Ann Shukman (Oxford: Holdan, 1977), pp. 13–48. A useful synthesis of Russian Formalist ideas on genre also forms part of BORIS TOMASHEVSKY's *Theory of Literature:*

Poetics (1928); for a translation of the relevant section, see TOMASHEVSKY, 'Literary Genres', trans. L.M. O'Toole, in *Russian Poetics in Translation*, vol. 5: *Formalism: History, Comparison, Genre*, ed. L.M. O'Toole and A. Shukman (Oxford: Holdan, 1978), pp. 52–93.

23. BORIS EIKHENBAUM, 'The Theory of the "Formal Method"', in *Russian Formalist Criticism: Four Essays*, ed. and trans. Lee T. Lemon and Marion J. Reis (Lincoln: University of Nebraska Press, 1965), p. 135.

24. See VICTOR ERLICH, *Russian Formalism: History – Doctrine*, 3rd edn (New Haven, Conn.: Yale University Press, 1981), pp. 118–39. The course of this polemic can be charted in the contemporary documents assembled in *The Futurists, the Formalists, and the Marxist Critique*, ed. Christopher Pike (London: Ink Links, 1979). The most famous attack was that of LEON TROTSKY, who devoted a chapter of his classic book *Literature and Revolution* (1924) to a critique of the Formalist school; for a sensitive treatment of the theoretical issues involved, see TONY BENNETT, *Formalism and Marxism* (London: Methuen, 1979), ch. 2.

25. ERLICH, *Russian Formalism: History – Doctrine*, p. 114.

26. See MIKHAIL BAKHTIN/PAVEL MEDVEDEV, *The Formal Method in Literary Scholarship: A Critical Introduction to Sociological Poetics*, trans. Albert J. Wehrle (Cambridge, Mass.: Harvard University Press, 1985), ch. 7.

27. One example is the notion of a genre's 'orientation to reality' as distinct from its orientation to the literary system: the distinction is central to Bakhtin's critique, but is already operative in, for instance, Tynyanov's essay on 'The Ode as a Rhetorical Genre'.

28. RAYMOND WILLIAMS, *Marxism and Literature* (Oxford: Oxford University Press, 1977); LUCIEN GOLDMANN, *Towards a Sociology of the Novel* (London: Tavistock, 1975) and his *Method in the Sociology of Literature*, ed. William Q. Boelhower (Oxford: Blackwell, 1980); FRANCO MORETTI, *Signs Taken for Wonders: Essays in the Sociology of Literary Forms*, trans. David Forgacs (London: Verso, 1983); JOHN FROW, *Marxism and Literary History* (Oxford: Blackwell, 1986); TONY BENNETT, *Outside Literature* (London: Routledge, 1990). For a useful survey of this impressive intellectual tradition, see ALAN SWINGEWOOD, *Sociological Poetics and Aesthetic Theory* (Basingstoke: Macmillan, 1986).

29. DAVID LODGE, 'After Bakhtin', in *The Linguistics of Writing: Arguments between Language and Literature* (Manchester: Manchester University Press, 1987), p. 97.

30. In *Art and Answerability: Early Philosophical Essays by M.M. Bakhtin*, ed. Michael Holquist and Vadim Liapunov (Austin: University of Texas Press, 1990).

31. GARY MORSON and CARYL EMERSON, *Mikhail Bakhtin: Creation of a Prosaics* (Stanford, Calif.: Stanford University Press, 1990).

32. In addition to the texts already mentioned and those reprinted below, the relevant sources are MIKHAIL BAKHTIN, *Problems of Dostoevsky's Poetics*, 2nd edn, ed. and trans. Caryl Emerson (Minneapolis: University of Minnesota Press, 1984), ch. 4; and 'Response to a Question from the *Novy Mir* Editorial Staff' (1970) and 'From Notes Made in 1970–71', both in M.M. BAKHTIN, *Speech Genres and Other Late Essays*, ed. Caryl Emerson and Michael Holquist, trans. Vern W. McGee (Austin: University of Texas Press, 1986), pp. 1–9, 132–58. For critical commentaries on Bakhtinian genre theory, see the titles listed in my headnotes to Chapters 4 and 5.

33. KATERINA CLARK and MICHAEL HOLQUIST, *Mikhail Bakhtin* (Cambridge, Mass.: Belknap, 1984), pp. 99, 271. See also MICHEL AUCOUTURIER, 'The Theory of the

Novel in Russia in the 1930s: Lukács and Bakhtin', in *The Russian Novel from Pushkin to Pasternak*, ed. John Garrard (New Haven, Conn.: Yale University Press, 1983).

34. WALTER ONG, *Orality and Literacy: The Technologizing of the Word* (New York: Routledge, 1982), esp. ch. 6.

35. KENNETH BURKE, *Attitudes Toward History* (Berkeley: University of California Press, 1937, rev. edn 1959), ch. 2: 'Poetic Categories'. See also BURKE's *The Philosophy of Literary Form* (Berkeley: University of California Press, 1973). The relevance of Burke's work to genre theory is addressed in FREDRIC JAMESON, 'Symbolic Inference; or, Kenneth Burke and Ideological Analysis', *Critical Inquiry*, 4 (1978), 507–23. Jameson's own conception of narrative as 'a socially symbolic act' (the subtitle of *The Political Unconscious*) is in many ways an extension of Burke's.

36. TODOROV extends this investigation in his important book *Mikhail Bakhtin: The Dialogical Principal*, trans. Wlad Godzich (Manchester: Manchester University Press, 1984), esp. ch. 6.

37. Propp's debt to and divergence from Formalist methodology are analysed by ANN SHUKMAN, 'The Legacy of Propp', *Essays in Poetics*, 1:2 (1976), 82–94.

38. The same statement ('Gestaltenlehre ist Verwandlungslehre') appears as an epigraph to MIKHAIL PETROVSKY's essay 'The Morphology of the Folktale' (1927). For the background to contemporary literary interest in the concept of morphology, see PETER STEINER, *Russian Formalism: A Metapoetics* (Ithaca, NY: Cornell University Press, 1984), pp. 80–98; V.N. TOPOROV, 'A Few Remarks on Propp's *Morphology of the Folktale*' in *Russian Formalism: A Retrospective Glance*, ed. Robert Louis Jackson and Stephen Rudy (New Haven, Conn.: Yale Center for International and Area Studies, 1985), pp. 252–71; and DOLOZEL, *Occidental Poetics*, ch. 6. The omission of the Goethean epigraphs from the original English translation of Propp's *Morphology of the Folktale* was regarded as an 'inadmissible liberty' by Propp, who claimed that they revealed the methodological basis of his work, and its essential originality. Propp also maintained that the suppression of the epigraphs contributed to what he believed was the serious misunderstanding of his work displayed by Lévi-Strauss in the review to which I have already alluded. Propp's somewhat acrimonious response to Lévi-Strauss, which elicited a tactful reply from the latter, is reprinted under the title 'Study of the Folktale: Structure and History' in *Dispositio*, 1:3 (1976), 277–92. For Lévi-Strauss's commentary and reply, see CLAUDE LÉVI-STRAUSS, *Structural Anthropology*, vol. 2, trans. Monique Layton (New York: Basic Books, 1976), pp. 115–45.

39. Reprinted in *Readings in Russian Poetics: Formalist and Structuralist Views*, ed. Ladislav Matejka and Krystyna Pomorska (Cambridge, Mass.: Massachusetts Institute of Technology Press, 1971).

40. On the continuities and discontinuities between Russian Formalism and Czech Structuralism, see PETER STEINER, 'The Roots of Structuralist Esthetics', in *The Prague School: Selected Writings, 1929–1946*, ed. Peter Steiner (Austin: University of Texas Press, 1982), pp. 174–219; JURIJ STRIEDTER, *Literary Structure, Evolution and Value: Russian Formalism and Czech Structuralism Reconsidered* (Cambridge, Mass.: Harvard University Press, 1989); and F.W. GALAN, *Historic Structures: The Prague School Project, 1928–1946* (Austin: University of Texas Press, 1984).

41. Relevant works are listed in my Further Reading section. The standard commentary on Lotman and the Tartu school is ANN SHUKMAN, *Literature and Semiotics: A Study of the Writings of Yu. M. Lotman* (Amsterdam: North-Holland Publishing Company, 1977); his theory of genre is discussed on pp. 153–7.

42. NORTHROP FRYE, *Anatomy of Criticism: Four Essays* (Princeton: Princeton University Press, 1957), p. 104.

43. JONATHAN CULLER, *Structuralist Poetics: Structuralism, Linguistics and the Study of Literature* (London: Routledge and Kegan Paul, 1975), pp. 113–30.

44. E.D. HIRSCH, Jr, *Validity in Interpretation* (New Haven, Conn.: Yale University Press, 1967), ch. 3: 'The Concept of Genre'. For further discussion of the relevance of Wittgenstein's notion of 'language games' and 'family resemblances' to genre theory, see MAURICE MANDELBAUM, 'Family Resemblances and Generalisation Concerning the Arts', *American Philosophical Quarterly*, 2:3 (1965), 219–28; and ALASTAIR FOWLER, *Kinds of Literature: An Introduction to the Theory of Genres and Modes* (Oxford: Oxford University Press, 1982), pp. 41–2.

45. VINCENT B. LEITCH, '(De)Coding (Generic) Discourse', *Genre*, 24:1 (1991), 83–98.

46. GÜNTHER KRESS, review of Vijay K. Bhatia, *Analysing Genre: Language Use in Professional Settings* (London: Longman, 1993), *Times Higher Education Supplement*, 15 April 1994.

47. ADENA ROSMARIN, *The Power of Genre* (Minneapolis: University of Minnesota Press, 1985).

48. BETTY ROSENBERG, *Genreflecting: A Guide to Reading Interests in Genre Fiction* (Littleton, Colo.: Libraries Unlimited, 1982).

49. This term is used to describe the 'systemic-functional' school of linguistics developed by Michael Halliday at the University of Sydney in IAN REID, 'A Generic Frame for Debates about Genre', in *The Place of Genre in Learning: Current Debates*, ed. I. Reid (Deakin University: Centre for Studies in Literary Education, 1987), p. 1. Pedagogy is only one of the areas of applied linguistics in which genre theory has been used: VIJAY BHATIA's book *Analysing Genre*, cited above, extends the concept of genre to such items as sales promotion letters and job applications. KRESS's own book *Social Semiotics* (Oxford: Polity Press, 1988), co-authored with ROBERT HODGE, proposes an even wider extension of the techniques of genre analysis, while HODGE's *Literature as Discourse: Textual Strategies in English and History* (Cambridge: Polity Press, 1990) develops the notion of 'social semiotics' within these two disciplines in particular. The theoretical basis of such work – at least its linguistic aspects – is cogently summarised under the entry for 'genre analysis' in KRISTEN MALMKYER, ed., *The Linguistics Encyclopedia* (London: Routledge, 1991).

50. For these various developments, see the titles listed in the final section of my guide to Further Reading.

51. CLIFFORD GEERTZ, 'Blurred Genres: the Refiguration of Social Thought', *American Scholar*, 49:1 (1980), 65–79.

52. MICHEL FOUCAULT, *The Archaeology of Knowledge*, trans. A.M. Sheridan Smith (London: Tavistock, 1972), p. 22.

53. The new subtitle was adopted in 1992, in order, the editors of the journal inform us, to 'emphasise more fully the intricate relations between genre and the social, institutional, cultural, and political texts that constitute its discursive and cultural forms' (I quote from the announcement of the forthcoming change in vol. 24:2, Summer 1991, p. 221). As well as advertising the eclectic methodology characteristic of 'new historicism' (a term apparently coined in this journal), this reglossing of the term 'genre' indicates very clearly the intellectual expansion of the concept.

54. RENÉ WELLEK and AUSTIN WARREN, *Theory of Literature*, 3rd edn (Harmondsworth: Penguin Books, 1968), p. 231.

55. A term coined by PAUL VAN TIEGHEM in 'La question des genres littéraires', *Hélicon*, 1 (1938), 95–101 (99). WELLEK and WARREN in their *Theory of Literature* (p. 236) coin the English form, though it is rarely used.

56. For a definition of 'microgenres' and 'macrogenres', see JEAN MOLINO, 'Les genres littéraires', *Poétique*, 24:93 (1993), 3–27.

57. For an elaboration of this charge, see JENNIFER WISE, 'Marginalising Drama: Bakhtin's Theory of Genre', *Essays in Theatre*, 8:1 (1989), 15–22.

58. For a succinct statement of method by the Chicago school, see ELDER OLSON, 'An Outline of Poetic Theory', in *Critics and Criticism: Ancient and Modern*, ed. R.S. Crane et al. (Chicago: University of Chicago Press, 1952). For a shrewd assessment of the strengths and limitations of this approach to genre, see JOHN REICHERT, 'More than Kin and Less than Kind: The Limits of Genre Theory', in *Theories of Literary Genre*, ed. Strelka.

1 Criticism of the Theory of Artistic and Literary Kinds*

BENEDETTO CROCE

Benedetto Croce's forthright condemnation of the doctrine of artistic and literary kinds (genres), and of other supposed 'errors' of aesthetic theory, inaugurated the twentieth-century debate on genre and remains a standard point of reference, if only for the extremity of its views. In this brief extract from his famous treatise on the theory and history of aesthetics, the Italian philosopher presents his reasons for abandoning the whole idea of genres, except for purely pragmatic purposes such as arranging books on shelves. Theories of genre, he claims, especially when codified into definitions and rules, impoverish artistic creation and criticism alike, inhibiting originality, setting up erroneous standards of judgement, and belying the tendency of true art to break rules and violate norms. None of these arguments is entirely new, as Croce acknowledges in a later chapter of the *Aesthetic* (XIX, iii) where he surveys the history of genre theory and reveals the tradition of resistance to the doctrine of kinds; and in many respects his own position is simply an extreme version of the Romantic conception of art as self-expression. But Croce gives new force to the anti-generic view by grounding it in a distinction, fundamental to his whole philosophical system, between intuitive and logical knowledge, forms of thought which he sees as independent of and irreducible to one another. Aesthetic objects belong to the former, generic categories to the latter domain; to discuss a work of art in terms of genre is thus to falsify its nature, and commit what philosophers call a 'category mistake'. A history of genre is, likewise, an empty abstraction which Croce believes can tell us nothing about the nature of the aesthetic.

---

* Reprinted from Benedetto Croce, *Aesthetic as Science of Expression and General Linguistic*, trans. Douglas Ainslie, 2nd edn (London: Peter Owen, 1953), pp. 35–8. First published as *Estetica come scienza dell'espressione e linguitica generale: teoria e storia* (Bari, 1902).

For a more recent philosophical critique of the concept of genre, see Derrida (Chapter 13). Most of the other theorists in this anthology reject Croce's view; for a direct rebuttal, see Jauss (Chapter 8). The intellectual context of Croce's work is discussed by René Wellek, *Four Critics: Croce, Valéry, Lukács and Ingarden* (Seattle: University of Washington Press, 1981), and John Paul Russo, 'Antihistoricism in Benedetto Croce and I.A. Richards', in *Theoretical Issues in Literary History*, ed. David Perkins (Cambridge, Mass.: Harvard University Press, 1991).

[...] the greatest triumph of the intellectualist error lies in the theory of artistic and literary kinds, which still has vogue in literary treatises and disturbs the critics and the historians of art. Let us observe its genesis.

The human mind can pass from the aesthetic to the logical, just because the former is a first step in respect to the latter. It can destroy expression, that is, the thought of the individual, by thinking of the universal. It can gather up expressive facts into logical relations. We have already shown that this operation becomes in its turn concrete in an expression, but this does not mean that the first expressions have not been destroyed. They have yielded their place to the new aesthetico-logical expressions. When we are on the second step, we have left the first.

One who enters a picture gallery, or who reads a series of poems, having looked and read, may go further: he may seek out the nature and the relations of the things there expressed. Thus those pictures and compositions, each of which is an individual inexpressible in logical terms, are gradually resolved into universals and abstractions, such as *costumes, landscapes, portraits, domestic life, battles, animals, flowers, fruit, seascapes, lakes, deserts; tragic, comic, pathetic, cruel, lyrical, epic, dramatic, chivalrous, idyllic facts*, and the like. They are often also resolved into merely quantitative categories, such as *miniature, picture, statuette, group, madrigal, ballad, sonnet, sonnet sequence, poetry, poem, story, romance*, and the like.

When we think of the concept of *domestic life*, or *chivalry*, or *idyll*, or *cruelty*, or one of the quantitative concepts mentioned above, the individual expressive fact from which we started has been abandoned. From aesthetes that we were, we have changed into logicians; from contemplators of expression, into reasoners. Certainly no objection can be made to such a process. In what other way could science arise, which, if it have aesthetic expressions presupposed in it, must yet go beyond them in order to fulfil its function? The logical or scientific form, as such, excludes the aesthetic form. He who begins to think scientifically has already ceased to contemplate aesthetically;

although his thought assumes of necessity in its turn an aesthetic form, as has already been said, and as it would be superfluous to repeat.

Error begins when we try to deduce the expression from the concept, and to find in what takes its place the laws of the thing whose place is taken; when the difference between the second and the first step has not been observed, and when, in consequence, we declare that we are standing on the first step, when we are really standing on the second. This error is known as the *theory of artistic and literary kinds*.

'What is the *aesthetic* form of domestic life, of chivalry, of the idyll, of cruelty, and so forth? How should these contents be *represented*?' Such is the absurd problem implied in the theory of artistic and literary classes, when it has been shorn of excrescences and reduced to a simple formula. It is in this that consists all search after laws or rules of classes. Domestic life, chivalry, idyll, cruelty and the like, are not impressions, but concepts. They are not contents, but logical-aesthetic forms. You cannot express the form, for it is already itself expression. For what are the words cruelty, idyll, chivalry, domestic life, and so on, but the expression of those concepts?

Even the most refined of such distinctions, which possess the most philosophic appearance, do not resist criticism; as when works of art are divided into subjective and objective kinds, into lyric and epic, into works of feeling and decorative works. In aesthetic analysis it is impossible to separate subjective from objective, lyric from epic, the image of feeling from that of things.

From the theory of artistic and literary kinds derive those erroneous modes of judgement and of criticism, thanks to which, instead of asking before a work of art if it be expressive and what it expresses, whether it speak or stammer or is altogether silent, they ask if it obey the *laws* of epic or of tragedy, of historical painting or of landscape. While making a verbal pretence of agreeing, or yielding a feigned obedience, artists have, however, really always disregarded these *laws of the kinds*. Every true work of art has violated some established kind and upset the ideas of the critics, who have thus been obliged to broaden the kinds, until finally even the broadened kind has proved too narrow, owing to the appearance of new works of art, naturally followed by new scandals, new upsettings and – new broadenings.

To the same theory are due the prejudices, owing to which at one time (is it really passed?) people used to lament that Italy had no tragedy (until one arose who bestowed such a wreath, which alone of adornments was wanting to her glorious locks), nor France the epic poem (until the *Henriade*, which slaked the thirsty throats of the critics). Eulogies accorded to the inventors of new kinds are connected with these prejudices, so much so, that in the seventeenth century the invention of the *mock-heroic* poem seemed an important event, and the honour of it was disputed, as though it were the discovery of America. But the works adorned with this name (the *Secchia rapita* and the *Scherno degli Dei*) were still-born, because their authors (a slight drawback) had nothing new or original to say. Mediocrities racked their brains to invent new kinds artificially. The *piscatorial* eclogue was added to the *pastoral*, and finally the *military* eclogue. The *Aminta* was dipped and became the *Alceo*. Finally, there have been historians of art and literature, so much fascinated with these ideas of kinds, that they claimed to write the history, not of individual and real literary and artistic works, but of those empty phantoms, their kinds. They have claimed to portray, not the evolution of the *artistic spirit*, but the *evolution of kinds*.

The philosophical condemnation of artistic and literary kinds is found in the formulation and demonstration of what artistic activity has always done and good taste always recognized. What are we to do if good taste and the real fact, when reduced to formulas, sometimes assume the air of paradoxes?

It is not scientifically incorrect to talk of tragedies, comedies, dramas, romances, pictures of everyday life, battle-pieces, landscapes, seascapes, poems, versicles, lyrics, and the like, if it be only with a view to be understood, and to draw attention to certain groups of works, in general and approximately, to which, for one reason or another, it is desired to draw attention. To employ *words* and *phrases* is not to establish *laws* and *definitions*. The mistake only arises when the weight of a scientific definition is given to a word, when we ingenuously let ourselves be caught in the meshes of that phraseology. Pray permit me a comparison. The books in a library must be arranged in one way or another. This used generally to be done by a rough classification of subjects (among which the categories of miscellaneous and eccentric were not wanting); they are now generally arranged by sizes or by publishers. Who can deny the necessity and the utility of such arrangements? But what should we say if someone began seriously to seek out the literary laws of miscellanies and of eccentricities, of the Aldines or Bodonis, of shelf A or shelf B, that is to say, of those altogether arbitrary groupings whose sole object was their practical utility? Yet should any one attempt such an undertaking, he would be doing neither more nor less than those do who seek out the *aesthetic laws* which must in their belief control literary and artistic kinds.

2   The Literary Fact*

YURY TYNYANOV

Translated into English here for the first time, this seminal essay by Yury Tynyanov demonstrates the subtlety and depth of Russian Formalist thinking on the question of genre. Where earlier Formalist theory had concentrated on poetic language and adopted a synchronic perspective in order to analyse the notion of 'literariness', Tynyanov here explores the historical dimension of literature, focusing on the phenomenon of literary change. Historical considerations, he argues, severely complicate the quest for literariness, since what is deemed literary (a 'literary fact' as distinct from a fact of everyday life) is constantly shifting, not least because genres themselves perpetually evolve – through their own internal development, but also by competing with and modifying one another, and hence moving up or down the hierarchy of genres. The essay examines how and why these evolutionary processes occur, and in so doing reflects on the methodological problems of studying an object in continuous transition. Central to the discussion is the concept of 'system', a metaphor Tynyanov variously applies to the individual work, the individual genre, and literature as a whole, each of which he stresses is a *dynamic* rather than a static system, constituted not by the peaceful interaction of different elements, but by the supremacy or foregrounding of one element that subjugates and colours the rest (an extension of the Formalist concept of the 'dominant', previously applied to poetic language). One important methodological implication is that genres cannot be studied in isolation, only in relation to one another – a conclusion reinforced by Colie's work on Renaissance genre-systems (Chapter 9). Other important theoretical concepts introduced or elaborated by Tynyanov include genre-consciousness, orientation, function,

---

* Translated from Yury Tynyanov, *Poetika, istoriya literatury, kino* (Moscow: Nauka, 1977). First published as 'O Literaturnom fakte' in *Lef*, No. 2 (1924), 100–16, and reprinted in Tynyanov, *Arkhaisty i novatory* (Archaists and innovators) (Leningrad, 1929). Translated by Ann Shukman.

and the idea of a genre as a 'constructive principle', replacing the earlier Formalist conception of genre as a repertoire of 'devices'. Though his examples are mainly drawn from Russian literature, the aim of the essay is to establish general theoretical principles – in this case, nothing less than the fundamental laws of literary succession.

'The Literary Fact' opens Tynyanov's brilliant collection *Archaists and Innovators* (Leningrad, 1929), which combines essays in general theory with case studies of individual authors and genres. Two subsequent essays address closely related topics: 'On Literary Evolution' (in *Readings in Russian Poetics*, ed. Matejka and Pomorska, 1971) and 'The Ode as a Rhetorical Genre' (as yet untranslated). Other Formalist work on genre is listed in the Further Reading section, and discussed in my Introduction (pp. 6–8). For detailed commentary on Tynyanov's concept of system, see Steiner, *Russian Formalism: A Metapoetics* (1984), pp. 99–137, and Frow, *Marxism and Literary History* (1986), pp. 83–102. For more general appraisals of Formalist genre theory, see Jauss (Chapter 8); Erlich, *Russian Formalism* (1981), pp. 251–71; and Striedter, *Literary Structure, Evolution and Value* (1989). For other ideas on the competition and evolution of genres, see Bakhtin, Opacki, Todorov and Fowler (Chapters 4, 5, 7, 11, 14).

For Viktor Shklovsky

What is literature? What is genre?

All self-respecting textbooks of literary theory invariably begin by defining these terms. Theory of literature stubbornly competes with mathematics with its extremely condensed and confident static definitions: it forgets that mathematics is built on definitions, whereas in theory of literature definitions are not the foundation, but only an after-effect which is, moreover, constantly being altered by the evolving literary fact. And definitions get ever more difficult to make. In everyday speech the terms 'letters' (*slovesnost'*), 'literature' (*literatura*) and 'poetry' (*poeziya*) are current, and the need arises to nail them down and make them fit for science which so venerates definitions.

The result is three levels: the lowest is 'letters', the highest is 'poetry', and 'literature' is in the middle. It is rather difficult to distinguish them from each other.[a]

And then what if people write, as they used to in the olden days, that 'letters' simply means everything that has ever been written, and 'poetry' is thinking in images? What then, because it is clear that on the one hand poetry is not thinking in images, and on the other that thinking in images is not poetry?[b]

In fact, perhaps it's not worth bothering with a precise definition of all the terms in current use and elevating them to the rank of scientific definitions – especially since the definitions themselves have not had much success. Let's try for instance to define the concept *poema* ('long poem'), to define the concept of that genre. All attempts at a single, static definition will fail. We have only to cast a glance at Russian literature to realise that this is so. All the revolutionary essence of Pushkin's *poema* 'Ruslan and Lyudmila'[c] lay in the fact that it was a non-*poema* (the same can be said of his 'Prisoner in the Caucasus'). This claimant to the genre of the heroic *poema* turns out to be a frivolous 'tale' of the eighteenth century, one which, however, makes no excuse for its frivolity; the critics sensed that it was some kind of an exception to the genre-system. In fact the work was a *dislocation* of the system. The same can be said with regard to particular elements of the *poema*: the 'hero', the 'character' in 'The Prisoner in the Caucasus', was deliberately created by Pushkin 'for the critics', the plot was 'a tour de force'.[d] *And again the critics perceived this as an exception to the system, a mistake, and again this was a dislocation of the system.* Pushkin altered the significance of the hero, but the critics perceived the hero against the background of the noble hero and spoke of 'debasement'.

Pushkin wrote:

> One lady remarked of 'The Gipsies' that there is only one honourable person in the entire work, and that is the bear. The late lamented Ryleev was indignant that Aleko led the bear about and what is worse took money from the gaping crowds. Vyazemsky repeated the same comment. Ryleev asked me to make Aleko at least into a blacksmith which would be much more noble. Best of all would have been to make him into an official or a landowner, but not a gipsy. In that case, of course, there wouldn't have been the *poema* at all: *ma tanto meglio.*[e]

Not regular evolution, but a leap; not development, but a dislocation. The genre became unrecognisable, and yet sufficient was preserved in it so that this non-*poema* was still a *poema*. And this sufficiency lay not in the 'fundamental' or the 'important' distinctive features of the genre, but in the secondary ones, in those features which are as it were taken for granted and which seem not to characterise the genre at all. The distinctive feature which is needed to preserve the genre is, in this case, *size*.

The concept of size is primarily an energy concept: we tend to call a form on whose construction we have expended more energy a 'large form'. A 'large form', a *poema*, may be presented in a small quantity of lines (see Pushkin's 'The Prisoner in the Caucasus'). In its spatial extent, a 'large form' is the result of energy. But in certain historical periods it is indeed energy that determines the laws of construction. The novel is distinguished from the short story by the fact that it is a *large form*; the *poema* from the simple 'poem' in the same way. Our expectations of a 'large form' are not the same as of a small form: depending on the size of the construction, each detail, each stylistic device, has a different function, a different force, and a different load is laid upon it.

If this construction principle is preserved, the feeling of the genre is preserved in each instance; but, given that the principle is preserved, the construction can be dislocated endlessly: the lofty *poema* may be replaced by the frivolous tale, the noble hero by a prosaic hero (Pushkin parodies this by rhyming *senator* with *literator*[f]), the storyline may be pushed into the background, and so on.

It then becomes obvious that a *static* definition of a genre, one which would cover all its manifestations, is impossible: the genre dislocates itself; we see before us the broken line, not a straight line, of its evolution – and this evolution takes place precisely at the expense of the 'fundamental' features of the genre: of the epic as narrative, of the lyric as the art of the emotions, etc. The sufficient and necessary condition for the unity of a genre from epoch to epoch are the 'secondary' features such as the size of the construction.

But *genre* itself is not a constant, immobile system: it is interesting how the concept of genre fluctuates in cases when we are faced with a passage from a work, or a fragment. A passage from a *poema* may be perceived as a passage *from a poema*, that is, as a *poema*; but it may be perceived also as a passage, that is, we may be conscious of the fragment as a genre. This sense of a genre is not dependent on the whim of the perceiver, but on the prominence, or indeed the presence, of a particular genre: in the eighteenth century the passage was perceived as a *fragment*, in Pushkin's time as a *poema*. It is interesting that the functions of all stylistic means and devices are dependent on the definition of the genre: in a *poema* their functions will be different from those in a passage.

As a system, therefore, genre may fluctuate. It arises (out of the exceptions and vestiges in other systems) and it declines, turning into the rudimentary elements of other systems. The genre-function of a particular device is not something immobile.

It is impossible to conceive of genre as a static system for the reason that genre-consciousness itself arises as a result of a confrontation with a traditional genre (i.e. as a result of a sense that the traditional genre has been supplanted, even partially, by a 'new' one occupying its place). The point is that the new phenomenon *supplants* the old one, occupies its place, and, without being a 'development' of the old, is at the same time its substitute. When there is no 'substitution', the genre as such disappears and disintegrates.

The same can be said with regard to 'literature'. All fixed, static definitions of it are swept away by the fact of evolution.

Definitions of literature which operate with its 'fundamental' features come up against the living *literary fact*. Though it gets more and more difficult to give a firm *definition of literature*, any of our contemporaries can point out to you what a *literary fact* is. They will tell you that such and such a thing has nothing to do with literature, is a fact of everyday life or of the poet's personal life, while such and such, on the other hand, is indeed a *literary fact*. An older contemporary, one who has lived through one, or two, and sometimes even more, literary revolutions, will point out that in their time a certain phenomenon was not a literary fact but now has become one, and vice versa. Journals and almanacs existed before our times, but only in our times have they been recognised as special 'literary works', as a 'literary fact'.[8] Nonsense language has always existed – in children's speech, among the sectarians, etc. – but only in our times has it become a literary fact;[h] and so on. And the contrary is true: what today is a literary fact, tomorrow may be a mere fact of life and disappear from literature. Charades and logogriphs are children's games to us, but in Karamzin's time, when there was a taste for fun with words and games of devices, they were a literary genre. And it is not just that the *boundaries* of literature, its 'periphery', its frontier regions, are unstable: no, it is the very 'centre' we are talking about. It is not a case of one single age-old stream moving and evolving in uninterrupted succession in the centre of literature, while the new phenomena merely float in from the sides. No, these selfsame new phenomena actually occupy the centre itself, while the centre shifts down to the periphery.

At a period when a genre is disintegrating, it shifts from the centre to the periphery, and a new phenomenon floats in to take its place in the centre, coming up from among the trivia, out of the backyards and low haunts of literature. (This is the phenomenon of the 'canonisation of the younger genres' which Viktor Shklovsky has written about.) This is how the adventure novel became cheap reading matter, and how the same thing is happening now to the psychological tale.

The same thing happens when literary movements are replaced: in the 1830s and 1840s 'Pushkinian verse' (i.e. not Pushkin's verse, but its popular elements) passed into the hands of imitators and reached an extraordinary degree of jejuneness and vulgarity on the pages of the literary journals (Baron Rozen, V. Shchastny, A.A. Krylov, and others[i]). In the literal sense of the term it became the boulevard poetry of its time, while phenomena from other historical traditions and strata moved into the centre.

Historians of literature, drawing up their 'fixed', 'ontological' definition of literature as an 'essence', have been obliged to treat instances of historical supplantation too as though they were instances of peaceful succession, the peaceful and regular unfolding of this 'essence'. The picture is an orderly one: 'Lomonosov begat Derzhavin. Derzhavin begat Zhukovsky, Zhukovsky begat Pushkin, Pushkin begat Lermontov'.

Pushkin's unambiguous remarks about his alleged progenitors were overlooked (Derzhavin, said Pushkin, was 'an eccentric who didn't know how to write Russian', Lomonosov 'had a baneful influence on literature'[j]). It escaped notice too that Derzhavin succeeded to Lomonosov only when he had *dislocated Lomonosov's ode*, that Pushkin succeeded to the eighteenth-century large form *by making the trivia of the Karamzinists into a large form,* and that they all of them were able to succeed their predecessors only because they *dislocated* the style and the genres of those predecessors. It escaped notice that each new phenomenon *supplanted* the old, and that each instance of supplanting was an unusually complex phenomenon, that *uninterrupted succession should be spoken of only with regard to things like a school, or movement of imitation, but not with regard to literary evolution, the principle of which is struggle and supplanting.* Moreover, certain phenomena which are endowed with exceptional dynamism and whose significance in the evolution of literature is enormous were entirely overlooked: we have in mind phenomena which do not use the normal, habitual material of literature, and which for this reason do not leave enough striking, static 'traces' behind them; phenomena whose construction is so different from that of earlier literature that they find no place in the 'textbook'. Examples of this are nonsense language, or the *vast* field of nineteenth-century letter-writing, both of which operate with unusual material; they have enormous significance for the evolution of literature, but escape any static definition of the literary fact. This too demonstrates the error of the static approach.

You cannot judge a bullet by its colour, taste or smell, but from the point of view of its dynamics. It is rash to discuss a work of literature in terms of its aesthetic qualities in general. (Incidentally, we are hearing more and more talk of 'aesthetic values in general', of 'beauty in general', from the most unexpected quarters.)

The researcher who studies a work of literature out of context is in no way setting it beyond the reach of historical projections, he is merely approaching it with the wretched, imperfect historical apparatus of a contemporary from another age.[k]

In no way is the literary period, literary contemporaneity, an immobile system to be opposed to the moving, evolving historical order.

The same historical struggle between different strata and different formations goes on in contemporaneity as it does at all times of the historical order. Like all contemporaries, we place an equals sign between 'new' and 'good'. And there are periods when all poets write 'well' and when therefore the 'bad' poet will be the genius. Nekrasov's 'impossible', unacceptable form, his 'awful' verses, were good because they ousted poetry that had become automatised, because they were *new*. Without taking account of the evolutionary factor, the work is lost to literature; and though we may study its devices, we risk studying them apart from their functions, for *the whole point of a new construction may be in the new use to which old devices are put, in their new constructive significance*, and this is just what is overlooked if we adopt a 'static' approach.

(This does not mean that works of literature cannot 'live through the ages'. Automatised things can be made use of. Each period foregrounds some phenomena from the past, ones it feels akin to, and forgets others. But these are of course secondary phenomena, new work on ready-made material. The historical Pushkin is different from the Pushkin of the Symbolists, but the Pushkin of the Symbolists cannot be compared with the evolutionary significance of Pushkin in Russian literature;[l] each period selects the material it needs, but the way this material is used characterises only the period itself.)

By taking the literary work or author out of context, we cannot reach the author's individuality either. The author's individuality is not a static system, the literary personality is dynamic, like the literary epoch with which and in which it moves. The author's individuality is not like a closed space in which something can be seen, it is more like a broken line, which the literary epoch keeps breaking and redirecting.

(Incidentally, it is very fashionable nowadays to substitute the question of the 'writer's individuality' for the question of 'literary individuality'. The question of the psychological genesis of each phenomenon is substituted for the question of the evolution and the supplanting of literary phenomena, and instead of literature we are supposed to study 'the creative personality'.[m] It is obvious that the genesis of each phenomenon is one question, while the evolutionary significance of that phenomenon, its place in the evolutionary order, is another. To talk of the personal psychology of the creator and to find there the uniqueness of the phenomenon and its evolutionary literary significance is like explaining the origin and significance of the Russian revolution by saying that it came about as a result of the personal characteristics of the leaders on the opposing sides.)

An interesting corroboration of the view that one should treat 'the psychology of creation' extremely cautiously, even in questions of 'theme' and 'thematics' which can readily be associated with the author's psychology, is Vyazemsky's response to A. Turgenev, who had detected personal experiences in Vyazemsky's poetry:

If I had been in love as you think, if I did believe in the immortality
of the soul, then probably I would not have said openly to you:
'*The soul, never dying, will live beyond life, in the immortality of love.*'
   For instance I have often remarked that when my heart is furious
my tongue dries up; though it will blurt out something to a passer-
by. Diderot says: 'Why look for the author in his characters? What
do Racine and Athalie have in common, or Molière and Tartuffe?'
What he said about dramatists, holds true of every writer. The
chief mark of an author lies not in his choice of topics, but in his
treatment of them: how, from what point of view does he regard
the thing, what does he see in it, and what does he find in it, that
is unnoticed by another? You can't judge a singer by the words he
sings . . . Batyushkov in reality is hardly the same as he is in his
verses. He has not a scrap of voluptuousness about him.[1]

A static, context-free study is quite unable to provide the way-in to
the literary personality of an author and merely palms off the concept
of psychological genesis for the concepts of literary evolution and
literary genesis.

Pushkin studies demonstrate the result of this static and isolated
approach. Pushkin is emphasised instead of period and of evolutionary
line, he is studied in isolation from it (usually the entire literary
epoch is studied under the heading 'Pushkin'). And for this reason
(and this reason alone) many literary historians continue to declare
that the last period of Pushkin's lyrics is the highest point in the
development of his lyric writing, without noticing that Pushkin's
lyric production was declining at this time and that he was shifting
into para-literary fields: the journal and history.

Many significant and valuable literary phenomena have been
condemned to be studied from a static point of view instead of an
evolutionary one. The talentless literary critic who now mocks at
early Futurism wins a cheap victory: to judge a dynamic fact from a
static point of view is the same as judging the qualities of a shot
apart from its trajectory. The 'shot' may be very nice to look at and
not fly, i.e. not be a shot, or it may be 'clumsy' and 'ugly' but fly
well, i.e. be a shot.

And it is uniquely in evolution that we can analyse the 'definition'
of literature; whereupon we discover that the qualities of *literature*
which seemed to be *fundamental* and primary are endlessly changing,
and do not describe literature as such. Concepts like 'aesthetic', in the
sense of 'beautiful', are of this kind.

The constant factor is something that has all along been taken for
granted, namely that literature is a speech construction, perceived
precisely as a construction, i.e. literature is a *dynamic speech construction.*[n]

The need for ceaseless dynamism is what gives rise to evolution, because every dynamic system inevitably becomes automatised, and dialectically delineates the opposite constructive principle.[2]

The uniqueness of the literary work lies in the way the constructive factor is applied to the material, in the way it 'gives form to' (i.e., in effect, deforms°) the material. Every work is like an off-centre disc, where the constructive factor is not dissolved in the material, does not 'correspond' to it, but is connected to it eccentrically, stands out against it.

Moreover, naturally, 'material' is not to be opposed to 'form' because it is also 'formal' and does not exist apart from constructive material. Attempts to get outside the construction lead to results like those of Potebnya's theory: at point X (the idea), towards which the image is striving, many images may obviously converge, and this mixes the most disparate, specific constructions into one.[p] Material is the subservient element of form owing to the foregrounded constructive elements.

In poetry this pivotal constructive factor is *rhythm* and the material, in the broad sense, is the *semantic groups*; in prose, the *semantic grouping* (the plot) is the constructive factor, and the material is the rhythmical (in the broad sense) elements of discourse.

Every constructive principle establishes its own specific connections within these constructive series, a particular relationship of the constructive factor towards the subservient elements. (A constructive principle may also include a deliberate *orientation* towards a particular function or use of the construction: to take a simple example, orientation towards the *spoken* word is part of the constructive principle of oratorical speech and even of the oratorical lyric, and so on.)

Thus while 'constructive factor' and 'material' are constant concepts for certain constructions, the constructive principle is a concept which is always changing, which is complex and evolving. The whole essence of a 'new form' lies in the new principle of construction, in the new use made of the relationship between the constructive factor and the subservient factors – the material.

The interaction of constructive factor and material must continually diversify, fluctuate, take new shapes, in order to be dynamic.

It is easy to approach an automatised work from another period with one's own perceptual baggage and to see not the original constructive principle but only connections which have become deadened and indistinguishable, and which we colour with our own perceptual lenses. But a *contemporary* always senses these relationships, these interactions, in their dynamism; he or she does not separate 'metre' from 'vocabulary', but always knows the novelty of their relationship. And this novelty is consciousness of evolution.

One of the laws of the dynamism of form is that there should be the greatest fluctuation, the greatest variability in the correlation of constructive principle and material.

Pushkin, for instance, has recourse to *blank spaces* in poems with a particular stanza structure. (These are not 'omissions', because the lines are omitted in this case for constructional reasons, and in some instances the blank spaces are completely without a text, as, for instance, in *Eugene Onegin*.) The same thing can be found in Annensky and in Mayakovsky ('About This').

These are not pauses, but actually verse without speech material; the semantics are what you will, 'anything'; as a result the constructive factor, the metre, is laid bare and its role emphasised.[q]

The construction is here worked out on zero speech material. The frontiers of the material in verbal art are so broad; such deep cleavages and ruptures are admissible – the constructive factor welds them together. The leaps over the material, this zero-material, only emphasise the tenacity of the constructive factor.[r]

And so when we analyse literary evolution we find the following stages: (1) an opposing constructive principle takes shape in dialectical relationship to an automatised principle of construction; (2) it is then applied – the constructive principle seeks out the readiest field of application; (3) it spreads over the greatest mass of phenomena; (4) it becomes automatised and gives rise to opposing principles of construction.

At a time when the dominant central trends are disintegrating, a dialectically new constructive principle takes shape. Large forms, when they become automatised, show up the significance of small forms (and vice versa); the image consisting of a verbal ornamentation, a semantic fracturing, once automatised, shows up the significance of the image which is motivated by an object (and vice versa).

But it would be fanciful to imagine that a new trend, a new supplanting, comes into being all at once, like Minerva from the head of Jupiter.

No, this important fact of evolutionary supplanting is preceded by a complex process.

First of all an opposing constructive principle takes shape. It takes shape from *'chance' results and 'chance' exceptions and errors*. For example, when the *small* form is predominant in lyric poetry – the sonnet and quatrain, etc. – the action of collecting the sonnets or quatrains and so on into a *volume* may be just such a 'chance result'.

But once the small form has become automatised, this *chance result becomes established* and the volume itself is felt to be a construction, i.e. a large form comes into being.

August Schlegel, for instance, called Petrarch's sonnets a lyric novel; and Heine, a poet of the small form in *Buch der Lieder* and other cycles of 'small poems', supposed that one of the most important constructive moments came when these poems were *united* in a volume; this was the moment of connection, and he created the volumes – the lyrical novels – in which each small poem served as a chapter.

Conversely, one of the 'chance' results of the large form is the recognition that the device of leaving things unfinished, leaving blanks, is a method of construction which leads directly to the small form. But obviously, leaving things unfinished, leaving blanks, will be perceived as an error, as an exception to the system, and only when the system itself becomes automatised will this mistake be perceived, against the background of the system, as a new constructive principle.

Strictly speaking, every blemish, every 'mistake', every 'misdemeanour' in normative poetics is, potentially, a new constructive principle (this is what happened, for example, when the Futurists used linguistic slips and 'mistakes' to make semantic shifts).[3]

As it develops, a constructive principle seeks to apply itself. Certain special, highly favourable conditions are needed for this application to come about in fact.

This is what is happening in our days with the Russian adventure novel. The principle of the plot-based novel emerged as a dialectical contradiction to the principle of the plotless tale and short story; but the constructive principle has not yet found the field of application it needs. It is still being applied to foreign material; and in order to fuse with Russian material it needs certain special circumstances. The union cannot be achieved all that simply: plot and style get going together when conditions are right, and that's the whole secret. If these conditions are not met the phenomenon will remain merely an endeavour.

The more 'subtle', the more unusual, the phenomenon, the more clearly will the new constructive principle take shape.

Art finds the phenomena it needs in the field of everyday *life*.[5] Life swarms with the rudimentary elements of different kinds of intellectual activity. Everyday life is made up of rudimentary science, rudimentary art and technology; it differs from developed science, art and technology by the method of dealing with them. 'Artistic life' then is something different from art because the function of art in it is different, though both art and artistic life share the same phenomena. Their different methods of dealing with the same phenomena make their selection of these phenomena different, and so the actual forms of artistic life are different from art. But at that moment when a fundamental central constructive principle is developing in art, it seeks out phenomena that are 'someone else's', 'new', fresh. These phenomena must not be the old, familiar ones which have been associated with a constructive principle that is now disintegrating.

So the new constructive principle falls upon fresh phenomena of everyday life, ones which are close at hand.

Let us take an example:

In the first half of the eighteenth century, letter-writing was more or less what it was until recently with us – a phenomenon only of everyday life. Letters did not intrude into literature. They borrowed a lot from literary prose style, but were far from being literature; they consisted of notes, receipts, petitions, announcements to friends, and so on.

Poetry was predominant in literature; and in poetry the high genres held sway. There was no opening, no crack, through which the letter could become a literary fact. But then this trend wore itself out; interest in prose and the lesser genres pushed out the lofty ode.

The ode, the predominant genre, began to sink to the level of sycophantic verses, that is, doggerel addressed by petty clerks to their superiors; it sank into everyday life. The constructive principle of a new tendency began to be felt dialectically.

The chief principle of the grand ode (*grandiozari*) of the eighteenth century was the oratorical, emotionally blinding function of the poetic word. Lomonosov's images were constructed according to the principle of transferring the thing to an 'improper' place, one which was not appropriate for it; the principle of 'harnessing together distant ideas' legitimised the combination of words which were distant in meaning; the image became a kind of semantic 'demolition job', and not a 'picture' (at the same time the principle of harnessing together words according to their sound grew to prominence).

Emotion ('grandiose' emotion) intensified and slackened in turn – 'rest periods', 'weak places', paler sections, were part of the plan.

Hence the allegorism and anti-psychologism of eighteenth-century high literature.

The oratorical ode evolved into Derzhavin's ode in which the grandeur of the ode with its mixture of 'high' and 'low' words was joined with the comic elements of satirical verse.

The end of the grand lyric came in the time of Karamzin. In opposition to oratorical discourse, the song and the romance grew in significance. The image as a semantic demolition became automatised and gave rise to the appeal of the image based on the most immediate associations.

The small form came to the fore, and with it the small emotion; psychologism supplanted the allegories. This is how constructive principles dialectically cast themselves off from the old ones.

But for these principles to be applied they need the most transparent, the handiest phenomena – and they found them in everyday life.

In drawing-rooms, in the small talk of the 'dear ladies', in albums, the small form of 'trifles' became the rage: 'songs', quatrains, rondos, acrostics, charades, bouts-rimés and games were transformed into important literary phenomena.

And finally, *the letter*.

Letters turned out to be the handiest, the easiest, the most needed phenomena, and here the new principles of construction were displayed with unusual emphasis: leaving things unsaid, being fragmentary, hinting, the 'domestic' small form of the letter motivated the introduction of trifles and stylistic devices quite the opposite of the 'grandiose' devices of the eighteenth century. This much-needed material lay outside literature in everyday life. And the letter was lifted out of everyday life where it had functioned as a document into the very centre of literature. Karamzin's letters to Petrov[t] overtook his own experiments in the old oratorical canonic prose and resulted in *Letters of a Russian Traveller*, the work in which the travel letter became a *genre*. The travel letter became the justification for the genre, and the genre's way of welding together the new devices. See Karamzin's preface:

> The colourfulness and unevenness of his style are the consequence of the different objects which impress the soul of the traveller; he describes his impressions not at leisure, not in the quiet of his study, but wherever and however he may, on the road, on scraps of paper, with a pencil. Much, I admit, is not serious, mere trifles, but why not forgive the traveller some idle details? The man in travelling garb, staff in hand, pack on his shoulders, has no need to speak with the careful nicety of a courtier in the company of other courtiers, or of a professor, sitting in his Spanish wig on his great cathedra.[u]

But alongside the traveller's letter the everyday letter continued to exist: the centre of literature was occupied not only and not wholly by the printed genres but also by the everyday letter with its snatches of poems, its jokes, its anecdotes – for it no longer consisted just of 'announcements' and 'receipts'.

The former document was becoming a fact of literature.[v]

Among the younger Karamzinists, A. Turgenev, P. Vyazemsky, the everyday letter was in ceaseless evolution. Their letters were read not only by the addressees; their responses were evaluated and analysed like literary works. The type of the Karamzin letter which was a mosaic with its inserted verses, unexpected shifts, and well-rounded aphorisms lasted for a long time. (See Pushkin's first letters to

Vyazemsky and V. Pushkin.) But the style of the letter was evolving. From the very beginning a place was found in the letter for an intimate joke between friends, a joking periphrasis, for parody and for teasing each other, for hints at eroticism; all these elements stressed the intimacy and non-literary nature of the genre. This was how the letter developed, but with A. Turgenev, Vyazemsky and especially with Pushkin it evolved along other lines.

Affectation disappeared and was frowned upon, periphrasis was dropped, there was a tendency towards coarse simplicity (in Pushkin's case this was not without the influence of the archaisers who stood up for 'primeval simplicity' against the aestheticism of the Karamzinists). This was not the neutral simplicity of a document, an announcement, a receipt, this was a newly found literary simplicity. The non-literary nature of the genre, its private nature, was still stressed, but it was stressed with deliberate coarseness, intimate bad language, coarse eroticism.

Yet at the same time the writers were aware of the genre as a profoundly literary genre: the letters were read and shared. Vyazemsky planned to write a Russian *Manuel du style épistolaire*.[w] Pushkin wrote rough drafts for modest private letters. He assiduously cultivated his epistolary style, guarding his simplicity from a relapse into the affectations of the Karamzinists ('Adieu, prince Numbskull and princess Giddyhead. You see I haven't enough of my own simplicity left for writing': Letter to Vyazemsky, 1826).

The spoken language was mostly French, but Pushkin tells off his brother for mixing French and Russian in his letters, like a Moscow girl cousin.[x]

So the *letter*, while it remained a private, non-literary fact, was at the same time also, and for this very reason, a literary fact of the greatest significance. This literary fact gave rise to the canonised genre of 'literary correspondence', but even in its pure form it still remained a fact of literature.

We can easily trace epochs when the letter, having played out its literary role, sinks once more into everyday life, no longer impinging on literature, and becomes a fact of everyday life, a document, a receipt. But when circumstances are right this fact of life can again become a fact of literature.

It is intriguing to see how those historians and theoreticians of literature who work with fixed definitions of literature deal with the enormous significance of a literary fact which emerges out of everyday life and then sinks into it again. To date, Pushkin's letters have been used only as a source of information or by those seeking the erotic. The letters of Vyazemsky, A. Turgenev and Batyushkov have never been studied by anyone as a literary fact.[4]

In the case we looked at, that of Karamzin, the letter was the justification for certain devices of construction: as something fresh out of everyday life, 'not ready-made', it met the needs of the new constructive principle better than any 'ready-made' literary things.

But there is another way by which something from everyday life can become part of literature, there is another way of transforming a fact of life into a fact of literature.

Once a constructive principle is applied to any one field it strives to enlarge itself and to spread over as wide an area as possible.

We might call this the 'imperialism' of the constructive principle. One can observe this imperialism, this urge to take over the widest area, in any sector. An example pointed out by Veselovsky is how an epithet may become generalised: if one day poets write 'golden sun', 'golden hair', then on the next they will have 'golden sky', 'golden land' and 'golden blood'.[y] A fact of a similar kind is the tendency of a victorious order or genre to affect other fields: thus periods when rhythmic prose is common coincide with periods when poetry predominates over prose. The prevalence of *vers libres* proves that the constructive principle of rhythm has so penetrated consciousness that it can spread to phenomena of the widest possible order.

A constructive principle strives to exceed its normal bounds, for if it stays confined to the usual phenomena it soon becomes automatised. This explains why poets change their themes.

To take an example: Heine constructed his art on dissonance and breakdown. He breaks the straight line of an entire poem in the last line with a *pointe*; he constructs an image on the principle of contrast. This is how he treats the theme of love. Gotschall writes:

> Heine took these contrasts between 'sacred' and 'vulgar' love to the extreme; they threatened to escape from the poem. Eventually these variations ceased to 'have resonance', these endless self-mockeries seemed like the clown in the circus. His humour had to seek out new fields, had to leave the narrow field of 'love' and take the state, literature, art, the objective world as its theme.[5]

When a constructive principle spreads over the widest possible material, it eventually strives to break through the boundary of what is specifically literary, what is 'second-hand', and finally falls upon everyday life. For example, the dynamics of *plot*, the constructive principle of prose, comes to predominance and seeks maximum development. Then things with a *minimal storyline*, without a plot, are taken as plot-based. (See Viktor Shklovsky, 'Tristram Shandy';[z] we might compare this process with the phenomenon of *vers libres* which, being unlike the normal system of verse, for this very reason emphasise verse.)

And nowadays this constructive principle is moving into everyday life. Newspapers and journals have existed for many years as a fact of everyday life. But nowadays there is an awakened interest in newspapers, journals and almanacs as special works of literature, as constructions.

A fact of everyday life gives vitality through its own constructive aspect. We are not indifferent to the motivation of a newspaper or journal. A journal may be fine with regard to its material and yet we may still judge it to be inept with regard to its construction, its motivation, and so condemn it as a journal. If one follows the evolution of the journal, and its replacement by the almanac and so on, it becomes clear that the line of this evolution is not a straight one: at one time the journal is a neutral fact of everyday life, its motivation is without significance, at another it grows into a literary fact. At a time of intensive effort, when such things as 'sugar-lump composition' are becoming widespread in the short story and novel (i.e. when the plot is composed of deliberately unconnected sections),[aa] this principle of construction naturally extends to neighbouring, and then more distant, phenomena.

There is another telling occurrence when one can see a constructive principle which is feeling cramped on purely literary material passing on to material of everyday life. I am speaking of the 'literary persona'.

Certain stylistic features point to the *person* of the author. One can find vestiges of this in the ordinary tale: peculiarities of lexis, syntax, and above all of intonational phrasing, all contribute certain elusive and yet concrete features of the narrator; if the tale is told with emphasis on the narrator, from his persona, then these elusive features become glaringly concrete and form themselves into an image. (Of course this is a particular kind of concreteness, very different from that of a pictorial representation; and if one were asked for instance what this narrator *looks like*, then our answer would have to be subjective.[bb]) The final stroke that gives this stylistic persona literary specificity is the *name*.

When a person is designated, a mass of small features are immediately evoked, which reach far beyond the concepts actually expressed. When a nineteenth-century writer signed his article 'A Dweller of New Village' instead of his name,[cc] he was not of course wanting to tell the reader that he lived in New Village because there would have been no point at all in the reader knowing this fact.

But precisely because of this 'pointlessness' the designation acquired other features: the reader selected from the concepts only what was *typical*, only what gave some kind of an idea of the author's characteristics, and applied these features to those features which had emerged for him from the author's style, from the idiosyncrasies of his narration, or from the assortment of ready-made similar names. So New Village would imply 'a remote place' and the author of the article would be 'a hermit'.

Name and surname have even greater expressive qualities. In everyday life a name, a surname, are identical to their bearer. When someone mentions an unfamiliar surname, we say: 'That name means nothing to me.' But in a work of literature there are no unfamiliar names. All names mean something. Every name or title in a work of literature is a designation which plays with all the hues of which it is capable. With maximum intensity it evokes nuances which in life we overlook. 'Ivan Petrovich Ivanov' is not a drab name for a literary character, because its drabness is a negative feature only in life while in a construction it immediately becomes a positive feature.

Signatures such as 'A Dweller of the Village of Tentel'evo' or 'The Old Man of Luzhnitsky',[dd] which appear to be simple designations of place (or age), are very typical and very specific names not only because of features expressed by the phrases 'old man' and 'village dweller', but also because of the expressive force of the place-names 'Tentel'evo' and 'Luzhnitsky'.

Then there is also the institution of the *pseudonym* in artistic practice. Looked at from its everyday aspect the pseudonym is a phenomenon similar to anonymity. The life conditions and historical causes that gave rise to it are complex and not our concern here. But in periods of literature when the 'persona of the author' is made prominent, this life phenomenon is made use of in literature.

In the 1820s, pseudonyms such as the examples given above 'grew denser', more specific, as the stylistic features of *skaz* developed. In the 1830s this phenomenon led to the creation of the literary personage of Baron Brambeus.[ee]

Later the 'personage' of Kuz'ma Prutkov was created. A fact of law, which was primarily concerned with an author's rights and responsibilities, a name tag displayed in the writers' union, became under certain specific conditions of literary evolution a *literary fact*.

Within literature there are phenomena of different strata; in this sense there is never a complete supplanting of one literary movement by another. But in another sense such a change does take place – the paramount movements and paramount genres are replaced.

However broad and numerous the branches of literature are, however many individual features are characteristic of particular branches of literature, history leads them along certain defined paths: there is no avoiding the moments when what seemed like an endlessly diversified current grows shallow and when new phenomena, at first small-scale and barely noticeable, come to take its place.

Endlessly diversified is the 'fusion of a constructive principle with the material' of which I have spoken, and it takes place in a mass of diversified forms, but for every literary movement there comes the inevitable moment of historical generalisation, when it is reduced to the simple and uncomplicated.

The emergence of schools of imitators who hasten the replacement of the main current is a phenomenon of this order. And when this supplanting occurs there are revolutions of different dimensions, different profundity. There are domestic revolutions, 'political' ones, there are 'social' revolutions, *sui generis*. And these revolutions usually burst through what is strictly speaking 'literature' and seize hold of the domain of everyday life.

We should bear in mind how diversified the make-up of the literary fact is every time we speak of 'literature'.

The literary fact has a complex make-up, and in this sense literature is a ceaselessly evolving order.

Every term in theory of literature must be the specific result of specific facts. You cannot take your starting point from the extra- or supra-literary heights of metaphysical aesthetics and forcibly 'choose' the data that 'match' the term. A term is specific: every definition evolves just as the literary fact itself evolves.

Author's notes

1. Ostaf'ev archive, vol. 1, St Petersburg, 1899, p. 382; letter of 1819.

2. On the functions of the literary order, see the article 'On Literary Evolution' in this volume [*Archaists and Innovators* (1929)]. The definition of literature as a dynamic speech construction does not of itself presuppose the laying bare of the device. There are periods when the device which has been laid bare, like any other device, becomes automatised, and when it naturally gives rise to the demand for the dialectically opposite, the device that is smoothed over. This smoothed-over device is more dynamic in such circumstances than one that is laid bare, because it replaces that correlation of constructive principle and material which had become normal, and therefore emphasises it. The 'negative feature' of a smoothed-over form may be powerful when the 'positive feature' of a form laid bare has become automatised.[ff]

3. For this reason any 'purism' is a specific purism, a purism founded on a given system, and not 'purism in general'. The same is true of linguistic purism. The archaisers' journal *Galateya* (1829 and 1830) carried whole pages with long lists of Pushkin's 'mistakes' and 'errors'. Modern Russian prose shows its prudishness in two directions: a fear of the simple phrase and an avoidance of fully motivated linguistic slips. Pisemsky, who was not afraid of such things, wrote: 'The stench of cheap tobacco you could feel and some kind of cabbage soup which had gone off made life almost unbearable in that place'[gg] (A.F. PISEMSKY, *Polnoe sobranie sochinenii*, St Petersburg, 1910, vol. 4, pp. 46–7).

4. This was written in 1924. The article by N. Stepanov and others has appeared since then.[hh]

5. R. GOTSCHALL, *Die deutsche National-Literatur des 19. Jahrhunderts* (Breslau, 1872), vol. 2, p. 92. To say that these changes are brought about by extra-literary causes (for instance, personal experiences) is to confuse the concepts of genesis and evolution into one thing. The psychological genesis of a phenomenon in no way corresponds to its evolutionary significance.

Translator's notes

a   A reference to the ideas of A.A. Smirnov, which Tynyanov had criticised in a review of the previous year.

b   A reference to Shklovsky's polemic against the ideas of Potebnya that poetry is 'thinking in images', See V. SHKLOVSKY, 'Art as Technique', in *Russian Formalist Criticism: Four Essays*, trans. L.T. Lemon and M.J. Reis (Lincoln: University of Nebraska Press, 1965).

c   'Ruslan and Lyudmila', nearly 3000 lines long, was begun in 1817 when Pushkin was 18 years old, and published in 1820. It was Pushkin's first published work. 'The Prisoner of the Caucasus', some 700 lines long, was written in 1820–1.

d   Pushkin created the shockingly cold and insensitive character of the Prisoner 'for the critics' (letter to L.S. Pushkin of October 1822); the phrase 'tour de force', however, refers to the plot of another *poema*, 'The Robber Brothers' (1821) (letter to Vyazemsky of October 1823).

e   From 'A Refutation of the Critics' (1830).

f   From his parodic 'Ode to His Excellency Count D.I. Khvostov' (1825).

g   The question of the literary form of a journal was one which exercised the Formalists in the mid- to late 1920s.

h   Nonsense language (*zaum'*) was widely used in the experimental poetry of the Futurists.

i   Minor poets of the period. Tynyanov was wrong, however, to include Krylov, who died in 1829.

j   Tynyanov's quotations are not accurate.

k   Tynyanov's point was taken up in the *Theses* of the Prague Linguistic Circle (1929): 'The scholar must avoid egocentrism, the analysis and evaluation of poetic facts of other periods or nations from the perspective of his own poetic habits and artistic norms stressed in his education' (*The Prague School: Selected Writings, 1929–1946*, ed. P. Steiner (Austin: University of Texas Press, 1982), p. 17).

l   See for example the words of the Symbolist poet ALEXANDER BLOK at the Pushkin Commemoration in 1921: 'We know Pushkin the man, we know Pushkin the friend of the monarchy, we know Pushkin the friend of the Decembrists, but all this pales before Pushkin the poet. A poet is an immutable value. His language and his devices may become obsolete, but the essence of his concern does not . . . the poet's concern . . . is quite incommensurable with the order of the external world' ('The Poet's Role', in *Russian Views of Pushkin*, ed. and trans. D.J. Richards and C.R.S. Cockrell (Oxford: Meeuws, 1976), pp. 128, 132).

m   The Formalists were consistently anti-psychologist from the earliest days of *Opoyaz*. In this their approach was similar to that of the formal school of German art historians (Wöfflin and his school) and literary scholars (Dibelius,

Walzel, etc.), whose work was well known in Russia. The Formalists themselves were aware of the parallels, but inclined to stress the differences in problems and principles, as well as their own originality. See Y. TYNYANOV, *Poetika, istoriya literatury, kino* (Moscow: Nauka, 1977), pp. 515–16. Hereafter cited as PLK.

[n]   The similarity between some of Tynyanov's ideas, notably the idea of the dynamic construction, and those of Gestalt psychology has been pointed out by, e.g., K. POMORSKA, *Russian Formalist Theory and Its Poetic Ambiance* (The Hague: Mouton, 1968), pp. 39, 41, and V. ERLICH. *Russian Formalism: History, Doctrine* (The Hague: Mouton, 1955), pp. 133, 170–1. Here too there would seem to be more a case of a parallel development than of influence (see PLK, pp. 516–17).

[o]   In a letter to Vinokur of 7 November 1924 Tynyanov wrote: 'My term "deformation" is unfortunate, I should have written "transformation" and then everything would have been in place' (PLK, p. 517).

[p]   On the Formalists' criticism of Potebnya, see P. STEINER, *Russian Formalism: A Metapoetics* (Ithaca: Cornell University Press, 1984), pp. 140ff.; ERLICH, *Russian Formalism*, pp. 23–6; as well as SHKLOVSKY, 'Art as Technique'.

[q]   In the later cantos of Pushkin's *Eugene Onegin* there are numbered stanzas, occupying a space on the page, but which have no words. Tynyanov explores the significance of these 'blank stanzas' further in his book *The Problem of Verse Language* [1924], trans. M. Sosa and B. Harvey (Ann Arbor: Ardis, 1981).

[r]   YURY LOTMAN has developed the idea of the 'minus-device', the significance of an absence, in his book *The Structure of the Artistic Text*, trans. Ronald Vroon (Ann Arbor: University of Michigan, 1977).

[s]   The term *byt* ('everyday life'), frequently used by the Formalists, has connotations of human life as lived in its mundane and unremarkable course. *Byt* is to be contrasted with the world of culture and ideology, just as it is also not the same as the more general word for 'life', *zhizn'*.

[t]   Another of Tynyanov's slips: Karamzin's letters to Petrov were destroyed after Petrov's death by his brother (PLK, p. 517).

[u]   Abbreviated quotation from the preface to Karamzin's *Letters of a Russian Traveller* (1793).

[v]   Tynyanov is of course referring to the letter between friends, and not to the genre of the epistolary novel which was already in existence.

[w]   This was not Vyazemsky's intention, but A.I. Turgenev's.

[x]   Letter of 24 January 1822.

[y]   See A. VESELOVSKY, *Istoriceskaja poetika*, ed. V. Zirmunsky (Leningrad, 1940), p. 21.

[z]   V. SHKLOVSKY, 'Sterne's *Tristram Shandy*: Stylistic Commentary', in Lemon and Reis, *Russian Formalist Criticism*.

[aa]   One of several graphic terms used by the Formalists for describing plot constructions. See also Shklovsky's 'threading' and 'staircase' plots.

[bb]   The particular narrative device when a story is told through the words of a personified narrator was termed *skaz* by the Formalists.

[cc]   N.I. Gnedich.

[dd]   Pseudonyms used by Kachenovsky, Pogodin and Yakovlev.

[ee] Pseudonym of Marlinsky.

[ff] Here Tynyanov hints at a solution to the problem always raised by Formalist theory, namely, how to explain art that is not based on novelty, but on familiarity and repetition.

[gg] Literal translation of Pisemsky's awkward Russian.

[hh] N. STEPANOV, 'Druzheskaya perepiska 20-kh godov', in *Russkaya proza*, ed. B. Eikhenbaum and Yu. Tynyanov (Leningrad, 1926).

3 Fairy Tale Transformations*

VLADIMIR PROPP

Propp's famous book *The Morphology of the Folktale* (1928) is often
regarded as the first work of literary structuralism in that it uses
the concept of invariance to analyse the structural similarities which
underlie the superficial diversity of Russian fairy tales, arguing
that all such stories are basically variants of a single type, employing a fixed repertory of motifs or 'functions'. The companion essay
reprinted here, published in the same year, extends that investigation of the grammar of genre by explaining *how* those variants are
produced, Propp's aim being to identify both the formal mechanisms involved (he lists twenty different kinds of transformation,
distinguishing first between the 'basic' and the 'derived' form of a
'story element') and, more controversially, the ethnological and
historical processes which give rise to them. Though Propp was
not a member of the *Opoyaz* circle, this interest in the diachronic as
well as the synchronic aspects of genre is characteristic of the later
phase of Russian Formalism, as is the sustained application of the
concepts of 'system' and 'function' (compare Tynyanov, Chapter
2). But Propp, like Jakobson and Bogotyrev in their important
essay 'On the Boundary between Studies of Folklore and Literature' (in *Readings in Russian Poetics*, 1971), draws a firm distinction
between literary and folk narratives (the latter being a product of a
collective creativity, transmitted orally), and it is by no means certain how many of the transformational processes listed here also
occur in the development of *literary* genres: compare Fowler's typology of generic transformations (Chapter 14), Frye on 'displacement'
(Chapter 6), and Todorov on the origins of genre (Chapter 11).

To be understood fully, the essay needs to be read alongside
Propp's *Morphology of the Folktale*; some of Propp's other work on

* Reprinted from *Readings in Russian Poetics: Formalist and Structuralist Views*, ed.
Ladislav Matejka and Krystyna Pomorska (Cambridge, Mass.: Massachusetts
Institute of Technology Press, 1971), pp. 94–114. First published as 'Transformacii
volshebnyx skazok' in *Poetika*, 4 (1928), 70–89. Translated by C.H. Severens.

folk narrative is collected in his *Theory and History of Folklore* (1984). For his Russian context and influence, see Ann Shukman, 'The Legacy of Propp', *Essays in Poetics*, 1:2 (1976), 82–94; and Steiner, *Russian Formalism: A Metapoetics* (1984), pp. 80–98. For his influence on French structuralism, see Culler, *Structuralist Poetics* (1975), pp. 207–8; and the important exchange with Lévi-Strauss cited in the notes to my Introduction (p. 22). Jameson's essay (Chapter 10) incorporates a detailed critique of Propp's theory of genre, which he juxtaposes with Northrop Frye's. Notwithstanding the many criticisms of his theoretical model, Propp's impact on literary structuralism in general and on narratology in particular can hardly be overestimated: for evidence of the latter, see the volume in the present series on *Narratology: An Introduction*, ed. Susan Onega and José Angel García Landa (1996).

1

The study of the fairy tale may be compared in many respects to that of organic formation in nature. Both the naturalist and the folklorist deal with species and varieties which are essentially the same. The Darwinian problem of the origin of species arises in folklore as well. The similarity of phenomena both in nature and in our field resists any direct explanation which would be both objective and convincing. It is a problem in its own right. Both fields allow two possible points of view: either the internal similarity of two externally dissimilar phenomena does not derive from a common genetic root – the theory of spontaneous generation – or else this morphological similarity does indeed result from a known genetic tie – the theory of differentiation owing to subsequent metamorphoses or transformations of varying cause and occurrence.

In order to resolve this problem, we need a clear understanding of what is meant by similarity in fairy tales. Similarity has so far been invariably defined in terms of a plot and its variants. We find such an approach acceptable only if based upon the idea of the spontaneous generation of species. Adherents to this method do not compare plots; they feel such comparison to be impossible or, at the very least, erroneous.[1] Without our denying the value of studying individual plots and comparing them solely from the standpoint of their similarity, another method, another basis for comparison may be proposed. Fairy tales can be compared from the standpoint of their composition or structure; their similarity then appears in a new light.[2]

We observe that the actors in the fairy tale perform essentially the same actions as the tale progresses, no matter how different from one another in shape, size, sex, and occupation, in nomenclature and other static attributes. This determines the relationship of the constant factors to the variables. The functions of the actors are constant; everything else is a variable. For example:

1. The king sends Ivan after the princess; Ivan departs.
2. The king sends Ivan after some marvel; Ivan departs.
3. The sister sends her brother for medicine; he departs.
4. The stepmother sends her stepdaughter for fire; she departs.
5. The smith sends his apprentice for a cow; he departs.

The dispatch and the departure on a quest are constants. The dispatching and departing actors, the motivations behind the dispatch, and so forth, are variables. In later stages of the quest, obstacles impede the hero's progress; they, too, are essentially the same, but differ in the form of imagery.

The functions of the actors may be singled out. Fairy tales exhibit 31 functions, not all of which may be found in any one fairy tale; however, the absence of certain functions does not interfere with the order of appearance of the others. Their aggregate constitutes one system, one composition. This system has proved to be extremely stable and widespread. The investigator, for example, can determine very accurately that both the ancient Egyptian fairy tale of the two brothers and the tale of the firebird, the tale of *Morozka*, the tale of the fisherman and the fish, as well as a number of myths follow the same general pattern. An analysis of the details bears this out. Thirty-one functions do not exhaust the system. Such a motif as 'Baba-Jaga gives Ivan a horse' contains four elements, of which only one represents a function, while the other three are of a static nature.

In all, the fairy tale knows about 150 elements or constituents. Each of these elements can be labeled according to its bearing on the sequence of action. Thus, in the above example, Baba-Jaga is a donor, the word 'gives' signals the moment of transmittal, Ivan is a recipient, and the horse is the gift. If the labels for all 150 fairy tale elements are written down in the order dictated by the tales themselves, then, by definition, all fairy tales will fit such a table. Conversely, any tale which fits such a table is a fairy tale, and any tale which does not fit it belongs in another category. Every rubric is a constituent of the fairy tale, and reading the table vertically yields a series of basic forms and a series of derived forms.

It is precisely these constituents which are subject to comparison. This would correspond in zoology to a comparison of vertebra with vertebra, of tooth with tooth, etc. But there is a significant difference between organic formations and the fairy tale which makes our task easier. In the first instance, a change in a part or feature brings about a change in another feature, whereas each element of the fairy tale can change independently of the other elements. This has been noted by many investigators, although there have been so far no attempts to infer from it all the conclusions, methodological and otherwise.[3] Thus, Kaarle Krohn, in agreeing with Spiess on the question of constituent interchangeability, still considers it necessary to study the fairy tale in terms of entire structures rather than in terms of constituents. In so doing, Krohn does not (in keeping with the Finnish school) supply much in the way of evidence to support his stand. We conclude from this that the elements of the fairy tale may be studied independently of the plot they constitute. Studying the rubrics vertically reveals norms and types of transformations. What holds true for an isolated element also holds true for entire structures. This is owing to the mechanical manner in which the constituents are joined.

2

The present work does not claim to exhaust the problem. We will only indicate here certain basic guideposts which might subsequently form the basis of a broader theoretical investigation.

Even in a brief presentation, however, it is necessary before examining the transformations themselves to establish the criteria which allow us to distinguish between basic and derived forms. The criteria may be expressed in two ways: in terms of general principles and in terms of special rules.

First, the general principles. In order to establish these principles, the fairy tale has to be approached from a standpoint of its environment, that is, the conditions under which it was created and exists. Life and, in the broad sense of the word, religion are the most important for us here. The causes of transformations frequently lie outside the fairy tale, and we will not grasp the evolution of the tale unless we consider the environmental circumstances of the fairy tale.

The basic forms are those connected with the genesis of the fairy tale. Obviously, the tale is born out of life; however, the fairy tale reflects reality only weakly. Everything which derives from reality is of secondary formation. In order to determine the origins of the fairy tale, we must draw upon the broad cultural material of the past.

It turns out that the forms which, for one reason or another, are defined as basic are linked with religious concepts of the remote past. We can formulate the following premise: if the same form occurs both in a religious monument and in a fairy tale, the religious form is primary and the fairy tale form is secondary. This is particularly true of archaic religions. Any archaic religious phenomenon, dead today, is older than its artistic use in a current fairy tale. It is, of course, impossible to prove that here. Indeed, such a dependency in general cannot be *proved*; it can only be *shown* on the basis of a large range of material. Such is the first general principle, which is subject to further development. The second principle may be stated thus: if the same element has two variants, of which one derives from religious forms and the other from daily life, the religious formation is primary and the one drawn from life is secondary.

However, in applying these principles, we must observe reasonable caution. It would be an error to try to trace all basic forms back to religion and all derived ones to reality. To protect ourselves against such errors, we need to shed more light on the methods to be used in comparative studies of the fairy tale and religion and the fairy tale and life.

We can establish several types of relationships between the fairy tale and religion. The first is a direct genetic dependency, which in some cases is patently obvious, but which in other cases requires special historical research. Thus, if a serpent is encountered both in the fairy tale and in religion, it entered the fairy tale by way of religion, not the other way around.

However, the presence of such a link is not obligatory even in the case of very great similarity. Its presence is probable only when we have access to direct cult and *ritual* material. Such ritual material must be distinguished from a combination of religious and *epic* material. In the first case, we can raise the question of a direct kinship along descending lines, analogous to the kinship line of fathers and children; in the second case we can speak only of parallel kinship or, to continue the analogy, the kinship of brothers. Thus the story of Samson and Delilah cannot be considered the prototype of the fairy tale resembling their story: both the fairy tale and the biblical text may well go back to a common source.

The primacy of cult material should likewise be asserted with a certain degree of caution. Nonetheless, there are instances when this primacy may be asserted with absolute confidence. True, evidence is frequently not found in the document itself but in the concepts which are reflected there and which underlie the fairy tale. But we are often able to form our judgment about the concepts only by means of the documents. For example, the Rig-Veda, little studied by folklorists, belongs to such sources of the fairy tale. If it is true that the fairy tale knows approximately 150 constituents, it is noteworthy that the Rig-Veda contains no fewer than 60. True, their use is lyrical rather than epic, but it should not be forgotten that these are hymns of high

priests, not of commoners. It is doubtless true that in the hands of
the people (shepherds and peasants) this lyric took on features of the
epic. If the hymn praises Indra as the serpent-slayer (in which case
the details sometimes coincide perfectly with those of the fairy tale),
the people were able in one form or another to *narrate* precisely how
Indra killed the serpent.

Let us check this assertion with a more concrete example. We
readily recognise Baba-Jaga and her hut in the following hymn:

Mistress of the wood, mistress of the wood, whither do you
vanish? Why do you not ask of the village? Are you afraid then?

When the hue and cry of birds bursts forth, the mistress of the
wood imagines herself a prince riding forth to the sound of
cymbals.

Cattle seem to be grazing on the edge of the woods. Or is it a hut
which stands darkly visible there? In the night is heard a squeaking
and creaking as of a heavy cart. It is the mistress of the wood.

An unseen voice calls to the cattle. An axe rings out in the woods.
A voice cries out sharply. So fancies the nocturnal guest of the
mistress of the wood.

The mistress of the wood will do no harm unless alarmed. Feed on
sweet fruits and peacefully sleep to full contentment.

Smelling of spices, fragrant, unsowing but ever having plenty,
mother of the wild beasts, I praise the mistress of the wood.

We have certain fairy tale elements here: the hut in the woods, the
reproach linked with inquiry (in the fairy tale it is normally couched
in the form of direct address), a hospitable night's rest (she provides
food, drink, and shelter), a suggestion of the mistress of the wood's
potential hostility, an indication that she is the mother of the wild
beasts (in the fairy tale she calls them together); missing are the
chicken legs of her hut as well as any indication of her external
appearance, etc. One small detail presents a remarkable coincidence:
wood is apparently being chopped for the person spending the night
in the forest hut. In Afanas'ev (No. 99)[4] the father, after leaving his
daughter in the hut, straps a boot last to the wheel of his cart. The
last clacks loudly, and the girl says: *Se mij baten' ka drovcja rubae*
(Me pa be a-choppin' wood).

Furthermore, all of these coincidences are not accidental, for they
are not the only ones. These are only a few out of a great many
precise parallels between the fairy tale and the Rig-Veda.

The parallel mentioned cannot, of course, be viewed as proof that our Baba-Jaga goes back to the Rig-Veda. One can only stress that on the whole the line proceeds from religion to the fairy tale, not conversely, and that it is essential here to initiate accurate comparative studies.

However, everything said here is true only if religion and the fairy tale lie at a great chronological distance from each other, if, for example, the religion under consideration has already died out, and its origin is obscured by the prehistoric past. It is quite a different matter when we compare a living religion and a living fairy tale belonging to one and the same people. The reverse situation may occur, a dependency which is impossible in the case of a dead religion and a modern fairy tale. Christian elements in the fairy tale (the apostles as helpers, the devil as spoiler) are *younger* than the fairy tale, not older, as in the preceding example. In point of fact, we really ought not to call this relationship the reverse of the one in the preceding case. The fairy tale derives from ancient religions, but modern religions do not derive from the fairy tale. Modern religion does not create the fairy tale but merely *changes* its material. Yet there are probably isolated examples of a truly reversed dependency, that is, instances in which the elements of religion are derived from the fairy tale. A very interesting example is in the Western church's canonization of the miracle of St George the Dragon Slayer. This miracle was canonized much later than was St George himself, and it occurred despite the stubborn resistance of the Church.[5] Because the battle with the serpent is a part of many pagan religions, we have to assume that it derives precisely from them. In the thirteenth century, however, there was no longer a living trace of these religions, only the epic tradition of the people could play the role of transmitter. The popularity of St George on the one hand and his fight with the dragon on the other caused his image to merge with that of the dragon fight; the Church was forced to acknowledge the completed fusion and to canonize it.

Finally, we may find not only direct genetic dependency of the fairy tale on religion, not only parallelism and reversed dependency, but also the complete absence of any link despite outward similarity. Identical concepts may arise independently of one another. Thus the magic steed is comparable with the holy steeds of the Teutons and with the fiery horse Agni in the Rig-Veda. The former have nothing in common with Sivka-Burka, while the latter coincides with him in all respects. The analogy may be applied only if it is more or less complete. Heteronymous phenomena, however similar, must be excluded from such comparisons.

Thus the study of *basic* forms necessitates a comparison of the fairy tale with various religions.

Conversely, the study of *derived* forms in the fairy tale shows how it is linked with reality. A number of transformations may be explained as the intrusions of reality into the fairy tale. This forces us to clarify the problem concerning the methods to be used in studying the fairy tale's relationship to life.

In contrast to other types of tales (the anecdote, the novella, the fable, and so on), the fairy tale shows a comparatively sparse sprinkling of elements from real life. The role of daily existence in creating the fairy tale is often overrated. We can resolve the problem of the fairy tale's relationship to life only if we remember that artistic realism and the presence of elements from real life are two different concepts which do not always overlap. Scholars often make the mistake of searching for facts from real life to support a realistic narrative.

Nikolaj Lerner, for example, takes the following lines from Pushkin's 'Bova':

This is really a golden Council,
No idle chatter here, but deep thought:
A long while the noble lords all thought.
Arzamor, old and experienced,
All but opened his mouth (to give counsel,
Perhaps, was the old greybeard's desire),
His throat he loudly cleared, but thought better
And in silence his tongue did bite
[All the council members keep silent and begin to drowse.]

and comments:

In depicting the council of bearded senility we may presume the poem to be a satire on the governmental forms of old Muscovite Russia . . . We note that the satire might have been directed not only against Old Russia but against Pushkin's Russia as well. The entire assembly of snoring 'thinkers' could easily have been uncovered by the young genius in the society of his own day.[6]

In actual fact, however, this is strictly a *fairy tale* motif. In Afanas'ev (for example, in No. 140) we find: 'He asked once – the boyars were silent; a second time – they did not respond; a third time – not so much as half a word.' We have here the customary scene in which the supplicant entreats aid, the entreaty usually occurring three times. It is first directed to the servants, then to the boyars (clerks, ministers), and third to the hero of the story. Each party in this triad may likewise be trebled in its own right. Thus we are not dealing with real life but with the amplification and specification (added names, etc.) of a folklore element. We would be making the same mistake if we were to consider the Homeric image of Penelope and the conduct of her suitors as corresponding to the facts of life in ancient Greece and to Greek connubial customs. Penelope's suitors are *false suitors*, a well-known device in epic poetry throughout the world. We should first isolate whatever is folkloric and only afterward raise the question as to the correspondence between specifically Homeric moments and factual life in ancient Greece.

Thus we see that the problem which deals with the fairy tale's relationship to real life is not a simple one. To draw conclusions about life directly from the fairy tale is inadmissible.

But, as we will see below, the role of real life in the *transformation* of the fairy tale is enormous. Life cannot destroy the overall structure of the fairy tale, but it does produce a wealth of younger material which replaces the old in a wide variety of ways.

3

The following are the principal and more precise criteria for distinguishing the basic form of a fairy tale element from a derived form:

1. A fantastical treatment of a constituent in the fairy tale is older than its rational treatment. Such a case is rather simple and does not require special development. If in one fairy tale Ivan receives a magical gift from Baba-Jaga and in another from an old woman passing by, the former is older than the latter. This viewpoint is theoretically based on the link between the fairy tale and religion. Such a viewpoint, however, may turn out to be invalid with respect to other types of tales (fables, etc.) which on the whole may be older than the fairy tale. The realism of such tales dates from time immemorial and cannot be traced back to religious concepts.

2. Heroic treatment is older than humorous treatment. This is essentially a frequent variant of the preceding case. Thus the idea of entering into mortal combat with a dragon precedes that of beating it in a card game.

3. A form used logically is older that a form used nonsensically.[7]

4. An international form is older than national form.

Thus, if the dragon is encountered virtually the world over but is replaced in some fairy tales of the North by a bear or, in the South, by a lion, then the basic form is the dragon, while the lion and bear are derived forms.

Here we ought to say a few words concerning the methods of studying the fairy tale on an international scale. The material is so expansive that a single investigator cannot possibly study all the 100 elements in the fairy tales of the entire world. He must first work through the fairy tales of one people, distinguishing between their basic and their derived forms. He must then repeat the same procedure for a second people, after which he may proceed to a comparative study.

In this connection, the thesis on international forms may be narrowed and stated thus: a broadly national form is older than a regional or provincial form. But, if we once start along this path, we cannot refute the following statement: a widespread form predates an isolated form. However, it is theoretically possible that a truly ancient form has survived only in isolated instances and that all other occurrences of it are younger. Therefore great caution must be exercised when applying the quantitative principle (the use of statistics); moreover, *qualitative* considerations of the material under study must be brought into play. An example: in the fairy tale 'Pretty Vasilisa' (No. 104 in Afanas'ev) the figure of Baba-Jaga is accompanied by the appearance of three mounted riders who symbolize morning, day, and night. The question spontaneously arises: is this not a fundamental feature peculiar to Baba-Jaga, one which has been lost in the other fairy tales? Yet, after a rigorous examination of special considerations (which do not warrant mention at this point), this opinion must be rejected.

4

By way of example we will go through all the possible changes of a single element – Baba-Jaga's hut. Morphologically, the hut represents the abode of the donor (that is, the actor who furnishes the hero with the magical tool). Consequently, we will direct attention not only to the hut but to the appearance of all the donor's abodes. We consider the basic Russian form of the abode to be the hut on chicken legs; it is in the forest, and it rotates. But since *one* element does not yield all the changes possible in a fairy tale, we will consider other examples as well.

1. *Reduction.* Instead of the full form, we may find the following types of changes:

i.   The hut on chicken legs in the forest.
ii. The hut on chicken legs.
iii. The hut in the forest.
iv. The hut.
v.   The pine forest (Afanas'ev No. 95).
vi. No mention of the abode.

Here the basic form is truncated. The chicken legs, the rotation, and the forest are omitted, and finally the very hut is dispensed with. Reduction may be termed an incomplete basic form. It is to be explained by a lapse of memory which in turn has more complex causes. Reduction points to the lack of agreement between the fairy tale and the whole tenor of the life surrounding it; reduction points to the low degree of relevance of the fairy tale to a given environment, to a given epoch, or to the reciter of the fairy tale.

2. *Expansion*. We turn now to the opposite phenomenon, by which the basic form is extended and broadened by the addition of extra detail. Here is an expanded form: The hut on chicken legs in the forest rests on pancakes and is shingled with cookies.

More often than not, expansion is accompanied by reduction. Certain features are omitted, others are added. Expansion may be divided into categories according to origin (as is done below for substitutions). Some expanded forms derive from daily life, others represent an embellished detail from the fairy tale canon. This is illustrated by the preceding example. Examination reveals the donor to be a blend of hostile and hospitable qualities. Ivan is usually welcomed at the donor's abode. The forms this welcome may take are extremely varied. (She gave him food and drink. Ivan addresses the hut with the words: 'We'd like to climb up and have a bite to eat.' The hero sees in the hut a table laid, he samples all the food or eats his fill; he goes outside and slaughters some of the donor's cattle and chickens, etc.) This quality on the part of the donor is expressed by his very abode. In the German fairy tale *Hansel and Gretel*, this form is used somewhat differently, in conformance with the childlike nature of the story.

3. *Contamination*. In general, the fairy tale is in a state of decline today, and contamination is relatively frequent. Sometimes contaminated forms spread and take root. The idea that Baba-Jaga's hut turns continuously on its axis is an example of contamination. In the course of the action, the hut has a very specific purpose: it is a watchtower; the hero is tested to see whether or not he is worthy of receiving the magical tool. The hut greets Ivan with its closed side, and consequently it is sometimes called the 'windowless, doorless hut'. Its open side, that is, the side with the door, faces away from Ivan. It would appear that Ivan could very easily go around to the other side of the hut and enter through the door. But this Ivan cannot and in the fairy tale never does do. Instead, he utters the incantation: 'Stand with your back to the forest and your front to me', or 'Stand, as your mother stood you', and so on. The result was usually: 'The hut turned.' This 'turned' became 'spins', and the expression, 'When it has to, it turns this way and that' became simply, 'It turns this way

and that'. The expression thus lost its sense but was not deprived of a certain characteristic vividness.

4. *Inversion.* Often the basic form is reversed. Female members of the cast are replaced by males, and vice versa. This procedure may involve the hut as well. Instead of a closed and inaccessible hut, we sometimes get a hut with a wide-open door.

5–6. *Intensification and attenuation.* These types of transformation only apply to the *actions* of the cast. Identical actions may occur at various degrees of intensity. One example of intensification: the hero is exiled instead of merely being sent on a quest. Dispatch is one of the constant elements of the fairy tale; this element occurs in such a variety of forms that all degrees of dispatch intensity are demonstrable. The dispatch may be initiated in various ways. The hero is often asked to go and fetch some unusual thing. Sometimes the hero is given a task. ('Do me the service.') Often it is an order accompanied by threats, should he fail, and promises, should he succeed. Dispatch may also be a veiled form of exile: an evil sister sends her brother for the milk of a fierce animal in order to get rid of him; the master sends his helper to bring back a cow supposedly lost in the forest; a stepmother sends her stepdaughter to Baba-Jaga for fire. Finally, we have literal exile. These are the basic stages of dispatch, each of which allows a number of variations and transitional forms; they are especially important in examining fairy tales dealing with exiled characters. The order, accompanied by threats and promises, may be regarded as the basic form of dispatch. If the element of promise is omitted, such a reduction may be simultaneously considered an intensification – we are left with a dispatch *and* a threat. Omission of the threat will soften and weaken this form. Further attenuation consists in completely omitting the dispatch. As he prepares to leave, the son asks his parents for their blessing.

The six types of transformations discussed so far may be interpreted as very familiar *changes* in the basic form. There are, however, two other large groups of transformations: substitutions and assimilations. Both of them may be analyzed according to their origin.

7. *Internally motivated substitution.* Looking again at the donor's dwelling, we find the following forms:

i.   A palace.
ii. A mountain alongside a fiery river.

These are not cases of either reduction or expansion, etc. They are not changes but substitutions. The indicated forms, however, are not drawn from without; they are drawn from the fairy tale's own reserves. A dislocation, a rearrangement of forms and material, has taken place. The palace (often of gold) is normally inhabited by a princess. Subsequently this dwelling is ascribed to the donor. Such dislocations in the fairy tale play a very important role. Each element has its own peculiar form. However, this form is not always exclusively bound to the given element. (The princess, for example, usually a sought member of the cast, may play the role of the donor, or that of the helper, etc.) One fairy tale image suppresses another; Baba-Jaga's daughter may appear as the princess. In the latter case, appropriately enough, Baba-Jaga does not live in her hut but in a palace, that is, the abode normally associated with a princess. Linked to this one are the palaces of copper, silver, and gold. The maidens living in such palaces are simultaneously donor and princess. The palaces possibly came about as the result of trebling the golden palace. Possibly they arose in complete independence, having, for example, no connection whatsoever with the idea of the Ages of Gold, Silver, and Iron, etc.

Similarly, the mountain alongside the fiery river is no other than the abode of the dragon, an abode which has been attributed to the donor.

These dislocations play an enormous role in creating transformations. The majority of all transformations are substitutions or dislocations generated from within the fairy tale.

8. *Externally motivated substitutions.* If we have the forms:

i. An inn.
ii. A two-storied house,

it is apparent that the fantastic hut has been replaced by forms of dwelling normal to real life. The majority of such substitutions may be explained very easily, but there are substitutions which require a special ethnographic exegesis. Elements from life are always immediately obvious, and, more often than not, scholars center their attention upon them.

9. *Confessional substitutions.* Current religion is also capable of suppressing old forms, replacing them with new ones. Here we are involved with instances in which the devil functions as a winged messenger, or an angel is the donor of the magical tool, or an act of penance replaces the performance of a difficult task (the donor tests the hero). Certain legends are basically fairy tales in which all elements have undergone supporting substitutions. Every people has its own confessional substitutions. Christianity, Islam, and Buddhism are reflected in the fairy tales of the corresponding peoples.

10. *Substitution by superstition.* Obviously, superstition and local beliefs may likewise suppress the original material of a fairy tale.

However, we encounter this type of substitution much more rarely than we might expect at first glance (the errors of the mythological school). Pushkin was mistaken in saying that in the fairy tale:

Wonders abound, a wood-demon lurks,
Rusalka sits in the boughs.

If we encounter a wood-demon in the fairy tale, he almost always replaces Baba-Jaga. Water nymphs are met with but a single time in the entire Afanas'ev collection, and then only in an introductory flourish of dubious authenticity. In the collections by Ončukov, Zelinin, the Sokolovs, and others, there is not a single mention of Rusalka. The wood-demon only finds its way into the fairy tale because, as a creature of the forest, it resembles Baba-Jaga. The fairy tale accepts only those elements which can be readily accommodated in its construction.

11. *Archaic substitutions.* We have already mentioned that the basic forms of the fairy tale go back to extinct religious concepts. Based on this fact, we can sometimes separate the basic forms from the derived ones. In certain unique instances, however, the basic form (more or less normal in the fairy tale epic) has been replaced by a form no less ancient which can likewise be traced back to a religious source, but whose occurrence is unique. For example, rather than the battle with the dragon in the fairy tale 'The Witch and the Sun's Sister' (No. 93 in Afanas'ev), we have the following: the dragon's mate suggests to the prince, 'Let Prince Ivan come with me to the scales and we'll see who outweights whom.' The scales toss Ivan sky-high. Here we have traces of psychostasia (the weighing of souls). Where this form – well known in ancient Egypt – came from and how it came to be preserved in the fairy tale are questions which need study.

It is not always easy to distinguish between an archaic substitution and a substitution imposed by superstition. Both have their roots (sometimes) in deep antiquity. But if some item in the fairy tale is also found in a living faith, the substitution may be considered as a relatively new one (the wood-demon). A pagan religion may have two offshoots: one in the fairy tale and the other in a faith or custom. They may well have confronted each other in the course of centuries, and the one may have suppressed the other. Conversely, if a fairy tale element is not attested to in a living faith (the scales), the substitution has its origin in deep antiquity and may be considered archaic.

12. *Literary substitutions.* Literary material shows the same low degree of likelihood of being accepted by the fairy tale that current superstition does. The fairy tale possesses such resistance that other

genres shatter against it; they do not readily blend. If clash takes place, the fairy tale wins. Of all the various literary genres, that of the fairy tale is the most likely to absorb elements from legend and epic. On rare occasions the novel provides a substitution; but even in such a case, it is only the chivalric romance which plays a certain role. The chivalric romance itself, however, is frequently a product of the fairy tale. The process occurs in stages: fairy tale → romance → fairy tale. Therefore, works such as 'Eruslan Lazarevič' are among the 'purest' of fairy tales in terms of construction, despite the bookish nature of individual elements. The *Schwank*, the novella, and other forms of popular prose are more flexible and more receptive to elements from other genres.

13. *Modification*. There are substitutions whose origin is not readily ascertainable. More often than not, these are imaginative substitutions which came into being through the teller's own resourcefulness. Such forms defy ethnographic or historical specification. We should note, however, that these substitutions play a greater role in animal tales and other types of tales than in fairy tales. (The bear is replaced by the wolf, one bird by another, etc.) Of course, they may occur in the fairy tale too. Thus, as the winged messenger, we find an eagle, a falcon, a raven, geese, and others. As the sought-after marvel, we find a stag with antlers of gold, a steed with a mane of gold, a duck with feathers of gold, a pig with bristles of gold, and so on. Derived, secondary forms are generally those most likely to undergo modification. This may be shown by comparing a number of forms in which the sought wonder is simply a transformation of the sought princess with golden locks. If a comparison of the basic and the derived forms exhibits a certain descending line, a comparison of two derived forms reveals a certain parallelism. There are elements in the fairy tale having a particular variety of forms. One example is the 'difficult task'. If the task does not have a basic form, it makes little difference to the fairy tale, in terms of the unity of its construction, what kind of task is assigned. This phenomenon is even more apparent when we compare elements which have never belonged to a basic type of fairy tale. Motivation is one such element. But transformations sometimes create the need to motivate a certain act. As a result, we see a wide variety of motivations for one and the same act. Thus the hero's exile (exile is a secondary formation) is motivated by widely varied circumstances. On the other hand, the dragon's abduction of the maiden (a primary form) is hardly ever motivated externally but is motivated from within.

Certain features of the hut are also subject to modification. Instead of a hut on chicken legs, we encounter a hut on goat horns or on sheep legs.

14. *Substitutions of unknown origin.* We have been discussing substitutions from the point of view of their origin, but their origin is not always ascertainable; it does not always appear as a simple modification. Therefore we require a category for substitutions of unknown origin. For example, the little sister of the sun from the fairy tale 'Little Sister' (Afanas'ev No. 93) plays the donor's role and may be considered a rudimentary form of the princess. She lives in the 'solar rooms'. We cannot know whether this reflects a sun cult, or the creative imagination of the narrator, or some suggestion by the collector asking the storyteller whether he knows any fairy tales dealing with a particular subject, or whether thus and so can be found; in such a case, the teller sometimes fabricates something to please the collector.

This places a limitation on substitutions. We could, of course, set up several more varieties which might be applied to a given isolated case. However, there is no need for that now. The substitutions specified here are meaningful throughout the entire breadth of fairy tale material; their application to isolated cases may be easily inferred and demonstrated by employing the transformational types cited.

Let us turn to another class of changes, that of assimilations. By assimilation we understand an incomplete suppression of one form by another, the two forms merging into a single form. Because assimilations follow the same classification scheme as the substitutions, they will be enumerated in brief.

15. *Internally motivated assimilations.* An example occurs in the forms:

i. A hut under a golden roof.
ii. A hut by a fiery river.

In a fairy tale we often meet with a palace under a golden roof. A hut plus a palace under a golden roof equals a hut under a golden roof. The same is true in the case of the hut by the fiery river.

The fairy tale 'Fedor Vodovič and Ivan Vodovič' (Ončukov No. 4) provides a very interesting example. Two such very heterogeneous elements as the miraculous birth of the hero and his pursuit by the dragon's wives (sisters) have been drawn together by assimilation. The wives of the dragon, in pursuing the hero, usually turn into a well, a cloud, or a bed and situate themselves in Ivan's path. If he samples some fruit or takes a drink of water, etc., he is torn to pieces. For the miraculous birth, this motif is used in the following manner: the princess strolls about her father's courtyard, sees a well with a small cup, and by it a bed (the apple tree has been forgotten). She drinks a cupful and lies down on the bed to rest. From this she conceives and gives birth to two sons.

16. *Externally motivated assimilations*. These take the form:

i.   A hut on the edge of the village.
ii. A cave in the woods.

Here we find that the imaginary hut has become a real hut and a real cave, but the solitude of its inhabitant has been preserved. Indeed, in the second instance, the forest element is also preserved. Fairy tale plus reality produces an assimilation which favors real life.

17. *Confessional assimilations*. This process may be exemplified by the replacement of the dragon by the devil; however, the devil, like the dragon, dwells in a lake. The concept of evil beings of the deep does not necessarily have anything in common with the so-called lower mythology of the peasants; it is often explained as simply one type of transformation.

18. *Assimilation via superstition*. This is a relatively rare phenomenon. The wood-demon living in a hut on chicken legs is an example.

19–20. *Literary and archaic assimilations*. These are encountered even more rarely. Assimilations with the folk epic and legend are of some importance in the Russian fairy tale. Here, however, we are more likely to find suppression rather than the assimilation of one form by another, while the components of the fairy tale are preserved as such. Archaic assimilations require a detailed examination of each occurrence. They do occur, but identifying them is possible only after highly specialized research.

Our survey of the transformation of types can end at this point. It is impossible to assert that absolutely all fairy tale forms will be accommodated by our classificatory scheme, but at any rate a significant number clearly are. It would have been possible to bring in still other types of transformations, such as specification and generalization. In the first case, general phenomena become particularized (instead of the thrice-tenth kingdom, we find the city Xvalynsk); in the latter case, the opposite occurs (the thrice-tenth kingdom becomes simply a 'different, other' kingdom, etc.). But almost all types of specification may also be regarded as substitutions, and generalizations as reductions. This is true, too, for rationalization (a winged steed becomes an earthbound horse) as well as for the conversion of the fairy tale into an anecdote, etc. A correct and consistent application of the types of transformation indicated will give a firmer foundation to the study of the fairy tale in the process of its development.

What is true for the individual elements of the fairy tale is also true for the fairy tale as a whole. If an extra element is added, we have amplification; in the reverse case, we have reduction, etc.

Applying these methods to entire fairy tales is important for comparative studies on fairy tale plots.

One very important problem remains. If we write out all the occurrences (or at least a great many of them) of one element, not all the forms of one element can be traced back to some single basis. Let us suppose that we accept Baba-Jaga as the basic form of the donor. Such forms are a witch, Grannie-Behind-the-Door, Grandma-Widow, an old lady, an old man, a shepherd, a wood-demon, an angel, the devil, three maids, the king's daughter, etc. – all may be satisfactorily explained as substitutions and other transformations of Baba-Jaga. But then we encounter a 'fingernail-sized peasant with an elbow-length beard'. Such a form for the donor does not come from Baba-Jaga. If such a form does occur in a religion, we have a form which has been coordinated with Baba-Jaga; if not, we have a substitution of unknown origin. Each element may have several basic forms, although the number of such parallel, coordinated forms is usually insignificant.

Notes

1. ANTTI A. AARNE warns against such an 'error' in his *Leitfaden der vergleichenden Märchenforschung* (Hamina, 1913).

2. See PROPP's *Morphology of the Folktale* (Austin, Texas, 1968).

3. See F. PANZER, *Märchen, Sage und Dichtung* (Munich, 1905). 'Seine Komposition ist eine Mosaikarbeit, die das schildernde Bild aus deutlich abgegrenzten Steinchen gefügt hat. Und diese Steinchen bleiben umso leichter *auswechselbar*, die einzelnen Motive können umso leichter variieren, als auch nirgends für eine Verbindung in die Tiefe gesorgt ist.' (His composition is a mosaic that has fashioned the descriptive image out of clearly delineated pieces. And these pieces are more readily *interchangeable*, the individual *motifs* can vary more easily, since at no time is there any provision made for an interconnection in depth.) This is clearly a denial of the theory of stable combinations or permanent ties. The same thought is expressed even more dramatically and in greater detail by K. SPIESS in *Das deutsche Volksmärchen* (Leipzig, 1917). See also K.L. KROHN, *Die folkloristische Arbeitsmethode* (Oslo, 1926).

4. All references to Afanas'ev have been adjusted to the 1957 edition of *Narodnye russkie skazki A.N. Afanas'eva* (Moscow, 1957).

5. J.B. AUFHAUSER, *Das Drachenwunder des heiligen Georg* (Leipzig, 1911).

6. NIKOLAI LERNER, 'Primečanija k "Bove"' ('Notes on "Bova"'), in A.S. PUSHKIN, *Sočinenija*, vol. 1 (St Petersburg: Brokganf-Efron, 1907), p. 204.

7. For other examples, see I.V. KARNAUXOVA in *Krest'janskoe iskusstvo SSSR* (Peasant Art in the USSR) (Leningrad, 1927).

4 Epic and Novel: Toward a Methodology for the Study of the Novel*

MIKHAIL BAKHTIN

Since the earliest attempts to define it in the eighteenth century, the novel has always posed special problems for genre theorists, not only because it does not fit traditional literary categories but also because it puts in question the notions of literariness on which such categories are based. In this extract from his 1941 essay 'Epic and Novel', the Russian critic Mikhail Bakhtin attempts to explain what it is about the novel that so radically differentiates it from other literary genres, and makes it seem, as he memorably puts it, like 'a creature from an alien species'. There are several strands to the argument. Part of the discussion is focused, as the title indicates, on an historical comparison between the novel and the epic, a comparison which owes something to Georg Lukács's *Theory of the Novel* (1920), which Bakhtin had started to translate in the 1920s, as well as to the German Romantic theorists (Goethe, Schiller, Friedrich Schlegel, Hegel and others) who instigated the tradition of philosophical genre theory to which both Lukács and Bakhtin, in different ways, belong. Although unacknowledged here, there are also important continuities with the work of the Russian Formalists on the theory of literary evolution, especially regarding the competition and transformation of genres, the role of parody, and the relation between literary and extraliterary genres. Bakhtin's concept of 'novelisation', for instance, is essentially an extension of these ideas (with echoes too of Schlegel). A third strand involves the sociology of genres, a methodology which in the 1920s had aligned Bakhtin with Marxist detractors of the Formalist school, but which here incorporates his own highly unorthodox theory of the carnivalesque, with its subversive account of the tension between high and low, official and unofficial cultural forms. Underlying

---

* Reprinted from M.M. Bakhtin, *The Dialogic Imagination: Four Essays*, ed. Michael Holquist, trans. Caryl Emerson and Michael Holquist (Austin: University of Texas Press, 1981), pp. 3–13, 18–21. Written in 1941 and first published in Bakhtin's *Voprosy literatury i estetiki* (Problems of literature and aesthetics)(Moscow, 1975).

all these arguments is Bakhtin's 'dialogic' conception of language, whose implications for genre theory are directly addressed in Bakhtin's essay on 'speech genres' (Chapter 5). By weaving together these various explanatory models, and, where necessary, devising new terminology of his own (polyglossia, heteroglossia, novelisation), Bakhtin attempts to forge a critical idiom sufficiently flexible to describe this most protean of forms, and sufficiently complex to probe the deep sociological factors which account for its unique position among literary genres.

For Bakhtin's further ideas on the concept of genre, see the texts cited and discussed in my Introduction (pp. 8–11). Despite the enormous interest in Bakhtin, there is relatively little commentary on this aspect of his work, but see Clive Thomson, 'Bakhtin's "Theory" of Genre', *Studies in Twentieth-Century Literature*, 9: 1 (1984), 29–40; Evelyn Cobley, 'Mikhail Bakhtin's Place in Genre Theory', *Genre*, 21 (1988), 321–38; and Tzvetan Todorov, *Mikhail Bakhtin: The Dialogical Principle*, trans. Wlad Godzich (Manchester: Manchester University Press, 1984), ch. 6. The best general introductions to Bakhtin's work are Todorov's book, and Michael Holquist, *Dialogism: Bakhtin and His World* (London: Routledge, 1990). Also useful is Sue Vice, *Introducing Bakhtin* (Manchester: Manchester University Press, 1997), which highlights key concepts and gives straightforward examples of their application.

The study of the novel as a genre is distinguished by peculiar difficulties. This is due to the unique nature of the object itself: the novel is the sole genre that continues to develop, that is as yet uncompleted. The forces that define it as a genre are at work before our very eyes: the birth and development of the novel as a genre take place in the full light of the historical day. The generic skeleton of the novel is still far from having hardened, and we cannot foresee all its plastic possibilities.

We know other genres, as genres, in their completed aspect, that is, as more or less fixed pre-existing forms into which one may then pour artistic experience. The primordial process of their formation lies outside historically documented observation. We encounter the epic as a genre that has not only long since completed its development, but one that is already antiquated. With certain reservations we can say the same for the other major genres, even for tragedy. The life they have in history, the life with which we are familiar, is the life they have lived as already completed genres, with a hardened and no longer flexible skeleton. Each of them has developed its own canon that operates in literature as an authentic historical force.

All these genres, or in any case their defining features, are considerably older than written language and the book, and to the present day they retain their ancient oral and auditory characteristics. Of all the major genres only the novel is younger than writing and the book: it alone is organically receptive to new forms of mute perception, that is, to reading. But of critical importance here is the fact that the novel has no canon of its own, as do other genres; only individual examples of the novel are historically active, not a generic canon as such. Studying other genres is analogous to studying dead languages; studying the novel, on the other hand, is like studying languages that are not only alive, but still young.

This explains the extraordinary difficulty inherent in formulating a theory of the novel. For such a theory has at its heart an object of study completely different from that which theory treats in other genres. The novel is not merely one genre among other genres. Among genres long since completed and in part already dead, the novel is the only developing genre. It is the only genre that was born and nourished in a new era of world history and therefore it is deeply akin to that era, whereas the other major genres entered that era as already fixed forms, as an inheritance, and only now are they adapting themselves – some better, some worse – to the new conditions of their existence. Compared with them, the novel appears to be a creature from an alien species. It gets on poorly with other genres. It fights for its own hegemony in literature; wherever it triumphs, the other older genres go into decline. Significantly, the best book on the history of the ancient novel – that by Erwin Rohde[1] – does not so much recount the history of the novel as it does illustrate the process of disintegration that affected all major genres in antiquity.

The mutual interaction of genres within a single unified literary period is a problem of great interest and importance. In certain eras – the Greek classical period, the Golden Age of Roman literature, the Neoclassical period – all genres in 'high' literature (that is, the literature of ruling social groups) harmoniously reinforce each other to a significant extent; the whole of literature, conceived as a totality of genres, becomes an organic unity of the highest order. But it is characteristic of the novel that it never enters into this whole, it does not participate in any harmony of the genres. In these eras the novel has an unofficial existence, outside 'high' literature. Only already completed genres, with fully formed and well-defined generic contours, can enter into such a literature as a hierarchically organized, organic whole. They can mutually delimit and mutually complement each other, while yet preserving their own generic natures. Each is a unit, and all units are interrelated by virtue of certain features of deep structure that they all have in common.

The great organic poetics of the past – those of Aristotle, Horace, Boileau – are permeated with a deep sense of the wholeness of literature and of the harmonious interaction of all genres contained within this whole. It is as if they literally hear this harmony of the genres. In this is their strength – the inimitable, all-embracing fullness and exhaustiveness of such poetics. And they all, as a consequence, ignore the novel. Scholarly poetics of the nineteenth century lack this integrity: they are eclectic, descriptive; their aim is not a living and organic fullness but rather an abstract and encyclopedic comprehensiveness. They do not concern themselves with the actual possibility of specific genres coexisting within the living whole of literature in a given era; they are concerned rather with their coexistence in a maximally complete anthology. Of course these poetics can no longer ignore the novel – they simply add it (albeit in a place of honor) to already existing genres (and thus it enters the roster as merely one genre among many; in literature conceived as a living whole, on the other hand, it would have to be included in a completely different way).

We have already said that the novel gets on poorly with other genres. There can be no talk of a harmony deriving from mutual limitation and complementariness. The novel parodies other genres (precisely in their role as genres); it exposes the conventionality of their forms and their language; it squeezes out some genres and incorporates others into its own peculiar structure, reformulating and re-accentuating them. Historians of literature sometimes tend to see in this merely the struggle of literary tendencies and schools. Such struggles of course exist, but they are peripheral phenomena and historically insignificant. Behind them one must be sensitive to the deeper and more truly historical struggle of genres, the establishment and growth of a generic skeleton of literature.

Of particular interest are those eras when the novel becomes the dominant genre. All literature is then caught up in the process of 'becoming', and in a special kind of 'generic criticism.' This occurred several times in the Hellenic period, again during the late Middle Ages and the Renaissance, but with special force and clarity beginning in the second half of the eighteenth century. In an era when the novel reigns supreme, almost all the remaining genres are to a greater or lesser extent 'novelized': drama (for example Ibsen, Hauptmann, the whole of Naturalist drama), epic poetry (for example, *Childe Harold* and especially Byron's *Don Juan*), even lyric poetry (as an extreme example, Heine's lyrical verse). Those genres that stubbornly preserve their old canonic nature begin to appear stylised. In general any strict adherence to a genre begins to feel like a stylization, a stylization taken to the point of parody, despite the artistic intent of the author.

71

In an environment where the novel is the dominant genre, the conventional languages of strictly canonical genres begin to sound in new ways, which are quite different from the ways they sounded in those eras when the novel was *not* included in 'high' literature.

Parodic stylizations of canonized genres and styles occupy an essential place in the novel. In the era of the novel's creative ascendency – and even more so in the periods of preparation preceding this era – literature was flooded with parodies and travesties of all the high genres (parodies precisely of genres, and not of individual authors or schools) – parodies that are the precursors, 'companions' to the novel, in their own way studies for it. But it is characteristic that the novel does not permit any of these various individual manifestations of itself to stabilize. Throughout its entire history there is a consistent parodying or travestying of dominant or fashionable novels that attempt to become models for the genre: parodies on the chivalric romance of adventure (*Dit d'aventures*, the first such parody, belongs to the thirteenth century), on the Baroque novel, the pastoral novel (Sorel's *Le Berger extravagant*),[2] the Sentimental novel (Fielding, and *The Second Grandison*[3] of Musäus), and so forth. This ability of the novel to criticize itself is a remarkable feature of this ever-developing genre.

What are the salient features of this novelization of other genres suggested by us above? They become more free and flexible, their language renews itself by incorporating extraliterary heteroglossia and the 'novelistic' layers of literary language, they become dialogized, permeated with laughter, irony, humor, elements of self-parody and finally – this is the most important thing – the novel inserts into these other genres an indeterminacy, a certain semantic openendedness, a living contact with unfinished, still-evolving contemporary reality (the openended present). As we will see below, all these phenomena are explained by the transposition of other genres into this new and peculiar zone for structuring artistic models (a zone of contact with the present in all its openendedness), a zone that was first appropriated by the novel.

It is of course impossible to explain the phenomenon of novelization purely by reference to the direct and unmediated influence of the novel itself. Even where such influence can be precisely established and demonstrated, it is intimately interwoven with those direct changes in reality itself that also determine the novel and that condition its dominance in a given era. The novel is the only developing genre and therefore it reflects more deeply, more essentially, more sensitively and rapidly, reality itself in the process of its unfolding. Only that which is itself developing can comprehend development as a process. The novel has become the leading hero in the drama of literary development in our time precisely because it best of all reflects the tendencies of a new world still in the making; it is, after all, the only genre born of this new world and in total affinity with it. In many respects the novel has anticipated, and continues to anticipate, the future development of literature as a whole. In the process of becoming the dominant genre, the novel sparks the renovation of all other genres, it infects them with its spirit of process and inconclusiveness. It draws them ineluctably into its orbit precisely because this orbit coincides with the basic direction of the development of literature as a whole. In this lies the exceptional importance of the novel, as an object of study for the theory as well as the history of literature.

Unfortunately, historians of literature usually reduce this struggle between the novel and other already completed genres, all these aspects of novelization, to the actual real-life struggle among 'schools' and 'trends'. A novelized poem, for example, they call a 'romantic poem' (which of course it is) and believe that in so doing they have exhausted the subject. They do not see beneath the superficial hustle and bustle of literary process the major and crucial fates of literature and language, whose great heroes turn out to be first and foremost genres, and whose 'trends' and 'schools' are but second- or third-rank protagonists.

The utter inadequacy of literary theory is exposed when it is forced to deal with the novel. In the case of other genres literary theory works confidently and precisely, since there is a finished and already formed object, definite and clear. These genres preserve their rigidity and canonic quality in all classical eras of their development; variations from era to era, from trend to trend or school to school are peripheral and do not affect their ossified generic skeleton. Right up to the present day, in fact, theory dealing with these already completed genres can add almost nothing to Aristotle's formulations. Aristotle's poetics, although occasionally so deeply embedded as to be almost invisible, remains the stable foundation for the theory of genres. Everything works as long as there is no mention of the novel. But the existence of novelized genres already leads theory into a blind alley. Faced with the problem of the novel, genre theory must submit to a radical restructuring.

Thanks to the meticulous work of scholars, a huge amount of historical material has accumulated and many questions concerning the evolution of various types of novels have been clarified – but the problem of the novel genre as a whole has not yet found anything like a satisfactory principled resolution. The novel continues to be seen as one genre among many; attempts are made to distinguish it as an already completed genre from other already completed genres, to discover its internal canon – one that would function as a well-defined system of rigid generic factors. In the vast majority of cases, work on the novel is reduced to mere cataloging, a description of all variants on the novel – albeit as comprehensive as possible. But the results of these descriptions never succeed in giving us as much as a hint of comprehensive formula for the novel as a genre. In addition, the experts have not managed to isolate a single definite, stable characteristic of the novel – without adding a reservation, which immediately disqualifies it altogether as a generic characteristic.

Some examples of such 'characteristics with reservations' would be: the novel is a multi-layered genre (although there also exist magnificent single-layered novels); the novel is a precisely plotted and dynamic genre (although there also exist novels that push to its literary limits the art of pure description); the novel is a complicated genre (although novels are mass-produced as pure and frivolous entertainment like no other genre); the novel is a love story (although the greatest examples of the European novel are utterly devoid of the love element); the novel is a prose genre (although there exist excellent novels in verse). One could of course mention a large number of additional 'generic characteristics' for the novel similar to those given above, which are immediately annulled by some reservation innocently appended to them.

Of considerably more interest and consequence are those normative definitions of the novel offered by novelists themselves, who produce a specific novel and then declare *it* the only correct, necessary and authentic form of the novel. Such, for instance, is Rousseau's foreword to his *La Nouvelle Héloïse*, Wieland's to his *Agathon*,[4] Wezel's to his *Tobias Knouts*;[5] in such a category belong the numerous declarations and statements of principle by the Romantics on *Wilhelm Meister, Lucinda* and other texts. Such statements are not attempts to incorporate all the possible variants of the novel into a single eclectic definition, but are themselves part and parcel of the living evolution of the novel as a genre. Often they deeply and faithfully reflect the novel's struggle with other genres and with itself (with other dominant and fashionable variants of the novel) at a particular point in its development. They come closer to an understanding of the peculiar position of the novel in literature, a position that is not commensurate with that of other genres.

Especially significant in this connection is a series of statements that accompanied the emergence of a new novel type in the eighteenth century. The series opens with Fielding's reflections on the novel and its hero in *Tom Jones*. It continues in Wieland's foreword to *Agathon*, and the most essential link in the series is Blankenburg's *Versuch über den Roman*.[6] By the end of this series we have, in fact, that theory of the novel later formulated by Hegel. In all these statements, each reflecting the novel in one of its critical stages (*Tom Jones, Agathon,*

Wilhelm Meister), the following prerequisites for the novel are characteristic: (1) the novel should not be 'poetic', as the word 'poetic' is used in other genres of imaginative literature; (2) the hero of a novel should not be 'heroic' in either the epic or the tragic sense of the word: he should combine in himself negative as well as positive features, low as well as lofty, ridiculous as well as serious; (3) the hero should not be portrayed as an already completed and unchanging person but as one who is evolving and developing, a person who learns from life; (4) the novel should become for the contemporary world what the epic was for the ancient world (an idea that Blankenburg expressed very precisely, and that was later repeated by Hegel).

All these positive prerequisites have their substantial and productive side – taken together, they constitute a criticism (from the novel's point of view) of other genres and of the relationship these genres bear to reality: their stilted heroizing, their narrow and unlifelike poeticalness, their monotony and abstractness, the pre-packaged and unchanging nature of their heroes. We have here, in fact, a rigorous critique of the literariness and poeticalness inherent in other genres and also in the predecessors of the contemporary novel (the heroic Baroque novel and the Sentimental novels of Richardson). These statements are reinforced significantly by the practice of these novelists themselves. Here the novel – its texts as well as the theory connected with it – emerges consciously and unambiguously as a genre that is both critical and self-critical, one fated to revise the fundamental concepts of literariness and poeticalness dominant at the time. On the one hand, the contrast of novel with epic (and the novel's opposition to the epic) is but one moment in the criticism of other literary genres (in particular, a criticism of epic heroization); but on the other hand, this contrast aims to elevate the significance of the novel, making of it the dominant genre in contemporary literature.

The positive prerequisites mentioned above constitute one of the high points in the novel's coming to self-consciousness. They do not yet of course provide a theory of the novel. These statements are also not distinguished by any great philosophical depth. They do however illustrate the nature of the novel as a genre no less – if perhaps no more – than do other existing theories of the novel.

I will attempt below to approach the novel precisely as a genre-in-the-making, one in the vanguard of all modern literary development. I am not constructing here a functional definition of the novelistic canon in literary history, that is, a definition that would make of it a system of fixed generic characteristics. Rather, I am trying to grope my way toward the basic structural characteristics of this most fluid of genres, characteristics that might determine the direction of its peculiar capacity for change and of its influence and effect on the rest of literature.

I find three basic characteristics that fundamentally distinguish the novel in principle from other genres: (1) its stylistic three-dimensionality, which is linked with the multi-languaged consciousness realized in the novel; (2) the radical change it effects in the temporal coordinates of the literary image; (3) the new zone opened by the novel for structuring literary images, namely, the zone of maximal contact with the present (with contemporary reality) in all its openendedness.

These three characteristics of the novel are all organically interrelated and have all been powerfully affected by a very specific rupture in the history of European civilization: its emergence from a socially isolated and culturally deaf semipatriarchal society, and its entrance into international and interlingual contacts and relationships. A multitude of different languages, cultures and times became available to Europe, and this became a decisive factor in its life and thought.

In another work [i.e. the article 'From the Prehistory of Novelistic Discourse' in *The Dialogic Imagination*] I have already investigated the first stylistic peculiarity of the novel, the one resulting from the active polyglossia of the new world, the new culture and its new creative literary consciousness. I will summarize here only the basic points.

Polyglossia had always existed (it is more ancient than pure, canonic monoglossia), but it had not been a factor in literary creation; an artistically conscious choice between languages did not serve as the creative center of the literary and language process. Classical Greeks had a feeling both for 'languages' and for the epochs of language, for the various Greek literary dialects (tragedy is a polyglot genre), but creative consciousness was realized in closed, pure languages (although in actual fact they were mixed). Polyglossia was appropriated and canonized among all the genres.

The new cultural and creative consciousness lives in an actively polyglot world. The world becomes polyglot, once and for all and irreversibly. The period of national languages, coexisting but closed and deaf to each other, comes to an end. Languages throw light on each other: one language can, after all, see itself only in the light of another language. The naive and stubborn coexistence of 'languages' within a given national language also comes to an end – that is, there is no more peaceful coexistence between territorial dialects, social and professional dialects and jargons, literary language, generic languages within literary language, epochs in language and so forth.

All this set into motion a process of active, mutual cause and effect and interillumination. Words and language began to have a different feel to them; objectively they ceased to be what they had once been. Under these conditions of external and internal interillumination, each given language – even if its linguistic composition (phonetics, vocabulary, morphology, etc.) were to remain absolutely unchanged – is, as it were, reborn, becoming qualitatively a different thing for the consciousness that creates in it.

In this actively polyglot world, completely new relationships are established between language and its object (that is, the real world) – and this is fraught with enormous consequences for all the already completed genres that had been formed during eras of closed and deaf monoglossia. In contrast to other major genres, the novel emerged and matured precisely when intense activization of external and internal polyglossia was at the peak of its activity; this is its native element. The novel could therefore assume leadership in the process of developing and renewing literature in its linguistic and stylistic dimension.

In the above-mentioned work I tried to elucidate the profound stylistic originality of the novel, which is determined by its connection with polyglossia.

Let us move on to the two other characteristics, both concerned with the thematic aspect of structure in the novel as a genre. These characteriztics can be best brought out and clarified through a comparison of the novel with the epic.

The epic as a genre in its own right may, for our purposes, be characterized by three constitutive features: (1) a national epic past – in Goethe's and Schiller's terminology the 'absolute past' – serves as the subject for the epic;[7] (2) national tradition (not personal experience and the free thought that grows out of it) serves as the source for the epic; (3) an absolute epic distance separates the epic world from contemporary reality, that is, from the time in which the singer (the author and his audience) lives.

[. . .] The three characteristics of the epic posited by us above are, to a greater or lesser extent, also fundamental to the other high genres of classical antiquity and the Middle Ages. At the heart of all these already completed high genres lie the same evaluation of time, the same role for tradition, and a similar hierarchical distance. Contemporary reality as such does not figure in as an available object of representation in any of these high genres. Contemporary reality may enter into the high genres only in its hierarchically highest levels, already distanced in its relationship to reality itself. But the events, victors and heroes of 'high' contemporary reality are, as it were, appropriated by the past as they enter into these high genres (for example, Pindar's odes or the works of Simonides); they are woven by various intermediate links and connective tissue into the unified fabric of the heroic past and tradition. These events and heroes receive their value and grandeur precisely through this association with the past, the source of all authentic reality and value. They withdraw themselves, so to speak, from the present day with all its inconclusiveness, its indecision, its openness, its potential for rethinking and re-evaluating. They are raised to the valorized plane of the past, and assume there a finished quality. We must not forget that 'absolute past' is not to be confused with time in our exact and limited sense of the word; it is rather a temporally valorized hierarchical category.

It is impossible to achieve greatness in one's own time. Greatness always makes itself known only to descendants, for whom such a quality is always located in the past (it turns into a distanced image); it has become an object of memory and not a living object that one can see and touch. In the genre of the 'memorial', the poet constructs his image in the future and distanced plane of his descendants (cf. the inscriptions of oriental despots, and of Augustus). In the world of memory, a phenomenon exists in its own peculiar context, with its own special rules, subject to conditions quite different from those we meet in the world we see with our own eyes, the world of practice and familiar contact. The epic past is a special form for perceiving people and events in art. In general the act of artistic perception and representation is almost completely obscured by this form. Artistic representation here is representation *sub specie aeternitatis*. One may, and in fact one must, memorialize with artistic language only that which is worthy of being remembered, that which should be preserved in the memory of descendants; an image is created for descendants, and this image is projected on to their sublime and distant horizon. Contemporaneity for its own sake (that is to say, a contemporaneity that makes no claim on future memory) is molded in clay; contemporaneity for the future (for descendants) is molded in marble or bronze.

The interrelationship of times is important here. The valorized emphasis is not on the future and does not serve the future, no favors are being done it (such favors face an eternity outside time); what is served here is the future memory of a past, a broadening of the world of the absolute past, an enriching of it with new images (at the expense of contemporaneity) – a world that is always opposed in principle to any *merely transitory* past.

In the already completed high genres, tradition also retains its significance – although under conditions of open and personal creativity, its role becomes more conventionalized than in the epic.

In general, the world of high literature in the classical era was a world projected into the past, on to the distanced plane of memory, but not into a real, relative past tied to the present by uninterrupted temporal transitions; it was projected rather into a valorized past of beginnings and peak times. This past is distanced, finished and closed like a circle. This does not mean, of course, that there is no movement within it. On the contrary, the relative temporal categories within it are richly and subtly worked out (nuances of 'earlier', 'later', sequences of moments, speeds, durations, etc.); there is evidence of a high level of artistic technique in matters of time. But within this time, completed and locked into a circle, all points are equidistant from the real, dynamic time of the present; insofar as this time is whole, it is not localised in an actual historical sequence; it is not relative to the present or to the future; it contains within itself, as it were, the entire fullness of time. As a consequence, all high genres of the classical era, that is, its entire high literature, are structured in the zone of the distanced image, a zone outside any possible contact with the present in all its openendedness.

As we have said, contemporaneity as such (that is, one that preserves its own living contemporary profile) cannot become an object of representation for the high genres. Contemporaneity was reality of a 'lower' order in comparison with the epic past. Least of all could it serve as the starting point for artistic ideation or evaluation. The focus for such an idea of evaluation could only be found in the absolute past. The present is something transitory, it is flow, it is an eternal continuation without beginning or end; it is denied an authentic conclusiveness and consequently lacks an essence as well. The future as well is perceived either as an essentially indifferent continuation of the present, or as an end, a final destruction, a catastrophe. The temporally valorized categories of absolute beginning and absolute end are extremely significant in our sense of time and in the ideologies of past times. The beginning is idealized, the end is darkened (catastrophe, 'the twilight of the gods'). This sense of time and the hierarchy of times described by us here permeate all the high genres of antiquity and the Middle Ages. They permeated so deeply into the basic foundation of these genres that they continue to live in them in subsequent eras – up to the nineteenth century, and even further.

This idealization of the past in high genres has something of an official air. All external expressions of the dominant force and truth (the expression of everything conclusive) were formulated in the valorised-hierarchical category of the past, in a distanced and distant image (everything from gesture and clothing to literary style, for all are symbols of authority). The novel, however, is associated with the eternally living element of unofficial language and unofficial thought (holiday forms, familiar speech, profanation).

The dead are loved in a different way. They are removed from the sphere of contact, one can and indeed must speak of them in a different style. Language about the dead is stylistically quite distinct from language about the living.

In the high genres all authority and privilege, all lofty significance and grandeur, abandon the zone of familiar contact for the distanced plane (clothing, etiquette, the style of a hero's speech and the style of speech about him). It is in this orientation toward completeness that the classicism of all non-novel genres is expressed.

Contemporaneity, flowing and transitory, 'low', present – this 'life without beginning or end' – was a subject of representation only in the low genres. Most importantly, it was the basic subject matter in that broadest and richest of realms, the common people's creative culture of laughter. In the aforementioned work I tried to indicate the enormous influence exercised by this realm – in the ancient world as well as the Middle Ages – on the birth and formation of novelistic language. It was equally significant for all other historical factors in the novelistic genre, during their emergence and early formation. Precisely here, in popular laughter, the authentic folkloric roots of the novel are to be sought. The present, contemporary life as such, 'I myself' and 'my contemporaries', 'my time' – all these concepts were originally the objects of ambivalent laughter, at the same time cheerful and annihilating. It is precisely here that a fundamentally new attitude toward language and toward the word is generated. Alongside direct representation – laughing at living reality – there flourish parody and travesty of all high genres and of all lofty models embodied in national myth. The 'absolute past' of gods, demigods and heroes is here, in parodies and even more so in travesties, 'contemporized': it is brought low, represented on a plane equal with contemporary life, in an everyday environment, in the low language of contemporaneity.

Notes

1. ERWIN ROHDE (1845–1898), *Der Griechesche Roman und seine Vorläufer* (1876, but many later editions, most recently that published by F. Olds (Hildesheim, 1960)), one of the greatest monuments of nineteenth-century classical scholarship in Germany. It has never really ever been superseded. But see BEN F. PERRY, *The Ancient Romances* (Berkeley, 1967), and ARTHUR HEISERMAN, *The Novel before the Novel* (Chicago, 1977).

2. CHARLES SOREL (1599–1674), an important figure in the reaction to the *preciosité* of such figures as HONORÉ d'URFÉ (1567–1625), whose *L'Astrée* (1607–27), a monstrous 5500-page volume overflowing with highflown language, is parodied in *Le Berger extravagant* (1627). The latter book's major protagonist is a dyed-in-the-wool Parisian who reads too many pastoral novels; intoxicated by these, he attempts to live the rustic life as they describe it – with predictably comic results.

3. JOHANN KARL AUGUST MUSÄUS (1735–1787), along with Tieck and Brentano, one of the great collectors of German folk tales and author of several *Kunstmärchen* of his own (translated into English by Carlyle). Reference here is to his *Grandison der Zweite* (1760–62, rewritten as *Der deutsche Grandison*, 1781–2), a satire on Richardson.

4. CHRISTOPH MARTIN WIELAND (1733–1813) is the author of *Geschichte des Agathon* (1767, first of many versions), an autobiographic novel in the guise of a Greek romance, considered by many to be the first in the long line of German *Bildungsromane*.

5. Reference here is to JOHANN CARL WEZEL (1747–1819), *Lebensgeschichte Tobias Knouts, des Weisen, sonst der Stammler genannt* (1773), a novel that has not received the readership it deserves. A four-volume reprint was published by Metzler (Stuttgart, Afterword by Viktor Lange) in 1971. See also ELIZABETH HOLZBEG-PFENNIGER, *Der desorientierte Erzähler: Studien zu J.C. Wezels Lebensgeschichte des Tobias Knouts* (Bern, 1976).

6. FRIEDRICH VON BLANKENBURG (1744–1796), *Versuch über den Roman* (1774), an enormous work (over 500 pages) that attempts to define the novel in terms of a rudimentary psychology, a concern for *Tugend* in the heroes. A facsimile edition was published by Metzler (Stuttgart) in 1965. Little is known about Blankenburg, who is also the author of an unfinished novel with the imposing title *Beytrage zur Geschichte deutschen Reichs und deutschen Sitten*, the first part of which appeared a year after the *Versuch* in 1775.

7. Reference here is to 'Über epische und dramatische Dichtung', cosigned by SCHILLER and GOETHE, but probably written by the latter in 1797, although not published until 1827. The actual term used by Goethe for what Bakhtin is calling 'absolute past' is *vollkommen vergangen*, which is opposed not to the novel, but to drama, which is defined as *vollkommen gegenwärtig*. The essay can be found in Goethe's *Sämtliche Werke* (Jubiläums-Ausgabe, Stuttgart and Berlin, 1902–7), vol. 36, pp. 149–52.

5 The Problem of Speech Genres*

Mikhail Bakhtin

In this fascinating essay, part of a projected book on *The Genres of Speech* which he never completed, Bakhtin calls for a dramatic expansion of the field of genre theory to embrace the entire spectrum of verbal activity. At one level, this is clearly an extension of his previous argument about the role of 'extraliterary' genres in the formation of the novel, a thesis which Bakhtin here broadens into a more comprehensive account of the relation between 'primary' and 'secondary' genres. But the rationale for the proposal is ultimately linguistic rather than literary. As the full text of the essay makes clear, Bakhtin's revolutionary theory of genre, like other aspects of his 'dialogism', rests on his critique of the Saussurean theory of language, whose seminal distinction between 'langue' (the language system) and 'parole' (the individual utterance) ignores the *subsystems* of language or *types* of utterance (oral or written) which Bakhtin calls 'speech genres'. These, Bakhtin argues, are a precondition for meaningful communication, since they 'organise our speech in almost the same way as grammatical (syntactical) forms do' (p. 90), conveying expectations of content, style and structure which help to shape any verbal exchange, from the simplest conversational rejoinder to the most complex scientific statement. Yet, except for the special case of literary genres and the oratorical forms once studied by theorists of rhetoric, speech genres remain a largely unexplored and, indeed, unnoticed feature of verbal life. Using many suggestive examples, Bakhtin's essay thus sets the agenda for what is in effect a new branch of knowledge.

Although the essay was not published until 1979, certain aspects of this agenda have now been implemented, in some cases independently of Bakhtin. The composition of the essay in the early

* Reprinted from M.M. Bakhtin, *Speech Genres and Other Late Essays*, trans. Vern W. McGee, ed. Caryl Emerson and Michael Holquist (Austin: University of Texas Press, 1986), pp. 60–7, 78–81, 96–101. Written in 1952–53 and first published in Bakhtin's *Estetika slovesnogo tvorchestva* (Aesthetics of verbal creativity) (Moscow, 1979).

1950s coincided almost exactly with the development of speech-act theory and the linguistic procedure known as 'discourse analysis', both of which have interesting parallels with Bakhtinian genre theory: see Todorov (Chapter 11). Sociopolitical, as distinct from purely linguistic, analysis of a wide range of popular discourses and genres is also an integral part of the emerging discipline of cultural studies, which has been much influenced by Bakhtin: see *Bakhtin and Cultural Theory*, ed. Ken Hirschkop and David Shepherd (Manchester: Manchester University Press, 1989), which includes an excellent bibliographical essay. Theoretical interest in the 'forms of combination' of human utterance is illustrated too by the spectacular success across many disciplines of the concept of intertextuality, a term invented by Julia Kristeva in direct response to Bakhtin's work: see Kristeva, *Desire in Language* (1980); and, for some recent applications, *Intertextuality: Theories and Practices*, ed. Worton and Still (1990). Each of these developments, however, involves a shift of focus from the category of genre *per se*, and in this sense the central thrust of Bakhtin's programme arguably still remains unfulfilled.

All the diverse areas of human activity involve the use of language. Quite understandably, the nature and forms of this use are just as diverse as are the areas of human activity. This, of course, in no way disaffirms the national unity of language.[a] Language is realized in the form of individual concrete utterances (oral and written) by participants in the various areas of human activity. These utterances reflect the specific conditions and goals of each such area not only through their content (thematic) and linguistic style, that is, the selection of the lexical, phraseological, and grammatical resources of the language, but above all through their compositional structure. All three of these aspects – thematic content, style, and compositional structure – are inseparably linked to the *whole* of the utterance and are equally determined by the specific nature of the particular sphere of communication. Each separate utterance is individual, of course, but each sphere in which language is used develops its own *relatively stable types* of these utterances. These we may call *speech genres*.

The wealth and diversity of speech genres are boundless because the various possibilities of human activity are inexhaustible, and because each sphere of activity contains an entire repertoire of speech genres that differentiate and grow as the particular sphere develops and becomes more complex. Special emphasis should be placed on the extreme *heterogeneity* of speech genres (oral and written). In fact, the category of speech genres should include short rejoinders of daily dialogue (and these are extremely varied depending on the subject matter, situation, and participants), everyday narration, writing (in all its various forms), the brief standard military command, the elaborate and detailed order, the fairly variegated repertoire of business documents (for the most part standard), and the diverse world of commentary (in the broad sense of the word: social, political). And we must also include here the diverse forms of scientific statements and all literary genres (from the proverb to the multivolume novel). It might seem that speech genres are so heterogeneous that they do not have and cannot have a single common level at which they can be studied. For here, on one level of inquiry, appear such heterogeneous phenomena as the single-word everyday rejoinder and the multivolume novel, the military command that is standardized even in its intonation and the profoundly individual lyrical work, and so on. One might think that such functional heterogeneity makes the common features of speech genres excessively abstract and empty. This probably explains why the general problem of speech genres has never really been raised. Literary genres have been studied more than anything else. But from antiquity to the present, they have been studied in terms of their specific literary and artistic features, in terms of the differences that distinguish one from the other (within the realm of literature), and not as specific types of utterances distinct from other types, but sharing with them a common *verbal* (language) nature. The general linguistic problem of the utterance and its types has hardly been considered at all. Rhetorical genres have been studied since antiquity (and not much has been added in subsequent epochs to classical theory). At that time, more attention was already being devoted to the verbal nature of these genres as utterances: for example, to such aspects as the relation to the listener and his influence on the utterance, the specific verbal finalization of the utterance (as distinct from its completeness of thought), and so forth. But here, too, the specific features of rhetorical genres (judicial, political) still overshadowed their general linguistic nature. Finally, everyday speech genres have been studied (mainly rejoinders in everyday dialogue), and from a general linguistic standpoint (in the school of Saussure and among his later followers – the Structuralists, the American behaviorists, and, on a completely different linguistic basis, the Vosslerians).[b] But this line of inquiry could not lead to a correct determination of the general linguistic nature of the utterance either, since it was limited to the specific features of everyday oral speech, sometimes being directly and deliberately oriented toward primitive utterances (American behaviorists).

The extreme heterogeneity of speech genres and the attendant difficulty of determining the general nature of the utterance should in no way be underestimated. It is especially important here to draw attention to the very significant difference between primary (simple) and secondary (complex) speech genres (understood not as a functional difference). Secondary (complex) speech genres – novels, dramas, all kinds of scientific research, major genres of commentary, and so forth – arise in more complex and comparatively highly developed and organized cultural communication (primarily written) that is artistic, scientific, sociopolitical, and so on. During the process of their formation, they absorb and digest various primary (simple) genres that have taken form in unmediated speech communion. These primary genres are altered and assume a special character when they enter into complex ones. They lose their immediate relation to actual reality and to the real utterances of others. For example, rejoinders of everyday dialogue or letters found in a novel retain their form and their everyday significance only on the plane of the novel's content. They enter into actual reality only via the novel as a whole, that is, as a literary-artistic event and not as everyday life. The novel as a whole is an utterance just as rejoinders in everyday dialogue or private letters are (they do have a common nature), but unlike these, the novel is a secondary (complex) utterance.

The difference between primary and secondary (ideological) genres is very great and fundamental,[c] but this is precisely why the nature of the utterance should be revealed and defined through analysis of both types. Only then can the definition be adequate to the complex and profound nature of the utterance (and encompass its most important facets). A one-sided orientation toward primary genres inevitably leads to a vulgarization of the entire problem (behaviorist linguistics is an extreme example). The very interrelations between primary and secondary genres and the process of the historical formation of the latter shed light on the nature of the utterance (and above all on the complex problem of the interrelations among language, ideology, and world view).

A study of the nature of the utterance and of the diversity of generic forms of utterances in various spheres of human activity is immensely important to almost all areas of linguistics and philology. This is because any research whose material is concrete language – the history of a language, normative grammar, the compilation of any kind of dictionary, the stylistics of language, and so forth – inevitably deals with concrete utterances (written and oral) belonging to various spheres of human activity and communication: chronicles, contracts, texts of laws, clerical and other documents, various literary, scientific, and commentarial genres, official and personal letters, rejoinders in everyday dialogue (in all of their diverse subcategories), and so on. And it is here that scholars find the language data they need. A clear idea of the nature of the utterance in general and of the peculiarities of the various types of utterances (primary and secondary), that is, of various speech genres, is necessary, we think, for research in any special area. To ignore the nature of the utterance or to fail to consider the peculiarities of generic subcategories of speech in any area of linguistic study leads to perfunctoriness and excessive abstractness, distorts the historicity of the research, and weakens the link between language and life. After all, language enters life through concrete utterances (which manifest language) and life enters language through concrete utterances as well. The utterance is an exceptionally important node of problems. We shall approach certain areas and problems of the science of language in this context.

First of all, stylistics. Any style is inseparably related to the utterance and to typical forms of utterances, that is, speech genres. Any utterance – oral or written, primary or secondary, and in any sphere of communication – is individual and therefore can reflect the individuality of the speaker (or writer); that is, it possesses individual style. But not all genres are equally conducive to reflecting the individuality of the speaker in the language of the utterance, that is, to an individual style. The most conducive genres are those of artistic literature: here the individual style enters directly into the very task of the utterance, and this is one of its main goals (but even within artistic literature various genres offer different possibilities for expressing individuality in language and various aspects of individuality). The least favorable conditions for reflecting individuality in language obtain in speech genres that require a standard form, for example, many kinds of business documents, military commands, verbal signals in industry, and so on. Here one can reflect only the most superficial, almost biological aspects of individuality (mainly in the oral manifestation of these standard types of utterances). In the vast majority of speech genres (except for literary-artistic ones), the individual style does not enter into the intent of the utterance, does not serve as its only goal, but is, as it were, an epiphenomenon of the utterance, one of its by-products. Various genres can reveal various layers and facets of the individual personality, and individual style can be found in various interrelations with the national language. The very problem of the national and the individual in language is basically the problem of the utterance (after all, only here, in the utterance, is the national language embodied in individual form). The very determination of style in general, and individual style in particular, requires deeper study of both the nature of the utterance and the diversity of speech genres.

The organic, inseparable link between style and genre is clearly revealed also in the problem of language styles, or functional styles. In essence, language, or functional, styles are nothing other than generic styles for certain spheres of human activity and communication. Each sphere has and applies its own genres that correspond to its own specific conditions. There are also particular styles that correspond to these genres. A particular function (scientific, technical, commentarial, business, everyday) and the particular conditions of speech communication specific for each sphere give rise to particular genres, that is, certain relatively stable thematic, compositional, and stylistic types of utterances. Style is inseparably linked to particular thematic unities and – what is especially important – to particular compositional unities: to particular types of construction of the whole, types of its completion, and types of relations between the speaker and other participants in speech communication (listeners or readers, partners, the other's speech, and so forth). Style enters as one element into the generic unity of the utterance. Of course, this does not mean that language style cannot be the subject of its own independent study. Such a study, that is, of language stylistics as an independent discipline, is both feasible and necessary. But this study will be correct and productive only if based on a constant awareness of the generic nature of language styles, and on a preliminary study of the subcategories of speech genres. Up to this point the stylistics of language has not had such a basis. Hence its weakness. There is no generally recognized classification of language styles. Those who attempt to create them frequently fail to meet the fundamental logical requirement of classification: a unified basis.[d] Existing taxonomies are extremely poor and undifferentiated.[1] For example, a recently published academy grammar of the Russian language gives the following stylistic subcategories of language: bookish speech, popular speech, abstract-scientific, scientific-technical, journalistic-commentarial, official-business, and familiar everyday speech, as well as vulgar common parlance. In addition to these linguistic styles, there are the stylistic subcategories of dialect words, archaic words, and occupational expressions. Such a classification of styles is completely random, and at its base lies a variety of principles (or bases) for division into styles. Moreover, this classification is both inexhaustive and inadequately differentiated. All this is a direct result of an inadequate understanding of the generic nature of linguistic styles, and the absence of a well-thought-out classification of speech genres in terms of spheres of human activity (and also ignorance of the distinction between primary and secondary genres, which is very important for stylistics).

It is especially harmful to separate style from genre when elaborating historical problems. Historical changes in language styles are inseparably linked to changes in speech genres. Literary language is a complex, dynamic system of linguistic styles. The proportions and interrelations of these styles in the system of literary language are constantly changing. Literary language, which also includes nonliterary styles, is an even more complex system, and it is organized on different bases. In order to puzzle out the complex historical dynamics of these systems and move from a simple (and, in the majority of cases, superficial) description of styles, which are always in evidence and alternating with one another, to a historical explanation of these changes, one must develop a special history of speech genres (and not only secondary, but also primary ones) that reflects more directly, clearly, and flexibly all the changes taking place in social life. Utterances and their types, that is, speech genres, are the drive belts from the history of society to the history of language. There is not a single new phenomenon (phonetic, lexical, or grammatical) that can enter the system of language without having traversed the long and complicated path of generic-stylistic testing and modification.[2]

In each epoch certain speech genres set the tone for the development of literary language. And these speech genres are not only secondary (literary, commentarial, and scientific), but also primary (certain types of oral dialogue – of the salon, of one's own circle, and other types as well, such as familiar, family-everyday, sociopolitical, philosophical, and so on). Any expansion of the literary language that results from drawing on various extraliterary strata of the national language inevitably entails some degree of penetration into all genres of written language (literary, scientific, commentarial, conversational, and so forth) to a greater or lesser degree, and entails new generic devices for the construction of the speech whole, its finalization, the accommodation of the listener or partner, and so forth. This leads to a more or less fundamental restructuring and renewal of speech genres. When dealing with the corresponding extraliterary strata of the national language, one inevitably also deals with the speech genres through which these strata are manifested. In the majority of cases, these are various types of conversational-dialogical genres. Hence the more or less distinct dialogization of secondary genres, the weakening of their monological composition, the new sense of the listener as a partner-interlocutor, new forms of finalization of the whole, and so forth. Where there is style there is genre. The transfer of style from one genre to another not only alters the way a style sounds, under conditions of a genre unnatural to it, but also violates or renews the given genre.

Thus, both individual and general language styles govern speech genres. A deeper and broader study of the latter is absolutely imperative for a productive study of any stylistic problem.

However, both the fundamental and the general methodological question of the interrelations between lexicon and grammar (on the one hand) and stylistics (on the other) rests on the same problem of the utterance and of speech genres.

Grammar (and lexicon) is essentially different from stylistics (some even oppose it to stylistics), but at the same time there is not a single grammatical study that can do without stylistic observation and excursus. In a large number of cases the distinction between grammar and stylistics appears to be completely erased. There are phenomena that some scholars include in the area of grammar while others include them in the area of stylistics. The syntagma is an example.

One might say that grammar and stylistics converge and diverge in any concrete language phenomenon. If considered only in the language system, it is a grammatical phenomenon, but if considered in the whole of the individual utterance or in a speech genre, it is a stylistic phenomenon. And this is because the speaker's very selection of a particular grammatical form is a stylistic act. But these two viewpoints of one and the same specific linguistic phenomenon should not be impervious to one another and should not simply replace one another mechanically. They should be organically combined (with, however, the most clear-cut methodological distinction between them) on the basis of the real unity of the language phenomenon. Only a profound understanding of the nature of the utterance and the particular features of speech genres can provide a correct solution to this complex methodological problem.

It seems to us that a study of the nature of the utterance and of speech genres is of fundamental importance for overcoming those simplistic notions about speech life, about the so-called speech flow, about communication and so forth – ideas which are still current in our language studies. Moreover, a study of the utterance as a *real unit of speech communion* will also make it possible to understand more correctly the *nature of language units* (as a system): words and sentences.

[. . .] Let us turn to the third and, for us, most important aspect: the stable *generic* forms of the utterance. The speaker's speech will is manifested primarily in the *choice of a particular speech genre*. This choice is determined by the specific nature of the given sphere of speech communication, semantic (thematic) considerations, the concrete situation of the speech communication, the personal composition of its participants, and so on. And when the speaker's speech plan with all its individuality and subjectivity is applied and adapted to a chosen genre, it is shaped and developed within a certain generic form. Such genres exist above all in the great and multifarious sphere of everyday oral communication, including the most familiar and the most intimate.

We speak only in definite speech genres, that is, all our utterances have definite and relatively stable typical *forms of construction of the whole*. Our repertoire of oral (and written) speech genres is rich. We use them confidently and skillfully *in practice*, and it is quite possible for us not even to suspect their existence *in theory*. Like Molière's Monsieur Jourdain who, when speaking in prose, had no idea that was what he was doing, we speak in diverse genres without suspecting that they exist. Even in the most free, the most unconstrained conversation, we cast our speech in definite generic forms, sometimes rigid and trite ones, sometimes more flexible, plastic, and creative ones (everyday communication also has creative genres at its disposal). We are given these speech genres in almost the same way that we are given our native language, which we master fluently long before we begin to study grammar. We know our native language – its lexical composition and grammatical structure – not from dictionaries and grammars but from concrete utterances that we hear and that we ourselves reproduce in live speech communication with people around us. We assimilate forms of language only in forms of utterances and in conjunction with these forms. The forms of language and the typical forms of utterances, that is, speech genres, enter our experience and our consciousness together, and in close connection with one another. To learn to speak means to learn to construct utterances (because we speak in utterances and not in individual sentences, and, of course, not in individual words). Speech genres organize our speech in almost the same way as grammatical (syntactical) forms do. We learn to cast our speech in generic forms and, when hearing others' speech, we guess its genre from the very first words; we predict a certain length (that is, the approximate length of the speech whole) and a certain compositional structure; we foresee the end; that is, from the very beginning we have a sense of the speech whole, which is only later differentiated during the speech process. If speech genres did not exist and we had not mastered them, if we had to originate them during the speech process and construct each utterance at will for the first time, speech communication would be almost impossible.

The generic forms in which we cast our speech, of course, differ essentially from language forms. The latter are stable and compulsory (normative) for the speaker, while generic forms are much more flexible, plastic, and free. Speech genres are very diverse in this respect. A large number of genres that are widespread in everyday life are so standard that the speaker's individual speech will is manifested only in its choice of a particular genre, and, perhaps, in its expressive intonation. Such, for example, are the various everyday genres of greetings, farewells, congratulations, all kinds of wishes, information about health, business, and so forth. These genres are so diverse because they differ depending on the situation, social position, and personal interrelations of the participants in the communication. These genres have high, strictly official, respectful forms as well as familiar ones.³ And there are forms with varying degrees of familiarity, as well as intimate forms (which differ from familiar ones). These genres also require a certain tone; their structure includes a certain expressive intonation. These genres, particularly the high and official ones, are compulsory and extremely stable. The speech will is usually limited here to a choice of a particular genre. And only slight nuances of expressive intonation (one can take a drier or more respectful tone, a colder or warmer one; one can introduce the intonation of joy, and so forth) can express the speaker's individuality (his emotional speech intent). But even here it is generally possible to re-accentuate genres. This is typical of speech communication: thus, for example, the generic form of greeting can move from the official sphere into the sphere of familiar communication, that is, it can be used with parodic-ironic re-accentuation. To a similar end, one can deliberately mix genres from various spheres.

In addition to these standard genres, of course, freer and more creative genres of oral speech communication have existed and still exist: genres of salon conversations about everyday, social, aesthetic, and other subjects, genres of table conversation, intimate conversations among friends, intimate conversations within the family, and so on. (No list of oral speech genres yet exists, or even a principle on which such a list might be based.) The majority of these genres are subject to free creative reformulation (like artistic genres, and some, perhaps, to a greater degree). But to use a genre freely and creatively is not the same as to create a genre from the beginning; genres must be fully mastered in order to be manipulated freely.

Many people who have an excellent command of a language often feel quite helpless in certain spheres of communication precisely because they do not have a practical command of the generic forms used in the given spheres. Frequently a person who has an excellent command of speech in some areas of cultural communication, who is able to read a scholarly paper or engage in a scholarly discussion, who speaks very well on social questions, is silent or very awkward in social conversation. Here it is not a matter of an impoverished vocabulary or of style, taken abstractly: this is entirely a matter of the inability to command a repertoire of genres of social conversation, the lack of a sufficient supply of those ideas about the whole of the utterance that help to cast one's speech quickly and naturally in certain compositional and stylistic forms, the inability to grasp a word promptly, to begin and end correctly (composition is very uncomplicated in these genres).

The better our command of genres, the more freely we employ them, the more fully and clearly we reveal our own individuality in them (where this is possible and necessary), the more flexibly and precisely we reflect the unrepeatable situation of communication – in a word, the more perfectly we implement our free speech plan.

Thus, a speaker is given not only mandatory forms of the national language (lexical composition and grammatical structure), but also forms of utterances that are mandatory, that is, speech genres. The latter are just as necessary for mutual understanding as are forms of language. Speech genres are much more changeable, flexible, and plastic than language forms are, but they have a normative significance for the speaking individuum, and they are not created by him but are given to him. Therefore, the single utterance, with all its individuality and creativity, can in no way be regarded as a *completely free combination* of forms of language, as is supposed, for example, by Saussure (and by many other linguists after him), who juxtaposed the utterance (*la parole*), as a purely individual act, to the system of language as a phenomenon that is purely social and mandatory for the individuum.[4] The vast majority of linguists hold the same position, in theory if not in practice. They see in the utterance only an individual combination of purely linguistic (lexical and grammatical) forms and they neither uncover nor study any of the other normative forms the utterance acquires in practice.

Ignoring speech genres as relatively stable and normative forms of the utterance inevitably led to the confusion we have already pointed out between the utterance and the sentence, and it had to lead them to the position (which, to be sure, was never consistently defended) that our speech is cast solely in stable sentence forms that are given to us; and the number of these interrelated sentences we speak in a row and when we stop (end) – this is completely subject to the individual speech will of the speaker or to the caprice of the mythical 'speech flow'.

When we select a particular type of sentence, we do so not for the sentence itself, but out of consideration for what we wish to express with this one given sentence. We select the type of sentence from the standpoint of the *whole* utterance, which is transmitted in advance to our speech imagination and which determines our choice. The idea of the form of the whole utterance, that is, of a particular speech genre, guides us in the process of our speaking. The plan of the utterance as a whole may require only one sentence for its implementation, but it may also require a large number of them. The chosen genre predetermines for us their type and their compositional links.

[. . .] Finer nuances of style are determined by the nature and degree of *personal* proximity of the addressee to the speaker in various familiar speech genres, on the one hand, and in intimate ones, on the other. With all the immense differences among familiar and intimate genres (and, consequently, styles), they perceive their addressees in exactly the same way: more or less outside the framework of the social hierarchy and social conventions, 'without rank', as it were. This gives rise to a certain *candor* of speech (which in familiar styles sometimes approaches cynicism). In intimate styles this is expressed in an apparent desire for the speaker and addressee to merge completely. In familiar speech, since speech constraints and conventions have fallen away, one can take a special unofficial, volitional approach to reality.[5] This is why during the Renaissance familiar genres and styles could play such a large and positive role in destroying the official medieval picture of the world. In other periods as well, when the task was to destroy traditional official styles and world-views that had faded and become conventional, familiar styles became very significant in literature. Moreover, familiarization of styles opened literature up to layers of language that had previously been under speech constraint. The significance of familiar genres and styles in literary history has not yet been adequately evaluated. Intimate genres and styles are based on a maximum internal proximity of the speaker and addressee (in extreme instances, as if they had merged). Intimate speech is imbued with a deep confidence in the addressee, in his sympathy, in the sensitivity and goodwill of his responsive understanding. In this atmosphere of profound trust, the speaker reveals his internal depths. This determines the special expressiveness and internal candor of these styles (as distinct from the loud street-language candor of familiar speech). Familiar and intimate genres and styles (as yet very little studied) reveal extremely clearly the dependence of style on a certain sense and understanding of the addressee (the addressee of the utterance) on the part of the speaker, and on the addressee's actively responsive understanding that is anticipated by the speaker. These styles reveal especially clearly the narrowness and incorrectness of traditional stylistics, which tries to understand and define style solely from the standpoint of the semantic and thematic content of speech and the speaker's expressive attitude toward this content. Unless one accounts for the speaker's attitude toward the *other* and his utterances (existing or anticipated), one can understand neither the genre nor the style of speech. But even the so-called neutral or objective styles of exposition that concentrate maximally on their subject matter and, it would seem, are free of any consideration of the other still involve a certain conception of their addressee. Such objectively neutral styles select language vehicles not only from the standpoint of their adequacy to the subject matter of speech, but also from the standpoint of the presumed apperceptive background of the addressee. But this background is taken into account in as generalized a way as possible, and is abstracted from the expressive aspect (the expression of the speaker himself is also minimal in the objective style). Objectively neutral styles presuppose something like an identity of the addressee and the speaker, a unity of their viewpoints, but this identity and unity are purchased at the price of almost complete forfeiture of expression. It must be noted that the nature of objectively neutral styles (and, consequently, the concept of the addressee on which they are based) is fairly diverse, depending on the differences between the areas of speech communication.

This question of the concept of the speech addressee (how the speaker or writer senses and imagines him) is of immense significance in literary history. Each epoch, each literary trend and literary-artistic style, each literary genre within an epoch or trend, is typified by its own special concepts of the addressee of the literary work, a special sense and understanding of its reader, listener, public, or people. A historical study of changes in these concepts would be an interesting and important task. But in order to develop it productively, the statement of the problem itself would have to be theoretically clear.

It should be noted that, in addition to those real meanings and ideas of one's addressee that actually determine the style of the utterances (works), the history of literature also includes conventional or semiconventional forms of address to readers, listeners, posterity, and so forth, just as, in addition to the actual author, there are also conventional and semiconventional images of substitute authors, editors, and various kinds of narrators. The vast majority of literary genres are secondary, complex genres composed of various transformed primary genres (the rejoinder in dialogue, everyday stories, letters, diaries, minutes, and so forth). As a rule, these secondary genres of complex cultural communication *play out* various forms of primary speech communication. Here also is the source of all literary/conventional characters of authors, narrators, and addressees. But the most complex and ultra-composite work of a secondary genre as a whole (viewed as a whole) is a single integrated real utterance that has a real author and real addressees whom this author perceives and imagines.

Thus, addressivity, the quality of turning to someone, is a constitutive feature of the utterance; without it the utterance does not and cannot exist. The various typical forms this addressivity assumes and the various concepts of the addressee are constitutive, definitive features of various speech genres.

As distinct from utterances (and speech genres), the signifying units of a language – the word and the sentence – lack this quality of being directed or addressed to someone: these units belong to nobody and are addressed to nobody. Moreover, they in themselves are devoid of any kind of relation to the other's utterance, the other's word. If an individual word or sentence is directed at someone, addressed to someone, then we have a completed utterance that consists of one word or one sentence, and addressivity is inherent not in the unit of language, but in the utterance. A sentence that is surrounded by context acquires the addressivity only through the entire utterance, as a constituent part (element) of it.[6]

Language as a system has an immense supply of purely linguistic means for expressing formal address: lexical, morphological (the corresponding cases, pronouns, personal forms of verbs), and syntactical (various standard phrases and modifications of sentences). But they acquire addressivity only in the whole of a concrete utterance. And the expression of this actual addressivity is never exhausted, of course, by these special language (grammatical) means. They can even be completely lacking, and the utterance can still reflect very clearly the influence of the addressee and his anticipated responsive reaction. The choice of *all* language means is made by the speaker under varying degrees of influence from the addressee and his anticipated response.

When one analyzes an individual sentence apart from its context, the traces of addressivity and the influence of the anticipated response, dialogical echoes from others' preceding utterances, faint traces of changes of speech subjects that have furrowed the utterance from within – all these are lost, erased, because they are all foreign to the sentence as a unit of language. All these phenomena are connected with the whole of the utterance, and when this whole escapes the field of vision of the analyst they cease to exist for him. Herein lies one of the reasons for that narrowness of traditional stylistics we commented upon above. A stylistic analysis that embraces all aspects of style is possible only as an analysis of the *whole* utterance, and only in that chain of speech communion of which the utterance is an inseparable *link*.

Author's notes

1. The same kinds of classifications of language styles, impoverished and lacking clarity, with a fabricated foundation, are given by A.N. Gvozdev in his book *Ocherki po stilistike russkogo jazyka* (Essays on the stylistics of the Russian language) (Moscow, 1952), pp. 13–15. All of these classifications are based on an uncritical assimilation of traditional ideas about language styles.

2. This thesis of ours has nothing in common with the Vosslerian idea of the primacy of the stylistic over the grammatical. Our subsequent exposition will make this completely clear.

3. These and other phenomena have interested linguists (mainly language historians) in the purely stylistic level as a reflection in language of

historically changed forms of etiquette, courtesy, and hospitality. See, for example, F. BRUNOT, *Histoire de la langue française des origines à 1900*, 10 vols (Paris: A. Colin, 1905).

4. Saussure defines the utterance (*la parole*) as an 'individual act. It is willful and intellectual. Within the act, we should distinguish between (1) the combinations by which the speaker uses the language code for expressing his own thought; and (2) the psychological mechanism that allows him to exteriorize those combinations' (*Course in General Linguistics* (New York: McGraw-Hill, 1966), p. 14). Thus, Saussure ignores the fact that in addition to forms of language there are also *forms of combinations* of these forms, that is, he ignores speech genres.

5. The loud candor of the streets, calling things by their real names, is typical of this style.

6. We note that interrogatory and imperative types of sentences, as a rule, act as completed utterances (in the appropriate speech genres).

Editors' notes

[a] 'National unity of language' is a shorthand way of referring to the assemblage of linguistic and translinguistic practices common to a given region. It is, then, a good example of what Bakhtin means by an open unity. See also OTTO JESPERSON, *Mankind, Nation, and Individual* (Bloomington: Indiana University Press, 1964).

[b] Saussure's teaching is based on a distinction between language (*la langue*) – a system of interconnected signs and forms that normatively determine each individual speech act and are the special object of linguistics – and speech (*la parole*) – individual instances of language use. Bakhtin discusses Saussure's teachings in *Marxism and the Philosophy of Language* as one of the two main trends in linguistic thought (the trend of 'abstract objectivism') that he uses to shape his own theory of the utterance. See V.N. VOLOSHINOV, *Marxism and the Philosophy of Language*, tr. Ladislav Matejka and I.R. Titunik (New York: Seminar Press, 1973), esp. pp. 58–61.

'Behaviorists' here refers to the school of psychology introduced by the Harvard physiologist J.B. Watson in 1913. It seeks to explain animal and human behavior entirely in terms of observable and measurable responses to external stimuli. Watson, in his insistence that behavior is a physiological reaction to environmental stimuli, denied the value of introspection and of the concept of consciousness. He saw mental processes as bodily movements, even when unperceived, so that thinking in his view is subvocal speech. There is a strong connection as well between the behaviorist school of psychology and the school of American descriptive linguistics, which is what Bakhtin is referring to here. The so-called descriptivist school was founded by the eminent anthropologist Franz Boas (1858–1942). Its closeness to behaviorism consists in its insistence on careful observation unconditioned by presuppositions or categories taken from traditional language structure. Leonard Bloomfield (1887–1949) was the chief spokesman for the school and was explicit about his commitment to a 'mechanist approach' (his term for the behaviorist school of psychology): 'Mechanists demand that the facts be presented without any assumption of such auxiliary factors [as a version of the mind]. I have tried to meet this demand . . .' (*Language* (New York: Holt, Rinehart, and Winston, 1933), p. vii). Two prominent linguists sometimes associated with the descriptivists, Edward Sapir (1884–1939) and his pupil Benjamin Lee Whorf (1897–1941), differ from Bloomfield insofar as behaviorism plays a relatively minor role in their work.

'Vosslerians' refers to the movement named after the German philologist Karl Vossler (1872–1949), whose adherents included Leo Spitzer (1887–1960). For Vosslerians, the reality of language is the continuously creative, constructive activity that is prosecuted through speech acts; the creativity of language is likened to artistic creativity, and stylistics becomes the leading discipline. Style takes precedence over grammar, and the standpoint of the speaker takes precedence over that of the listener. In a number of aspects, Bakhtin is close to the Vosslerians, but differs in his understanding of the utterance as the concrete reality of language life. Bakhtin does not, like the Vosslerians, conceive the utterance to be an individual speech act; rather, he emphasises the 'inner sociality' in speech communication – an aspect that is objectively reinforced in speech genres. The concept of speech genres is central to Bakhtin, then, in that it separates his translinguistics from both Saussureans and Vosslerians in the philosophy of language.

c   'Ideology' should not be confused with the politically oriented English word. Ideology as it is used here is essentially any system of ideas. But ideology is semiotic in the sense that it involves the concrete exchange of signs in society and history. Every word/discourse betrays the ideology of its speaker; every speaker is thus an ideologue and every utterance an ideologeme.

d   A unified basis for classifying the enormous diversity of utterances is an obsession of Bakhtin's, one that relates him directly to Wilhelm von Humboldt (1767–1835), the first in the modern period to argue systematically that language is the vehicle of thought. He calls language the 'labor of the mind' (*Arbeit des Geistes*) in his famous formulation '[language] itself is not [mere] work (*ergon*), but an activity (*energeia*) . . . it is in fact the labor of the mind that otherwise would eternally repeat itself to make articulated sound capable of the expression of thought' (*Über die Verschiedenheit des menschlichen Sprachbaues*, in *Werke*, vol. 7 (Berlin: De Gruyter, 1968), p. 46). What is important here is that for Bakhtin, as for von Humboldt, the diversity of languages *is itself of philosophical significance*, for if thought and speech are one, does not each language embody a unique way of thinking? It is here that Bakhtin also comes very close to the work of Sapir and, especially, of Whorf. See BENJAMIN LEE WHORF, *Language, Thought, and Reality*, ed. John B. Carroll (Cambridge, Mass.: MIT Press, 1956), esp. pp. 212–19 and 239–45.

6 The Mythos of Summer: Romance*

NORTHROP FRYE

No critic of the postwar era has had greater influence in the English-speaking world on the study of literary genres than the Canadian critic Northrop Frye, whose *Anatomy of Criticism* (1957) has been called the most original contribution to poetics since Aristotle. That influence, however, is fraught with paradox. Frye's brilliant development of the concept of the archetype, his encyclopaedic range of reference, and his ability to uncover the mythical substratum of even the most seemingly 'realistic' literature, led to an enormous enrichment of our understanding of literary forms, especially his four fundamental categories: comedy, tragedy, romance and irony/satire. On the other hand, many of the structural patterns he identifies – the formal analogies and 'associative clusters' of symbolism that link works of literature with one another and with other archetypal phenomena – cut across traditional distinctions of genre, with the result that, in Frye's taxonomy, each of these four categories undergoes so large an expansion as to cease to be the discrete entity it has functioned as historically. The *Anatomy of Criticism* emphasised this conceptual and terminological shift by defining those four categories as '*pre*-generic' and referring to them as *mythoi* (he also calls them 'modes'), while reserving the term 'genre' for the four 'radicals of presentation': drama, epic, lyric and – Frye's addition to the familiar triad – fiction. The two kinds of structuring principle are treated separately by Frye, *mythoi* being the province of what he terms 'archetypal criticism', genres of 'rhetorical criticism'. Although Genette (Chapter 12) has endorsed this division as being faithful to Aristotle's distinction between genre and mode (albeit reversing the terms), most have rejected or simply ignored it, and the 'theory of genres' most commonly ascribed to Frye – and unquestionably the most original aspect of his work – is what the *Anatomy* itself terms his 'theory of myths', his account of the

---

* Reprinted from Northrop Frye, *Anatomy of Criticism: Four Essays* (Princeton: Princeton University Press, 1957), pp. 186–206.

four *mythoi* or modes, each of which he links with one of the seasons. It is the second of these, romance or the 'mythos of summer', that is the subject of the following extract: a piece of archetypal criticism which, in its rich synthesis of psychological, anthropological and literary insights, as well as its stunning array of examples, illustrates better than any purely abstract definition Frye's distinctive understanding of literary form.

Like other aspects of his work, Frye's archetypal theory of genres has provoked intense debate: see Jameson's illuminating comparison with Propp (Chapter 10); Hernadi, *Beyond Genre* (1972), pp. 131–52; Todorov, *The Fantastic* (1973), pp. 8–23; Scholes, *Structuralism in Literature* (1974), pp. 117–41; and Brooke-Rose, 'Historical Genres/Theoretical Genres' (1976). The central place of romance in Frye's thinking is attested by his later book *The Secular Scripture: A Study of the Structure of Romance* (1976), where he defines romance as 'the structural core of all fiction' (p. 15), a claim that has helped to establish romance as a focal point of modern genre theory: see, for instance, Bloom, 'The Internalization of Quest Romance' (1971); Patricia Parker, *Inescapable Romance: Studies in the Poetics of a Mode* (Princeton: Princeton University Press, 1979); and Jameson (Chapter 10). For general assessments of Frye's work, see A.C. Hamilton, *Northrop Frye: Anatomy of his Criticism* (Toronto: University of Toronto Press, 1990); and Jonathan Hart, *Northrop Frye: The Theoretical Imagination* (London: Routledge, 1994).

The romance is nearest of all literary forms to the wish-fulfilment dream, and for that reason it has socially a curiously paradoxical role. In every age the ruling social or intellectual class tends to project its ideals in some form of romance, where the virtuous heroes and beautiful heroines represent the ideals and the villains the threats to their ascendancy. This is the general character of chivalric romance in the Middle Ages, aristocratic romance in the Renaissance, bourgeois romance since the eighteenth century, and revolutionary romance in contemporary Russia. Yet there is a genuinely 'proletarian' element in romance too which is never satisfied with its various incarnations, and in fact the incarnations themselves indicate that no matter how great a change may take place in society, romance will turn up again, as hungry as ever, looking for new hopes and desires to feed on. The perennially childlike quality of romance is marked by its extraordinarily persistent nostalgia, its search for some kind of imaginative golden age in time or space. There has never to my knowledge been any period of Gothic English literature, but the list of Gothic revivalists stretches completely across its entire history, from the *Beowulf* poet to writers of our own day.

The essential element of plot in romance is adventure, which means that romance is naturally a sequential and processional form, hence we know it better from fiction than from drama. At its most naive it is an endless form in which a central character who never develops or ages goes through one adventure after another until the author himself collapses. We see this form in comic strips, where the central characters persist for years in a state of refrigerated deathlessness. However, no book can rival the continuity of the newspaper, and as soon as romance achieves a literary form, it tends to limit itself to a sequence of minor adventures leading up to a major or climacteric adventure, usually announced from the beginning, the completion of which rounds off the story. We may call this major adventure, the element that gives literary form to the romance, the quest.

The complete form of the romance is clearly the successful quest, and such a completed form has three main stages: the stage of the perilous journey and the preliminary minor adventures; the crucial struggle, usually some kind of battle in which either the hero or his foe, or both, must die; and the exaltation of the hero. We may call these three stages respectively, using Greek terms, the *agon* or conflict, the *pathos* or death-struggle, and the *anagnorisis* or discovery, the recognition of the hero, who has clearly proved himself to be a hero even if he does not survive the conflict. Thus the romance expresses more clearly the passage from struggle through a point of ritual death to a recognition scene that we discovered in comedy. A threefold structure is repeated in many features of romance – in the frequency, for instance, with which the successful hero is a third son, or the third to undertake the quest, or successful on his third attempt. It is shown more directly in the three-day rhythm of death, disappearance and revival which is found in the myth of Attis and other dying gods, and has been incorporated in our Easter.

A quest involving conflict assumes two main characters, a protagonist or hero, and an antagonist or enemy. (No doubt I should add, for the benefit of some readers, that I have read the article 'Protagonist' in Fowler's *Modern English Usage*.) The enemy may be an ordinary human being, but the nearer the romance is to myth, the more attributes of divinity will cling to the hero and the more the enemy will take on demonic mythical qualities. The central form of romance is dialectical: everything is focussed on a conflict between the hero and his enemy, and all the reader's values are bound up with the hero. Hence the hero of romance is analogous to the mythical Messiah or deliverer who comes from an upper world, and his enemy is analogous to the demonic powers of a lower world. The conflict however takes place in, or at any rate primarily concerns, *our* world, which is in the middle, and which is characterized by the cyclical movement of nature.

Hence the opposite poles of the cycles of nature are assimilated to the opposition of the hero and his enemy. The enemy is associated with winter, darkness, confusion, sterility, moribund life, and old age, and the hero with spring, dawn, order, fertility, vigor, and youth. As all the cyclical phenomena can be readily associated or identified, it follows that any attempt to prove that a romantic story does or does not resemble, say, a solar myth, or that its hero does or does not resemble a sun-god, is likely to be a waste of time. If it is a story within this general area, cyclical imagery is likely to be present, and solar imagery is normally prominent among cyclical images. If the hero of a romance returns from a quest disguised, flings off his beggar's rags, and stands forth in the resplendent scarlet cloak of the prince, we do not have a theme which has necessarily descended from a solar myth; we have the literary device of displacement. The hero does something which we may or may not, as we like, associate with the myth of the sun returning at dawn. If we are reading the story as critics, with an eye to structural principles, we shall make the association, because the solar analogy explains why the hero's act is an effective and conventional incident. If we are reading the story for fun, we need not bother: that is, some murky 'subconscious' factor in our response will take care of the association.

We have distinguished myth from romance by the hero's power of action: in the myth proper he is divine, in the romance proper he is human. This distinction is much sharper theologically than it is poetically, and myth and romance both belong in the general category of mythopoeic literature. The attributing of divinity to the chief characters of myth, however, tends to give myth a further distinction, already referred to, of occupying a central *canonical* position. Most cultures regard certain stories with more reverence than others, either because they are thought of as historically true or because they have come to bear a heavier weight of conceptual meaning. The story of Adam and Eve in Eden has thus a canonical position for poets in our tradition whether they believe in its historicity or not. The reason for the greater profundity of canonical myth is not solely tradition, but the result of the greater degree of metaphorical identification that is possible in myth. In literary criticism the myth is normally the metaphorical key to the displacements of romance, hence the importance of the quest-myth of the Bible in what follows. But because of the tendency to expurgate and moralize in canonical myth, the less inhibited area of legend and folk tale often contains an equally great concentration of mythical meaning.

The central form of quest-romance is the dragon-killing theme exemplified in the stories of St George and Perseus [. . .]. A land ruled by a helpless old king is laid waste by a sea-monster, to whom

101

one young person after another is offered to be devoured, until the lot falls on the king's daughter: at that point the hero arrives, kills the dragon, marries the daughter, and succeeds to the kingdom. Again, as with comedy, we have a simple pattern with many complex elements. The ritual analogies of the myth suggest that the monster *is* the sterility of the land itself, and that the sterility of the land is present in the age and impotence of the king, who is sometimes suffering from an incurable malady or wound, like Amfortas in Wagner. His position is that of Adonis overcome by the boar of winter, Adonis's traditional thigh-wound being as close to castration symbolically as it is anatomically.

In the Bible we have a sea-monster usually named leviathan, who is described as the enemy of the Messiah, and whom the Messiah is destined to kill in the 'day of the Lord'. The leviathan is the source of social sterility, for it is identified with Egypt and Babylon, the oppressors of Israel, and is described in the Book of Job as 'king over all the children of pride'. It also seems closely associated with the natural sterility of the fallen world, with the blasted world of struggle and poverty and disease into which Job is hurled by Satan and Adam by the serpent in Eden. In the Book of Job God's revelation to Job consists largely of descriptions of the leviathan and a slightly less sinister land cousin named behemoth. These monsters thus apparently represent the fallen order of nature over which Satan has some control. (I am trying to make sense of the meaning of the Book of Job as we now have it, on the assumption that whoever was responsible for its present version had some reason for producing that version. Guesswork about what the poem may originally have been or meant is useless, as it is only the version we know that has had any influence on our literature.) In the Book of Revelation the leviathan, Satan, and the Edenic serpent are all identified. This identification is the basis for an elaborate dragon-killing metaphor in Christian symbolism in which the hero is Christ (often represented in art standing on a prostrate monster), the dragon Satan, the impotent old king Adam, whose son Christ becomes, and the rescued bride the Church.

Now if the leviathan is the whole fallen world of sin and death and tyranny into which Adam fell, it follows that Adam's children are born, live, and die inside his belly. Hence if the Messiah is to deliver us by killing the leviathan, he releases us. In the folk tale versions of dragon-killing stories we notice how frequently the previous victims of the dragon come out of him alive after he is killed. Again, if we are inside the dragon, and the hero comes to help us, the image is suggested of the hero going down the monster's open throat, like Jonah (whom Jesus accepted as a prototype of himself), and returning with his redeemed behind him. Hence the symbolism of the Harrowing of Hell, hell being regularly represented in iconography by the 'toothed gullet of an aged shark', to quote a modern reference to it. Secular versions of journeys inside monsters occur from Lucian to our day, and perhaps even the Trojan horse had originally some links with the same theme. The image of the dark winding labyrinth for the monster's belly is a natural one, and one that frequently appears in heroic quests, notably that of Theseus. A less displaced version of the story of Theseus would have shown him emerging from the labyrinth at the head of a procession of the Athenian youths and maidens previously sacrificed to the Minotaur. In many solar myths, too, the hero travels perilously through a dark labyrinthine underworld full of monsters between sunset and sunrise. This theme may become a structural principle of fiction on any level of sophistication. One would expect to find it in fairy tales or children's stories, and in fact if we 'stand back' from *Tom Sawyer* we can see a youth with no father or mother emerging with a maiden from a labyrinthine cave, leaving a bat-eating demon imprisoned behind him. But in the most complex and elusive of the later stories of Henry James, *The Sense of the Past*, the same theme is used, the labyrinthine underworld being in this case a period of past time from which the hero is released by the sacrifice of a heroine, an Ariadne figure. In this story, as in many folk tales, the motif of the two brothers connected by sympathetic magic of some sort is also employed.

In the Old Testament the Messiah-figure of Moses leads his people out of Egypt. The Pharaoh of Egypt is identified with the leviathan by Ezekiel, and the fact that the infant Moses was rescued by Pharaoh's daughter gives to the Pharaoh something of the role of the cruel father-figure who seeks the hero's death, a role also taken by the raging Herod of the miracle plays. Moses and the Israelites wander through a labyrinthine desert, after which the reign of the law ends and the conquest of the Promised Land is achieved by Joshua, whose name is the same as that of Jesus. Thus when the angel Gabriel tells the Virgin to call her son Jesus, the typological meaning is that the era of the law is over, and the assault on the Promised Land is about to begin. There are thus two concentric quest-myths in the Bible, a Genesis-apocalypse myth and an Exodus-millennium myth. In the former Adam is cast out of Eden, loses the river of life and the tree of life, and wanders in the labyrinth of human history until he is restored to his original state by the Messiah. In the latter Israel is cast out of his inheritance and wanders in the labyrinths of Egyptian and Babylonian captivity until he is restored to his original state in the Promised Land. Eden and the Promised Land, therefore, are typologically identical, as are the tyrannies of

Egypt and Babylon and the wilderness of the law. *Paradise Regained* deals with the temptation of Christ by Satan, which is, Michael tells us in *Paradise Lost*, the true form of the dragon-killing myth assigned to the Messiah. Christ is in the situation of Israel under the law, wandering in the wilderness: his victory is at once the conquest of the Promised Land typified by his namesake Joshua and the raising of Eden in the wilderness.

The leviathan is usually a sea-monster, which means metaphorically that he *is* the sea, and the prophecy that the Lord will hook and land the leviathan in Ezekiel is identical with the prophecy in Revelation that there shall be no more sea. As denizens of his belly, therefore, we are also metaphorically under water. Hence the importance of fishing in the Gospels, the apostles being 'fishers of men' who cast their nets into the sea of this world. Hence, too, the later development, referred to in *The Waste Land*, of Adam or the impotent king as an ineffectual 'fisher king'. In the same poem the appropriate link is also made with Prospero's rescuing of a society out of the sea in *The Tempest*. In other comedies, too, ranging from *Sakuntala* to *Rudens*, something indispensable to the action or the *cognitio* is fished out of the sea, and many quest-heroes, including Beowulf, achieve their greatest feats under water. The insistence on Christ's ability to command the sea belongs to the same aspect of symbolism. And as the leviathan, in his aspect as the fallen world, contains all forms of life imprisoned within himself, so as the sea he contains the imprisoned life-giving rainwaters whose coming marks the spring. The monstrous animal who swallows all the water in the world and is then teased or tricked or forced into disgorging it is a favorite of folk tales, and a Mesopotamian version lies close behind the story of Creation in Genesis. In many solar myths the sun-god is represented as sailing in a boat on the surface of our world.

Lastly, if the leviathan is death, and the hero has to enter the body of death, the hero has to die, and if his quest is completed the final stage of it is, cyclically, rebirth, and, dialectically, resurrection. In the St George plays the hero dies in his dragon-fight and is brought to life by a doctor, and the same symbolism runs through all the dying-god myths. There are thus not three but four distinguishable aspects to the quest-myth. First, the *agon* or conflict itself. Second, the *pathos* or death, often the mutual death of hero and monster. Third, the disappearance of the hero, a theme which often takes the form of *sparagmos* or tearing to pieces. Sometimes the hero's body is divided among his followers, as in Eucharist symbolism: sometimes it is distributed around the natural world, as in the stories of Orpheus and more especially Osiris. Fourth, the reappearance and recognition of the hero, where sacramental Christianity follows the metaphorical logic: those who in the fallen world have partaken of their redeemer's divided body are united with his risen body.

The four *mythoi* that we are dealing with, comedy, romance, tragedy, and irony, may now be seen as four aspects of a central unifying myth. *Agon* or conflict is the basis or archetypal theme of romance, the radical of romance being a sequence of marvellous adventures. *Pathos* or catastrophe, whether in triumph or in defeat, is the archetypal theme of tragedy. *Sparagmos,* or the sense that heroism and effective action are absent, disorganized or foredoomed to defeat, and that confusion and anarchy reign over the world, is the archetypal theme of irony and satire. *Anagnorisis,* or recognition of a newborn society rising in triumph around a still somewhat mysterious hero and his bride, is the archetypal theme of comedy.

We have spoken of the Messianic hero as a redeemer of society, but in the secular quest-romances more obvious motives and rewards for the quest are more common. Often the dragon guards a hoard: the quest for buried treasure has been a central theme of romance from the Siegfried cycle to *Nostromo,* and is unlikely to be exhausted yet. Treasure means wealth, which in mythopoeic romance often means wealth in its ideal forms, power and wisdom. The lower world, the world inside or behind the guarding dragon, is often inhabited by a prophetic sibyl, and is a place of oracles and secrets, such as Woden was willing to mutilate himself to obtain. Mutilation or physical handicap, which combines the themes of *sparagmos* and ritual death, is often the price of unusual wisdom or power, as it is in the figure of the crippled smith Weyland or Hephaistos, and in the story of the blessing of Jacob. The Arabian Nights are full of stories of what may be called the etiology of mutilation. Again, the reward of the quest usually is or includes a bride. This bride-figure is ambiguous: her psychological connection with the mother in an Oedipus fantasy is more insistent than in comedy. She is often to be found in a perilous, forbidden, or tabooed place, like Brunnhilde's wall of fire or the sleeping beauty's wall of thorns, and she is, of course, often rescued from the unwelcome embraces of another and generally older male, or from giants or bandits or other usurpers. The removal of some stigma from the heroine figures prominently in romance as in comedy, and ranges from the 'loathly lady' theme of Chaucer's *Wife of Bath's Tale* to the forgiven harlot of the Book of Hosea. The 'black but comely' bride of the Song of Songs belongs in the same complex.

The quest-romance has analogies to both rituals and dreams, and the rituals examined by Frazer and the dreams examined by Jung show the remarkable similarity in form that we should expect of two symbolic structures analogous to the same thing. Translated into dream terms, the quest-romance is the search of the libido or desiring self for a fulfilment that will deliver it from the anxieties of reality but will still contain that reality. The antagonists of the quest are often sinister figures, giants, ogres, witches and magicians, that clearly have a parental origin; and yet redeemed and emancipated paternal figures are involved too, as they are in the psychological quests of both Freud and Jung. Translated into ritual terms, the quest-romance is the victory of fertility over the waste land. Fertility means food and drink, bread and wine, body and blood, the union of male and female. The precious objects brought back from the quest, or seen or obtained as a result of it, sometimes combine the ritual and the psychological associations. The Holy Grail, for instance, is connected with Christian Eucharist symbolism; it is related to or descended from a miraculous food-provider like the cornucopia, and, like other cups and hollow vessels, it has female sexual affinities, its masculine counterpart being, we are told, the bleeding lance. The pairing of solid food and liquid refreshment recurs in the edible tree and the water of life in the biblical apocalypse.

We may take the first book of *The Faerie Queene* as representing perhaps the closest following of the biblical quest-romance theme in English literature: it is closer even than *The Pilgrim's Progress,* which resembles it because they both resemble the Bible. Attempts to compare Bunyan and Spenser without reference to the Bible, or to trace their similarities to a common origin in *secular* romance, are more or less perverse. In Spenser's account of the quest of St George, the patron saint of England, the protagonist represents the Christian Church in England, and hence his quest is an imitation of that of Christ. Spenser's Redcross Knight is led by the lady Una (who is veiled in black) to the kingdom of her parents, which is being laid waste by a dragon. The dragon is of somewhat unusual size, at least allegorically. We are told that Una's parents held 'all the world' in their control until the dragon 'Forwasted all their land, and them expelled'. Una's parents are Adam and Eve; their kingdom is Eden or the unfallen world, and the dragon, who is the entire fallen world, is identified with the leviathan, the serpent of Eden, Satan, and the beast of Revelation. Thus St George's mission, a repetition of that of Christ, is by killing the dragon to raise Eden in the wilderness and restore England to the status of Eden. The association of an ideal England with Eden, assisted by legends of a happy island in the western ocean and by the similarity of the Hesperides story to that of Eden, runs through English literature at least from the end of Greene's *Friar Bacon* to Blake's 'Jerusalem' hymn. St George's wanderings with Una, or without her, are parallel to the wandering of the Israelites in the wilderness, between Egypt and the Promised

Land, bearing the veiled ark of the covenant and yet ready to worship a golden calf.

The battle with the dragon lasts, of course, three days: at the end of each of the first two days St George is beaten back and is strengthened, first by the water of life, then by the tree of life. These represent the two sacraments which the reformed church accepted; they are the two features of the garden of Eden to be restored to man in the apocalypse, and they have also a more general Eucharist connection. St George's emblem is a red cross on a white ground, which is the flag borne by Christ in traditional iconography when he returns in triumph from the prostrate dragon of hell. The red and white symbolize the two aspects of the risen body, flesh and blood, bread and wine, and in Spenser they have a historical connection with the union of red and white roses in the reigning head of the church. The link between the sacramental and the sexual aspects of the red and white symbolism is indicated in alchemy, with which Spenser was clearly acquainted, in which a crucial phase of the production of the elixir of immortality is known as the union of the red king and the white queen.

The characterization of romance follows its general dialectic structure, which means that subtlety and complexity are not much favored. Characters tend to be either for or against the quest. If they assist it they are idealized as simply gallant or pure; if they obstruct it they are caricatured as simply villainous or cowardly. Hence every typical character in romance tends to have his moral opposite confronting him, like black and white pieces in a chess game. In romance the 'white' pieces who strive for the quest correspond to the *eiron* group in comedy, though the word is no longer appropriate, as irony has little place in romance. Romance has a counterpart to the benevolent retreating *eiron* of comedy in its figure of the 'old wise man', as Jung calls him, like Prospero, Merlin, or the palmer of Spenser's second quest, often a magician who affects the action he watches over. The Arthur of *The Faerie Queene*, though not an old man, has this function. He has a feminine counterpart in the sibylline wise mother-figure, often a potential bride like Solveig in *Peer Gynt*, who sits quietly at home waiting for the hero to finish his wanderings and come back to her. This latter figure is often the lady for whose sake or at whose bidding the quest is performed: she is represented by the Faerie Queene in Spenser and by Athene in the Perseus story. These are the king and queen of the white pieces, though their power of movement is of course reversed in actual chess. The disadvantage of making the queen-figure the hero's mistress, in anything more than a political sense, is that she spoils his fun with the distressed damsels he meets on his journey, who are often enticingly tied naked to rocks or trees, like Andromeda or Angelica in Ariosto. A polarization may thus be set up between the lady of duty and the lady of pleasure – we have already glanced [in an earlier section of *Anatomy of Criticism*] at a late development of this in the light and dark heroines of Victorian romance. One simple way out is to make the former the latter's mother-in-law: a theme of reconciliation after enmity and jealousy most commonly results, as in the relations of Psyche and Venus in Apuleius. Where there is no reconciliation, the older female remains sinister, the cruel stepmother of folk tale.

The evil magician and the witch, Spenser's Archimago and Duessa, are the black king and queen. The latter is appropriately called by Jung the 'terrible mother', and he associates her with the fear of incest and with such hags as Medusa who seem to have a suggestion of erotic perversion about them. The redeemed figures, apart from the bride, are generally too weak to be strongly characterized. The faithful companion or shadow figure of the hero has his opposite in the traitor, the heroine her opposite in the siren or beautiful witch, the dragon his opposite in the friendly or helping animals that are so conspicuous in romance, among which the horse who gets the hero to his quest has naturally a central place. The conflict of son and father that we noted in comedy recurs in romance: in the Bible the second Adam comes to the rescue of the first one, and in the Grail cycle the pure son Galahad accomplishes what his impure father Lancelot failed in.

The characters who elude the moral antithesis of heroism and villainy generally are or suggest spirits of nature. They represent partly the moral neutrality of the intermediate world of nature and partly a world of mystery which is glimpsed but never seen, and which retreats when approached. Among female characters of this type are the shy nymphs of classical legends and the elusive half-wild creatures who might be called daughter-figures, and include Spenser's Florimell, Hawthorne's Pearl, Wagner's Kundry, and Hudson's Rima. Their male counterparts have a little more variety. Kipling's Mowgli is the best known of the wild boys; a green man lurked in the forests of medieval England, appearing as Robin Hood and as the knight of Gawain's adventure; the 'salvage man', represented in Spenser by Satyrane, is a Renaissance favorite, and the awkward but faithful giant with unkempt hair has shambled amiably through romance for centuries.

Such characters are, more or less, children of nature, who can be brought to serve the hero, like Crusoe's Friday, but retain the inscrutability of their origin. As servants or friends of the hero, they impart the mysterious rapport with nature that so often marks the central figure of romance. The paradox that many of these children of nature are 'supernatural' beings is not as distressing in romance as in logic. The helpful fairy, the grateful dead man, the wonderful servant who has just the abilities the hero needs in a crisis, are all folk tale commonplaces. They are romantic intensifications of the comic tricky slave, the author's *architectus*. In James Thurber's *The Thirteen Clocks* this character type is called the 'Golux', and there is no reason why the word should not be adopted as a critical term.

In romance, as in comedy, there seem to be four poles of characterization. The struggle of the hero with his enemy corresponds to the comic contest of *eiron* and *alazon*. In the nature-spirits just referred to we find the parallel in romance to the buffoon or master of ceremonies in comedy: that is, their function is to intensify and provide a focus for the romantic mood. It remains to be seen if there is a character in romance corresponding to the *agroikos* type in comedy, the refuser of festivity or rustic clown.

Such a character would call attention to realistic aspects of life, like fear in the presence of danger, which threaten the unity of the romantic mood. St George and Una in Spenser are accompanied by a dwarf who carries a bag of 'needments'. He is not a traitor, like the other bag-carrier Judas Iscariot, but he is 'fearful', and urges retreat when the going is difficult. This dwarf with his needments represents, in the dream world of romance, the shrunken and wizened form of practical waking reality: the more realistic the story, the more important such a figure would become, until, when we reach the opposite pole in *Don Quixote*, he achieves his apotheosis as Sancho Panza. In other romances we find fools and jesters who are licensed to show fear or make realistic comments, and who provide a localized safety valve for realism without allowing it to disrupt the conventions of romance. In Malory a similar role is assumed by Sir Dinadan, who, it is carefully explained, is really a gallant knight as well as a jester: hence when he makes jokes 'the king and Launcelot laughed that they might not sit' – the suggestion of excessive and hysterical laughter being psychologically very much to the point.

Romance, like comedy, has six isolatable phases, and as it moves from the tragic to the comic area, the first three are parallel to the first three phases of tragedy and the second three to the second three phases of comedy, already examined from the comic point of view. The phases form a cyclical sequence in a romantic hero's life.

The first phase is the myth of the birth of the hero, the morphology of which has been studied in some detail in folklore. This myth is often associated with a flood, the regular symbol of the beginning and the end of a cycle. The infant hero is often placed in an ark or chest floating on the sea, as in the story of Perseus; from there he drifts to land, as in the exordium to *Beowulf*, or is rescued from among reeds and bulrushes on a river bank, as in the story of Moses. A landscape of water, boat, and reeds appears at the beginning of Dante's journey up the mount of Purgatory, where there are many suggestions that the soul is in that stage a newborn infant. On dry land the infant may be rescued either from or by an animal, and many heroes are nurtured by animals in a forest during their nonage. When Goethe's Faust begins to look for his Helena, he searches in the reeds of the Peneus, and then finds a centaur who carried her to safety on his back when she was a child.

Psychologically, this image is related to the embryo in the womb, the world of the unborn often being thought of as liquid; anthropologically, it is related to the image of seeds of new life buried in a dead world of snow or swamp. The dragon's treasure hoard is closely linked with this mysterious infant life enclosed in a chest. The fact that the real source of wealth is potential fertility or new life, vegetable or human, has run through romance from ancient myths to Ruskin's *King of the Golden River*, Ruskin's treatment of wealth in his economic works being essentially a commentary on this fairy tale. A similar association of treasure hoard and infant life appears in more plausible guise in *Silas Marner*. The long literary history of the theme of mysterious parentage from Euripides to Dickens has already been mentioned [elsewhere in *Anatomy of Criticism*].

In the Bible the end of a historical cycle and the birth of a new one is marked by parallel symbols. First we have a universal deluge and an ark, with the potency of all future life contained in it, floating on the waters; then we have the story of the Egyptian host drowned in the Red Sea and the Israelites set free to carry their ark through the wilderness, an image adopted by Dante as the basis of his purgatorial symbolism. The New Testament begins with an infant in a manger, and the tradition of depicting the world outside as sunk in snow relates the Nativity to the same archetypal phase. Images of returning spring soon follow: the rainbow in the Noah story, the bringing of water out of a rock by Moses, the baptism of Christ, all show the turning of the cycle from the wintry water of death to the reviving waters of life. The providential birds, the raven and dove in the Noah story, the ravens feeding Elijah in the wilderness, the dove hovering over Jesus, belong to the same complex.

Often, too, there is a search for the child, who has to be hidden away in a secret place. The hero being of mysterious origin, his true paternity is often concealed, and a false father appears who seeks the child's death. This is the role of Acrisius in the Perseus story, of the Cronos of Hesiodic myth who tries to swallow his children, of the child-killing Pharaoh in the Old Testament, and of Herod in the New.

In later fiction he often modulates to the usurping wicked uncle who appears several times in Shakespeare. The mother is thus often the victim of jealousy, persecuted or calumniated like the mother of Perseus or like Constance in the *Man of Law's Tale*. This version is very close psychologically to the theme of the rivalry of the son and a hateful father for possession of the mother. The theme of the calumniated girl ordered out of the house with her child by a cruel father, generally into the snow, still drew tears from audiences of Victorian melodramas, and literary developments of the theme of the hunted mother in the same period extend from Eliza crossing the ice in *Uncle Tom's Cabin* to *Adam Bede* and *Far from the Madding Crowd*. The false mother, the celebrated cruel stepmother, is also common: her victim is of course usually female, and the resulting conflict is portrayed in many ballads and folk tales of the Cinderella type. The true father is sometimes represented by a wise old man or teacher: this is the relation of Prospero to Ferdinand, as well as of Chiron the centaur to Achilles. The double of the true mother appears in the daughter of Pharaoh who adopts Moses. In more realistic modes the cruel parent speaks with the voice of, or takes the form of, a narrow-minded public opinion.

The second phase brings us to the innocent youth of the hero, a phase most familiar to us from the story of Adam and Eve in Eden before the Fall. In literature this phase presents a pastoral and Arcadian world, generally a pleasant wooded landscape, full of glades, shaded valleys, murmuring brooks, the moon, and other images closely linked with the female or maternal aspect of sexual imagery. Its heraldic colors are green and gold, traditionally the colors of vanishing youth: one thinks of Sandburg's poem *Between Two Worlds*. It is often a world of magic or desirable law, and it tends to center on a youthful hero, still overshadowed by parents, surrounded by youthful companions. The archetype of erotic innocence is less commonly marriage than the kind of 'chaste' love that precedes marriage; the love of brother for sister, or of two boys for each other. Hence, though in later phases it is often recalled as a lost happy time or Golden Age, the sense of being close to a moral taboo is very frequent, as it is of course in the Eden story itself. Johnson's *Rasselas*, Poe's *Eleanora*, and Blake's *Book of Thel* introduce us to a kind of prison-Paradise or unborn world from which the central characters long to escape to a lower world, and the same feeling of malaise and longing to enter a world of action recurs in the most exhaustive treatment of the phase in English literature, Keats's *Endymion*.

The theme of the sexual barrier in this phase takes many forms: the serpent of the Eden story recurs in *Green Mansions*, and a barrier of fire separates Amoret in Spenser from her lover Scudamour. At the end of the *Purgatorio* the soul reaches again its unfallen childhood or lost Golden Age, and Dante consequently finds himself in the garden of Eden, separated from the young girl Matelda by the river Lethe. The dividing river recurs in William Morris's curious story *The Sundering Flood*, where an arrow shot over it has to do for the symbol of sexual contact. In *Kubla Khan*, which is closely related both to the Eden story in *Paradise Lost* and to *Rasselas*, a 'sacred river' is closely followed by the distant vision of a singing damsel. Melville's *Pierre* opens with a sardonic parody of this phase, the hero still dominated by his mother but calling her his sister. A good deal of the imagery of this world may be found in the sixth book of *The Faerie Queene*, especially in the stories of Tristram and Pastorella.

The third phase is the normal quest theme that we have been discussing, and needs no further comment at this point. The fourth phase corresponds to the fourth phase of comedy, in which the happier society is more or less visible throughout the action instead of emerging only in the last few moments. In romance the central theme of this phase is that of the maintaining of the integrity of the innocent world against the assault of experience. It thus often takes the form of a moral allegory, such as we have in Milton's *Comus*, Bunyan's *Holy War*, and many morality plays, including *The Castell of Perseveraunce*. The much simpler scheme of the *Canterbury Tales*, where the only conflict is to preserve the mood of holiday and festivity against bickering, seems for some reason to be less frequent.

The integrated body to be defended may be individual or social, or both. The individual aspect of it is presented in the allegory of temperance in the second book of *The Faerie Queene*, which forms a natural sequel to the first book, dealing as it does with the more difficult theme of consolidating heroic innocence in this world after the first great quest has been completed. Guyon, the knight of temperance, has as his main antagonists Acrasia, the mistress of the Bower of Bliss, and Mammon. These represent 'Beauty and money', in their aspects as instrumental goods perverted into external goals. The temperate mind contains its good within itself, continence being its prerequisite, hence it belongs to what we have called the innocent world. The intemperate mind seeks its good in the external object of the world of experience. Both temperance and intemperance could be called natural, but one belongs to nature as an order and the other to nature as a fallen world. Comus's temptation of the Lady is based on a similar ambiguity in the meaning of nature. A central image in this phase of romance is that of the beleaguered castle, represented in Spenser by the House of Alma, which is described in terms of the economy of the human body.

The social aspect of the same phase is treated in the fifth book of *The Faerie Queene*, the legend of justice, where power is the prerequisite of justice, corresponding to continence in relation to temperance. Here we meet, in the vision of Isis and Osiris, the fourth-phase image of the monster tamed and controlled by the virgin, an image which appears episodically in Book One in connection with Una, who tames satyrs and a lion. The classical prototype of it is the Gorgon's head on the shield of Athene. The theme of invincible innocence or virginity is associated with similar images in literature from the child leading the beasts of prey in Isaiah to Marina in the brothel in *Pericles*, and it reappears in later fictions in which an unusually truculent hero is brought to heel by the heroine. An ironic parody of the same theme forms the basis of Aristophanes' *Lysistrata*.

The fifth phase corresponds to the fifth phase of comedy, and like it is a reflective, idyllic view of experience from above, in which the movement of the natural cycle has usually a prominent place. It deals with a world very similar to that of the second phase except that the mood is a contemplative withdrawal from or sequel to action rather than a youthful preparation for it. It is, like the second phase, an erotic world, but it presents experience as comprehended and not as a mystery. This is the world of most of Morris's romances, of Hawthorne's *Blithedale Romance*, of the mature, innocent wisdom of *The Franklin's Tale*, and of most of the imagery of the third book of *The Faerie Queene*. In this last, as well as in the late Shakespearean romances, notably *Pericles*, and even *The Tempest*, we notice a tendency to the moral stratification of characters. The true lovers are on top of a hierarchy of what might be called erotic imitations, going down through the various grades of lust and passion to perversion (Argante and Oliphant in Spenser; Antiochus and his daughter in *Pericles*). Such an arrangement of characters is consistent with the detached and contemplative view of society taken in this phase.

The sixth or *penseroso* phase is the last phase of romance as of comedy. In comedy it shows the comic society breaking up into small units or individuals; in romance it marks the end of a movement from active to contemplative adventure. A central image of this phase, a favorite of Yeats, is that of the old man in the tower, the lonely hermit absorbed in occult or magical studies. On a more popular and social level it takes in what might be called cuddle fiction: the romance that is physically associated with comfortable beds or chairs around fireplaces or warm and cosy spots generally. A characteristic feature of this phase is the tale in quotation marks, where we have an opening setting with a small group of congenial people, and then the real story told by one of the members. In *The Turn of the Screw* a large party is telling ghost stories in a country house; then some people leave, and a much smaller and more intimate circle gathers around the crucial tale. The opening dismissal of catechumens is thoroughly in the spirit and conventions of this phase. The effect of such devices is to present the story through a relaxed and contemplative haze as something that entertains us without, so to speak, confronting us, as direct tragedy confronts us.

Collections of tales based on a symposium device like the *Decameron* belong here. Morris's *Earthly Paradise* is a very pure example of the same phase: there a number of the great archetypal myths of Greek and Northern culture are personified as a group of old men who forsook the world during the Middle Ages, refusing to be made either kings or gods, and who now interchange their myths in an ineffectual land of dreams. Here the themes of the lonely old men, the intimate group, and the reported tale are linked. The calendar arrangement of the tales links it also with the symbolism of the natural cycle. Another and very concentrated treatment of the phase is Virginia Woolf's *Between the Acts*, where a play representing the history of English life is acted before a group. The history is conceived not only as a progression but as a cycle of which the audience is the end, and, as the last page indicates, the beginning as well.

From Wagner's *Ring* to science fiction, we may notice an increasing popularity of the flood archetype. This usually takes the form of some cosmic disaster destroying the whole fictional society except a small group, which begins life anew in some sheltered spot. The affinities of this theme to that of the cosy group which has managed to shut the rest of the world out are clear enough, and it brings us around again to the image of the mysterious newborn infant floating on the sea.

One important detail in poetic symbolism remains to be considered. This is the symbolic presentation of the point at which the undisplaced apocalyptic world and the cyclical world of nature come into alignment, and which we propose to call the point of epiphany. Its most common settings are the mountain-top, the island, the tower, the lighthouse, and the ladder or staircase. Folk tales and mythologies are full of stories of an original connection between heaven or the sun and earth. We have ladders of arrows, ropes pecked in two by mischievous birds, and the like: such stories are often analogues of the biblical stories of the Fall, and survive in Jack's beanstalk, Rapunzel's hair, and even the curious bit of floating folklore known as the Indian rope trick. The movement from one world to the other may be symbolized by the golden fire that descends from the sun, as in the mythical basis of the Danae story, and by its human response, the fire kindled on the sacrificial altar. The 'gold bug' in Poe's story, which reminds us that the Egyptian scarab was a solar emblem, is dropped from above on the end of a string through the eyehole of a skull on a tree and falls on top of a buried treasure: the archetype here is closely related to the complex of images we are dealing with, especially to some alchemical versions of it.

In the Bible we have Jacob's ladder, which in *Paradise Lost* is associated with Milton's cosmological diagram of a spherical cosmos hanging from heaven with a hole in the top. There are several mountain-top epiphanies in the Bible, the Transfiguration being the most notable, and the mountain vision of Pisgah, the end of the road through the wilderness from which Moses saw the distant Promised Land, is typologically linked. As long as poets accepted the Ptolemaic universe, the natural place for the point of epiphany was a mountain-top just under the moon, the lowest heavenly body. Purgatory in Dante is an enormous mountain with a path ascending spirally around it, on top of which, as the pilgrim gradually recovers his lost innocence and casts off his original sin, is the garden of Eden. It is at this point that the prodigious apocalyptic epiphany of the closing cantos of the *Purgatorio* is achieved. The sense of being between an apocalyptic world above and a cyclical world below is present too, as from the garden of Eden all seeds of vegetable life fall back into the world, while human life passes on.

In *The Faerie Queene* there is a Pisgah vision in the first book, when St George climbs the mountain of contemplation and sees the heavenly city from a distance. As the dragon he has to kill is the fallen world, there is a level of the allegory in which his dragon is the space between himself and the distant city. In the corresponding episode of Ariosto the link between the mountain-top and the sphere of the moon is clearer. But Spenser's fullest treatment of the theme is the brilliant metaphysical comedy known as the *Mutabilitie Cantoes*, where the conflict of being and becoming, Jove and Mutability, order and change, is resolved at the sphere of the moon. Mutability's evidence consists of the cyclical movements of nature, but this evidence is turned against her and proved to be a principle of order in nature instead of mere change. In this poem the relation of the heavenly bodies to the apocalyptic world is not metaphorical identification, as it is, at least as a poetic convention, in Dante's *Paradiso*, but likeness: they are still within nature, and only in the final stanza of the poem does the real apocalyptic world appear.

The distinction of levels here implies that there may be analogous forms of the point of epiphany. For instance, it may be presented in erotic terms as a place of sexual fulfilment, where there is no apocalyptic vision but simply a sense of arriving at the summit of experience in nature. This natural form of the point of epiphany is called in Spenser the Gardens of Adonis. It recurs under that name in Keats's *Endymion* and is the world entered by the lovers at the end of Shelley's *Revolt of Islam*. The Gardens of Adonis, like Eden in Dante, are a place of seed, into which everything subject to the cyclical order of nature enters at death and proceeds from at birth. Milton's early poems are, like the *Mutabilitie Cantoes*, full of the sense of a distinction between nature as a divinely sanctioned order, the nature of the music of the spheres, and nature as a fallen and largely chaotic world. The former is symbolized by the Gardens of Adonis in *Comus*, from whence the attendant spirit descends to watch over the Lady. The central image of this archetype, Venus watching over Adonis, is (to use a modern distinction) the analogue in terms of Eros to the Madonna and Son in the context of Agape.

Milton picks up the theme of the Pisgah vision in *Paradise Regained*, which assumes an elementary principle of biblical typology in which the events of Christ's life repeat those of the history of Israel. Israel goes to Egypt, brought down by Joseph, escapes a slaughter of innocents, is cut off from Egypt by the Red Sea, organizes into twelve tribes, wanders 40 years in the wilderness, receives the law from Sinai, is saved by a brazen serpent on a pole, crosses the Jordan, and enters the Promised Land under 'Joshua, whom the Gentiles Jesus call'. Jesus goes to Egypt in infancy, led by Joseph, escapes a slaughter of innocents, is baptized and recognized as the Messiah, wanders 40 days in the wilderness, gathers twelve followers, preaches the Sermon on the Mount, saves mankind by dying on a pole, and thereby conquers the Promised Land as the real Joshua. In Milton the temptation corresponds to the Pisgah vision of Moses, except that the gaze is turned in the opposite direction. It marks the climax of Jesus' obedience to the law, just before his active redemption of the world begins, and the sequence of temptations consolidates the world, flesh, and devil into the single form of Satan. The point of epiphany is here represented by the pinnacle of the temple, from which Satan falls away as Jesus remains motionless on top of it. The fall of Satan reminds us that the point of epiphany is also the top of the wheel of fortune, the point from which the tragic hero falls. This ironic use of the point of epiphany occurs in the Bible in the story of the Tower of Babel.

The Ptolemaic cosmos eventually disappeared, but the point of epiphany did not, though in more recent literature it is often ironically reversed, or brought to terms with greater demands for credibility. Allowing for this, one may still see the same archetype in the final mountain-top scene of Ibsen's *When We Dead Awaken* and in the central image of Virginia Woolf's *To the Lighthouse*. In the later poetry of Yeats and Eliot it becomes a central unifying image. Such titles as

The Tower and *The Winding Stair* indicate its importance for Yeats, and the lunar symbolism and the apocalyptic imagery of *The Tower* and *Sailing to Byzantium* are both thoroughly consistent. In Eliot it is the flame reached in the fire sermon of *The Waste Land*, in contrast to the natural cycle which is symbolized by water, and it is also the 'multifoliate rose' of *The Hollow Men. Ash Wednesday* brings us back again to the purgatorial winding stair, and *Little Gidding* to the burning rose, where there is a descending movement of fire symbolized by the Pentecostal tongues of flame and an ascending one symbolized by Hercules' pyre and 'shirt of flame'.

7 Royal Genres*

IRENEUSZ OPACKI

In this previously untranslated essay, the Polish Formalist scholar Ireneusz Opacki (pronounced Opatski) returns to the vexed question of the historical evolution of genres, and focuses on an issue that had remained obscure in earlier accounts of the evolutionary process, namely the phenomenon of 'hybridisation'. By this, Opacki means not just the particular type of genre-mixing for which Alastair Fowler reserves the term, but the many different kinds of cross-fertilisation which occur when, in the course of their historical development, other genres enter into the sphere of influence of what Opacki calls a 'royal genre' (a 'dominant' genre, in Russian Formalist terms). So powerful is the force field exerted by a royal genre, argues Opacki, and so great is its transformative influence, that hybridisation should be regarded not as a side-effect of the evolutionary process, but as a major cause of it. Similarly, the proliferation of 'genre variants', or 'hybrids', is often the clearest indication we have of a shift in the hierarchy of genres, or the establishment of a new literary trend. This raises further questions, some of which are explored in detail in earlier parts of the essay (not included here): for instance, at what point in its evolutionary development does, say, Greek tragedy cease to be Greek tragedy? When does a hybrid become a genre in its own right? What factors (internal or external) determine the *speed* of evolution of a particular genre, and why are certain genres apparently more stable than others? The purpose of the essay is not to provide definitive answers to these questions but to bring new clarity and precision to the discussion of literary evolution, while also adding significantly to our understanding of the mechanisms involved. As such,

* Translated from *Problemy teorii literatury*, 2nd edn, ed. Henryk Markiewicz (Wrocław: Ossolineum, 1987), vol. 1, pp. 161–7. First published as 'Krzyżowanie się postaci gatunkowych jako wyznacznik ewolucji poezji' (The hybridisation of genre forms as a determinant of the evolution of poetry) in *Pamiętnik Literacki*, 54:4 (1963). Translated by David Malcolm.

it represents an important contribution to the dynamic or 'morphological' theory of genre.

Although its nominal point of departure is Wellek and Warren's *Theory of Literature* (1949), Opacki's essay is clearly an extension of Russian Formalist work on the evolution of genres: compare Tynyanov (Chapter 2). On Polish Formalism, see Zbigniew Folejewski, '"Formalism" in Polish Literary Scholarship', *Slavic Review*, 32 (1972), 574–82; and Wiktor Weintraub, 'A Political Gloss to the History of the Polish Formalist Movement', in *Russian Formalism: A Retrospective Glance. A Festschrift in Honor of Victor Erlich*, ed. Robert Louis Jackson and Stephen Rudy (New Haven: Yale Center for International and Area Studies, 1985), pp. 6–14. For the larger context, see Wellek, *History of Modern Criticism*, Vol. 7: *German, Russian and Eastern European Criticism, 1900–1950* (1991). For further Polish work on the theory of genre, see the journal *Zagadnienia Rodzajów Literackich* (Problems of Literary Genre), founded in 1958, which publishes articles in English, French and German.

Every literary trend – or a phase of it – has underlying it certain defined socio-historical factors, which shape a specific attitude towards the world and a certain sphere of interests and problems. In turn, this brings with it the creation of a specific system of poetics, an ensemble of means of expression, of ways of structurally linking them, which – growing out of the 'extraliterary' environment of the trend – carry in them historically specific meanings and functions. Kazimierz Wyka put it concisely thus: 'A set of new socio-political conditions brings about the rise of a literary trend, not directly however, but translated into the internal tasks and problems of literature itself, and indeed the trend only arises when that translation actually takes place.'[1]

The language into which that translation is made is the language of literary genres: here is the basis of their evolution. This translation appears, in the most general terms, in three forms. The first is the creation of completely new elements of the language of poetry, in keeping with a completely new set of problems introduced by a given stage of history. Thus there arise new motifs, vocabulary, compositional devices. The second form is a semantic modification of the elements of poetics up to that time, as with a 'change in the meaning of an expression' in the evolution of language. In the history of the genre at this point two externally similar forms may appear – at different stages of its development; however they will be different forms, endowed with different meanings – like a pair of homonyms. And then it is impossible to combine them in a whole, in one variant or model of the genre; this is why the temporal boundaries of a specific genre model are so important. The third variety of evolution is the introduction within the field of one generic trend of elements belonging to specific, historically defined models of other genres. This is the issue which was demonstrated by the analyses of concrete works carried out earlier [in a section of the essay not printed here]. This seems to be a central issue, opening the broadest perspectives for studying the evolution of poetry. And it is now time to put forward a few hypotheses on the basis of the concrete literary phenomena analyzed earlier.

A further truism is valid here: every literary current introduces for its own use a certain hierarchy of literary genres – there are genres which are dominant in it, and 'secondary' genres which are less representative of it. This is an important phenomenon in literary history, a phenomenon which the study of genre history is beginning to look at. It is this phenomenon which explains why the greatest achievements of Polish drama occur during the second phase of Romanticism, and why the social novel has its most splendid achievements in the last decades of the nineteenth century. Quite simply those genres stood at the peak of the contemporary hierarchy of literary genres; they best rendered the aspirations of the period; they were the most appropriate 'language of translation' for socio-political phenomena into 'the internal tasks and problems of literature'. In eighteenth-century Classicism the 'crown' of literary genres was the ode, the satire and the fable. In the period of Sentimentalism it was the pastoral. In early Romanticism it was the poetic novel, and in its second phase it was the drama. In the period of *Młoda Polska* it was the lyric and the lyric fairy tale/legend (*baśń*). These are only examples of a few literary currents, examples which are necessary for our comments on the texts we have analyzed.

When we analyzed Zmorski's *Dziwa*, we discovered two logically sketched-out genre conventions, each of which shaped a different 'layer' of the text. We established that Zmorski's poem differs from earlier Romantic ballads (such as Mickiewicz's *Lilia*) in the limitation of the freedom of the epic narrator in favour of dramatic construction. In the context of the poetry of the period, this is in keeping with changes in the 'hierarchy of genres' which appear between the first and the second phases of Polish Romanticism. In the first phase the royal genre is the poetic novel. In the second phase it is the drama.[2] The difference between Zmorski's ballad and earlier ballads is not without cause, it seems, but is in keeping with these very changes in the hierarchy of genres.

When we analyzed Staff's *Królestwo*, we discovered three genological layers: the form of the Romantic (lyric) pastoral and the current of the fairy tale/legend. Let us cite here Kazimierz Wyka's formulation of the 'hierarchy of genres' in *Młoda Polska* and its consequences:

'This development [of the literature of *Młoda Polska*] can be presented in terms of a moving column of soldiers. First the head, that is poetry, moved, then after a certain time, prose, and then in turn drama. And when poetry, along with all the issues connected with it, has covered a considerable part of the road, this means that the units following behind are compelled to follow the distinctive route which it has marked out.'[3]

In practice, this means that poetry – and with *Młoda Polska* this means above all lyric poetry – as the royal genre, affected the form of the other literary genres. Indeed, when we consider the considerable degree of lyricisation of the novel of *Młoda Polska* – very clearly different from the positivist and naturalist novel – Wyka's comparison seems most convincing.

Staff's *Królestwo* also illustrates it well. As we have shown [in an earlier section of the essay], it follows the example of the old-Russian pastoral because it fits well with the common *Młoda Polska* slogan of 'the flight from the city' into the bosom of nature, the illustration of which is Kasprowicz's *Księga ubogich*. So in this context, the reason for the appearance of the level of the eighteenth-century pastoral is quite clear, as the pastoral could serve similar ideas as an adequate 'language of translation'. At the same time, however, the basic language of *Młoda Polska* was – as the contemporary hierarchy of genres indicates – the language of the lyric. Hence the construction in 'images' which overlays the adoption of the Romantic pastoral. And finally, in the *Młoda Polska* period the fairy tale/legend is very prominent and is in keeping with the expression of a strictly internal experience. And this element appears in Staff's poem.

Finally, Karpiński's text. Here there are two genological layers: the pastoral and the fable. Each of these genres was the 'jewel in the crown' of a different, but contemporary, literary trend: Classicism and Sentimentalism. So this is a phenomenon which is similar to the two previous ones: the classical fable, in its adaptation to suit Sentimental tastes, was given over to the operations of the main convention of this current, the convention which constituted the expression of the 'language of translation', the convention of the pastoral.

Thus the following hypothesis presents itself: *a literary genre, entering, in the course of evolution, the field of a particular literary trend, will enter into a very close 'blood relationship' with the form of the royal genre that is particular to that current.*

In this sense, the hybridisation of genre forms is a determinant of the evolution of poetry.[4]

But we must still answer – also in the form of hypotheses – some questions which emerge against the background of the conjectures we have just sketched out.

Does a literary genre which enters into these close 'blood relations' with the form of another genre, typical of a given literary trend, not become thereby another literary genre? If our concept of genre is based on the invariability of the features of its structure, the answer would have to be yes. But in our formulation, the answer is no. For the 'royal' genre of a given literary trend is, as it were, the 'sum' of its poetics, the most complete compendium of the current 'language of translation'. In this sense, it is representative for the general poetics of that trend. Let us once more quote Wyka's words here: 'the unity of a literary trend is determined by a relative unity, a predominant similarity of a common poetics. In the case of *Młoda Polska*, this relative unity was imposed by means of expression worked out and propounded via poetry.'[5]

In other words – as we see from Wyka's further arguments – via the lyric. This is a repetition of the thesis sketched out above. But it is worth looking at another aspect of it here: thanks to this the royal genre draws towards itself all the remaining literary genres of a given period. But this does not lead to the fusion of all literature into one genre. The distinguishing features of the various genres survive. They come from other areas of the work, from other levels of the structure which do not undergo transformation into new ones, in this way maintaining the evolutionary sequence and making it possible to divide works among different genres in a given period. If we formulate the model (form) of a given genre in a series of letters, which symbolise the components of its structure: $a\ b\ c\ d\ e\ f$; and if the royal genre of the subsequent literary trend has, by common consent, the form: $k\ l\ m\ n\ o\ p$, among which $m\ n\ o$ are the main constitutive features of the genre; then the earlier literary genre, entering into the literary trend, will take on these important new features, at the same time keeping part of the former ones: $b\ c\ d\ m\ n\ o\ f$. A new form of the genre arises which lasts while the given literary current does. The features $m\ n\ o$ draw to themselves all the genres on this stage of evolution; the remaining features make for differences among the genres.

A second question presents itself: are those 'differentiating' features not constant features of the genre in question? And here we have to answer no in principle. In principle, because tradition distinguishes ossified genre forms such as the sonnet or the fable which do indeed have their constant features (although this does not prevent them entering into relations with other genres).[6] But the overwhelming majority of genres do not have such features. The evolutionary path set out here is not the only path, but even it can lead to a complete transformation of the genre. Quite simply, every literary trend brings forward and emphasises a different genre (or different genres), in which different elements play a constitutive role. Sometimes, it will be a question of 'generic' shape – then different genres will in this regard modify their previous form, as, for example, Zmorski's ballad. On another occasion, it will be the type of 'created world' – then the changes will take place in this segment of the structure, as, for example, in Sentimentalism's adaptation of the fable. In time, this path, after running through different literary trends, may lead to a complete transformation of a given genre. The evolutionary sequence, however, will be maintained. It can be grasped (by observing the rules about analysing a trend in chronological terms) thanks to the slow speed of transformation in transitional periods, in periods of the 'friction' of antagonistic currents, which ensures the unity of the genre trend, and makes it easy to distinguish it among other trends.

The third question is as follows: if a genre, passing from one literary current to another, enters into a close 'blood relation' with another genre, then in concrete instances (with regard to concrete texts) one must speak of a multi-generic construction. If this is so, is taxonomy possible – for the text then belongs to at least two genres? This is a very troublesome question which requires further studies to obtain an answer. It seems, however, that the direction the answer might take can be sketched out fairly clearly. Where the concept of genre is based on fixed constants, the necessity of 'simultaneously counting' a work among different genological groups certainly does not exist. However, with a dynamic formulation of genre the direction of a solution to the problem should look something like the following:

Genres do not have unchanging, fixed constitutive features. First of all, because of the 'transformation' which occurs in the course of evolution. Second – and this is more important in this case – because of the shifts in importance of distinguishing individual features of structure, depending on the literary context of the epoch or literary trend. In the course of evolution, not only does one genre change, but they all do, constituting as they do a context for that genre. And at the point of transition from one literary trend to another, there takes place a revaluation of the hierarchy of genres: a previously secondary genre, because it possesses features which are especially serviceable to the new trend, rises to the top. Its promotion was determined by its distinctive features in the earlier phase of development. Now, once it becomes a royal genre, it imparts these distinctive features, which brought about its promotion, to other genres. They become features characteristic of the entire literary trend, thereby ceasing to be something distinctive for that genre, becoming non-distinguishing features. They become rather features which make it similar to other

genres.[7] In connection with this, other features of this genre achieve
the status of distinctive features, and the former ones lose their generic
particularity. And indeed, as such, now no longer genre markers,
they become part of other literary genres. If we view the problem in
this light, the phenomenon of the mixing of genres does not arise,
and thus one cannot speak of the multi-generic nature of a concrete
literary work. One can, however, speak of its genological multiplicity
of form, in the sense that one can detect the presence, in the work, of
several earlier consolidated genre forms which, at a given stage of
development, lost their clear generic identification, an identification
which was strictly limited by the borders of the literary trend in
which that form established itself, or 'took shape', as Mickiewicz puts
it. In this sense, a work is heterogeneous in form, but generically
homogeneous, because generic homogeneity is measured by the
current stage of literary development and the development of the
genre itself.

Raising the matter of the multiplicity of forms in concrete literary
works does not undermine, it seems, the matter of the unity of a
genre. On the contrary, it allows one to examine issues from the
evolution of poetry on the basis of genre studies. It shows the
concrete text against the background of the poetic tradition, and
demonstrates how the hybridisation, the interweaving of past genre
forms, determines poetic development, leading to new forms of
poetry, often based on the close fusion of differing traditional forms.
Here, it seems, is the essence of the special usefulness of this way of
looking at literature. We are drawing near what Wellek and Warren
call the 'inner life of literature'.[8] Grasping the literary work in its
multiplicity of form allows us, on one hand, to discover its individual
face, which depends on the nature of the genological forms used in
it and the way in which they are combined into a structural unity.
On the other hand, however, 'it also brings this advantage, that by
necessarily making reference to and assembling data on a wide range
of other works [forms], it makes us realise the field of a work's
literary tradition and points to that work's place within that tradition.
Thus it helps to fix its role in the development of literary culture,
which gives it its special quality as a literary phenomenon and
defines its historical-cultural importance.'[9] Let us add a third
benefit to all this: when we observe the hybridisation of genre
forms in concrete literary organisms, this understanding of genre
and literature permits a synthetic grasp of the principles of the
evolution of a genre; however, following on immediately from
this – if we connect our studies closely with the history of literary
trends – it allows us to establish some important principles of the
evolution of poetry as a whole.

Notes

1. K. WYKA, *Młoda Polska* (1961), part 1, pp. 1–2. (All quotations are taken from a manuscript copy of this work.)

2. For this phase of Romanticism, the second 'royal genre' is the *gaweda* (yarn). This also influences the evolution of the ballad, the main (and most numerous) variant of which adopts many elements of the *gawęda*. See I. OPACKI, *Ewolucje balladowej opowieści. Zagadnienie narratora i narracji w balladzie lat 1822–1920* (Evolution of the balladic tale: the issue of the narrator and narration in the ballad, 1822–1920) (Lublin, 1961), pp. 46–61.

3. WYKA, *Młoda Polska*, part 1, p. 26.

4. Of course, this does not mean that it is only in this way that the hybridisation of 'genre forms' takes place. Another type of hybridisation, which is the result of other tendencies, is the type of hybridisation seen in conscious stylisation. This is connected with the introduction – into the heart of one genre – of stylistic elements of a second genre. This issue remains within the sphere of the 'determinants of evolution' (conscious stylisation can only take place after a 'model of stylisation' has become fixed), but of course on a different basis. I can do no more than allude to this issue here.

5. WYKA, *Młoda Polska*, part 1, p. 34.

6. Here we can see a way towards a taxonomy of genres in terms of their 'evolutionary receptivity'. There are more and less elastic genres, and this issue offers a rich range of possibilities for research into the principles of the evolution of poetry. It points, indeed, to the variety of paths which evolution can take. See n. 7 below for further discussion of this matter.

7. There is space here only to sketch out the issue which raises, it appears, the most important qualification to the above. At several points in this essay I have declared that fixed and invariable features are not part of literary genres, although in many cases this is clearly not true. There are groups of fixed features on the basis of which one can construct a definition of, for example, the pastoral, the fable, the comedy, the fairy tale 'in general', a definition which will hold good for every stage of the historical development of these genres. This will often be the case (although not always – there are genres which are more or less 'flexible', e.g. the ballad – see n. 6 above) – but only when the genres in question are observed in isolation from the context of the whole of literature. Once we place these in their context, however, the construction of such definitions raises some problems. The pastoral 'in itself' has certain fixed features (type of poetic world, for example), but it imparts these features to other literary genres, thus losing in the context of these genres its 'pastoral distinctiveness' – in the sense of a distinctiveness which allows one to gather all these works together into one genre group. Thus, this fixed feature, as a result of its moving into the territory of other genres, stops being useful for constructing a concept of the pastoral, for although it is invariably part of the pastoral, it is not only a part of the pastoral alone. And it is this aspect of the matter which prompts one to formulate the hypothesis that fixed features are no part of literary genres; either there are no such features, or, if there are, they do not always keep the fixity of genre distinctiveness.
    This question touches upon the issue of how appropriate it is to create the concept of a specific genre, an issue which goes beyond the scope and possibilities of this essay, focusing as it does principally on the practical possibilities for research suggested by the particular understanding of genre phenomena set out above. But this issue demands reflection and rethinking

with regard to creating concepts for use in literary studies. When we formulate a concept, we consider above all the nature of the phenomenon as 'the thing in itself', leaving aside the aspect of its existence within the context of a specific reality. When constructing concepts of genre in literary studies, this aspect of its existence should be considered; the genre's nature should be defined from the point of view of the context in which it exists. This is why it is sometimes necessary to create two differing genre definitions for identical phenomena which exist, however, in two different contexts. An extreme example should illustrate this: a certain variant of the ballad possesses both in early Romanticism and in Positivism the element of 'miraculousness' and 'strangeness'. Within the context of early Romantic literature this feature is not a generically distinctive feature for the ballad, for it also appears in other literary genres. On the other hand, in the Positivist period, this may be a specifically balladic feature, for this is no part of other literary genres at this time, and in this context it becomes a determinant of a text's balladic status. This issue deserves further discussion, since it has a bearing on the appropriateness of the creation of genre concepts within literary studies, and on the question of the relativisation of definitions in relation to the context of the reality within which a defined phenomenon exists.

8. René Wellek and Austin Warren, *Theory of Literature*, 3rd edn (Harmondsworth: Penguin Books, 1968).

9. S. Skwarczyńska, 'Struktura rodzajowa "Genesis z Ducha" Słowackiego', in *Juliusz Słowacki. W stopięcdziesięcolecie urodziń. Materiały i szkice* (Warsaw, 1959), p. 279.

8 Theory of Genres and Medieval Literature*

Hans Robert Jauss

Despite obvious methodological differences, the three following essays, all of which date from the early 1970s, have in common the aim of enlarging our understanding of how literary genres and genre theory have functioned historically – an issue often marginalised in the structuralist approaches to genre then in vogue. For the German literary historian and theorist Hans Robert Jauss, one of the founders of the Konstanz school of 'reception aesthetics', this task is basically twofold: first, to rediscover, by means of empirical scholarship, the genre concepts and classification systems that have shaped the writing and reading of literature in the past; and secondly, to construct a theoretical model that satisfactorily explains the way such mechanisms operate. Medieval literature poses a particular challenge since its generic categories in no way correspond to those of modern genre-systems, and even basic facts about medieval literary theory remain obscure. In part, Jauss's essay is an attempt to recover this information, explain the medieval conception of literary genre, and assemble an historically accurate typology of medieval genres. This detailed case study in historical poetics, though, is framed within a more general theoretical discussion which involves the appraisal of a series of modern theories of genre, ranging from Croce's anti-generic hypothesis to the work of the Russian Formalists and Czech Structuralists. In these last two, especially, Jauss finds much to commend, and to incorporate into his own theoretical model – for instance, ideas on generic hierarchies, the 'dominant', and literary evolution (Tynyanov is his major source; cf. Chapter 2). But what he finds missing from all previous theories of genre is an adequate modelling of 'the function,

---

* Reprinted from Hans Robert Jauss, *Toward an Aesthetic of Reception*, trans. Timothy Bahti, with an introduction by Paul de Man (Minneapolis: University of Minnesota Press, 1982), pp. 76–80, 94–7, 99–109. First published in French in *Poétique* (1970), 79–101; reprinted in German in *Grundriss der Romanischen Literaturen des Mittelalters*, vol. 6 (Heidelberg: Karl Winter Üniversitäts Verlag, 1972).

reception, and influence of literary works and genres in their historical reality and social environment' (p. 143), a deficiency he seeks to remedy with his own brand of *Rezeptionsästhetik*, grounded in the versatile concept of the 'horizon of expectation'.

Though enormously influential in West Germany since the 1970s, and more recently in other parts of the world, Jauss's work has attracted fierce criticism from Marxist scholars like Robert Weimann for ignoring questions of literary production in favour of those of consumption or 'reception': the arguments are reviewed in Robert C. Holub, *Reception Theory: A Critical Introduction* (London: Methuen, 1984), pp. 121–34; and in Paul de Man's introductory essay to *Toward an Aesthetic of Reception* (1982). The latter volume also contains Jauss's key methodological statement 'Literary History as a Challenge to Literary Theory'. For other discussions of medieval genre theory, see W.H.H. Atkins, *English Literary Criticism: The Medieval Phase* (Cambridge: Cambridge University Press, 1943); Johannes A. Huisman, 'Generative Classifications in Medieval Literature', in *Theories of Literary Genre*, ed. Strelka (1978); Minnis, *Medieval Theory of Authorship* (1988); and Butterfield, 'Medieval Genres and Modern Genre Theory' (1990).

The development of a theory not infrequently has an unrecognized or essentially unreflected dependency on the kind and the limitations of the object through which the theory is to be exemplified or to which it is to be applied. This is especially the case with the theory of literary genres. On the one hand, traditional philologists developed it with preference for examples from the classical literary periods – that offered the advantage that the form of a genre could be determined according to canonized rules, and its history followed from work to work according to the intentions and accomplishments of their authors. Structuralist studies opposed this individualizing consideration with a theory that was primarily developed from primitive genres such as, for example, the narrative of myths or the 'conte populaire'; from such examples without an individualized artistic character, the theory could demonstrate those simplest structures, functions, and sequences that constitute and differentiate various genres on the basis of a narrative logic.

In contrast to this polarization, it seemed worthwhile to develop a theory of literary genres within a field of inquiry that lies between the opposites of singularity and collectivity, of the artistic character of literature and its merely purposive or social character. Medieval vernacular literatures are especially appropriate for such an attempt. For in this area philological studies have barely gotten beyond individual monographs, themselves often only overviews. These genres are a long way from being sufficiently delimited, let alone historically represented in their historical contemporaneity and sequence. The generic divisions of the handbooks rest on a convention of the discipline that is scarcely called into question any longer, according to which one promiscuously uses original characterizations, classical genre concepts, and later classifications. In international discussion, Romance literary studies have for a long time failed to advance any contribution to a historical systematics or to the general development of a theory of literary genres.[1] This failure has its material reasons, but also its scholarly-historical ones.

A history and theory of vernacular genres in the Middle Ages bumps up against the particular problem that the structural characteristics of the literary forms – from which the history and theory would begin – themselves first have to be worked out from texts that are, chronologically, highly diffuse. Here we have newly developing literatures that are not immediately dependent on the preceding Latin literature, as concerns either a humanist principle of strict imitation or the canon of a binding poetics. In the Romance vernacular, there was at first scarcely any poetological reflection on genres. 'The Vulgate languages and their long-developed typologies only come into the view of the theorists after 1300 with Dante, Antonio da Tempo, and Eustache Deschamps.'[2] But medieval theorists judged poetry primarily according to styles, and not according to generic norms.

On the other hand, the modern system of the three basic kinds or 'natural forms of literature' (*Dichtung*) would want to do more than exclude the majority of medieval genres as impure or pseudo-poetic forms.[3] For even the vernacular epic or lyric is difficult to describe within the distinction provided by the modern triad of epic, lyric, and dramatic – and the passion play simply cannot be so described. Basic distinctions such as purposive or purposeless, didactic or fictional, imitative or creative, traditional or individual – which have governed literary understanding since the emancipation of the 'fine arts' – were not yet perceived and reflected on; thus it makes no sense to work with a triadic division of literature owed to this emancipatory process, and to heap together with the didactic the remainder of a problematic fourth 'literary kind' (*Dichtart*) – in the Middle Ages, surely the larger part – that doesn't fit into the triadic schema.

In view of such difficulties, a heightened significance was given to the critique that began shortly after 1900 against the pseudo-normative concept of genre in positivistic literary history (understood as 'evolutionary' by Brunetière). Croce's aesthetics, which in view of the expressive uniqueness of each work of art still recognized only art itself (or intuition) as a 'genre', seemed to free the philologies from the genre problem altogether – a problem that Croce dissolved into the simple question of the utility of various classifications for books. But of course the cutting of a Gordian knot does not lead to any enduring solution to a scholarly problem. Croce's 'solution' would certainly not have been accorded any such tenacious success with enthusiasts and opponents if the reaction against the normative genre concept had not been led by the rise of modern stylistics,[4] which similarly declared the 'verbal work of art' to be autonomous, and developed methods of ahistorical interpretation for which an initial observation of historical genre-forms appeared superfluous.

With the turn away from the aestheticism of the 'work-immanent' method, which produced a record harvest of scholarly monographs but left unanswered the question of the diachronic and synchronic coherence of literary works, began the process of a new, historico-hermeneutic and structuralist development of theory – within which we still stand today. The theory of literary genres is at the point of seeking a path between the Scylla of nominalist skepticism that allows for only aposteriori classifications, and the Charybdis of regression into timeless typologies, a path along which the historicization of genre poetics and of the concept of form are upheld.[5] To initiate a justification of this path with a critique of Croce recommends itself not merely on the grounds of an intradisciplinary discussion. For Croce pushed to an extreme the critique of the universal validity of the canon of genres, a critique that had been growing since the eighteenth century, so that the necessity of founding a historical systematics of literary genres once again becomes apparent.

* * *

'Every true work of art has violated an established genre, and in this way confounded the ideas of critics who thus found themselves compelled to broaden the genre.'[6] What Croce provides here as an annihilating attack upon the normative genre concept once again presupposes (however unconsciously) that precise state of affairs in which the historical reality, the function (understood within the aesthetics of production), and the hermeneutic achievement of the genre concept would be demonstrable. For how else can one answer in a controllable manner the single question considered legitimate by Croce – whether a work of art is a perfectly achieved expression, or only half so, or even not at all[7] – if not through an aesthetic judgment that knows to distinguish within the work of art the unique expression from the expected and generic?

Even a perfect work of art (as the unity of intuition and expression, to use Croce's terms) could be absolute (isolated from everything *expected*) only at the expense of its comprehensibility. Croce considered art a matter of pure individual expression, thereby employing a form of the aesthetics of experience and of genius[8] that is linked to a specific period but was illegitimately generalized by him. But even considered as such, the literary work is conditioned by 'alterity', that is, in relation to another, an understanding consciousness. Even where a verbal creation negates or surpasses all expectations, it still presupposes preliminary information and a trajectory of expectations (*Erwartungsrichtung*) against which to register the originality and novelty. This horizon of the expectable is constituted for the reader from out of a tradition or series of previously known works, and from a specific attitude, mediated by one (or more) genre and dissolved through new works. Just as there is no act of verbal communication that is not related to a general, socially or situationally conditioned norm or convention,[9] it is also unimaginable that a literary work set itself into an informational vacuum, without indicating a specific situation of understanding. To this extent, every work belongs to a genre – whereby I mean neither more nor less than that for each work a preconstituted horizon of expectations must be ready at hand (this can also be understood as a relationship of 'rules of the game' (*Zusammenhang von Spielregeln*)) to orient the reader's (public's) understanding and to enable a qualifying reception.

The continually new 'widening of the genre', in which Croce saw the supposed validity of definitional and normative genre concepts led ad absurdum, describes from another perspective the processlike appearance and 'legitimate transitoriness' of literary genres,[10] as soon as one is prepared to desubstantialize the classical concept of genre. This demands that one ascribe no other generality to literary 'genres' (no longer so called, indeed, except metaphorically) than that which manifests itself in the course of its historical appearance. By no means must everything generically general – what allows a group of texts to appear as similar or related – be dismissed, along with the timeless validity of the concept of an essence (*Wesensbegriff*) implicit in the classical genre poetics. One may refer here to the differentiation in linguistics as well of a generality that assumes a middle position between the universal and the individual.[11] Following this line of thought, literary genres are to be understood not as *genera* (classes) in the logical senses, but rather as *groups* or *historical families*.[12] As such, they cannot be deduced or defined, but only historically determined, delimited, and described. In this they are analogous to historical languages, for which it likewise holds that German or French, for example, do not allow themselves to be defined, but rather only synchronically described and historically investigated.

[. . .] If one follows the fundamental rule of the historicization of the concept of form, and sees the history of literary genres as a temporal process of the continual founding and altering of horizons, then the metaphorics of the courses of development, function, and decay can be replaced by the nonteleological concept of the playing out of a limited number of possibilities.[13] In this concept a masterwork is definable in terms of an alteration of the horizon of the genre that is as unexpected as it is enriching; the genre's prehistory is definable in terms of a trying and testing of possibilities; and its arrival at a historical end is definable in terms of formal ossification, automatization, or a giving up or misunderstanding of the 'rules of the game', as is often found in the last epigones.[14] But the history of genres in this perspective also presupposes reflection on that which can become visible only to the retrospective observer: the beginning character of the beginnings and the definite character of an end; the norm-founding or norm-breaking role of particular examples; and finally, the historical as well as the aesthetic significance of masterworks, which itself may change with the history of their effects and later interpretations, and thereby may also differently illuminate the coherence of the history of their genre that is to be narrated. For in the dimension of their reception, literary genres as well stand under the dialectic of after-history and prehistory, insofar as, according to Walter Benjamin, because of their after-history 'their prehistory also becomes recognizable as conceived in continual change'.[15]

* * *

The theory of literary genres cannot remain within the structures of self-enclosed histories of genres, but rather must also consider the possibility of a historical systematics. If for centuries no attempt has been undertaken to bring the totality of literary genres of a period into a system of contemporary phenomena, the reason may be that the normative doctrine of genres has been profoundly discredited and, along with it, any systematics decried as speculative. In the meantime, the modern theory of genres can proceed only descriptively, and not by definition; this insight in no way excludes the possibility that, along the path of synchronic description and historical investigation, one may arrive, though not at a generically determined system of communication, nonetheless at a historical sequence of such systems. Even the literature of the Middle Ages is no arbitrary sum of its parts, but rather a latent ordering or sequence of orderings of literary genres. After all, several references by medieval authors and the (in this respect, still unevaluated) selection and arrangement of texts and genres in collected manuscripts point to this ordering.

The Latin poetics, with its rhetorical categories and classifications of style, might well also be brought to bear heuristically on an establishing and delimitation of generic characteristics, even though for the most part it contains only traditional didactic material and was not normative for the vernacular literature.

From the transmission of ancient rhetoric and theory of poetry, there were in the Middle Ages basically four schemata of division at one's disposal that could, in varying degree, serve the explanation of genres: modes of discourse (*genus demonstrativum, deliberativum, iudicialis*), levels of style (*genera dicendi: humile, medium, sublime*), forms of delivery (*genus dramaticum, narrativum, mixtum*), and finally objects (*tres status hominum: pastor otiosus, agricola, miles dominans*).[16] The doctrine of the three modes of discourse, each with two submodes, is admittedly not developed into a system for the division of corresponding literary genres in the rhetorical handbooks; it remains to be investigated whether they provided anything for the oratorical literature that first appeared in Italy. In the ancient tradition the three *genera dicendi* were distinguished above all according to formal elements of the level of style (vocabulary, meter, imagery, ornamentation). Here the medieval reception took a step beyond the ancient theory. Twelfth- and thirteenth-century authors introduced the concept of 'style' ('*sunt igitur tres styli: humilis, mediocris, grandiloqus*'), which they no longer defined solely according to the means of representation, but also according to its object (i.e., the social class of the represented characters and the elements of their environment).[17] The model for this system was the interpretation of Virgil's works going back to Servius and Donat, which had him in the *Bucolica, Georgica*, and *Aeneid* representing three stages of human society (shepherd, farmer, warrior) in the appropriate, that is, similarly leveled, style. Of the Virgilian genres, admittedly only the bucolic is cultivated in the Middle Ages, and not the georgic: and the *Aeneid* is also nowhere identified with the chanson de geste.[18] And yet the principle of classification according to the social class of the characters carried out by Johannes de Garlandia has its correspondence at least in the strictly class-ordered 'rules of the game' of the Old French epic and romance, if one ignores the missing ordering in the levels of style.

The theory of the three forms of delivery according to the system of the grammarian Diomedes (*narrativum* when the poet himself speaks, *dramaticum* when the characters alone speak, *mixtum* when poet and characters alternately have the voice) achieved particular influence in the Middle Ages through Bede and Isidore. Diomedes' tripartite division, proceeding from the most superficial formal characteristics, did more to cause confusion concerning the function of ancient genres (for example, concerning that of the ancient theater, so that the structure of plays to be performed had to be sought and developed anew) than it did to establish productive new distinctions.[19] Johannes de Garlandia brought order into this transmission. His *Poetria*, a synthesis of the *Artes dictaminis* and the *Artes poeticae*, fit Diomedes' tripartite division into a new *summa* of literary genres, which is systematically arranged according to four perspectives: 1. according to the verbal form (*prosa* and *metrum*, the first arranged into four genres: the technographic or scholarly, the historical, the epistolary, the rhythmic and musical); 2. according to the form of delivery (*quicumque loquitur*: Diomedes' tripartite division); 3. according to the degree of reality of the narrative (three *species narrationis*: res gesta or *historia*, res ficta or *fabula*, res ficta quae tamen fieri potuit or *argumentum*); 4. according to the feeling expressed in the poetry (*de differentia carminum*, a fourfold arrangement that develops a differentiation of the *genera tragica*, *comica*, *satyrica*, and *mimica* that is mentioned by Diomedes and in the *Tractatus coisilianus*).[20] The system of genres of Johannes de Garlandia's *Poetria* did not arise purely deductively, but rather, in its richness in definitions related to content, perhaps sought to order the state of literary genres arrived at in the reality of the thirteenth century: this is a hypothesis for which at least two arguments seem to speak. A. Adler has pointed out that the *historicum* in Johannes's definition (that is, the satiric genre in the fourth rubric) quite precisely expresses the perimeters and the function of the thirteenth-century literary forms that one may distinguish as the beginnings of political satire. And the distinction, thematic as well as stylistic, between tragedy (*carmen quod incipit a gaudio et terminat in lucto*) and comedy (*carmen iocusum incipiens a tristitia et terminans in gaudium*) returns in the genre theory of Dante's letter to Can Grande and corresponds to the structure as well as to the (later) title of the *Divina Commedia*.[21] [. . .]

*   *   *

The question of the reality of literary genres in the historical everyday world, or that of their social function, has been ignored in medieval scholarship, and not because of a lack of documents. Resisting any insight into this question, there has long been the humanist overemphasis on the written and printed tradition, a Platonic aesthetics according to which past literature can really be 'present' for us in a book at any moment,[22] and the naively objectivist equation of philological interpretation with the experience of the original reader or hearer. The necessary reorientation of scholarship was first introduced by Jean Rychner for the chanson de geste.[23] His programmatic slogan referring to the 'oral style', the epic technique, and the oral dissemination of the Old French epic – 'The *chanson de geste*, diffused under these conditions, ought to have been composed for these conditions'[24] – should also be emphasized for most of the other genres of vernacular literature, for which the problem of their conditions of influence (*Wirkungsbedingungen*) and social function still remains an open one. For this scholarly task, Romance philology can garner advice from a discipline that for more than 50 years has been developing methods for this, and testing them on a material that is furthermore exemplary for the literature of the Middle Ages: namely, theological research into literary criticism of the Bible.

During the same time that Romance philology stood under the spell of 'work-immanent' methods, and Croce's suspicion of literary genres was rarely contradicted, a scholarly tendency blossomed within theology that made a philological principle into one of its own: namely, that 'the literature in which the life of a community – thus, also the original Christian congregation – plays itself out arises out of very definite expressions and needs of the life of this community, which in turn present a certain style, certain forms and certain genres'.[25] Literary forms and genres are thus neither subjective creations of the author, nor merely retrospective ordering-concepts, but rather primarily social phenomena, which means that they depend on functions in the lived world. The Bible is also a *literary* monument that bears witness to the life of a community; it can no longer remain withdrawn from historical understanding as 'genus illud singulare, transcendens, nullam cum aliis comparationem ferens, quod est ipsa Scriptura sacra'.[26] Accordingly, the understanding of the Bible is no longer thinkable without a literary-critical scholarship that takes account of the environment and its languages, the personality of the author, and the literary genres known to the original addressees of the books.[27] This literary-historical scholarship has been brought under way by the so-called 'form-historical school' of Protestant theology (H. Gunkel, M. Dibelius, R. Bultman), and has since found its way into Catholic doctrine. The principle 'that research into the author and the literary genre of a determinate work has as its goal the exact understanding of the message which the work contains'[28] also lies at the basis of the Catholic handbooks on biblical scholarship,[29] which can draw support from the fact that Pope Pius XII, in the encyclical *Divino afflante spiritu* of 30 September 1943, recognized the modern theory of literary genres as an aid in biblical exegesis.

It is instructive for the problems of genre arising in the face of texts from the Romance Middle Ages that theological scholarship has a concept of genre that is structural as well as sociological: at first such scholarship inquires into the generically conditioned form, and the function in the lived world, of a given literary product in order then to consider it in its historical dimension. The literary genre becomes defined as a 'structural ensemble into which everything comes to insert itself in order to arrive at a particular meaning'; 'each of these literary genres communicates a certain truth to the reader, but in different orders'.[30] The recognition of such structures must meanwhile be preceded by 'the question of the presupposed situation, of the speaker, his intention, his listeners, and of the whole disposition: in short, the question of the "locus in life"' (Gunkel).[31] With the phrase 'locus in life' one understands a typical situation or mode of behavior in the life of a community, such as, for example, the festival of a sacrifice at sacred sites for the literary form of the hymn, but also such noncultic situations as work, hunting, and war; it is from these situations that the presupposed motifs that were constitutive for the form and intention of a genre first become comprehensible. For 'only the history of a genre proves whether the form of a literary work is not an accidental product, but rather a form capable of development which has its own life'.[32] The form-historical method that developed from this concept first determines 'the origin and affiliation of a specific literary genre in and to typical situations and behaviors of a community', and then follows the rise, alteration, and transition of the form so constituted in its history as a literary genre. As an example of this one may here cite Rudolf Bultmann's representation of the *apophthegmata*.[33]

* * *

But the 'literary history of the Bible' is also of great importance for medieval Romance philology from a thematic point of view. In recent decades one looked above all at the prototype of classical antiquity – its rhetoric and literary *topoi*, and its model authors – when asking about the origins of Romance literature. But the new literary genres of the Romance vernaculars in no way proceeded from this tradition in a linear development or an immediate 'appropriative transformation of the ancient heritage'. Concerning the 'afterlife of antiquity', the scholarship on tradition, believing in continuity, intentionally ignored the question of how the literature of the Christian era might actually be compatible with ancient literary theory, and whether there was something like a Christian aesthetics. In opposition to this attitude, Erich Auerbach variously demonstrated that the new demands and contents of the Christian faith had to break through the ancient literary system with its practice of a hierarchy of styles related to objects: 'humble everyday things . . . lose their baseness in the Christian context and become compatible with the lofty style; and conversely . . . the highest mysteries of the faith may be set forth in the simple words of the lowly style which everyone can understand. This was such a radical departure from the rhetorical, and indeed from the entire literary, tradition that it nearly signifies the destruction of its foundation.'[34] The consequences of the formation of a new Christian discursive art – a 'low rhetoric in the sense of the *sermo humilis'* established in Augustine's *De doctrina christiana* – for the forms of literature in late-Latin Christian antiquity and, later, in the Middle Ages, are still scarcely investigated. This is especially the case for the new formation of tradition in didactic literature, the genres of which bear the imprint of Christian eloquence, 'edification', and instruction. But the realm of *sermo humilis* also reaches into the epic and dramatic genres, which are determined by the model of the Bible not only thematically – through Christian dogma, through typology and the moral doctrine, as well as through the authority of the exempla – but also formally in manifold ways.

If one looks at the results of the 'literary history of the Bible', then one can only wonder why medieval studies have not yet undertaken any systematic attempt to investigate the possible model that literary genres found in the Bible may provide for medieval literature. The abundance of literary forms and genres ascertainable in the Old and New Testaments is astonishing, and leads directly to the discovery of Romance parallels. The Bible contains worldly lyrics (songs of work, ridicule, drinking, burial, and war) as well as spiritual ones (the hymn or the lament). It developed the most varied forms of narrative prose: etiological, historical, and also heroic sagas (the legendary garland for Samson); legends of martyrs and novellas (the Kings novellas, but also the Book of Ruth). It contains the model for various forms of historiography (tribal legend, genealogy, royal chronicle), historical prose (documents, letters, contracts, war reports), and biography (the self-disclosures of the prophets). All imaginable forms of wisdom literature (proverb, riddle, parable, fable, debate, allegory) and religious instruction (sermon, exhortation, epistle) are also found in it.

Finally, the method of the form-historical school also places the still-current distinction between the genres of 'spiritual' and 'worldly' literature in a problematic light. With this distinction, a literary understanding that arises only with the emancipation of the fine arts from their ties to cultic and social functions is transferred to a period that did not yet feel any separation between religious life and literary culture, the contents of faith and the forms of art. In the Middle Ages, all literature is still functionally determined through its 'locus in life'. What is generic in it arises from such immediately realized, self-evident, and therefore (for the most part) unreflected functions;

and thus, not from a reflected relationship with form as an aesthetic means, which can only appear with the developed generic consciousness of a literature that has become autonomous.[35] Two methodological consequences are to be drawn from this, according to M. Waltz: the object of research is here 'not the genre as it existed in the consciousness of contemporaries, but the function of the works'; but then a further object of study is the process, already beginning in the Middle Ages with the courtly lyric, in which a reflected generic consciousness appears with the problematization of the function, and leads in the Renaissance to the liberation of the autonomy of literature.[36] The distinction between 'spiritual' and 'worldly', functional constraint and 'literariness', has meaning in the Middle Ages only when it is understood as the *process* of a gradual literarization of genres that originally are tied to cultic, religious, and social functions.

For the application of the form-historical method to medieval literature, one can rightly claim that it is not satisfactory to explain the form of a genre directly from its 'locus in life' – on the one hand, because the genre can just as well form the 'locus of life' as the latter can the former, and on the other hand, because the function of a genre depends not only on its relation to a real, lived procedure, but also on its position within a comprehensive symbolic system familiar to contemporaries.[37] For the literary genre the question of the 'locus in life' has a synchronic as well as a diachronic dimension: it implies its function within the comprehensive ordering of the symbolic forms of expression of a culture and, at the same time, its position in the historical change of this symbolic system. For our period, this latter aspect means the process of the beginning literarization and individualization of generic conventions.

This process should not be misunderstood as an organic development, nor as secularization. Instead, the later, 'profane' history of a genre originally tied to religious or cultic functions does not need to develop immanently and linearly *out* of its original structural characteristics, but rather can be brought under way through heterogeneous impulses. Thus, the process of literarization or subjectification can fulfill itself precisely *counter to* the original purposeful orientation of the genre, that is, counter to its spirituality or edifying convention. For example, although Guillaume de Lorris's *Roman de la rose* in many respects appears only to further develop – under 'profane' symptoms – the spiritual traditions of the *bellum intestinum* (*Psychomachia*) and allegorical poetry in the mode of the *Roman de miserere* (of Reclus de Molliens, with numerous motivic analogies),[38] the structurally related first great worldly allegory nonetheless arises from an opposing process. Toward the end of the twelfth century the separation of allegorical poetry from biblical exegesis stood under the aegis of the contradiction that connected the spiritual author with the new allegorical form (*duplex sententia*) of the dit (from *veritatem dicere*) but against the brand-new contes and fables of worldly-courtly poetry. But now Guillaume de Lorris took up this challenge in that he lay claim to the same allegorical truth for the poetry of courtly love that the spiritual tradition of textual exegesis had reserved for itself: 'Faced with the absolute Book, at once model and rival, poetry in search of its autonomy forces itself to bring forth a *word* of authority (Love, for example) which it opposes to that of the Bible.'[39] The allegorization of poetry appearing in the thirteenth century is neither an immanent generic development nor a mere secularization of religious content, but rather the ostentatious appropriation and conscious literarization of a method proper to the spiritual tradition through poets like Guillaume de Lorris who sought an autonomous worldly literature.

The history of the development of the passion play offers a further example. Its development, which can be traced *ab ovo* from the famous interpolation of the Easter mass (*Quem quaeritis in sepulchro . . .*) in the tenth century up to the monstrous vernacular passion mysteries of the fifteenth century, is commonly seen as the prototype of a homogeneous process of progressive secularization, in which the originally liturgical event is increasingly secularized through scenes of increasingly worldly content until it finally degrades into a mere dramatic play. In opposition to this interpretation, Rainer Warning has brought to light heterogeneous impulses in the history of the genre that cannot be brought under the rubric of a process of secularization.[40] It is not incidental that the passion play shifts the sacred plot *extra muros*: as a 'mass in the marketplace' it produces ritual forms that distance themselves from church doctrine and finally even contradict it. Mimetic image-making already had brought church criticism upon the liturgical play; with the beginning of the vernacular tradition, the devil was introduced as a dramatic-dualistic counterpart, which approaches a remythification of the dogma of the incarnation when viewed against the background of Anselm of Canterbury's doctrine of satisfaction. In consequence of this dualistic structure, there finally arises the drastic arrangement of the martyrdom of the crucifixion, which brings the ostensible representation of the incarnation into the theologically ambiguous light of an archaic-magical scapegoat-ritual: 'To the extent that play and reality fuse together, God himself is ridiculed, spat upon, whipped and nailed to the cross in the stage figure of Jesus.'[41] In light of this interpretation, the history of the genre shows an opposing process behind the supposed secularization, which sprang from the latent protest of the dualistic-pagan folk piety against the monotheistic dogmatics, and explains the heretic tendency of the plays; this tendency may have led to the prohibition of further performances by the Parisian parliament's edict of 1548.

* * *

The last step in a theory of literary genres can proceed from the fact that a literary genre exists for itself alone as little as does an individual work of art. This fact is less self-evident than it may at first appear, if one retains an image of how genres commonly appear in literary histories; they are seen as a sequence of generic developments, closed within themselves, that for the most part are held together only through the outer framework of some general characteristics of the period. But the basic principle of a historicization of the concept of form demands not only that one relinquish the substantialist notion of a constant number of unchangeable essential characteristics for the individual genres. It also demands that one dismantle the correlative notion of a sequence of literary genres closed within themselves, encapsulated from one another, and inquire into the reciprocal relations that make up the literary system of a given historical moment. For the task of discovering diachronic and synchronic interrelations between the literary genres of a period, the Russian Formalists found methodological approaches that well deserve to be applied to the field of medieval literature.[42]

The Formalist conception of genre as a historical system of relations participates in the attempt to replace the classical notion of literary tradition – as a steady, unilinear, cumulative course – with the dynamic principle of literary *evolution*, by which they do not mean an analogy to organic growth or to Darwinian selection. For here 'evolution' is supposed to characterize the phenomenon of literary 'succession' 'not in the sense of a continuous "development," but rather in the sense of a "struggle" and "break" with immediate predecessors through a contemporary recourse to something older'.[43] In the historical evolution of literature thus understood, literary genres can be grasped in the periodic alternation of the dominating role as well as in a sequence of rivalries. At the basis of this idea lies the notion of a self-changing 'hierarchy of genres': 'For the Formalists the "period" is also a system with a system-specific "attitude" and its corresponding "dominants." On the basis of the general attitude or intention the genres – which to an especially large extent are able to give expression to this attitude – arrive at the top of the hierarchy of genres and become the "dominating" genres of the period. These can be entirely new genres, but also richly traditional genres can become restructured in respect to the new basic intention'.[44]

From a diachronic perspective the historical alternation of the dominating genre manifests itself in the three steps of canonization, automatization, and reshuffling. Successful genres that embody the 'high point' of the literature of a period gradually lose their effective power through continual reproduction; they are forced to the periphery by new genres often arising from a 'vulgar' stratum if they cannot be reanimated through a restructuring (be it through the playing up of previously suppressed themes or methods, or through the taking up of materials or the taking-over of functions from other genres).[45] In the realm of the Romance literature of the Middle Ages, the following examples offer themselves for an explanation in terms of the theory of the 'high point': the new appearance of the courtly romance, which around the middle of the twelfth century struggles for the dominating position with the older chanson de geste; then the rise of the prose romance, which around the turn of the thirteenth century makes its way with a new claim to truth;[46] and finally the triumph of allegory, which around 1234/35 (as Huon de Méry in the prologue to the *Tournoiement de l'Antéchrist* testifies, along with Guillaume de Lorris) presents itself as *novel pensé* and as yet unknown *matire*, and replaces the courtly epic and Arthurian world of the models of Chrétien de Troyes, Raoul de Houdenc, and their epigones, which are now felt as past. But as distinguished from the examples of the Formalists, for the most part chosen from modern literature, the history of genres in the twelfth and thirteenth centuries lacks a comparable stratum of subliterature. The new genres of the courtly verse-romance, the first prose romances, and the allegorical epic are not canonizations of lower genres, but rather proceed from a shift of functions (the paired or, respectively, narrative eight-syllabic line was found in rhymed chronicles; the prose in historiography; and the allegorical form in spiritual poetry).

The shift or taking over of function from other genres allows one to see the synchronic dimension in the literary system of a period. Literary genres do not exist alone, but rather form the various functions of a given period's system, to which they connect the individual work: 'A work which is ripped out of the context of the given literary system and transposed into another one receives another coloring, clothes itself with other characteristics, enters into another genre, loses its genre; in other words, its function is shifted.'[47] This process may also be demonstrated with the 'matière de Bretagne': since its significance within the system of the Celtic–Cymric mythology and legendary world was no longer understood by the French narrators and their audience, its fables received the other 'tone' of the fairy tale-like miraculous. Through this fictionalization conditioned by reception, the Arthurian romance distinguishes itself most sharply from the chanson de geste which arises from the historical saga and the martyr legends. From the perspective of their rivalry, new aspects of the history of these two genres may still be gained. Similarly, the history of courtly poetry could surely still be enriched if it were sketched within the historical relational-system of the genres that surround and, above all, also negate it: the Renart parts with their laughing satire of the whole courtly-knightly world; the verse farces (fabliaux) with their drastic and not infrequently grotesque perversions of courtly mores; the dits, sermons, and moral treatises with the existential earnestness of their doctrine of virtue and their scattered anticourtly polemics. Especially desirable would be research into the functional divisions in the didactic 'small genres' and the narrative 'short forms'; here one could make a sidepiece to André Jolles's *Einfache Formen*, the system of which would surely receive richly explanatory historical variants and extensions within the Romance sphere.[48]

* * *

The Formalist theory imposed upon itself the limitation of considering and describing the evolution of literary genres and forms as a unilinear process. It disregards the function of literary genres in quotidian history, and dismissed the questions of their reception by and influence on the contemporary and later audiences as mere sociologism and psychologism. The historicity of literature nonetheless is not absorbed into the succession of aesthetic-formal systems and the changing of hierarchies of genres. It does not suffice to set the 'literary series' only in relation with language as the nearest 'extraliterary series'. Since literary genres have their 'locus in life' and therefore their social function, literary evolution must also, beyond its own relationship between diachrony and synchrony, be determinable through its social function within the general process of history. Since the 1930s, Jan Mukařovský and the so-called Prague Structuralism have accomplished this further development of Formalist theory in ground-breaking studies, the reception of which is still lacking in Western European scholarship.[49] This step from formalism to a dialectical structuralism is interesting for a theory of literary genres above all because here the work of art is understood as a sign and carrier of meaning for a social reality, and the aesthetic is defined as a principle of mediation and a mode of organization for extra-aesthetic meanings. On the other hand, a theory of genres grounded in an aesthetics of reception necessarily will add to the study of the structural relations between literature and society, work and audience, where the historical system of norms of a 'literary public' lies hidden in a distant past; there it can most readily still be reconstructed through the horizon of expectations of a genre system that pre-constituted the intention of the works as well as the understanding of the audience.

The testimonies of older literatures often remain mute and the documents of social history also rarely give a direct answer to the questions that must be asked to obtain information about the function, reception, and influence of literary works and genres in their historical reality and social environment. Thus structuralism and hermeneutics are here related to one another to an especially great extent. Their mediation through the methods of an aesthetics of reception is necessary to enable one to become at all aware of the social function (by means of the synchronic system of genres, norms, and values) and – connected with this – the 'answering character' (by means of an analysis of the history of reception) of works of past art.[50] Along this path our epistemological interest in the literature of the Middle Ages will also be grounded anew: the opportunity for a renaissance in medieval studies appears today to lie much less in the significance of the Middle Ages as a homogeneous member of our familiar Western tradition than in the fact that its monuments have preserved only a fragmentary picture of a historically distant culture and life-world that are often foreign to us.

If one looks back on the scholarship of recent decades, there is no longer any mistaking that the humanist faith in an unbreakable tradition of literary forms and in the timeless presence of masterworks has deceived us about the historical distance and otherness of medieval literature. No perceptible historical continuity exists between the forms and genres of the Middle Ages and the literature of our present. Here the reception of the ancient poetics and canon of genres in the Renaissance unmistakably cut through the threads of the formation of tradition. The rediscovery of medieval literature by Romantic philology produced only the ideology of new continuities in the form of the essential unity of each national literature, but did not enable one to draw the medieval canon of genres and works back into a new literary productivity. The forms and genres of modern literature arose as a counter-thrust to the canon of classicist-humanist aesthetics: troubadour lyrics were as little an impulse for the *Fleurs du mal* as was the knightly epic for the *Education sentimentale* or the passion play for the modern 'non-Aristotelian' theater.

But from this one should not now conclude that the theory and history of the literary genres of the Middle Ages can no longer contribute to the understanding of the literature of our present. What they may achieve, and wherein they may once again arrive at an actuality, can rather first emerge when our relationship to the Middle Ages is liberated from the illusion of beginnings, that is, from the perspective that in this period one might find the first stage of our literature, the beginning that conditions all further development. The literature of the Middle Ages can once again become an irreplaceable paradigm, not as a beginning that receives its significance only through an end that is distant from it – the developed national literatures – but rather through its 'beginningness', significant in itself. Through the 'beginningness' of a literature newly forming itself in the vernacular languages, its archaic genres provide testimony for the ideal *and* reality of a unique political as well as cultural historical-world closed in itself, and offer us elementary structures in which the socially formative and communicative power of literature has manifested itself.

Notes

1. This was revived by the Third International Congress of Modern Literary History, held in Lyon in May 1939 ('Travaux du 3e Congrès international d'Histoire littéraire moderne', *Helicon 2* (1940)), which was devoted to the genre problem that had been declared dead by Croce and that thereby provoked his scornful protest. Cf. G. ZACHARIAS, 'B. Croce und die literarischen Gattungen', dissertation, University of Hamburg, 1951. For further discussion cf. J. POMMIER, 'L'idée de genre', *Publications de l'École Normale Supérieure*, Section des Lettres, II (Paris, 1945), pp. 47–81; RENÉ WELLEK and AUSTIN WARREN, *Theory of Literature* (New York, 1942), ch. 17: 'Literary Genres'; and W. RUTTKOWSKI, *Die literarischen Gattungen* (Bern, 1968), useful for its bibliography.

2. H. KUHN, 'Gattungsprobleme der mittelhochdeutschen Literatur', in *Dichtung und Welt im Mittelalter*, 2nd edn (Stuttgart, 1969), p. 45.

3. Cf. ibid., p. 7: 'But what does one do with the unsung maxim, rhymed discourse, the fable, with all the types that play, without boundaries, across the didactic, the novelistic, the allegorical, from the smallest forms up to the great forms? Should the passion play function as tragedy, the *Fasnachtspiel* as comedy? Can the didactic and the religious literature of all forms constitute their own genres, since, as "epic", "lyric" or "dramatic", they are only pseudotypes. And once again, prose of all kinds, literary and pragmatic, religious and scholarly and practical, with the most varied transitions into poetry: rhymed prefaces to *Lucidarius* and *Sachsenspiegel*, rhymed and prose chronicles world-historical as well as locally historical, the ritual literature?'

4. Croce's aesthetics were mediated in the United States through J.E. Spingarn, who counts among the ground-breakers of New Criticism; cf. SPINGARN, 'The New Criticism' (1910), in *The Achievement of American Criticism*, ed. C.A. Brown (New York, 1954), pp. 525–46, and J. HERMAND, 'Probleme der heutigen Gattungsgeschichte', in *Jahrbuch für internationale Germanistik* 2 (1970), pp. 85–94.

5. On the founding of an historical aesthetics, cf. PETER SZONDI, 'Einleitung' to *Theorie des modernen Dramas* (Frankfurt a.M., 1956), and his 'La théorie des genres poétiques chez Friedrich Schlegel', *Critique* (March 1968), 264–92 [Eng. 'Friedrich Schlegel's Theory of Poetical Genres: A Reconstruction from The Posthumous Fragments', in SZONDI, *On Textual Understanding and Other Essays*, trans. Harvey Mendelsohn (Manchester, 1986)].

6. BENEDETTO CROCE, *Estetica*, 2nd edn (Bari, 1902), p. 40 [see above, p. 27].

7. Ibid., pp. 40, 75.

8. The two names, *Erlebnisästhetik* and *Genieästhetik*, refer, respectively, to criticism represented by Dilthey's *Das Erlebnis und die Dichtung* (1907), and the late eighteenth-century theories of Hamann, Herder, and 'Sturm und Drang' (Tr.).

9. WOLF-DIETER STEMPEL, 'Pour une description des genres littéraires', in *Actes du XIIe Congrès international de linguistique Romane* (Bucharest, 1968), p. 565, on the fundamental condition of any theory of discourse: 'Every act of linguistic communication is reducible to a generic and conventional norm, composed, on the level of the spoken language, of the social index and the situational index as a unity of behavior.'

10. F. SENGLE, *Die literarische Formenlehre* (Stuttgart, 1966), p. 19.

11. According to E. COSERIU, 'Thesen zum Thema "Sprache und Dichtung"', in *Beiträge zur Textlinguistik*, ed. Wolf-Dieter Stempel (Munich, 1971), pp. 183–8, esp. section II, 2; cf. STEMPEL, 'Pour une description': 'Thus the genre, as it were, is at once of the system and of the utterance [*parole*], a status corresponding to that which Coseriu calls "norm"'.

12. What CROCE, *Estetica*, p. 78, called 'the family atmosphere' (to indicate the similarity of expressions) and played against the concept of genre, thus receives a positive meaning.

13. Cf. KUHN, 'Gattungsprobleme', pp. 46, 56f., 61.

14. On this last aspect I can refer to my studies of the Renart-epigones: cf. *Untersuchungen zur mittelalterlichen Tierdichtung* (Beihefte zur Zeitschrift für romanische Philologie C) (Tübingen, 1959), ch. V; also *Cultura neolatina*, 21 (1961), 214–19, and *Mélanges Delbouille* (1964), vol. II, pp. 291–312.

15. WALTER BENJAMIN, 'Eduard Fuchs, der Sammler und Historiker', in *Angelus Novus* (Frankfurt a.M., 1966) p. 303.

16. I. BEHRENS, *Die Lehre von der Einteilung der Dichtkunst* (Beihefte zur Zeitschrift für romanischen Philologie XCII) (Halle, 1940); E. FARAL, *Les arts poétiques du XIIe et du XIIIe siècles* (Paris, 1924); E. DE BRUYNE, *Etudes d'esthétique mediévale*, 3 vols (Brugge, 1946), esp. 2.42.

17. According to FARAL, *Les arts poétiques*, p. 82: 'That which was a matter of style for the first critics became a matter of social dignity for the school of the twelfth and thirteenth centuries. It is the quality of the characters, and not that of the elocution, that furnishes the principle of classification'; and DE BRUYNE, *Etudes*, 2.41 ff.

18. WERNER KRAUSS, 'Die literarishchen Gattungen', *Essays zur französischen Literatur* (Berlin and Weimar, 1968), p. 15.

19. E.R. CURTIUS, *Europäische Literatur und lateinisches Mittelalter*, 3rd edn (Bern, 1961), 'Exkurs V: Spätantike Literaturwissenschaft'; Eng. *European Literature and the Latin Middle Ages*, trans. Willard R. Trask (New York, 1953).

20. DE BRUYNE, *Etudes*, 2.18 ff.

21. CURTIUS, *Europaïsche Literatur*, ch. 17, sec. 5: 'Die *Commedia* und die literarischen Gattungen'.

22. For a critique of these premises for E.R. CURTIUS's research into tradition (e.g. his *Europaïsche Literatur*, ch. 1), cf. W. BULST, 'Bedenken eines Philologen', in *Medium Aevum Vivum*, ed. H.R. JAUSS and W. SCHALLER (Heidelberg, 1960),

pp. 7–10, and HANS ROBERT JAUSS, 'Literary History as a Challenge to Literary Theory', in *Toward an Aesthetic of Reception* (Minneapolis, 1982).

23. J. RYCHNER, *La chanson de geste: Essai sur l'art épique des jongleurs* (Société de publications romanes et françaises LXXX) (Geneva, 1955); cf. 'La technique littéraire des Chansons de geste', *Actes du Colloque de Liège*, September 1957 (Bibliothèque de la Faculté de philologie et de lettres de l'Université de Liège CL), ed. M. DELBOUILLE (Paris, 1959); also the report of the Congrès de Poitiers (July 1959) of the Société Rencesvals, in *Bulletin bibliographique de la Société Rencesvals*, 2 (1960), 59–122.

24. RYCHNER, *La chanson de geste*, p. 48.

25. RUDOLF BULTMANN, *Die Geschichte der synoptischen Tradition*, 6th edn (Göttingen, 1964), p. 4.

26. Cf. ibid., p. vii.

27. A. ROBERT and A. FEUILLET, *Introduction à la Bible* (Tournai, 1959), p. 150.

28. Ibid., p. 150.

29. A. ROBERT and A. FEUILLET, *Los géneros literarios de la Sagrada Escritura* (Congreso de ciencias eclesiásticas, Salamanca, 1954) (Barcelona, 1957); also A. LODS, *Histoire de la littérature hébraïque et juive* (Paris, 1950); A. BENIZEN, *Introduction to the Old Testament*, 2nd edn (Copenhagen, 1952); H.C. DODD, *The Apostolic Preaching and its Developments*, 7th edn (1957); K. KOCH, *Was ist Formengeschichte? Neue Wege der Bibelexegese*, 2nd edn (Neukirchen-Vluyn, 1967).

30. ROBERT and FEUILLET, *Los géneros*, p. 123.

31. C. KUHL and G. BORNKAMM, 'Formen und Gattungen', in *Religion in Geschichte und Gegenwart: Handwörterbuch für Theologie und Religionswissenschaft*, 3rd edn (Tübingen, 1958), vol. 2, cols 996–1005.

32. BULTMANN, *Die Geschichte*, p. 40.

33. Ibid., pp. 40, 41.

34. ERICH AUERBACH, *Literatursprache und Publikum in der lateinischen Spätantike und im Mittelalter* (Bern, 1958), p. 32; cf. Eng., *Literary Language and Its Public in Late Latin Antiquity and in the Middle Ages*, trans. Ralph Manheim (Princeton, NJ, 1965), p. 37.

35. Cf. BULTMANN, *Die Geschichte*, p. 4: 'Just as the *locus in life* is not a unique historical event, but rather a typical situation or mode of behavior in the life of a community, the literary genre – or respectively, the *form* through which a particular piece is coordinated with a genre – is similarly a sociological concept and not an aesthetic one, however much such forms may be used in a later development as aesthetic means for an individualizing literature.'

36. M. WALTZ, 'Zum Problem der Gattungsgeschichte im Mittelalter', in *Zeitschrift für romanische Philologie*, 86 (1970), 32, 33 n. 17, on the autonomy of courtly poetry, which sets in rather early: 'The courtly forms also prefigure in other ways the stable genres of the later period: they live in a symbolic world (which they essentially carry with them) that is separated from the official religious one, and its socio-cultural function is less immediately comprehensible.'

37. Ibid., p. 35.

38. See the *Grundriss der Romanischen Literaturen des Mittelalters*, vol. VI, C (1972), pp. 160, 233.

39. ROGER DRAGONETTI, *Revue belge de philologie et d'histoire*, 43 (1965), 118; cf. *GRLMA*, VI, C, p. 151.

40. RAINER WARNING, 'Ritus, Mythos and geistliches Spiel', in *Poetica*, 3 (1970), 83–114.

41. Ibid., p. 102.

42. Summarised by JURIJ STRIEDTER, ed., *Texte der russischen Formalisten*, vol. 1 (Theorie und Geschichte der Literatur und der schönen Künste VI, Munich, 1969), pp. lx–lxx.

43. Ibid., p. lxvi.

44. Ibid., p. lxv.

45. YURY TYNYANOV provided the model of such an analysis of the history of a genre for the ode in 'Die Ode als oratorisches Genre' (1922), in *Texte der russischen Formalisten*, vol. 2, ed. W.-D. STEMPEL (Munich, 1972), pp. 273–337; BORIS TOMASHEVSKY provides examples for the 'penetration of the procedures of the vulgar genre into the higher genre' in 'Thématique' (1925), in *Théorie de la littérature: Textes des formalistes russes*, ed. Tzvetan Todorov (Paris, 1965), pp. 263–307 [Eng. 'Thematics', in LEE T. LEMON and MARION J. REIS, eds, *Russian Formalist Criticism: Four Essays* (Lincoln: University of Nebraska Press, 1965)].

46. Cf. ERICH KÖHLER, 'Zur Entstehung des altfranzösischen Prosaromans', in *Trobadorlyrik und höfischer Roman* (Berlin, 1962), pp. 213–23.

47. TYNYANOV, 'Die Ode als oratorisches Genre'.

48. ANDRÉ JOLLES, *Einfache Formen: Legende, Sage, Mythe, Rätsel, Spiel, Kasus, Morabile, Märchen, Witz* (1930; 2nd edn Halle, 1956).

49. JAN MUKAŘOVSKÝ, *Kapitel aus der Poetik* (Frankfurt a.M., 1967), and *Kapitel aus der Asthetik* (Frankfurt a.M., 1970); on these see STRIEDTER, ed., *Texte der russischen Formalisten*, 1.lxi, lxxix; JAUSS, 'Literary History'.

50. Concerning the 'answering character' of the work of art, as well as the hermeneutic logic and tradition-forming function of the procedure of question and answer, I refer the reader to JAUSS, 'Literary History'.

147

9 Genre-Systems and the Functions of Literature*

ROSALIE COLIE

In this witty and erudite essay, the first in a series of lectures delivered at Berkeley in 1972, the American scholar Rosalie Colie explores the role of genre in the literary theory and practice of the Renaissance. Colie was not the first to tackle this large and complex topic, but she brings it into focus in new and unexpected ways, marshalling her knowledge of the European literary tradition with a lightness of touch rarely found among historians of genre theory. (The informal tone owes something to the fact that this is the unrevised text of a lecture, which also explains the absence of footnotes: Colie died in a boating accident soon after delivering the lectures.) The interest of this and the three other essays in *The Resources of Kind*, however, goes beyond their distinguished contribution to Renaissance scholarship. Colie's probing of the tension between official and unofficial codes of practice, her subtle illustrations of how generic conventions actually work (or, in some cases, don't), and, above all, her brilliant demonstration of the many different contexts in which the resources of genre are utilised within a 'book culture' (not just by writers, readers and critics but also printers, booksellers, librarians, teachers), have major implications for the methodology of genre studies and for our understanding of the concept of genre. The concrete particularity she brings to the notion of 'genre-system', for example, may serve to enrich and adjust the more abstract formulations of Tynyanov and Frye (Chapters 2 and 6), while her account of the interaction and competition of genres usefully extends the ideas of Bakhtin (Chapter 4). The fact that Colie doesn't feel the need to engage in polemic with other modern theorists of genre (the only two she cites, in both cases approvingly, are E.D. Hirsch and Claudio Guillén) in no way diminishes the theoretical importance of her work.

---

* Reprinted from Rosalie Colie, *The Resources of Kind: Genre-Theory in the Renaissance*, ed. Barbara K. Lewalski (Berkeley: University of California Press, 1973), pp. 2–31.

The books to which she alludes are Hirsch's *Validity in Inter-pretation* (1967) and Guillén's *Literature as System* (1971); the latter includes several important essays on Renaissance genre theory, brilliantly illuminated by modern structuralism. Many of Colie's (and Guillén's) ideas are discussed in Fowler's *Kinds of Literature* (1982) and Dubrow's *Genre* (1982), both of which, though intended to serve as general introductions, are particularly strong on Renaissance genre theory. For further work in this historical field, see *Renaissance Genres: Essays on Theory, History, and Interpretation*, ed. Lewalski (1986); Lewalski's *Paradise Lost and the Rhetoric of Literary Forms* (1985), which contains general discussion on Renaissance poetics; and the chapters on genre in Colie's own *Shakespeare's Living Art* (Princeton: Princeton University Press, 1974). For the classical foundations of Renaissance genre theory, see Donohue, *The Theory of Literary Kinds* (1943, 1949). As a model for the historical investigation of genre, Colie's essay can be usefully compared with Jauss and Jameson (Chapters 8 and 10).

It has gradually dawned on me that one way to understand some of the interconnections of Renaissance literature, a bulk of magnificent writing that somehow seems to belong culturally together, is to tackle notions of literary kind: what kinds of 'kind' did writers recognize, and why? Why should there have been such bitter critical battles in sixteenth-century Italy over Dante's *Commedia*, Speroni's un-Sophoclean tragedy *Canace e Macareo*, Ariosto's and Tasso's epics, Guarini's tragicomical play? Since three of these works are self-evidently masterpieces and the other two by no means bad, why weren't critics and readers able to take them gratefully for whatever they were, instead of making them objects of critical inquiry and even disapproval?

Part of the answer lies in the hold that concepts of genre had on writers and their readers in the Renaissance – a period which, for purposes of discussion, I take to begin with Petrarch and to end with Swift. For reasons that may seem familiar to us in one way and with results that seem very odd, literate young men in the Renaissance turned to a cultural ideal which they defined as other and better than their own, very much as alternative lifestyles to our own are now sought in Eastern, primitive, or remote cultures. All around us we see Eastern modes of thought and belief, Eastern arts and crafts: to the anthropologist or the historian lamentably detached from their cultural habitat – but loved as symbols for the virtues attributed to that habitat. With something of the same enthusiasm and the same synchronic selectivism with which other cultural elements are now defined as alternative value-systems to our own, generation after generation of Renaissance young men were willing to turn to antiquity, adapting to their needs and desires those elements in antiquity which they could recognize as useful or symbolically relevant.

It was a book revolution: texts were overwhelmingly the sources from which the new liberation came, although visual sources were also enormously important in stimulating the painting, sculpture and (especially) architecture of the time. The longer we work with ancient texts, however, the more obvious it is that word governed visual image, even then. Vitruvius was as important as Roman ruins visible and tangible. The texts in question were recovered from oblivion, published on the new-fangled presses, edited and quarreled over – and endlessly imitated. Why such models, and whence came their peculiar power? To be able to answer that question is to understand the Renaissance, I think: I do not pretend to offer answers to this here, but only to take – as do all the articles in paperbacks called 'Six Lectures on Renaissance Thought', 'The Renaissance: Aspects of its Culture', etc. – this glorification of ancient culture as a given. Certainly, in literature it *was* a given: from the fifteenth century on, those interested in the new learning (that is, the old learning restored) insisted on imitating; they made models of classical texts, chiefly Cicero, translated and imitated them. Rhetorical education, always a model-following enterprise, increasingly stressed *structures* as well as styles to be imitated in the humane letters – epistles, orations, discourses, dialogues, histories, poems – always discoverable to the enthusiastic new man of letters by kind.

Such classification, I think, was rhetorically based, but it tended toward a new kind, *poetics*, a kind which, when Aldus published the text of Aristotle's *Poetics*, did not yet exist; that epoch-making discourse appeared in a volume called 'Ancient Rhetoricians'. In one generation, however, Aristotle's *Poetics*, together with Horace's long-known *Ars poetica*, the epistle to the Pisos, had established a Renaissance genre, on which this study fundamentally relies. I shall refer from time to time to some of the many *artes poeticae* written in the period, since from them we can recover the ideas consciously held, governing the written criticism and theory of the Renaissance. From 'real' literature as opposed to criticism and theory, of course, we recover what is far more important, the *unwritten* poetics by which writers worked and which they themselves created.

At this point you may be saying: but is she suggesting that literary kinds, genres, are peculiar to ancient literature and Renaissance literature? What is *The Canterbury Tales* but a magnificent repertory of medieval narrative kinds? Were not poetic forms highly developed in the Provençal and Spanish schools of the twelfth and thirteenth centuries, and in the chambers of rhetoric of the late Middle Ages?

Of course: and there are always kinds, forms, schemata, in all the arts, even now, when we flee from them that sometime did them seek. (If a Campbell's soup tin, then, obviously, a Brillo box.) In the last 50 years we have learnt a good deal about our perceptions of anything at all, notably, that these perceptions are mediated by forms, collections, collocations, associations; we have learnt, even, that we learn so naturally by forms and formulae that we often entirely fail to recognize them for what they are.

[. . .] It is much as musical forms mean to us that literary forms 'meant' to Renaissance writers – a genre was, in Claudio Guillén's nice phrase, 'a challenge to match an imaginative structure to reality'. With that last word I have introduced the shibboleth and stumbling block of Renaissance Aristotelianism, the idea of mimesis, or the imitation of *reality*. It was in the service of this mimesis that Aristotle contributed a social dimension, or decorum, to the literary modes he canonized, narrative, dramatic, and lyric, modes then subdivided into genres – epic, tragic, comic, etc. In the imitation of reality, a high style befits its high subject – epic or tragic; a low style a low subject, comedy or some lyric forms. Since Cicero expressed outright what is implied in Aristotle's formula, namely that styles must not be mixed (comic style is a defect in tragedy, tragic style in comedy, etc.), we can understand why subscribers to this theory fussed so over Guarini's *Il pastor fido*, which did what Sidney complained of English plays' doing in mingling 'Kings and Clownes'. The breaking of decorum, in this case, has to do with social as well as with aesthetic premises.

It seems to me that even though the chief concept of mimesis may often have acted as a constraint upon literary innovation in the Renaissance, another version of imitation, simply the imitation of formal models, was in spite of its inbuilt conservatism a factor for literary change and imaginative experiment. Further, though I insist that there were concepts of kind which *did* govern imitation in both senses, there were many more kinds than were recognized in official literary philosophy; and it is by these competing notions of kind that the richness and variety of Renaissance letters were assured.

By looking at Renaissance notions of genre and generic system, I hope to convey also some of the social importance of generic systems for writers as members of a profession, a profession which changed over time but maintained a consensus of values which – however different specific opinions were at different times and in different places – offered a ready code of communication both among professionals and to their audiences. That generic concepts may be indispensable to literature in general E.D. Hirsch's interesting book more than suggests; E.H. Gombrich's theory of perception based on received and receivable schemata has implications far wider than the field of visual arts. Although I think and hope that these theorists are right, my own attempt remains narrower – simply to try to define some of the ways in which the idea of genre governed (– a vile phrase) and contributed to (– an OK phrase) writers and writing in one of the great outbursts of literary growth and change.

Although it seems obvious that a genre-system offers a set of interpretations, of 'frames' or 'fixes' on the world, and that some Renaissance genre-critics tried to fix those fixes hard, it was not entirely obvious in the Renaissance what the genres of literature surely were, nor yet how to identify them. From Aristotle onward, we keep hearing what 'poetry', or imaginative literature, *isn't*: for Aristotle it wasn't oratory, or history, or philosophy; for most Renaissance critics it wasn't medieval poetry and therefore wasn't Dante; for Ronsard and the Pléiade in sixteenth-century France it wasn't Rabelais' *Gargantua et Pantagruel*; for Sidney, often generous in his categories, it wasn't plays which 'be neither right Tragedies nor right Comedies; mingling Kings and Clownes' – a dictum which, taken seriously, would remove *Henry IV* and *King Lear* from critical attention. Nor was meter always enough to insure that a work was 'poetry', even though many ancient genres were designated simply by their metrical arrangements – elegiacs, iambics, sapphics, alcaics, etc. Aristotle removed Empedocles from the canon, metrics and all, because philosophy did not involve *mimesis*, imaginative imitation, of reality, but describes truth, whereas history simply describes 'fact'. A modern Aristotelian, Julius Caesar Scaliger, let Empedocles back into the canon, together with other philosophical poets, and generalized the doctrine of mimesis to include in the epic category Heliodorus' prose *Ethiopian History*. Aristotle's stress on the categories of *poetry*, as distinct from other verbal conventions or systems, was Horace's stress also: from a mingling of these great texts grew the major tenets of Renaissance literary criticism. But neither these systems nor their components were identical – which meant that confusion underlay all Renaissance genre theory, even the simplest.

Certainly critics could find evidence for the idea of genre in ancient texts wherever they looked, evidence which could be systematized and generalized in various ways. There were the *genera dicendi*, divisions into high and middle and low styles; there were metrical genres, which gave rise to many Renaissance theoretical experiments in vernacular quantitative verse; there were genres based on the rendering of a poem – sung or spoken, accompanied or unaccompanied by what instrument; genres based on speaker or 'voice' – the poet's own or his characters'. Virgil's dominance in medieval and later theory accounted for one application of the *genera dicendi* to his kinds in ascending order – low style-pastoral, middle-georgic, high-epic – which may in part explain to us why there is so very much pastoral poetry in the period, the kind with which poets officially 'began', and beyond which many never passed. By Aristotle's law, though, georgics were not poetry at all, since they were descriptive rather than mimetic: the middle style must be reassigned. Tragedy-high style, comedy-middle, satire-low was one way of doing it – but then, where do the lyric genres go? Some, dithyramb or ode, seem higher in style than the pastoral lyric – or, to put it another way, odes seem more like heroic poetry and therefore candidates for a higher style than lyrics of love or banqueting.

In spite of the fact that Aristotle gave so good a model for literary definition that his editor Robortello could, simply by extrapolation, produce an Aristotelian definition for comedy matching the original definition for tragedy; in spite of the fact that Guarini could defend his uncanonical pastoral tragicomedy on impeccably Aristotelian lines against his Aristotelian enemies; in spite of the fact that the *Poetics* stated firmly what was poetry and what wasn't, offering reasons in each case; in spite of the fact that in that document an hierarchy of literary forms was set up, Aristotle was nonetheless far from an absolute or even a consistent guide to ancient genre practice. Two kinds of institutions favor category and order, even in literature: schools, in one of which Aristotle was a distinguished teacher, and libraries. From the great library at Alexandria we can find traces of generic system – a familiar Dewey-decimal model, really, designed to store books and therefore to store knowledge. A poet, Callimachus, was charged with preparing the catalogue of the library (in the lost *Pinakes*). From the fragmentary references to this huge work and from Callimachus's own poetry, arranged categorically in Heroics, Hymns, Iambics, Epigrams, etc., we can read something of how that system worked: literary works were organized by groups, sometimes thematic (as in the category *Comic Poets*, of which the poet Lycophron was later keeper), sometimes metrical, sometimes topical; within a given group, works were organized by author when known, then generically; within genres they were alphabetically aligned. Apparently this sort of organization (most obviously reflected in the manuscripts of the Greek Anthology of epigrams recovered in the Renaissance) was understood and taken for granted by Horace and other Roman writers, engaged in imitating not only reality but (even more important) the literary forms in which their Greek models had imitated reality – hence Horace's relative clarity about generic forms in his *Ars poetica*.

We can understand these practical ways of keeping writing straight, since our own libraries are based on much the same principles, and there is considerable evidence elsewhere of both generic categorization and generic ranking. In the *Ion,* it is taken for granted that poetry comes in kinds, and in the *Republic* also. We find generic histories – Aristotle's of tragedy, Cicero's and Tacitus's short histories of oratory. Velleius Paterculus discussed the growth and decline of all the arts, in particular literature, and drew the parallel between the flowerings of fifth-century Athens and his native Rome. Cicero divided poetry into tragic, comic, epic, melic, and dithyrambic in the *De optimo genere oratorum,* where his famous regulation against mixing styles occurs: 'in the kinds, each to his own tone and voice, which the educated recognize'. Organization of this sort naturally encouraged the idea of competition, of overgoing – Cicero awarded prizes to particular poets for epic, tragic, and comic poetry; so did Horace, though to different winners. The potato race, the sack race, the three-legged race, are competitions of like ritual kind, but in the low style. Horace tells of his own development in a genre – first he wrote in Greek, then in his own Latin in imitation of Lucilius, beside whose satires, he says, his own are mere trifles. Still, his 'trifles' draw fire: he tells us that some critics found his satires 'nerveless', others that they exceeded the bounds set by the norm ('ultra legem tendere opus'). 'Set by the norm' – there were, then, understood norms, with bounds, as we might also gather from Cicero's phrase about decorum in style, a decorum 'known to the educated'. The fact that the *concept* of generic form was taken for granted is more important than any definition of a specific generic norm could ever be, I think: Propertius seems to be speaking in thoroughly known categories when he tells us that he left the 'buskin' of Aeschylus for his own 'poems turned on a smaller lathe' – that is, his love-elegies. We can find in Pliny comments on the genre of comedy, and Statius wrote about funeral themes and their forms. Ovid showed how his naughty subject, love, had invaded other genres (epic, tragic, comedy, etc.) and compared his verse, particularly the *Ars amatoria,* favorably with the *capricci* written on gambling, ball-games, swimming, cosmetics, and feasts – themes taken up in the Latin verse of the Renaissance and often very amusingly developed.

As is the case with anything taken for granted, tantalizingly little is explained of the literary system. We can tell, though, that imitation of Greek models was de rigueur for Roman poets, and that there were *kinds* of poetry to imitate. From Propertius's remark and from Callimachus's categories, we suspect, too, that the *size* of a poem was important in generic definition. Moreover, the thematic stress of generic comment hinted sufficiently to Renaissance writers that cultural transfer was achieved by generic means; that Roman authors had so proceeded to domesticate Greek values, and that they might accomplish the same task in the same way.

To read the moving letters of Petrarch, obsessed with domesticating ancient literature in his own period and milieu, is to recognize how powerful was his conviction that *kind* offered the way to re-educate his generation. The correspondence between Boccaccio and Petrarch on literary themes conveys an eerie sense of their conviction of control over 'everything' – they knew which texts were important, they trusted their diligent art to accommodate those crucial elements of ancient culture to their own world. Merely glancing down a list of their works, we can see how they accomplished this transfer in generic terms. Petrarch was romantic, or mythic, about it, writing his *Africa* in Latin, his Provençal love-lyrics in the vernacular – writing his *Africa*, indeed, mostly in Italy, his *Canzoniere* partly in Provence. His Scipio, symbol for the epic world, for Roman grandeur, and for the fusion of earthly and heavenly experience, was more than an epic hero for him, rather a hero transferring across time and space antique *numen* to Petrarch and by Petrarch's means to his own age. Geography counted: Boccaccio drew the Sicilian Muse from Sicily to that other Sicily, Naples, and thence to Florence in his *Ninfale Fiesolano*; Petrarch worked to endow his Helicon, the Sorgue, and his Tempe, the Vaucluse, with the numen of poetic significance. King Hugo of Cyprus, King Robert of Sicily, were invoked by these poets as imperial patrons had been, as imperial patrons to be: Petrarch arranged for his laureateship on the Capitoline, the archaeologically proper place for such crowning: he made himself into his myth.

But they were businesslike too: following what they believed to be Virgil's prescriptive model in the Eclogues, Petrarch and Boccaccio provided the Eclogues of their Carmina buc(c)olica with hidden meanings, which they scrupulously revealed to their correspondents. In prose forms and poetic – in discourse, dialogue, biography, geography, epistle, as well as comedy, pastoral narrative, eclogues, triumphs, verse epistles, etc. – these two men labored to present new models for good literature to Europe as a whole and Florentines in particular, always in generic form. Petrarch was fussy about genre: not just any old 'kind' pleased him; it had to be classical. Late in life, he wrote to thank Boccaccio for the gift of the *Decameron*, but dismissed it as an early work of Boccaccio's youth, before he had seen the light: the *Decameron* was written for an audience of ladies, on trivial topics – so much for Boccaccio's generic distinction in the preface to the *Decameron*, 'cento novelle, ò favole, ò parabole, ò historie'. It was Boccaccio's later work, the missionary work for antiquity, that Petrarch honored, urging his friend to even greater efforts on behalf of humanism.

Petrarch insisted that the forms be restored in their purity, and inveighed against the habit of florilegia, of anthologizing piecemeal, which robbed readers, he felt, of any sense of a work of literature as a made thing, as, literally, a poem. We may note, too, that these two, at the beginning, were blissfully unaware that certain ancient forms might not be fully poetic – the dialogue, the discourse, the epistle: good humanists *avant la lettre*, they took the forms they found and imitated them. So the work, *mutatis mutandis*, was done everywhere: Du Bellay runs through the acceptable kinds in his *Deffense*, Ronsard in his *Abrégé de l'art poétique française* and in the introductions to his various volumes of verse. In the Pléiade poets' work we can read the care with which they categorized their poetry and produced proper poetic models for France. Sometimes they are exact and scholarly – so the effort in epigram and ode; sometimes they exploit the metaphorical thematics of a kind – *Gaietez, les Soupirs, les Regrets* are the titles of sonnet collections; Du Bellay honored Petrarch in calling his love-sonnets *Olive*. Ronsard's *Franciade*, Camoens's *Os Lusiadas* follow the Virgilian pattern in recording cultural transfer from one civilization to its successor; even as Virgil made Aeneas come from Troy to Latium, so Francion and Lusus came from Troy to France and Portugal. Lusus's descendant, Vasco da Gama, sailed out epically to transfer Portuguese culture in his turn. Geography mattered culturally, as it did for Petrarch, who mooned about Mantua thinking programmatically of Virgil. Ronsard's origins in the Vendôme, Du Bellay's in Anjou were constantly stressed in their poetry and by their readers; whose woods these are we know when Ronsard laments the felling in the Gâtine. It is Naples and its countryside which Sannazaro pastoralizes in his *Arcadia* – and from the notion of Naples, too, perhaps, he made his shepherds into fishermen. In Virgil's honor a writer of eclogues whose name was Spagnuoli called himself Mantuanus. Spenser mythicizes the Thames in the *Prothalamion*, the Irish landscape in the *Epithalamion*, Michael Drayton makes a geographical myth of his whole island in the historical-geographical-epical *Polyolbion*. Johannes Secundus's title, 'Basia', makes generic metaphor of Catullus's wonderful word. Ronsard's *Bocages*, Jonson's *Timber* and *Underwoods* adapt the already metaphorical *Sylvae*, or mixed matter and mixed forms, of Statius, Poliziano, and others.

The idea of genre governed in another area too: the work of the great *librarii*, the booksellers, was no less organized by kind than the Alexandrian library had been. From the editions of Aldus Manutius and his sons, Henri Estienne and his sons, we see how automatically they organized by kind. Estienne's generic publications are particularly helpful for students of literature, then and now: in his huge collection of the Greek heroic poets, he included Bion, Moschus, and Theocritus, although he soon removed them along with a covering essay on Virgil's eclogues which brought the genre from Greece to Rome, to a book called *Bucolica*. In one extra-Aristotelian commentary, *Poesis Philosophica*, Estienne collected fragments of Empedocles, Parmenides, Pythagoras, Musaeus, and others, together with the letters of Heraclitus and Democritus: genre is governed by subject here, in a volume important for several subsequent Renaissance efforts to write philosophy in verse. As he had with his eclogue collection, Estienne extended the category of philosophical poetry to include Lucretius. After publishing Aulus Gellius's *Attic Nights*, Estienne published his notes to that text as *Parisian Nights*, joking about the scholarly vigils he devoted to Aulus Gellius. The point is, these notes sketch an essay on kind: Estienne stressed the likeness in form – or better, in non-form – between the compendia of Aulus Gellius and Macrobius, and lamented that he had not managed to publish them together in one book (which would have been immense, of course). That is, his concern to put like works together extended beyond officially poetic forms to grant a principle of kind to all and any writing, an attitude characteristic of humanists who refused to allow some literary works to be considered more literary than others. Further, we can recognize in Estienne's notion a scholarly desire not yet entirely extinct: he wanted to put into a student's hands, within two covers, 'all' the material on any given subject.

I caught on to this first – much later than I should have – when looking up material on horticulture as part of an effort to understand the background of allusion in Marvell's little poem 'The Garden'; and found Cato, Varro, Columella, the ancient authorities on agriculture, reliably printed together for my convenience in volumes usually called *De re rustica.* Gradually I found Virgil's *Georgics* joining the first triad, occasionally also Poliziano's poem on gardens and Palladio's text on the proper organization of country estates. Looking up books on military theory, in order to write one clause in the third lecture of this series, I found ancient authorities together in volumes called *De re militaria*, and not only learnt about Sir Thomas Browne, my *point de départ*, but also understood a good deal more about Fluellen, that country gentleman whose hobby was the discipline of ancient warfare, in which boys were not needlessly killed. In my long preoccupation with the subliterary form of rhetorical paradox, I became accustomed to finding the same authorities invoked in the apologetic prefaces to new paradoxes, but found as well various combinations of these same authorities dished up categorically in volumes designed for delectation and imitation. It made my work easier – as it did Robert Burton's, who owned a book in which Erasmus's *Praise of Folly*, together with his defense of it to Martinus Dorp, was bound up with Seneca's, Calcagnini's, and Synesius's paradoxes against received opinion, all ready to hand for the *Anatomy of Melancholy*.

We may take it, then, that literary invention – both 'finding' and 'making' – in the Renaissance was largely generic, and that transfer of ancient values was largely in generic terms, accomplished by generic instruments and helps. So the work was done elsewhere – in Lyons with the early printers, in Paris with the Pléiade, even in England by the Sidney circle and more independent souls. Very late in the Renaissance, at the beginning of the seventeenth century, Pieter Cornelisz Hooft determined to bring the vernacular literature of his young country, the hardly-United Netherlands, into the modern world. To do so he set to work, civic humanist that he was, by translating great works, notably Tacitus's history, which he then made the formal and moral model for his own *History of the Netherlands*. He produced formal tragedies and a Plautine comedy, a romantic Ariostan tragedy, and an interlude on the Judgment of Paris: the range, then, of dramatic forms. If we add to this his *Joyeuse Entrée* for the young Mary Stuart, come to marry William II, we reach into the area of triumphal pageant-drama of medieval celebration, brought up to date by the decorations of classical triumphs. Hooft wrote in most of the modern lyric forms, too: songs, sonnets, emblems, verse epistles à la Ovid, eclogues, epigrams, epithalamia, anniversaries, elegies, genethliaca, odes, entertainments for public persons, celebrations of public events. What Hooft left undone (with one significant exception) his younger contemporary Constantijn Huygens scrupulously did. Huygens wrote a fine topographical poem in praise of his native town, The Hague; a long satire; and a pastoral lament which managed to incorporate public policy and a complex self-analytical dialogue between the now-silent shepherd and the poet himself. In addition, Huygens translated parts of Guarini's *Pastor Fido*; he wrote a highly successful farce in Antwerp dialect; and he provided the first character-poems in Europe. He worked in large forms, which he made very discursive; he contributed a great deal of autobiography to his poetry, writing a long poem on his tiny countryhouse, Hofwyck – a long paeon to his public enterprise in constructing a paved road between the fishing village Scheveningen and The Hague. His family poem managed to make compatible domestic economy (with prayers for family and servants) and cosmology; late in his life, he constructed a Latin verse-autobiography. With all this, he wrote epithalamia, genethliaca, elegies, epitaphs, epicedia, and epigrams by the hundred. He translated some of Donne's, Marino's, and Théophile's poems into Dutch; he wrote devotional poems of varying lengths, as well as important devotional sonnets; at the very end of his life, he wrote a physicotheological poem on the comet of 1680–81, in which he readjusted the Ptolemaic cosmology he had presented as true 50 years before, to make plain that he now dwelt in a new universe with his gifted son, the astronomer and physicist Christiaen Huygens.

We may note the absence of epic in the Dutch list: there is no unfinished *Franciade* or *Faerie Queene* here: there is, too, a reason for that lack, I think. Like Boccaccio and Petrarch, Hooft and Huygens turned their native literature around, forced it to take its place on the European continent as a respectable, sophisticated vernacular. But they did this 300 years after Petrarch began his ambitious project in the same line; in one generation, Hooft and Huygens traversed the accomplishment of those 300 years, so that not only were the forms and kinds introduced to Holland, but so also were the styles, developing over time, of those forms and kinds. By many scholars, Huygens is classed as a 'baroque' poet (whatever that may be) – not as 'Renaissance' at all. In his work much is telescoped: where Petrarch had insisted on the purity of each genre, unmixed with another, and Hooft had largely kept to that program, Huygens offers us *genera mista* in almost every case – self-conscious, carefully worked mixtures, which counterpoint against one another the separate genres Petrarch was trying to re-establish. 'If severed they be good, the conjunction cannot be hurtfull', Huygens learnt from Sidney.

I turn now to mixed genre as a mode of *thought* as well as of poetry, and to that same Cicero who was so firm in separating generic styles from one another. In Cicero's *De Oratore*, the orator Crassus laments the decay of the arts from that golden time in which Hippias of Elis could boast 'that there was nothing in any art at all that he did not know, that not only did he know all the arts of a liberal education – geometry, music, letters, and poetry, as well as the teachings of natural science, ethics, and politics, but indeed he had made with his own hands the ring he had on, the cloak he was clad in, the boots he wore'.

'There are', Crassus went on, 'other losses to the arts, by being split up into several parts. Do you imagine that in the time of Hippocrates of Cos, there were some doctors who specialized in medicine, others in surgery, still others in diseases of the eye? Or that geometry for Euclid or Archimedes, or music for Damon or Aristoxenus, or letters for Aristophanes or Callimachus were so separate that no one could comprehend the *genus universum* – culture as a whole, the total kind – but rather that everyone chose a different slice of a subject for his specialty?' It is this *genus universum*, culture as a whole, to which Sidney refers in his great topical paean to poetry as fundamental to all culture, any civilization; and, indeed, this is why the library at Alexandria was called Museion, because it housed *all* the muses, not just the literary ones. In a book published in 1541, Mario Equicola organized learning in nine categories, each governed by one of the muses; the cosmos, the topics of study and of poetry, the *coelicoli* were all related to one muse or another, and for each category there was also an assigned literary kind.

In his *Defence*, again and again Sidney reiterates, always in generic lists, his belief that the *paideia* is born *as* poetry and borne *by* poetry – Musaeus created dithyramb and prophecy, Homer heroic matter, Hesiod theogony and agriculture, Orpheus and Linus hymns and prophetic poetry, Amphion architecture, Thales, Empedocles and Parmenides philosophy, Pythagoras and Phocylides ethics, Solon politics, Plato philosophy and dramatic dialogue, Herodotus history ('entituled by the name of the nine Muses'): these are the heroes of civilization and of poetry, gigantic *inventores* and recorders of the kinds of knowledge and of art. Their efforts taken together make up the *genus universum*; along with Antonio Minturno, Scaliger, William Webbe and a host of others, Sidney presents the whole *paideia* as poetic topics.

And so thought many humanist literary theorists opposed to the limiting tendency of Renaissance Aristotelian-Horatians, who carefully defined the genres and wrote out of the poetic canon much of the matter given above in Sidney's list. Minturno insisted that philosophy and poetry *were* in fact poetic: Empedocles, Lucretius, Lucan were poets, and so were writers on various arts – Hesiod and Virgil on agriculture; Horace, Vida, Fracastoro on poetry. After listing the different literary kinds, Minturno proceeded to show how they were and could be mixed: epic, for instance, has parts that are elegiac, epigrammatic, hymnic; Petrarch's *Trionfi* are clearly heroic, if not epic; and bucolics, he thought, fronted on epic (he cited Boccaccio's *Ameto* and Sannazaro's *Arcadia*). His own *Amor innamorato*, a mixture of prose with poetry, treats of heroic love. A host of inclusionist critics could be grouped with Minturno and Sidney – Francesco Patrizi (like E.D. Hirsch) argued that every poem on any subject had its poetic kind; and that 'misti poemi' were valuable precisely because they combined various 'sets' on the world into a larger collective vision. Joannes Antonius Viperano suggested that it was always possible to make a new genre, as one could see from the many extant works which mixed the kinds. He noted (*pace* Thomas Rosenmeyer) that bucolics had become very mixed in subject matter and in form, and that the epic had always been so; Giovanni Pietro Capriano, Equicola, Benedetto Varchi, Speroni, Guarini and his allies variously defended a large number of genres – which they considered necessary instruments of interpreting reality, to render all there is, in heaven and on earth. Varchi also argued for adapting to literary kinds the categories of the other arts, music and painting in particular.

Though he contributed to the literature of *paragone*, of competition among the arts (see Aristotle's protracted argument about epic and tragic poetry), as well as the many Renaissance *paragoni* among the visual arts (a theme borrowed from antiquity), Varchi's chief interest lay not in the rivalries among art-forms and disciplines but in their contributions to one another. In one musician's borrowing from the literary genre-system as he understood it, I hope to show how solid and reliable this very indefinable system could be. Claudio Monteverdi, inheritor of a highly developed union of music and poetry in the dominant madrigal-form, recognized the stylistic changes in the lyric between Petrarch's time and Marino's sufficiently to exploit their possibilities for his madrigal art: most of his innovative work was done on texts by writers *he* considered to have been innovators in poetry, as he was an innovator in music. He chose Tasso, Guarini, and Marino as poets whose texts could lead him into more complex musical creations. When he turned later to texts by Petrarch and Bembo, set *ad infinitum* in the generation of madrigalists just preceding his own, Monteverdi deliberately tried to recognize their archaism in a stylistic 'progression' within the madrigal genre, and to overgo the achievements of earlier madrigalists who had set these same texts. He went farther, using Ovidian literary forms and rhetorical techniques to translate his *lamenti* into music – Arianna's for Baccho, Orfeo's for Euridice, the Virgin's for her dead Son. In his new form, *Tirsi e Clori*, Monteverdi consciously set himself to the pathos of pastoral rendering, moving into a new genre of music; he repeated the operations, higher on the stylistic scale, in his musical version of what amounts to a short epic, the episode from *Gerusalemme Liberata* of Tancredi's duel with Clorinda. By his accomplishment, we can recognize in the literary genre-system a sufficiently secure scheme for the invention – the finding – of a musical equivalent. From his understanding of the separate musical and literary kinds, too, we can the better understand how Monteverdi mixed the literary and musical kinds in what is *the* mixed genre in the arts, the opera.

From the clear and frank mixture of genres in the opera, we may appropriately look back upon the fountainhead of Western literature, to Homer once more. In a Plutarchian tradition, Renaissance theorists found 'all' in Homer – not only had he written an epic (the *Iliad*) which gave rise to the tragic genre, but also he had written an epic from which comedy sprang, in the *Odyssey*; from comedy to romance was but a short step. Even Aristotle recognized several 'kinds' in Homer's work, and derived comedy from the mock-epic *Margites* attributed to Homer in antiquity. Throughout the Renaissance, the kinds were fathered or grandfathered on Homer – satire (Scaliger), hymns (Minturno), orations (everyone), epigrams, as well as the history and philosophy banned by Aristotle from the canon. It is easy to sympathize with the anti-Aristotelian Patrizi's remark that, by

Aristotelian standards, only one half of the *Iliad* might be considered poetry. In other words, Homer *was* the *paideia*, the model for education; and the way to education, even with only Homer as a textbook, was by kind. Taken thematically, or as disciplines within the *paideia*, the poetic kinds had existed as long as civilization had: indeed, poets were the *inventores* of civilization. Sidney listed the vatic bards whose poems both formed and contained civilization: that the list was rattled off by Minturno, Equicola, Scaliger, William Webbe and many others only demonstrates the strength of that topical notion, and makes even plainer why Milton wanted to write a poem 'doctrinal to the nation'. If one wishes to be economical about the kinds, then they may all be seen as latent within the work of another mythic founder of a tradition, Homer. No wonder the epic seemed so mixed a form in the Renaissance – and, also, no wonder there were such battles over Dante, Ariosto, and Tasso! No wonder, too, that mock-epics began to make fun of such totality, and a comic prose-epic to criticize the criticism as well.

Within the idea of a genre-system, then, various notions of genre competed for attention and imitation – Sidney's *Defence* lists the kinds by substance as well as by form. In the *artes poeticae* of the late sixteenth and early seventeenth centuries, we often find a list of possible forms, with their distinctions drawn in terms of topic or content. [. . .] By this kind of definition, form implies context and, indeed, context implies a particular form. 'I sing' implies 'the wrath of Achilles', 'of Arms and the Man who', or 'Of Mans first Disobedience, and . . .', just as the reed pipe, the syrinx, *la sampogna*, implies the pastoral 'set'. The important thing about these generic phrases, taken as it were from the grammar of epic in this case, is that they imply each other; we can reverse the business too: 'Arma virumque' implies 'cano', and we must await Milton's 'I sing' at the end of the long, complicated clause with which *Paradise Lost* begins. Such reliance takes a genre-system for granted, as *donnée*: from genre so interpreted Monteverdi borrowed. Within its securities, Robert Herrick, supremely a poet of the little in subject and form, can write his variations:

> I sing of Brooks, of Blossomes, Birds, and Bowers:
> Of April, May, of June and July-flowers.
> I sing of May-poles, Hock-carts, Wassails, Wakes,
> Of Bride-grooms, Brides, and of their Bridall-cakes.
> I write of Youth, of Love, and have Accesse
> By these, to sing of cleanly-Wantonnesse.
> I sing of Dewes, of Raines, and piece by piece,
> Of Balme, of Oyle, of Spice, and Amber-Greece.

I sing of Times trans-shifting; and I write
How Roses first came Red, and Lillies White.
I write of Groves, of Twilights, and I sing
The Court of Mab, and of the Fairie-King.
I write of Hell; I sing (and ever shall)
Of Heaven, and hope to have it after all.

Nothing could less satisfactorily fulfill the epic 'I sing'; the brooks, blossoms, birds, bowers are the pastoral so radiant in Herrick's book *Hesperides*. The May-poles and Hock-carts refer to celebrations in the rhythm of a georgic year; brides and bridegrooms appear in pro- and epithalamia; dews and rains in philosophical or scientific poetry; times trans-shifting in allegorical, historical, or metamorphic poetry; and 'How Roses first came Red, and Lillies White' points not only to specific poems in the *Hesperides* but also to Herrick's distinguished exercise in diminution, reducing Ovidian metamorphic topics to epigram size. Groves are the numinous *loci* of supernatural presence; 'the Court of Mab, and of the Fairie-King' (Oberon) diminishes Spenser's epic story to thumbnail scale. With 'I write of Hell; I sing (and ever shall) Of Heaven', we return to the epic promise of the first words, now translated into sacred story – and realise that Herrick *has* in fact given all that he promised in the secular *Hesperides* (that mixed garden) and in the sacred *Noble Numbers*. By choosing the epigram as his major poetic form, Herrick has reduced the pretensions of genres 'large' in scope or theme or size – has mocked them, treated them as metaphors, even as he exploits their official topics. So with his invocation 'To His Muse': this 'Mad maiden' isn't invited to descend to the poet, rather she is urged to sit still, to stop running away from the poet (now decently countrified) to the wicked and seductive city whence he has come. He encourages her to sit still 'In poore and private Cottages', where her 'meaner Minstrelsie', called an intermixture of 'Eclogues and Beucolicks', will be appreciated for what it is and not subjected to the destructive comments of urban critics. That is, Herrick's pastoral muse is conceived as yearning for her generic and dialectic opposite, the city, even as the poet, discontented occasionally in Devon, has settled for Devon and its natural beauty.

Without a genre-system to play against, all this falls flat. Herrick relies upon a literary system readers can take for granted, works with professional commonplaces in a professionally common place, occupied by readers as well as writers who understand what is expected of them. Without awareness of the decorum supplied by a system of genres something like what Ronsard and North rattled off, such poetry as this makes almost no sense, and Herrick seems the poet of trivia so many have taken him for. With an awareness of the games played with his own poetic traditions, he can seem a considerable craftsman at the very least, and a considerable innovator at the very best. There are many other examples of similar reliance on the system which in fact subvert the system. Giambattista Marino showed his skill in various ways – in the short epic *La Strage de gli Innocenti*; in a long Ovidian poem, *L'Adone*; in lyric forms named for their proper instrument, *La Lira* and *La Sampogna*. But he wrote another book, unlike most books I know, called *La Galeria*. The subdivisions of this book are named for the topics of the poems – *Pittura, Scultura*. Within these broad terms there are more precise ones – ritratti, portraits of popes, princes, cardinals, captains, heroes, tyrants, pirates, magicians and heretics, Greek, Latin, and modern poets, beautiful women good and bad, as well as burlesque portraits (interestingly enough, of burlesque or mocking poets, Folengo and Pulci); historical paintings (really mythological, in our terminology); narrative paintings, chiefly of biblical subjects; and finally *capricci* (on an ant, a glowworm, a mosquito). The statues were also divided into categories – reliefs, medals, and again capricci, or grotesque topics. By this ecphrastic book, Marino raises the whole question of generic division; he divides and subdivides, affecting to suit style to subject – but in fact all these elaborately categorized poems are simply epigrams, written from the low style to the highest. Not only that, all these subjects are *normal* epideictic topics: we do not need the pictures and statues (some of them imaginary, others actual works of art) for such poems. Marino is playing a joke, pretending to categorical arrangement for which he had no real need. By asserting unnecessary categorical determinations, Marino makes us think back to recognize afresh that the arts have different semiotic systems, and that they are, as individual disciplines, important for that very difference. He is making fun of the doctrine *ut pictura poesis*, and catches us unaware by breaking down an apparent difference from art to art while keeping firmly to his own medium.

Taking the critic and theorist Julius Caesar Scaliger as a test-case for a moment, I want to discuss some of the ways in which a genre-system can maintain and also subvert its own rules. Scaliger's *Poetices libri septem* is generically organized. Sometimes he writes within one genre-system – metrics, for instance – but his chief interest in the genres was topical or thematic. Hence, though in one sense he is a good Renaissance Aristotelian critic, in other ways he was an unregenerate independent: for example, he allowed imaginative prose to be literature and refused to deny philosophy a place in poetics. Close definer that he was of the decorums of different genres, he also argued for works mixed in kind. Scaliger may have been one authority for Sidney's argument for *genera mista*:

Now in his parts, kindes, or Species (as you list to terme them),
It is to be noted that some Poesies have coupled together two or
three kindes, as Tragicall and Comicall, whereupon is risen the
Tragicomicall. Some in the like manner have mingled Prose and
Verse, as Sanazzar and Boetius. Some have mingled matters
Heroicall and Pastoral [Sidney himself, in his *Arcadia*]. But that
commeth all to one in this question, for if severed they be good,
the conjunction cannot be hurtfull.

Without losing sight of the specific requirements for generic division,
Scaliger at the same time defends the propositions that everything
utterable has its genre, and that a complex, large, inclusive utterance
may require mixture of the kinds. That is, I think Scaliger recognizes
the principle of invariancy, which assures a given genre its subject
and style, and in some cases shape also, as well as the inclusiveness
dictated by belief in the *paideia*; within his genre-system, he allows
for counter-genericism too. Not in the least discounting the importance
of formal arrangements, Scaliger nonetheless stresses subject matter
as the definer of kind, a stress which leads inevitably to the generic
thematics recognized by Monteverdi's adaptation to another art of
the literary genre-system. It leads as well out of genre to *mode*, where
thematics and style often predominate over form and forms.

Another way of saying all this is that Scaliger followed through
the implications of his *comparative* criticism. He took for granted the
periodization of literature, as well as the historical transfers of culture
effected by literary means; he recognized the rivalry as well as the
imitation of Greek writings by Romans, of ancient writings by moderns.
Not for nothing did he make his endless 'comparationes' of Virgil with
his Greek counterparts, Ennius with his, Ovid and Horace with theirs;
not for nothing, in a section called 'Hypercritica', did he compare
modern writers with the ancients. Recognizing generic distinctions –
that is to say, interpreting and criticizing texts categorically – Scaliger
allows himself to be a critic, to make judgments on the texts he
discussed. By multiplying his systematic examinations, he could
consider all the available writings of the three civilizations *as a
whole*, a universal kind, called 'literature'. That is, he can handle
literature synchronically or diachronically – and could have done
neither without a very strong sense of history, of alteration and
modification over time.

By ending this section on the generic inclusionism which we do
not always expect genre theory to permit, but which turns up constantly
in Renaissance genre commentary, I allow my own interests and
sympathies to show. I would like to present genre theory as a means
of accounting for connections between topic and treatment within the

literary system, but also to see the connection of the literary kinds with *kinds* of knowledge and experience; to present the kinds as a major part of that *genus universum* which is part of all literary students' heritage. The kinds honor aspects and elements of culture and in their conjunctions help make up culture as a whole. In the liminal poem to Herrick's *Hesperides* cited earlier, 'I sing of Brooks, etc.', we can see the Homeric *hubris* at work, as into those tiny forms which make up his book Herrick wrote in as many different kinds as Homer in his mighty epic. Conscious of his place in a poetic heritage and a poetic profession, Herrick demonstrated his poet's aims: aesthetically, to vary his work; professionally, to master his craft and to surprise us with that mastery; humanly, to render the variety, the *sylva* or mixed matter of experience. And all this not in a book called *Sylvae* or *Forrest* or *Underwoods*, but in a book whose title holds another kind of richness, more delicate, more cultivated, more various – *Hesperides*, the garden of the gods, of love, of generation, of reward.

Herrick's view of genre seems to me a good paradigm for my own: patterns, kinds, mental sets organize for us the lives we individually lead, much as these kinds, sets, patterns organized the vast body of literature. Experience can be seen as searching for its own form, after all: the kinds may act as myth or metaphor for a man's new vision of literary truth.

10 Magical Narratives: On the Dialectical Use of Genre Criticism*

Fredric Jameson

Of the many distinguished critics in the Marxist tradition who have practised what can loosely be called the sociology of genres, none has investigated more carefully the theoretical issues involved than the American critic Fredric Jameson. Acknowledging that, despite the resistance to genre theory which is part of 'the ideology of modernism', genre criticism 'has always maintained a privileged relationship with historical materialism', Jameson sets out in this essay to define the terms on which a properly 'dialectical' version of that criticism might be based: that is, one which would interpret literary genres in light of the historical conditions that sustain them, while simultaneously reflecting on the historicity of the act of interpretation itself. His starting point, however, is not the modern masters of dialectical thought (Adorno, Benjamin, Bloch, Lukács, and others) who were the subject of his earlier book *Marxism and Form* (1971), but two specifically literary theorists who between them represent what Jameson saw in 1975 as the dominant trends in modern genre criticism, Northrop Frye (cf. Chapter 6) and Vladimir Propp (cf. Chapter 3). Both of these marginalise historical considerations, Frye in the name of a universal grammar of the human imagination, Propp in pursuance of a synchronic methodology derived from structural linguistics. The purpose of Jameson's 'metacommentary' (his term) is not simply to expose the theoretical confusions and blindspots that result from this suspension of history, but also – in the best dialectical manner – to reappropriate the insights of what he calls the 'semantic' and 'structural' approaches within a genuinely historical theory of genre. The choice of romance as a test case for this new theoretical

* Reprinted from Fredric Jameson, *The Political Unconscious: Narrative as a Socially Symbolic Act* (1981; rpt. London: Routledge, 1989), pp. 107–31, 145–50. An earlier version of the essay was published as 'Magical Narratives: Romance as Genre' in *New Literary History*, 7:1 (1975), 135–63.

167

model is not arbitrary, since romance is both, as Frye had argued, 'the source and paradigm of all story-telling', embracing 'high' and 'low' narrative forms, and the genre that displays most forcibly the utopian impulses that, along with other factors, make literature part of 'the political unconscious' – the larger theme of his book. For reasons of space, the opening and penultimate sections of the essay (from where some of the quotations above are taken) have been omitted.

A more extended critique of Russian Formalist and structuralist methodology can be found in Jameson's *The Prison-House of Language* (1972). Questions of genre also feature prominently in his *Marxism and Form* (1971) and, more recently, *Postmodernism, or, The Cultural Logic of Late Capitalism* (1991). For an assessment of Jameson's dialectical theory of genre, see Frow, *Marxism and Literary History* (1986), pp. 30–41. For the broader context of sociological genre theory, see Alan Swingewood, *Sociological Poetics and Aesthetic Theory* (Basingstoke: Macmillan, 1986); and Tony Bennett's lucid critique of this tradition in *Outside Literature* (1990), pp. 78–114. Much recent work on romance, including popular forms, is indebted to Jameson: see, for instance, *The Progress of Romance: The Politics of Popular Fiction*, ed. Jean Radford (London: Routledge & Kegan Paul, 1986); and Laurie Langbauer, *Women and Romance: The Consolations of Gender in the English Novel* (Ithaca: Cornell University Press, 1990).

When we look at the practice of contemporary genre criticism, we find two seemingly incompatible tendencies at work, which we will term the *semantic* and the *syntactic* or structural, respectively, and which can conveniently be illustrated by traditional theories of comedy. For a first group, the object of study is less the individual comic text than some ultimate comic vision of which the texts of Molière, Aristophanes, Joyce, and Rabelais offer so many embodiments. Accounts of such a vision, to be sure, seem to oscillate between the repressive and the liberatory; thus for Bergson comedy has the function of preserving social norms by castigating deviancy with ridicule, while for Emil Staiger the comic serves to make the fundamental absurdity of human existence tolerable. Such approaches, whatever their content, aim to describe the essence or meaning of a given genre by way of the reconstruction of an imaginary entity – the 'spirit' of comedy or tragedy, the melodramatic or epic 'world view', the pastoral 'sensibility' or the satiric 'vision' – which is something like the generalized existential experience behind the individual texts. In what follows we will take Frye's work as the richest idiosyncratic elaboration of such an approach, for which genre is essentially apprehended as a *mode*.

The second, syntactic, approach to genre, which condemns the semantic option as intuitive and impressionistic, proposes rather to analyze the mechanisms and structure of a genre such as comedy, and to determine its laws and its limits. Analyses of this kind, which range from the lost chapters of Aristotle's *Poetics* to Freud's joke book, aim less at discovering the meaning of the generic mechanism or process than at constructing its model. The two approaches are thus no mere inversions of each other, but are fundamentally incommensurable, as may be judged from the fact that each projects a quite distinct dialectical opposite or negation. For the semantic or phenomenological approach, the contrary in terms of which comedy will be defined always proves to be another mode: tragedy, say, or irony. For structural analyses, the 'opposite' of comedy will simply be the noncomic or the unfunny, the joke that falls flat or the farce that remains a dead letter. Our basic text for this second approach to the generic problem will be Vladimir Propp's *Morphology of the Folk Tale*, where genre is apprehended in terms of a series of determinate functions, or what we will call a structure or a *fixed form*.

It will have become evident that these two approaches correspond to what [in the first chapter of *The Political Unconscious*] has been described as the rivalry between old-fashioned 'interpretation', which still asks the text what it *means*, and the newer kinds of analysis which, according to Deleuze, ask how it *works*. Yet similar methodological hesitations and alternations in stylistics and in the history of linguistics suggest that we can now locate the source of such antinomies in the very nature of language, which, uniquely ambiguous, both subject and object all at once, or in Humboldt's terms, both *energeia* and *ergon*, intentional meaning and articulated system, necessarily projects two distinct and discontinuous dimensions (or 'objects of study') which can never be conceptually unified.[1] We assume that the objective source of these twin projections, language, is somehow a unified phenomenon. Unfortunately, as the burden of Wittgenstein's later work teaches, any attempt prematurely to think it as such – in the form of Language – always reifies it. Thus, our meditation on language must henceforth take the mediatory path of the separate specialized disciplines which each of these perspectives on language has generated: logic and linguistics, semantics and grammar, phenomenology and semiotics.

This situation apparently condemns genre theory to a methodological double standard, an unavoidable shifting of gears between two irreconcilable options. At best, it would seem, we can make a virtue of necessity, and turn the problem into a relatively sterile hypothesis about the dual nature of genre; the latter would then be defined as that literary discourse which may be examined either in terms of a fixed form or in terms of a mode, but which *must* be susceptible of study from both these perspectives optionally.

In reality, however, this disappointing hypothesis marks a first step forward on the project of this chapter, which is, by rethinking both these interpretive methods dialectically, to historicize their findings, so as, thereby, not merely to gain some sense of the ideological significance and historical destiny of romance as a genre, but, beyond that, to get some feeling for the dialectical use of generic literary history as such.

Dialectical thinking can be characterized as historical reflexivity, that is, as the study of an object (here the romance texts) which also involves the study of the concepts and categories (themselves historical) that we necessarily bring to the object. In the present case these categories have already been described as the semantic and structural approaches. But how do you go about 'historicizing' such mental categories or conceptual operations? A first step in this direction has been taken when you come to understand that they are not the result of purely philosophic choices or options in the void, but are objectively determined: and this is what has happened when we come to understand that the apparently philosophical alternative between the two 'methods' was in reality the projection of objective antinomies in language.

Now we need to make a further step, which we can call the de-positivizing of these two positions. Every universalizing approach, whether the phenomenological or the semiotic, will from the dialectical point of view be found to conceal its own contradictions and repress its own historicity by strategically framing its perspective so as to omit the negative, absence, contradiction, repression, the *non-dit*, or the *impensé*. To restore the latter requires that abrupt and paradoxical dialectical restructuration of the basic problematic which has often seemed to be the most characteristic gesture and style of dialectical method in general, keeping the terms but standing the problem on its head. So we will show in what follows that Frye's entire discussion of romance turns on a presupposition – the ethical axis of good and evil – which needs to be historically problematized in its turn, and which will prove to be an ideologeme that articulates a social and historical contradiction. An interrogation of Propp's method will, meanwhile, disclose that it is contradictory in its own terms, and fails to come to grips with the basic underlying problem of the *subject*, which it assumes as nonproblematical and as a given from the outset. The dialectical critique of these methods is, however, not a merely negative and destructive one; it leads, as we shall see, to their fulfillment and completion, albeit in a very different spirit from the one they initially propose.

Frye's theory of romance, as has been suggested, is the fullest account of this genre as a mode. Romance is for Frye a wish-fulfillment or Utopian fantasy which aims at the transfiguration of the world of everyday life in such a way as to restore the conditions of some lost Eden, or to anticipate a future realm from which the old mortality and imperfections will have been effaced. Romance, therefore, does not involve the substitution of some more ideal realm for ordinary reality (as in mystical experience, or as might be suggested by the partial segments of the romance paradigm to be found in the idyll or the pastoral), but rather a process of *transforming* ordinary reality: 'the quest-romance is the search of the libido or desiring self for a fulfillment that will deliver it from the anxieties of reality *but will still contain that reality*'.[2]

Frye's initial emphasis on the transformation of ordinary reality already implies a corollary: if it is possible for the lineaments of the earthly paradise to emerge from ordinary life, then the latter must already have been conceived, not as some humdrum place of secular contingency and 'normal' existence, but rather as the end product of curse and enchantment, black magic, baleful spells, and ritual desolation. Romance is thus at once staged as the struggle between higher and lower realms, between heaven and hell, or the angelic and the demonic or diabolic:

> The hero of romance is analogous to the mythical Messiah or deliverer who comes from an upper world, and his enemy is analogous to the demonic powers of a lower world. The conflict however takes place in, or at any rate primarily concerns, *our* world, which is in the middle, and which is characterized by the cyclical movements of nature. Hence the opposite poles of the cycles of nature are assimilated to the opposition of the hero and his enemy. The enemy is associated with winter, darkness, confusion, sterility, moribund life, and old age, and the hero with spring, dawn, order, fertility, vigor, and youth.[3]

This description rewrites the form in terms of three distinct operative elements: its 'world', its twin protagonists (hero and villain), and its semic organization (high and low, angelic and demonic, white and black magic, winter and spring), each of which demands comment.

Frye's assimilation of the 'world' of romance to nature in its traditional acceptation conceals an interesting problem, which phenomenological accounts of this concept may help to dramatize. For phenomenology, the technical term *world* designates the ultimate frame or *Gestalt*, the overall organizational category or ultimate perceptual horizon, within which empirical, inner-worldly objects and phenomena are perceived and inner-worldly experience takes place; but in that case, 'world', in its phenomenological sense, cannot normally be an object of perception in its own right.[4] This view is indeed confirmed by conventional narrative realism, where events take place within the infinite space of sheer Cartesian extension, of the quantification of the market system: a space which like that of film extends indefinitely beyond any particular momentary 'still' or setting or larger vista or panorama, and is incapable of symbolic unification.

A first specification of romance would then be achieved if we could account for the way in which, in contrast to realism, its inner-worldly objects such as landscape or village, forest or mansion – mere temporary stopping places on the lumbering coach or express train itinerary of realistic representation – are somehow transformed into folds in space, into discontinuous pockets of homogeneous time and of heightened symbolic closure, such that they become tangible analoga or perceptual vehicles for *world* in its larger phenomenological sense. Heidegger's account goes on to supply the key to this enigma, and we may borrow his cumbersome formula to suggest that romance is precisely that form in which the *worldness* of *world* reveals or manifests itself, in which, in other words, *world* in the technical sense of the transcendental horizon of our experience becomes visible in an inner-worldly sense. Frye is therefore not wrong to evoke the intimate connection between romance as a mode and the 'natural' imagery of the earthly paradise or the waste land, of the bower of bliss or the enchanted wood. What is misleading is the implication that this 'nature' is in any sense itself a 'natural' rather than a very peculiar and specialised social and historical phenomenon.

The centrality of *worldness* in romance will now lead us to question the primacy Frye attributes to traditional categories of character – in particular, the role of the hero and the villain – in romance. We suggest, on the contrary, that the strangely active and pulsating vitality of the 'world' of romance, much like Stanislaw Lem's sentient ocean in *Solaris*, tends to absorb many of the act- and event-producing functions normally reserved for narrative 'characters'; to use Kenneth Burke's dramatistic terminology, we might say that in romance the category of Scene tends to capture and to appropriate the attributes of Agency and Act, making the 'hero' over into something like a registering apparatus for transformed states of being, sudden alterations of temperature, mysterious heightenings, local intensities, sudden drops in quality, and alarming effluvia, in short, the whole semic range of transformation scenes whereby, in romance, higher and lower worlds struggle to overcome each other.

It will be objected that Frye's description is predicated on his notion of the displacement of romance from some primary register in religious myth all the way to its degraded versions in the irony of a fallen world. We will have more to say about this concept of 'displacement' later. Even at present, however, we may suggest that Frye has here projected the later categories of religion – the ideology of centralized and hieratic power societies – back onto myth, which is rather the discourse of decentered, magic-oriented, tribal social formations. Any 'first-hand' contact with the original mythic narratives themselves (and for many readers, Lévi-Strauss's four-volume *Mythologiques* will have served as a vast introductory manual of these unfamiliar and unsettling strings of episodes, so utterly unlike what our childhood versions of Greek myth led us to expect) suggests that later notions of 'character' are quite inappropriate to the actants of these decentered and preindividual narratives.

Even the traditional heroes of Western art-romance, from Yvain and Parzival to Fabrice del Dongo and the Pierrot of Queneau, or the 'grand Meaulnes' of Alain-Fournier and the Oedipa Maas of Pynchon's *Crying of Lot 49*, far from striking us as emissaries of some 'upper world', show a naivete and bewilderment that marks them rather as mortal spectators surprised by supernatural conflict, into which they are unwittingly drawn, reaping the rewards of cosmic victory without ever having quite been aware of what was at stake in the first place. In a later study, indeed, Frye himself insists on the essential marginality of the most characteristic protagonists of romance, slaves or women, who, by their necessary recourse to fraud and guile rather than to sheer physical power, are more closely related to the Trickster than to the Solar Hero.[5]

If now we ask how such passive-contemplative *actants* can be conceived as functional units of a narrative system, it is clearly the peculiar semic organization of romance which mediates between character-positions and that more fundamental and narratively 'meaningful' entity which is worldness itself. Frye's works provide an immense table of the content of the basic semes of romance, of which it is sufficient for our present purposes to observe that they are all arrayed in binary opposition to one another. A dialectical study of this genre (and of Frye's reading of it) ought then logically to impose a historical re-examination of the binary opposition itself, as a form without content which nonetheless ultimately confers signification on the various types of content (geographical, sexual, seasonal, social, perceptual, familial, zoological, physiological, and so on) which it organizes. Such re-examination is in fact under way everywhere in post-structuralism today; we will mention only the influential version of Jacques Derrida, whose entire work may be read, from this point of view, as the unmasking and demystification of a host of unconscious or naturalized binary oppositions in contemporary and traditional thought, the best known of which are those which oppose speech and writing, presence and absence, norm and deviation, center and periphery, experience and supplementarity, and male and female. Derrida has shown how all these axes function to ratify the centrality of a dominant term by means of the marginalization of an excluded or inessential one, a process that he characterizes as a persistence of 'metaphysical' thinking.[6] On the face of it, however, it seems paradoxical to describe the ideologies of the decentered and serialized society of consumer capitalism as metaphysical survivals, except to underscore the ultimate origin of the binary opposition in the older 'centered' master code of theocentric power societies. To move from Derrida to Nietzsche is to glimpse the possibility of a rather different interpretation of the binary opposition, according to which its positive and negative terms are ultimately assimilated by the mind as a distinction between good and evil. Not metaphysics but ethics is the informing ideology of the binary opposition; and we have forgotten the thrust of Nietzsche's thought and lost everything scandalous and virulent about it if we cannot understand how it is ethics itself that is the ideological vehicle and the legitimation of concrete structures of power and domination.

Yet surely, in the shrinking world of the present day, with its gradual leveling of class and national and racial differences, and its imminent abolition of Nature (as some ultimate term of Otherness or difference), it ought to be less difficult to understand to what degree the concept of good and evil is a positional one that coincides with categories of Otherness. Evil thus, as Nietzsche taught us, continues to characterize whatever is radically different from me, whatever by virtue of precisely that difference seems to constitute a real and urgent threat to my own existence. So from the earliest times, the stranger from another tribe, the 'barbarian' who speaks an incomprehensible language and follows 'outlandish' customs, but also the woman, whose biological difference stimulates fantasies of castration and devoration, or in our own time, the avenger of accumulated resentments from some oppressed class or race, or else that alien being, Jew or Communist, behind whose apparently human features a malignant and preternatural intelligence is thought to lurk: these are some of the archetypal figures of the Other, about whom the essential point to be made is not so much that he is feared because he is evil; rather he is evil *because* he is Other, alien, different, strange, unclean, and unfamiliar.

The question of some immanent, nonconceptual ideological function of romance as a 'pure' narrative is thereby again raised with a vengeance. Meanwhile, our problematization of Frye's use of these oppositions has allowed us to complete his analysis in an unexpected and instructive way. We will therefore abstract the following working hypothesis: that the modal approach to genre must be pursued, until, by means of radical historicization, the 'essence', 'spirit', 'world-view', in question is revealed to be an ideologeme, that is, a historically determinate conceptual or semic complex which can project itself variously in the form of a 'value system' or 'philosophical concept', or in the form of a protonarrative, a private or collective narrative fantasy.

But we cannot leave this particular ideologeme – ethics, or the binary opposition between good and evil – without a word on the ringing and programmatic 'solution' ('beyond good and evil!') in which Nietzsche's diagnosis is cast. This goal, utterly to discredit and to transcend the ethical binary, remains intact even if we find unsatisfactory the visions through which Nietzsche tried to articulate it: the energy mutation of the *Übermensch* on the one hand, or the private and intolerable ethos of the eternal return on the other. In our present context, we may observe that this transcendence of ethics is in fact realized by other generic modes, which thereby in their very form rebuke the ideological core of the romance paradigm. The ethical opposition is, for instance, wholly absent from tragedy, whose fundamental staging of the triumph of an inhuman destiny or fate generates a perspective which radically transcends the purely individual categories of good and evil. This proposition may be demonstrated by our feeling, when, in something that looks like a tragedy, we encounter judgments of a more properly ethical type (re-emergence of 'heroes' and 'villains'), that the text in question is rather to be considered a melodrama, that is, a degraded form of romance. Neither Creon nor Iago can be read as villains without dispersing the tragic force of the plays; yet our irresistible temptation to do so tells us much about the hold of ethical categories on our mental habits. As for comedy, we will see shortly that its categories are also quite distinct from those of romance, and more resolutely social: the classical conflict in comedy is not between good and evil, but between youth and age, its Oedipal resolution aiming not at the restoration of a fallen world, but at the regeneration of the social order.

Tragedy and comedy are thus already in a special sense 'beyond good and evil'. As for conceptual thought, if we grasp the problem as one of escaping from the purely individualizing categories of ethics, of transcending the categories into which our existence as individual subjects necessarily locks us and opening up the radically distinct transindividual perspectives of collective life or historical process, then the conclusion seems unavoidable that we already have the ideal of a thinking able to go beyond good and evil, namely the dialectic itself. This is not to say that the inventors-discoverers of the dialectic were themselves completely successful in avoiding the entanglement of ethical categories. Hegel's designation of the ultimate horizon of historical and collective understanding as 'Absolute Spirit' still fatally projects the afterimage of the individual consciousness of the philosopher-sage; and the classical aporia of the Marxist vision of revolutionary change – objective social law or voluntarist and Leninist praxis – suggests that those locked into it have been unable fully to realize a vision of history in which the voluntarist actions of individuals and individual groups are themselves grasped as objective forces in history. Moreover, Marx and Engels' attempt, in the *Manifesto*, to formulate their vision of 'historical inevitability' by way of a mechanical alternation of older ethical categories (the bourgeoisie as both progressive and dehumanizing, both a necessary and a humanly intolerable stage in social development[7]) sufficiently conveys the hold of the older ethical categories and their language. Yet these historical texts are not the last word on the dialectic itself, but merely prodigious anticipations of the thought mode of a social formation of the future, which has not yet come into being.

A final step, however, needs to be taken if our presentation of the ideologeme is to have any completeness. To leave it at this point would, indeed, paradoxically reopen it to all the idealizing habits we wish to avoid, and in particular would suggest a perspective – the 'ethical binary' is 'wrong', that is to say, evil – in which the ideological closure in question would end up drawing the entire analysis back into itself. This paradox can be avoided only if we can grasp the ideologeme itself as a form of social praxis, that is, as a symbolic resolution to a concrete historical situation. What, on the level of the ideologeme, remains a conceptual *antinomy*, must now be grasped, on the level of the social and historical subtext, as a *contradiction*.

Nietzsche's analysis, which unmasks the concept of ethics as the sedimented or fossilized trace of the concrete praxis of situations of domination, gives us a significant methodological precedent. He demonstrated, indeed, that what is really meant by 'the good' is simply my own position as an unassailable power center, in terms of which the position of the Other, or of the weak, is repudiated and marginalized in practices which are then ultimately themselves formalized in the concept of evil. The Christian reversal of this situation, the revolt of the weak and the slaves against the strong, and the 'production' of the secretly castrating ideals of charity, resignation, and abnegation, are, according to the Nietzschean theory of *ressentiment*, no less locked into the initial power relationship than the aristocratic system of which they are the inversion. But Nietzsche's rewriting of ethics in terms of a concrete situation, suggestive as it is for the more fully developed theory of *sedimentation* we will present shortly, is evidently a mythic one, which has the weakness of taking the ethical code as a mere replication of its concrete subtext.

It would seem possible to perform this operation in a different way, by grasping the ideologeme, not as a mere reflex or reduplication of its situational context, but as the imaginary resolution of the objective contradictions to which it thus constitutes an active response. It is clear, for instance, that the positional notion of good and evil so central to romance narrative is not unique to this form alone, but also characterizes the *chanson de geste* from which romance emerged, as well as popular forms such as the American Western with which both have so much in common.[8] Such kinships suggest that this positional thinking has an intimate relationship to those historical periods sometimes designated as the 'time of troubles', in which central authority disappears and marauding bands of robbers and brigands range geographical immensities with impunity: this is certainly true of the late Carolingian period, when a population terrorized by barbarian incursions increasingly withdrew into the shelter of local fortresses.

When, in the twelfth century, this kind of social and spatial isolation was overcome, and the feudal nobility became conscious of itself as a universal class or 'subject of history', newly endowed with a codified ideology,[9] there must arise what can only be called a contradiction between the older positional notion of good and evil, perpetuated by the *chanson de geste*, and this emergent class solidarity. Romance in its original strong form may then be understood as an imaginary 'solution' to this real contradiction, a symbolic answer to the perplexing question of how my enemy can be thought of as being *evil* (that is, as other than myself and marked by some absolute difference), when what is responsible for his being so characterized is quite simply the *identity* of his own conduct with mine, the which – points of honor, challenges, tests of strength – he reflects as in a mirror image.

Romance 'solves' this conceptual dilemma by producing a new kind of narrative, the 'story' of something like a semic evaporation. The hostile knight, in armor, his identity unknown, exudes that insolence which marks a fundamental refusal of recognition and stamps him as the bearer of the category of evil, up to the moment when, defeated and unmasked, he asks for mercy by *telling his name*: 'Sire, Yidiers, li filz Nut, ai non' (*Erec et Enide*, 1042), at which point, reinserted into the unity of the social class, he becomes one more knight among others and loses all his sinister unfamiliarity. This moment, in which the antagonist ceases to be a villain, distinguishes the romance narrative from those of *chanson de geste* and the Western at the same time that it raises a new and productive dilemma for the future development and adaptation of this form. For now that the 'experience' or the seme of evil can no longer be permanently assigned or attached to this or that human agent, it must find itself expelled from the realm of interpersonal or inner-worldly relations in a kind of Lacanian *forclusion* and thereby be projectively reconstituted into a free-floating and disembodied element, a baleful optical illusion, in its own right: that 'realm' of sorcery and magical forces which constitutes the semic organization of the 'world' of romance and henceforth determines the provisional investment of its anthropomorphic bearers and its landscapes alike. With this development, something like a history of the form may be said already to have begun.

* * *

It is one matter to historicize Frye's interpretation of romance, and quite another to historicize Propp's 'structural' method, to which we now turn. Propp's seminal work, although explicitly limited to the Russian folk tale, has in fact generally been evoked as the paradigm of narrative as such, and of so-called quest-romance in particular, in that it allows us to reformulate or rewrite the episodes of individual romance texts as an invariable sequence of 'functions', or in other words, as a fixed form. Propp summarizes his findings as follows:

(1) Functions of characters serve as stable, constant elements in a tale, independent of how and by whom they are fulfilled.
(2) The number of functions known to the fairy tale is limited.
(3) The sequence of functions is always identical.
(4) All fairy tales are of one type in regard to their structure.[10]

This final proposition in particular, suggesting a circular movement whereby the analyst studies his corpus of tales in order to verify their structural homology with one another – that is to say, in order to exclude what does not belong, and thus triumphantly to validate the corpus with which he began! – seems to reduce Propp's method to a classificatory operation, thereby setting a direction for our own discussion as well. We will want to see, in what follows, whether any more productive (let alone historicizing) use can be found for Propp's scheme than the purely typologizing or classificatory.

Lévi-Strauss, in his important review article,[11] has shown that Propp's model suffers from a twofold (and paradoxical) weakness. On the one hand, even on its own terms, it is insufficiently formalized: Propp's 'functions', in other words, fail to attain an adequate level of abstraction.

Yet what was powerful and attractive about the method from the outset was precisely the possibility it offered of reducing a wealth of empirical or surface narrative events to a much smaller number of abstract or 'deep-structural' moments. Such a reduction allows us not only to compare narrative texts which seem very different from one another; it also allows us to simplify a single involved narrative into redundant surface manifestations of a single recurrent function. Thus it is useful to be able to rewrite Fabrice's episodic difficulties, in the early part of *La Chartreuse de Parme* – episodes that we might otherwise be tempted to lay out in the form of a picaresque narrative – as so many versions of one of Propp's basic functions: 'the hero is tested, interrogated, attacked, etc., which prepares the way for his receiving either a magical agent or helper (first function of the donor)'.[12] Thus, a significant remark by the Duchess, on Fabrice's departure for Napoleon's armies, helps us sort out some of the essential functions of the figures he meets in his adventures: 'Speak with more respect of the sex that will make your fortune: for you will always displease men, having too much fire for prosaic souls.'[13] The distinction then allows us to extend and to deepen this process of analytic reduction until donor and villain can at last be specified: women will be the donors in this quest-romance and men the villains.

Still, from Lévi-Strauss's point of view, Propp's functions are inadequately 'reduced' or formalized because they are still formulated in storytelling categories, no matter how general these may be. When we compare Propp's account of the function that inaugurates the main sequence of the tale ('one member of a family either lacks something or desires to have something [definition: *lack*]')[14] with its equivalents in Lévi-Strauss or Greimas (disequilibrium, contract broken, disjunction), it will be clear, not only that the latter are of a quite different level of abstraction – metalinguistic rather than merely generalizing – but also that a different type of narrative analysis will follow from such a starting point. Propp's follow-up can only be a set of subsequent episodes. That of Greimas or Lévi-Strauss moves at once to the level of semes and semic interactions of a more properly synchronic or systemic type, in which narrative episodes are no longer privileged as such, but play their part along with other kinds of semic transformations, inversions, exchanges and the like. To sum up this aspect of Lévi-Strauss's critique, then, we may say that Propp's series of functions is *still too meaningful*, or, in other words, is still not sufficiently distanced methodologically from the surface logic of the storytelling text.

Paradoxically, however, the other objection to be raised about Propp's method is the opposite one, namely that his analysis is *not yet meaningful enough*. This is Lévi-Strauss's charge of 'empiricism', which strikes at the discovery that constitutes the heart of Propp's book, namely the fixed and irreversible sequence of a limited number of functions. From Lévi-Strauss's standpoint, the observation that the sequence in the fairy tale is 'thus and not otherwise', even if true, confronts us with something as final and enigmatic, and as ultimately 'meaningless', as the constants of modern science, for example pi or the velocity of light. If we juxtapose Propp's narratological DNA with Lévi-Strauss's own reading of the Oedipus legend[15] in which functions are reshuffled like a deck of cards and laid out in suits which henceforth entertain purely logical or semic relations with one another – it becomes clear that what is ultimately irreducible in Propp's analysis is simply narrative diachrony itself, the movement of storytelling in time. To characterize this movement in terms of 'irreversibility' is then to produce not a solution, but rather the problem itself.

From the later, methodologically far more self-conscious points of view of Lévi-Strauss and Greimas, who insist on a radical distinction between the narrative surface (or manifestation) and some underlying deep narrative structure, the irreducible diachrony of Propp's version of the deep structure of the fairy tale is simply the shadow thrown by the surface manifestation upon his narrative model. The two objections are thus essentially the same: both the insufficient formalization of the model (its anthropomorphic traces) and the irreversibility it attributes to its functions are different aspects of the same basic error, namely to have rewritten the primary narratives *in terms of another narrative*, rather than in terms of a synchronic system. Paradoxically, in this Propp rejoins Frye, whose 'method' also amounts to the rewriting of a body of varied texts in the form of a single master narrative.

But Propp's model and the developments to which it has led, particularly in Greimassian semiotics, impose rather different questions from those we have raised about Frye. In particular, we will want to ask whether the ideal of formalization, projected by, yet imperfectly realized in, Propp's model, is ultimately realizable. We have already characterized Propp's findings as 'anthropomorphic'. It now remains to be seen whether a narrative system is conceivable from which the anthropomorphic or the traces of surface representation or narrative 'manifestation' have been completely eliminated. Both Propp and Greimas distinguish between narrative 'functions' and narrative characters, or between narrative unities and *actants*:[16] but it is clear that the former, as sheer event, present no real problems for some ultimate formalization, since events can always in one way or another be rewritten in terms of semic categories. I believe, therefore, that the ultimate blind spot or aporia of such *narrative analysis* is rather to be found in the problem of the character, or in even more basic terms, in its incapacity to make a place for the subject.

Yet this is already a paradoxical reproach: it will be objected that, on the contrary, the aim of the work of Propp and Greimas – and their signal achievement – has been precisely to displace the emphasis that an older, more representational narrative theory put on character. To insist on seeing characters in terms of those more basic unities which are narrative functions, or, in the case of Greimas, to propose the new concept of the *actant* for the structural 'operators' of underlying semic transformations, would seem to mark a real advance toward the deanthropomorphization of the study of narrative. Unfortunately, the relationship between function and *actant* necessarily works both ways; and if the latter is thereby displaced and made structurally subordinate to the former, the fact remains that, perhaps even more irrevocably than in less self-conscious interpretations of narrative such as Frye's, the concept of the narrative function is shackled to some ultimately irreducible nucleus of anthropomorphic representation – call it *actant*, structural role, character-effect, or whatever you like – which then fatally retransforms narrative function into so many acts or deeds of a human figure. The anthropomorphic figure, however, necessarily resists and is irreducible to the formalization that was always the ideal of such analysis.

We need to take seriously the more naive objection to such 'scientific' ideals: namely that stories are always about people and that it is perverse, even for purposes of analysis, to seek to eliminate the very anthropomorphism that uniquely characterizes narrative as such. But here the work of Lévi-Strauss has a useful lesson for us; the *Mythologiques* are unique in the way in which they achieve two things apparently incompatible from the point of view of this objection. For at the same time that this corpus of narrative analysis restores to us, as few other works have, an immense body of narratives which enlarge our reading habits and reconfirm the status of storytelling as the supreme function of the human mind, *Mythologiques* also performs the tour de force of eliminating precisely those working concepts of *actant* and of narrative diachrony which we have held to be the strategic weaknesses of Propp's model.

The key to this paradoxical achievement is, I think, to be found in the social origins of the narrative material with which Lévi-Strauss deals. These are evidently preindividualistic narratives; that is, they emerge from a social world in which the psychological subject has not yet been constituted as such, and therefore in which later categories of the subject, such as the 'character', are not relevant. Hence the bewildering fluidity of these narrative strings, in which human characters are ceaselessly transformed into animals or objects and back again; in which nothing like narrative 'point of view', let alone 'identification' or 'empathy' with this or that protagonist, emerges; in which not even the position of an individual storyteller or 'sender' (*destinataire*) can be conceptualized without contradiction.

But if the emergence of narrative characters requires such social and historical preconditions, then the dilemmas of Propp and Greimas are themselves less methodological than historical ones; they result from projecting later categories of the individual subject back anachronistically onto narrative forms which precede the subject's emergence when they do not unreflexively admit into the logic of their narrative analyses precisely those ideological categories that it was the secret purpose of later texts (for example, nineteenth-century novels) to produce and to project. This is to say that a dialectical critique of the categories of semiotic and narrative method must historicize these categories by relating what are apparently purely methodological issues and dilemmas to the whole current philosophical critique of the subject, as it emerges from Lacan, Freud, and Nietzsche, and is developed in post-structuralism. These philosophical texts, with their attacks on humanism (Althusser), their celebration of the 'end of Man' (Foucault), their ideas of *dissémination* or *dérive* (Derrida, Lyotard), their valorisation of schizophrenic writing and schizophrenic experience (Deleuze), may in the present context be taken as symptoms of or testimony to a modification of the experience of the subject in consumer or late monopoly capitalism: an experience which is evidently able to accommodate a far greater sense of psychic dispersal, fragmentation, drops in 'niveau', fantasy and projective dimensions, hallucinogenic sensations, and temporal discontinuities than the Victorians, say, were willing to acknowledge. From a Marxist point of view, this experience of the decentering of the subject and the theories, essentially psychoanalytic, that have been devised to map it are to be seen as the signs of the dissolution of an essentially bourgeois ideology of the subject and of psychic unity or identity (what used to be called bourgeois 'individualism'); but we may admit the descriptive value of the post-structuralist critique of the 'subject' without necessarily endorsing the schizophrenic ideal it has tended to project. For Marxism, indeed, only the emergence of a post-individualistic social world, only the reinvention of the collective and the associative, can concretely achieve the 'decentering' of the individual subject called for by such diagnoses; only a new and original form of collective social life can overcome the isolation and monadic autonomy of the older bourgeois subjects in such a way that individual consciousness can be lived – and not merely theorized – as an 'effect of structure' (Lacan).

How this historical perspective can be dialectically related to the problems of narrative analysis in such a way as to produce a more reflexive view of the operation of 'characters' in a narrative structure we will try to show in the next chapter [of *The Political Unconscious*]. For the moment, we must return to Greimas in order to underscore a certain gap between his narrative theory, as we have criticized it here, and his concrete practice of narrative analysis. We may now reformulate our earlier diagnosis of the semiotic ideal of formalization in the more practical terms of our objection to classificatory operations. From this point of view, what is problematical about Propp's character-functions (hero, donor, villain) or Greimas's more formalised *actants* emerges when it turns out that we are merely being asked to drop the various elements of the surface narrative into these various prepared slots. Thus, returning to Stendhal's narratives, we find that the functional or actantial reduction seems to involve little more than 'deciding' that this novelist's secondary male figures – l'Abbé Pirard, l'Abbé Blanès, Mosca, the Marquis de la Mole – as so many spiritual fathers of the protagonists of Stendhal's novels, are all to be classed as so many manifestations of the donor.

Yet this method celebrates its true triumphs, and proves to be a methodological improvement over Propp, precisely in those moments in which Greimas is able to show a disjunction between the narrative surface and the underlying actantial mechanisms. Actantial reduction is indeed particularly revealing in those instances in which the surface unity of 'character' can be analytically dissolved, by showing, as Greimas does in certain of his readings, that a single character in reality conceals the operation of two distinct *actants*.[17] This x-ray process could obviously also work in the other direction; thus, our scattered remarks about Stendhal, above, suggest that in his narratives, the function of the donor finds manifestation in two distinct groups of characters, the supportive or maternal women figures and the spiritual fathers. Such surface or narrative reduplication will evidently not be without important consequences for the ultimate shape of the narrative as a whole. What we can at once suggest is that both the Propp model and Greimas's more complex narrative system become productive at the moment when the narrative text in one way or another *deviates* from its basic schema; far less so in those instances where, the narrative proving to be its simple replication, the analyst is reduced to noting the conformity of the manifest text to the underlying theoretical schema.

I have in another place maintained that the originality and usefulness of Propp's model from an interpretive standpoint lay in his conception of the donor, which I argued to be the central mechanism of his reading of fairy tales.[18] It is now time to re-examine this proposition from our present perspective, according to which the value of such narrative models lies in their capacity to register a given text's specific deviation from them, and thereby to raise the more dialectical and historical issue of this determinate formal difference. We can better appreciate the usefulness of actantial reduction, if we reflect, for instance, on the 'character' of Heathcliff in *Wuthering Heights*, a figure whose ambiguous nature (romantic hero or tyrannical villain?) has remained an enigma for intuitive or impressionizing, essentially 'representational', criticism, which can only seek to resolve the ambiguity in some way (for example, Heathcliff as 'Byronic' hero). In terms of actantial reduction, however, the text would necessarily be read or rewritten, not as the story of 'individuals', nor even as the chronicle of generations and their destinies, but rather as an impersonal process, a semic transformation centering on the house, which moves from Lockwood's initial impressions of the Heights, and the archaic story of origins behind it, to that final ecstatic glimpse through the window, where, as in the final scene of Cocteau's *Orphée*, 'le décor monte au ciel' and a new and idyllic family takes shape in the love of Hareton and the second Cathy. But if this is the central narrative line of the work, or what Greimas would call its principal *isotopie*, then Heathcliff can no longer be considered the hero or the protagonist in any sense of the word. He is rather, from the very beginning – the abrupt introduction into the family of the orphan child, 'as dark almost as if it came from the devil' – something like a mediator or a catalyst, designed to restore the fortunes and to rejuvenate the anemic temperament of the two families. What is this to say but that 'Heathcliff' occupies in some complicated way the place of the donor in this narrative system: a donor who must wear the functional appearance of the protagonist in order to perform his quite different actantial function. The resolution of the narrative in fact undermines one's earlier impression that Heathcliff, by his passion for the first Cathy and his matrimonial alliance with the Lintons, was to be read as the protagonist of the romance. This misreading, deliberately projected by the text, serves in fact to disguise his twofold mission as donor, to restore money to the family and to reinvent a new idea of passion, which will serve as the model – in the sense of a Girardian triangular mediation – for the later and conclusive passion.

Hence the complex semic confusion between good and evil, love and money, the role of the 'jeune premier' and that of the patriarchal villain, which mark this 'character' who is in reality a mechanism for mediating these semes. Such a view at once leads us away from the narrative model of which a conventional semiotic reading of Heathcliff would simply provide a validation, and toward a historical inquiry into the reasons for this complex and unique deviation from it. What we have said earlier about such oppositions now allows us to sketch out the historical ground on which such a deviation could be understood as a meaningful symbolic act.

What has been called Byronic about Heathcliff could indeed with as much justice be termed Nietzschean: this peculiar character or actantial locus exasperates just that system of ethical judgments which are as unavoidable for the reader as they are unsatisfactory and nonfunctional. But this is because Heathcliff is the locus of *history* in this romance: his mysterious fortune marks him as a protocapitalist, in some other place, absent from the narrative, which then recodes the new economic energies as sexual passion. The aging of Heathcliff then constitutes the narrative mechanism whereby the alien dynamism of capitalism is reconciled with the immemorial (and cyclical) time of the agricultural life of a country squiredom; and the salvational and wish-fulfilling Utopian conclusion is bought at the price of transforming such an alien dynamism into a benign force which, eclipsing itself, permits the vision of some revitalization of the ever more marginalized countryside. To see 'Heathcliff' as a historical modification of the function of the donor thus allows us to glimpse the ideologeme – the conceptual antinomy but also the social contradiction – which generates the narrative, but which it is the latter's mission to 'resolve'.

Such a dialectical reappropriation of the semiotic model suggests that some more general sense of the historic adaptation of classical romance to nineteenth-century conditions – which include the new social content of nascent capitalism as well as its new forms, in particular the realistic novel – might be gained by further investigation of the role of the donor in these works. What we have said about Stendhal, in particular, leads to an unexpected view of the Utopian love-death which concludes *Le Rouge et le noir*: for Julien's discovery of his authentic self, his rediscovery of his 'true' love for Mme de Renal, must now clearly be seen as a fundamental modification in the actantial role of the latter, who has been transformed from the donor into the object of the protagonist's quest.

This transformation suggests that Stendhal's narrative must be seen as something more complex than a mere appropriation or replication of that romance structure whose analysis gave us the preliminary instruments to read it or rewrite it in such terms. Indeed, it is as though the semiotic equipment, whose use was predicated on the assumption that Stendhal's novel is simply another manifestation of Propp's narrative structure, now completes its work by discrediting itself and betraying its own typologising limits. The dialectical moment is upon us when, having first read Stendhal as an embodiment of the romance structure, we then find ourselves forced into the realization that what is historically specific about Stendhal's novel is precisely its deviation from that underlying structure which was the starting point of the analysis. Yet we would not have been able to

185

detect this feature of the work – in which its historicity becomes accessible to us for the first time – had we not begun by respecting the working convention of first-level semiotics, namely that the text was at the start to be analyzed and laid out *as though* it were the mere replication of Propp's narrative line or 'deep structure'.

We may now, therefore, see *Le Rouge et le noir* less as an example than as a kind of immanent critique of romance in its restructuration of the form. As we observed in a somewhat different way in *Wuthering Heights*, the complex transformation and foregrounding of the original 'function' of the donor amounts to something like a dialectical self-consciousness of romance itself. But whereas *Wuthering Heights* projected its 'critique' of the donor into the whole realm of instrumental history, Stendhal's dissociation of this function into the 'paternal' donor and the 'maternal' object of desire has a somewhat different emphasis, and tends to foreground the phenomenon of desire itself, thereby reflecting the emergence of a new commodity object-world in which the 'objects' of desire, necessarily degraded by their new status as commodities, tend to call the very authenticity of the quest-romance, organised around them, back into question. The later system of *La Chartreuse de Parme*, in which the figure of a more properly feminine donor, the Duchess Sanseverina, is gradually disjoined in a more explicit way from that of a more properly 'desirable' quest-object, in the person of Clélia, may then be seen as something like a second-degree recontainment of the earlier contradiction – one which, returning nostalgically to the original romance paradigm, releases that more archaic fairy tale atmosphere which is so striking in the later work.

* * *

With these twin reopenings upon history of our two approaches to genre, we are now in a better position to evaluate Frye's notion of generic history, which he describes in terms of the displacement of romance from one mimetic level or 'style' (high, low, mixed) to another. Transformations in the status of the hero ('superior in *kind* both to other men and to the environment of other men', 'superior in *degree* to other men and to his environment', 'superior in degree to other men but not to his natural environment', 'superior neither to other men nor to his environment', 'inferior in power or intelligence to ourselves'[19]) signal a modulation from some 'original' solar myth, through the levels of romance, epic and tragedy, comedy and realism, to that of the demonic and ironic, of the contemporary antihero, whence, as at the end of Vico or of the *Inferno* ('lasciò qui loco vòto/ quella ch'appar di qua, e sù ricorse') the whole storytelling system rotates on its axis and the original solar myth reappears. In this sense, *The Secular Scripture* is itself the strongest contemporary renewal of romance, and may be added into its own corpus in much the same way that Lévi-Strauss has suggested that all later interpretations of the Oedipus myth (including Freud's) be understood as variants on the basic text.

I have suggested elsewhere[20] that, despite the use of the Freudian concept of displacement, with its negative implications (repression, distortion, negation, and the like), the driving force of Frye's system is the idea of historical *identity*: his identification of mythic patterns in modern texts aims at reinforcing our sense of the affinity between the cultural present of capitalism and the distant mythical past of tribal societies, and at awakening a sense of the continuity between our psychic life and that of primitive peoples. Frye's is in this sense a 'positive' hermeneutic, which tends to filter out historical difference and the radical discontinuity of modes of production and of their cultural expressions. A negative hermeneutic, then, would on the contrary wish to use the narrative raw material shared by myth and 'historical' literatures to sharpen our sense of historical difference, and to stimulate an increasingly vivid apprehension of what happens when plot falls into history, so to speak, and enters the force fields of the modern societies.

From this point of view, then, the problem raised by the persistence of romance as a mode is that of substitutions, adaptations, and appropriations, and raises the question of what, under wholly altered historical circumstances, can have been found to replace the raw materials of magic and Otherness which medieval romance found ready to hand in its socioeconomic environment. A history of romance as a mode becomes possible, in other words, when we explore the substitute codes and raw materials, which, in the increasingly secularized and rationalized world that emerges from the collapse of feudalism, are pressed into service to replace the older magical categories of Otherness which have now become so many dead languages.

* * *

[. . .] The structural approach also knows its own specific opening onto history, which must now be described. We have already observed the play of structural norm and textual deviation which characterized such analysis at its best; but we have not yet observed that this analytical operation is not a two- but rather a three-term process, and that its greater complexity makes of structural analysis something quite different from the conventional systems of norm and deviation (as, for instance, in a host of theories of poetic language, or, in the area of the psychic, in theories of transgression). What is dialectical about this more complete structural model is that the third term is always absent, or, more properly, that it is nonrepresentable. Neither the manifest text, nor the deep structure tangibly mapped out before us in a spatial hieroglyph, the third variable in such analysis is necessarily history itself, as an absent cause.

The relationship between these three variables may be formulated as a permutational scheme or *combinatoire*, in which the systematic modification or commutation of any single term – by generating determinate variations in the other two – allows us to read the articulate relationships that make up the whole system. Thus, the deviation of the individual text from some deeper narrative structure directs our attention to those determinate changes in the historical situation which block a full manifestation or replication of the structure on the discursive level. On the other hand, the failure of a particular generic structure, such as epic, to reproduce itself not only encourages a search for those substitute textual formations that appear in its wake, but more particularly alerts us to the historical ground, now no longer existent, in which the original structure was meaningful. Finally, an a priori and experimental commutation of the historical term may stimulate our perceptions of the constitutive relationship of forms and texts to their historical preconditions by producing artificial laboratory situations in which such forms of texts are rigorously inconceivable. Thus, paradoxically, the ultimate model of such a *combinatoire* recalls the form of Hegel's reflections on epic ('our present-day machinery and factories together with the products they turn out . . . would . . . be out of tune with the background of life which the original epic requires')[21] save for the absence in Hegel's thought of the fundamental structural discovery, namely the twin variables of a deep structure and a manifest text.

What is paradoxical, of course, is that structural analysis should thus finally open out onto the third term of what I have elsewhere called 'the logic of content':[22] the semantic raw materials of social life and language, the constraints of determinate social contradictions, the conjunctures of social class, the historicity of structures of feeling and perception and ultimately of bodily experience, the constitution of the psyche or subject, and the dynamics and specific temporal rhythms of historicity. Where the interpretation of genre in terms of mode led us ultimately to the ideologeme, to the narrative paradigm, and to the sedimentation of various generic discourses – all essentially cultural or superstructural phenomena – structural analysis demands as its completion a kind of negative reconstruction, a postulation by implication and presupposition, of an absent or unrepresentable

infrastructural limiting system. Now ultimately perhaps we may
return to linguistics for a working projection of these discontinuities
which is more productive and less paralyzing and absolute than the
distinction between semantics and structure from which we started;
here, as so often, Hjelmslev's four-part mapping of the expression
and the content of what he sees as the twin dimensions of the form
and the substance of speech[23] is suggestive, and may be adapted to
genre theory as follows:

Form
- *expression*: the narrative structure of a genre
- *content*: the semantic 'meaning' of a generic mode

Substance
- *expression*: ideologemes, narrative paradigms
- *content*: social and historical raw material

It will be noted that each method, as it moves from the 'form' of a
text to the latter's relationship to 'substance', completes itself with the
complementary term. Thus, the semantic reading of genre ultimately
grounds itself in expressive materials, while structural analysis, through
the *combinatoire*, finds its ground in the text's 'logic of content'.

Still some final word must be added about the nature of the
relationship between text and context projected by the structural
combinatoire, if only because some readers may overhastily assimilate
this scheme to the mechanical Marxist notion of a determination of
superstructure by base (where 'determination' is read as simple
causality). In the generic model outlined here, the relationship of
the 'third term' or historical situation to the text is not construed
as causal (however that might be imagined) but rather as one of a
limiting situation; the historical moment is here understood to block
off or shut down a certain number of formal possibilities available
before, and to open up determinate new ones, which may or may
not ever be realised in artistic practice. Thus, the *combinatoire* aims
not at enumerating the 'causes' of a given text or form, but rather
at mapping out its objective, a priori conditions of possibility,
which is quite a different matter.

As for romance, it would seem that its ultimate condition of figuration,
on which the other preconditions we have already mentioned are
dependent – the category of worldness, the ideologeme of good and
evil felt as magical forces, a salvational historicity – is to be found in
a transitional moment in which two distinct modes of production, or
moments of socioeconomic development, coexist. Their antagonism is
not yet articulated in terms of the struggle of social classes, so that its

resolution can be projected in the form of a nostalgic (or less often, a Utopian) harmony. Our principal experience of such transitional moments is evidently that of an organic social order in the process of penetration and subversion, reorganization and rationalization, by nascent capitalism, yet still, for another long moment, coexisting with the latter. So Shakespearean romance (like its falling cadence in Eichendorff) opposes the phantasmagoria of 'imagination' to the bustling commercial activity at work all around it, while the great art-romances of the early nineteenth century take their variously reactive stances against the new and unglamorous social institutions emerging from the political triumph of the bourgeoisie and the setting in place of the market system. Late variants of romance like that of Alain-Fournier may be understood as symbolic reactions to the stepped-up pace of social change in the late nineteenth-century French countryside (laicization and the *loi Combes*, electrification, industrialization), while the production of Julien Gracq presupposes the regressive situation of Brittany within an otherwise 'modernized' state.

Yet the point of such correlations is not simply to establish something like Plekhanov's 'social equivalent' for a given form, but rather to restore our sense of the concrete situation in which such forms can be seized as original and meaningful protopolitical acts. This is the sense in which we have used the model of the *combinatoire* to locate marked or charged absences in Eichendorff's *Taugenichts*, and in particular the repression of comedy structure by way of the attenuation of authority figures (in this novella, indeed, authority is personified only by an older woman briefly glimpsed, the single villainous character being that secondary and grotesque Italian spy, who, galloping across the field in moonlight, 'looked like a ghost riding on a three-legged horse'). We might also have shown this text's repression of other basic functions in the romance structure as well: most notably the omission of what we have called the transformation scene, and the substitution for the basic conflict between Eichendorff's two worlds – the humdrum workaday world of the village and the enchanted space of the chateau, with its music and candelabra, its gardens and eyes twinkling through half-opened shutters – of compromise formations and mediatory combinations in which the two codes are playfully recombined (the flute-playing porter as a bourgeois with an aristocratic hobby, the old peasant with silver buckles, and so forth). On a narrative level, indeed, the two realms swap functions: that of work borrows its magic and its phantasmagorical elements from the aristocratic realm of leisure, while it proves to be in the latter that the various illusory plot complications – what in classic romance would be the force of evil and the malignant spell – originate. The resolution of the narrative thus cannot dramatise the triumph of either force over the other one, or enact any genuine ritual purification, but must produce a compromise in which everything finds its proper place again, in which the Taugenichts is reconciled through marriage to the world of work, while at the same time finding himself endowed with a miniature chateau of his own within the enchanted grounds of the aristocratic estate. It is because Eichendorff's opposition between good and evil threatens so closely to approximate the incompatibility between the older aristocratic traditions and the new middle-class life situation that the narrative must not be allowed to press on to any decisive conclusion. Its historical reality must rather be disguised and defused by the sense of moonlit revels dissolving into thin air, and conceal a perception of class realities behind the phantasmagoria of *Schein* and *Spiel*. But romance does its work well; under the spell of this wondrous text, the French Revolution proves to be an illusion, and the grisly class conflict of decades of Napoleonic world war fades into the mere stuff of bad dreams.

Notes

1. These two dimensions, and the methodological alternatives that accompany them, essentially correspond to what VOLOSHINOV/BAKHTIN calls the two tendencies or 'two trends of thought in the philosophy of language': see *Marxism and the Philosophy of Language*, trans. Ladislav Matejka and I.R. Titunik (Cambridge, Mass.: Harvard University Press, 1973), pp. 45–63.

2. NORTHROP FRYE, *Anatomy of Criticism: Four Essays* (Princeton: Princeton University Press, 1957), p. 193, italics mine. [See above, p. 106.]

3. Ibid., pp. 187–8. [See above, pp. 100–1.]

4. MARTIN HEIDEGGER, *Sein und Zeit* (Tübingen: Niemeyer, 1957), pp. 131–40.

5. NORTHROP FRYE, *The Secular Scripture: A Study of the Structure of Romance* (Cambridge, Mass.: Harvard University Press, 1976), pp. 68ff.

6. This theme is perhaps most explicitly stated in his attack on the concept of 'parasitism' in J.L. AUSTIN and JOHN SEARLE ('Limited Inc.', Supplement to *Glyph*, 2 (1977): 'You do not have to be a preacher or a pamphleteer calling for the expulsion of wicked parasites (either of language or of political life, effects of the unconscious, scapegoats, migrant workers, militants and spies) for your language to be ethico-political or – and this is really all I wanted to bring out about Austin – for your ostensibly theoretical discourse to reproduce the basic categories that ground all ethico-political statements' (p. 69)).

7. KARL MARX and FRIEDRICH ENGELS, 'Communist Manifesto', Part I (in K. MARX, *On Revolution*, ed. and trans. S.K. Padover (New York: McGraw-Hill, 1971)), esp. pp. 82–5.

8. And also that curious Brazilian 'high literary' variant of the Western which is GUIMARÃES ROSA's *Grande Sertão: Veredas* (translated as *The Devil to Pay in the Backlands* (New York: Knopf, 1963)).

9. MARC BLOCH, *Feudal Society*, trans. L.A. Manyon (Chicago: University of Chicago Press, 1961), pp. 320ff.

10. VLADIMIR PROPP, *Morphology of the Folktale*, trans. L. Scott (Austin: University of Texas Press, 1968), pp. 21–3.

11. 'La Structure et la forme', in CLAUDE LÉVI-STRAUSS, *Anthropologie structurale*, vol. 2 (Paris: Plon, 1973), 139–73 [Eng. *Structural Anthropology*, vol. 2, trans. Monique Layton (New York: Basic Books, 1976), pp. 115–45].

12. PROPP, *Morphology*: Function XII (p. 39).

13. STENDHAL, *La Chartreuse de Parme*, ch. 2 (Paris: Cluny, 1940), p. 34.

14. PROPP, *Morphology:* Function VIIIa (p. 35).

15. CLANDE LÉVI-STRAUSS, 'The Structural Study of Myth', in *Structural Anthropology* [vol. 1], trans. Claire Jacobson and Brooke Grundfest Schoepf (New York: Basic Books, 1963), pp. 213–16.

16. Greimas's conception of the *actant* is based on a distinction between narrative syntax (or 'deep structure') and that 'surface' narrative discourse in which 'actors' or recognizable 'characters' are the visible unities: *actants*, which correspond to the necessarily far more limited functions of the narrative syntagm, are generally reduced by Greimas to three groups: Sender/Receiver, Subject-Hero/Object-Value, and Auxiliary/Villain. See A.J. GREIMAS, *Sémantique structurale* (Paris: Larousse, 1966), pp. 172–91 [Eng. *Structural Semantics: An Attempt at a Method*, trans. Daniele McDowell, Ronald Schleifer and Alan Velie (Lincoln: University of Nebraska Press, 1983)]; or more recently, 'Les Actants, les acteurs, et les figures', in *Sémiotique narrative et textuelle*, ed. C. Chabrol (Paris: Larousse, 1973), pp. 161–76.

17. A.J. GREIMAS, 'La Structure des actants du récit', in *Du Sens* (Paris: Seuil, 1970), pp. 249–70 [Eng. *On Meaning: Selected Writings in Semiotic Theory*, trans. Paul J. Herron and Frank H. Collins (London: Pinter, 1987)].

18. F. JAMESON, *The Prison-House of Language: A Critical Account of Structuralism and Russian Formalism* (Princeton: Princeton University Press, 1972), pp. 65–9.

19. FRYE, *Anatomy of Criticism*, pp. 33–4.

20. F. JAMESON, 'Criticism in History', in *Weapons of Criticism: Marxism in America and the Literary Tradition*, ed. Norman Rudich (Palo Alto, Calif.: Ramparts Press, 1976), pp. 38–40.

21. 'What man requires for his external life, house and home, tent, chair, bed, sword and spear, the ship with which he crosses the ocean, the chariot which carries him into battle, boiling and roasting, slaughtering, drinking and eating – nothing of this must have become merely a dead means to an end for him; he must still feel alive in all these with his whole sense and self in order that what is in itself merely external be given a humanly inspired individual character by such close connection with the human individual' (G.W.F. HEGEL, *Aesthetik* (Frankfurt: Europäische Verlagsanstalt, 1955), vol. 2, 414, my translation).

22. In F. JAMESON, *Marxism and Form: Twentieth-Century Dialectical Theories of Literature* (Princeton: Princeton University Press, 1971), pp. 327–59.

23. LOUIS HJELMSLEV, *Prolegomena to a Theory of Language*, trans. F.J. Whitfield (Madison: University of Wisconsin Press, 1961), ch. 13.

11   The Origin of Genres*

T͟ZVETAN T͟ODOROV

Interpreter and guardian of what he once called 'the methodological heritage of (Russian) Formalism', Tzvetan Todorov, a native
Bulgarian who emigrated to Paris in 1963, is also the French
structuralist theorist who has concerned himself most consistently with questions of genre. His best-known contribution to
the subject is his early book on the Fantastic, which includes a
critique of Frye's *Anatomy of Criticism* (1957) centring on the charge
that Frye confused *historical* genres, which 'result from an observation of literary reality', with *theoretical* genres, which result
'from a deduction of a theoretical order' (*The Fantastic*, 1973,
pp. 13–14). This distinction recurs in various forms throughout
Todorov's work, and is now generally accepted by genre theorists (though see Genette, p. 214 below). In the present essay,
Todorov refines this argument, and seeks to clarify a number of
other vexed issues in genre theory, such as the relationship (al-
legedly severed in much modern literature) between individual
text and genre; the process by which new genres are formed out
of old ones; and – the topic to which most of the essay is devoted
– the similarities and differences between literary genres and
other 'speech acts'. In each case, Todorov tackles the problem by
going back to first principles, displaying the clarity of thought
and ease of expression that have made him one of the most accessible of modern literary theorists; but the essay is notable too
for its broad range of reference, both in the selection of examples
(from Joyce's *Ulysses* to African nicknames) and in its engagement with other genre theorists of the past and present. Although
unacknowledged here, his crucial theoretical source is Bakhtin,

* Reprinted from Todorov, *Genres in Discourse*, trans. Catherine Porter (Cambridge:
Cambridge University Press, 1990), pp. 13–26. First published as 'L'origine des
genres' in 1976, and reprinted with revisions in Todorov, *Les genres du discours*
(Paris, 1978).

whose concept of 'speech genres' (Chapter 5) Todorov is summarising and adjusting; and whose prospective title for an unfinished book – *The Genres of Discourse* – Todorov borrows for his own collection of essays. (The debt is amply repaid by Todorov's excellent monograph on Bakhtin: *The Dialogical Principle*, 1984.) Todorov's ideas on the genre-system and its 'constant transformations' also draw on Tynyanov (Chapter 2), some of whose essays Todorov had earlier translated into French.

Apart from the works already cited, Todorov's work on genre includes an essay on 'Literary Genres' in *Current Trends in Linguistics* (1974); *The Poetics of Prose* (1977); and the anthology he co-edited with Genette, *Théorie des genres* (1986). Critical responses to Todorov's theory include Brooke-Rose, 'Historical Genres/Theoretical Genres' (1976); Hawkes, *Structuralism and Semiotics* (1977), pp. 95–106; and Rosmarin, *The Power of Genre* (1985), pp. 32–3. For an introduction to literary applications of speech-act theory, see Sandy Petrey, *Speech Acts and Literary Theory* (1990); its particular relevance for genre theory is explored in Fishelov, *Metaphors of Genre* (1993), pp. 119–53.

To persist in paying attention to genres may seem to be a vain if not anachronistic pastime today. We all know that genres used to exist: in the good old days of classicism there were ballads, odes, sonnets, tragedies, and comedies; but do these exist today? Even the genres of the nineteenth century, poetry or novel (and these are no longer quite genres in our eyes), seem to be coming undone, at least in the literature 'that counts'. As Maurice Blanchot said of the undeniably modern Hermann Broch, 'like many other writers of our time, he has been subject to that impetuous pressure of literature that no longer recognises the distinction between genres and seeks to destroy their limits'.[1]

It is even considered a sign of authentic modernity in a writer if he ceases to respect the separation of genres. This idea, whose transformations can be traced back to the Romantic crisis of the early nineteenth century (despite the fact that the German Romantics themselves were major builders of generic systems), has found one of its most brilliant spokesmen in our day in the person of Maurice Blanchot. More forcefully than anyone else, Blanchot has said what others have not dared to think or have not known how to express: today there is no intermediate entity between the unique individual work and literature as a whole, the ultimate genre; there is none, for the evolution of modern literature consists precisely in making each work an interrogation of the very essence of literature. Let us reread a particularly eloquent passage:

The book is the only thing that matters, the book as it is, far from genres, outside of the categorical subdivisions – prose, poetry, novel, document – in which it refuses to lodge and to which it denies the power of establishing its place and determining its form. A book no longer belongs to a genre; every book stems from literature alone, as if literature held in advance, in their generality, the secrets and the formulas that alone make it possible to give to what is written the reality of a book. It would thus be as though, the genres having faded away, literature were asserting itself alone in the mysterious clarity that it propagates and that each literary creation sends back, multiplied – as if, then, there were an 'essence' of literature.[2]

And elsewhere:

The fact that literary forms, that genres, no longer have any genuine significance – that, for example, it would be absurd to ask whether *Finnegans Wake* is a prose work or not, or whether it can be called a novel – indicates the profound labor of literature which seeks to affirm itself in its essence by ruining distinctions and limits.[3]

Blanchot's statements seem to have the weight of self-evidence in their favor. A single point in his argument might give us pause: the privileging of the *here and now*. We know that every interpretation of history is based on the present moment, just as that of space starts with *here*, and that of other people with *I*. Nevertheless, when such an exceptional status – the culminating point of all history – is attributed to the *I-here-now*, one may wonder whether the egocentric illusion does not have something to do with it. (This delusion turns out to be a counterpart of what Paulhan called the 'explorer's illusion'.)

Moreover, in the very texts where Blanchot announces the disappearance of genres we find categories at work whose resemblance to generic distinctions is hard to deny. Thus one chapter of *Le Livre à venir* is devoted to the diary form, another to prophetic speech. Speaking of the same Broch ('who no longer acknowledges the distinction of genres'), Blanchot says that he 'indulges in all modes of expression – narrative, lyric, and discursive' (p. 141). Even more significantly, the book as a whole is based on a distinction between fundamental modes, the narrative and the novel: the narrative mode is characterised by the insistent search for its own place of origin – which the novel mode effaces and conceals. Thus 'genre' as such has not disappeared; the genres-of-the-past have simply been replaced by others. We no longer speak of poetry and prose, of documentary and fiction, but of novel and narrative, of narrative mode and discursive mode, of dialogue and journal.

The fact that a work 'disobeys' its genre does not mean that the genre does not exist. It is tempting to say 'quite the contrary', for two reasons. First because, in order to exist as such, the transgression requires a law – precisely the one that is to be violated. We might go even further and observe that the norm becomes visible – comes into existence – owing only to its transgressions. Blanchot himself says as much:

> If it is true that Joyce shatters the novelistic form by making it aberrant, he also hints that that form perhaps lives only through its alterations. It would develop not by engendering monsters, formless, lawless works lacking in rigor, but by provoking nothing but exceptions to itself, that constitute law and at the same time suppress it . . . One has to think that every time, in these exceptional works where a limit is reached, the exception alone is what reveals to us that 'law' of which it also constitutes the unexpected and necessary deviation. It is thus as if, in novelistic literature, and perhaps in all literature, we could never recognize the rule except by the exception that abolishes the rule, or more precisely, dislodges the center of which a certain work is the uncertain affirmation, the already destructive manifestation, the momentary and soon-to-be-negative presence. (pp. 133–4)

But there is more. Not only because, in order to be an exception, the work necessarily presupposes a rule; but also because no sooner is it recognized in its exceptional status than the work becomes a rule in turn, because of its commercial success and the critical attention it receives. Prose poems may have been exceptional in the days of Aloysius Bertrand and Baudelaire; today, who would dare write a poem in alexandrines, in rhymed verses – except perhaps as a new transgression of a new norm? Have not Joyce's exceptional wordplays become the rule for a certain modern literature? Does not the novel, however 'new' it may be, continue to exert its pressure on works being written today?

To go back to the German Romantics, and to Friedrich Schlegel in particular, in his writings, alongside certain Crocean assertions ('each poem, *sui generis*'), we find passages that tend in the opposite direction, establishing an equivalency between poetry and its genres. Poetry has certain things in common with the other arts: representation, expression, effect on the addressee. It has language use in common with everyday and scholarly language. Only the genres are its exclusive property. 'The theory of poetic types would be the doctrine of art specific to poetry.'[4] Poetry is its own genres, poetics is the theory of genres.[5]

In the process of arguing the legitimacy of a study of genres, we have come across an answer to the question raised implicitly in the title: the origin of genres. Where do genres come from? Quite simply from other genres. A new genre is always the transformation of an earlier one, or of several: by inversion, by displacement, by combination. Today's 'text' (which is also a genre, in one of its senses) owes as much to nineteenth-century 'poetry' as to the 'novel', just as *la comédie larmoyante* combined features of the comedy and the tragedy of the previous century. There has never been a literature without genres; it is a system in constant transformation, and historically speaking the question of origins cannot be separated from the terrain of the genres themselves. Saussure noted that 'the problem of the origin of language is not a different problem from that of its transformation'.[6] As Humboldt had already observed: 'When we speak of primitive languages, we employ such a designation only because of our ignorance of their earlier constituents.'[7]

The question of origin that I should like to raise, however, is not historical but systematic in nature; both questions seem to me equally legitimate, equally necessary. Not 'what preceded the genres in time?' but 'what presides over the birth of a genre, at any time?' More precisely, is there such a thing, in language (since we are dealing here with genres within discourse) as forms which, while they may foreshadow genres, are not yet included within them? And if so, how does the passage from the one to the other come about? In order to try to answer these questions, we must begin by asking just what a genre is.

At first glance, the answer seems self-evident: genres are classes of texts. But such a definition barely conceals its tautological nature behind the plurality of terms called into play: genres are classes, literature is textual. Rather than multiplying labels, then, we need to examine the content of these concepts.

Let us begin with the concept of *text*, or (to offer yet another synonym) *discourse*. We shall be told that discourse is a sequence of sentences. And here is where the first misunderstanding begins.

Where the acquisition of knowledge is concerned, an elementary truth is too often forgotten: that the viewpoint chosen by the observer reconfigures and redefines his object. So it is with language: one tends to forget that the linguist has a viewpoint from which she marks out an object, within the language material, that belongs to her; now this object will be altered if the viewpoint changes, even if the material remains the same.

A sentence is a unit belonging to language, and to the linguist. A sentence is a combination of possible words, not a concrete utterance. The same sentence may be uttered in various circumstances; for the linguist, its identity will not change even if, by virtue of altered circumstances, it changes meaning.

Discourse is not made up of sentences, but of uttered sentences, or, more succinctly, of utterances. Now the interpretation of an utterance is determined, on the one hand, by the sentence that is uttered, and on the other hand by the process of enunciation of that sentence. The enunciation process includes a speaker who utters, an addressee to whom the utterance is directed, a time and a place, a discourse that precedes and one that follows; in short, an enunciatory context. In still other terms, discourse is always and necessarily constituted by speech acts.[8]

Let us turn now to the other term of the expression 'class of texts', that is, *class*. This term poses a problem only in that it is too easy to apply: it is always possible to discover a property common to two texts, and thus to put them together in a class. Is there any virtue in calling the result of such a combination a 'genre'? I believe we will have a useful and operative notion that remains in keeping with the prevailing usage of the word if we agree to call genres only the classes of texts that have been historically perceived as such.[9] Evidence of such perception is found first and foremost in discourse dealing with genres (metadiscursive discourse) and, sporadically and indirectly, in literary texts themselves.

The *historical* existence of genres is signaled by discourse on genres; however, that does not mean that genres are simply metadiscursive notions and not discursive ones. As one example, we can attest to the historical existence of the genre known as tragedy in seventeenth-century France by pointing to discourse on tragedy (which begins with the existence of this word itself); but that does not mean that the tragedies themselves lack common features and that they could therefore not be described in other than historical terms. As we know, any class of objects may be converted into a series of properties by a passage from extension to comprehension. The study of genres, which has as its starting point the historical evidence of the existence of genres, must have as its ultimate objective precisely the establishment of these properties.[10]

Genres are thus entities that can be described from two different viewpoints, that of empirical observation and that of abstract analysis. In a given society, the recurrence of certain discursive properties is institutionalized, and individual texts are produced and perceived in relation to the norm constituted by that codification. A genre, whether literary or not, is nothing other than the codification of discursive properties.

This definition in turn needs to be explained through the two terms of which it is composed: *discursive property* and *codification*.

Discursive property is an expression I take in an inclusive sense. It is common knowledge that, even if we do not restrict ourselves to *literary* genres, we find that any aspect of discourse can be made obligatory. Songs are different from poems by virtue of phonetic features; sonnets differ from ballads in their phonology; tragedy is opposed to comedy by virtue of thematic elements; the suspense narrative differs from the classic detective story by the way its plot is structured; finally, an autobiography is different from a novel in that its author claims to be recounting facts and not constructing fictions. To categorise these various types of properties (though the categorization is not particularly important for my purposes), we might use the terminology of the semiotician Charles Morris, adapting it to our own uses: these properties stem either from the semantic aspect of the text, or from its syntactic aspect (the relation of the parts among themselves), or else from the verbal aspect (Morris does not use this term, but it can serve to encompass everything connected with the material manifestations of the signs themselves). The difference between one speech act and another, thus also between one genre and another, may be situated at any of these levels of discourse.

In the past, attempts have been made to distinguish 'natural' forms of poetry (for example, lyric, epic, or dramatic poetry) from its conventional forms (sonnets, ballads, odes), or even to oppose these two modes. We need to try to see on what level such an assertion may still have some meaning. One possibility is that lyric poetry, epic poetry, and so on, are universal categories and thus belong to discourse (which would not rule out their being complex – for example, they may be simultaneously semantic, pragmatic, and verbal), but then they belong to poetics in general, and not (specifically) to genre theory: they characterize possible modes of discourse in general, and not real modes of particular discourses. The other possibility is that such terms are used with regard to historical phenomena: thus the epic is what Homer's *Iliad* embodies. In the second case, we are indeed dealing with genres, but these are not qualitatively different on the discursive level from a genre like the sonnet (which for its part is also based on constraints: thematic, verbal, and so on). The most one can say is that certain discursive properties are more interesting than others: personally, I am more intrigued by the constraints that bear upon the pragmatic aspect of texts than by those involving their phonological structure.

It is because genres exist as an institution that they function as 'horizons of expectation' for readers and as 'models of writing' for authors. Here indeed we have the two sides of the historical existence of genres (some may prefer to speak of the metadiscursive discourse that has genres as its object). On the one hand, authors write in function of (which does not mean in agreement with) the existing generic system, and they may bear witness to this just as well within the text as outside it, or even, in a way, between the two – on the book cover; this evidence is obviously not the only way to prove the existence of models of writing. On the other hand, readers read in function of the generic system, with which they are familiar thanks to criticism, schools, the book distribution system, or simply by hearsay; however, they do not need to be conscious of this system.

Genres communicate indirectly with the society where they are operative through their institutionalization. This aspect of genre study is the one that most interests the ethnologist or the historian. In fact, the former will see in a genre-system first of all the categories that differentiate it from that of the neighboring peoples; correlations will have to be established between these categories and other elements of the same culture. The same is true for the historian: each epoch has its own system of genres, which stands in some relation to the dominant ideology, and so on. Like any other institution, genres bring to light the constitutive features of the society to which they belong.

The necessity for institutionalization makes it possible to answer another question we may be tempted to ask: even if we acknowledge that all genres stem from speech acts, how can we explain that not all speech acts produce literary genres? The answer is that a society chooses and codifies the acts that correspond most closely to its ideology; that is why the existence of certain genres in one society, their absence in another, are revelatory of that ideology and allow us to establish it more or less confidently. It is not a coincidence that the epic is possible in one period, the novel in another, with the individual hero of the novel opposed to the collective hero of the epic: each of these choices depends upon the ideological framework within which it operates.

We might establish the place of the notion of genre even more precisely by making two symmetrical distinctions. Since a genre is the historically attested codification of discursive properties, it is easy to imagine the absence of either of the two components of the definition: historical reality and discursive reality. In the absence of historical reality, we would be dealing with the categories of general poetics that are called – depending upon textual level – modes, registers, styles, or even forms, manners, and so on. The 'noble style' or 'first person narration' are indeed discursive realities; but they cannot be pinned down to a single moment in time: they are always possible. By the same token, in the absence of discursive reality, we would be dealing with notions that belong to literary history in the

broad sense, such as trend, school, movement, or, in another sense of
the word, 'style'. It is certain that the literary movement we know as
symbolism existed historically; but that does not prove that the works
of authors identified with symbolism have discursive properties in
common (apart from trivial ones); the unity of the movement may be
centered on friendships, common manifestations, and so on. Let us
allow that this may be the case; we would then have an example of
a historical phenomenon that has no precise discursive reality. This
does not make it inappropriate for study, but distinguishes it from
genres, and even more so from modes, and so on. Genres are the
meeting place between general poetics and event-based literary
history; as such, they constitute a privileged object that may well
deserve to be the principal figure in literary studies.

Such is the global framework of a study of genres.[11] Our current
descriptions of genres may be inadequate; that does not prove the
impossibility of a theory of genres, and the foregoing propositions
are offered as preliminaries to such a theory. In this connection I
should like to recall another fragment by Friedrich Schlegel, in
which he seeks to formulate a balanced view on the question and
wonders whether the negative impression one has when one becomes
familiar with genre distinctions cannot be attributed simply to the
imperfection of the systems proposed by the past.

> Must poetry simply be subdivided? or must it remain one and
> undivided? or alternate between separation and union? Most
> images of the universal poetic system are still as crude and
> childish as those that the ancients, before Copernicus, made of the
> astronomical system. The customary subdivisions of poetry are
> only a static construction for a limited horizon. What one knows
> how to do, or what has some value, these are the immobile earth
> in the center. But in the universe of poetry itself nothing is at rest,
> everything is in the process of becoming and changing and moving
> about harmoniously; and the comets too have immutable laws of
> movement. But before the course of these heavenly bodies can be
> calculated, before their return can be determined in advance, the
> true universal system of poetry has yet to be discovered.[12]

Comets too obey immutable laws . . . The old systems were capable
of describing only the static result; we have to learn how to present
genres as principles of dynamic production, or we shall never grasp
the true system of poetry. Perhaps the time has come to put Friedrich
Schlegel's program to work.

At this point we need to return to our initial question concerning
the systematic origin of genres. It has already been answered, in a

sense, since, as we have said, like all other speech acts genres arise from the codification of discursive properties. So our question has to be reformulated as follows: is there any difference at all between (literary) genres and other speech acts? Praying is a speech act; prayer is a genre (which may be literary or not): the difference is minimal. But to take another example, telling is a speech act, and the novel is a genre in which something is definitely being told; however, the distance between the two is considerable. Finally, there is a third case: the sonnet is surely a literary genre, but there is no verbal activity such as 'sonneting'; thus genres exist that do not derive from a simpler speech act.

Three possibilities may be envisaged, in short: either the genre, like the sonnet, codifies discursive properties as any other speech act would; or else the genre coincides with a speech act that also has a nonliterary existence, like prayer; or else it derives from a speech act by way of a certain number of transformations or amplifications (this would be the case for the novel, based on the act of telling). Only the third case actually presents a new situation: in the first two cases, a genre does not differ in any way from other speech acts. In the third case, on the contrary, we do not take discursive properties as a starting point, but we start rather with other already constituted speech acts, in a progression from a simple act to a complex one. This third case, too, is the only one that warrants being set apart from the other verbal actions. Thus our question about the origin of the genres becomes the following: what transformations do given speech acts undergo in order to produce given literary genres?

I shall try to respond by examining some concrete cases. This procedural choice already implies that the question of the systematic origin of genres cannot be maintained as a pure abstraction, any more than genres themselves can be viewed either as purely discursive or purely historical phenomena. Even if the order of our discussion leads us from the simple to the complex, in the interest of clarity, the order of discovery follows the opposite path: starting from the observed genres, we are attempting to find their discursive origin.

My first example comes from a culture different from our own: that of the Lubas, inhabitants of Zaire. I have chosen it because of its relative simplicity.[13] 'Inviting' is an extremely common speech act. The number of formulas used can be restricted; the result is a ritual invitation, such as is practiced in our society on certain solemn occasions. But among the Lubas a minor literary genre exists that is derived from the invitation, and which is practiced even outside its original context. In one example, 'I' invites his brother-in-law to come into the house. However, this explicit formula appears only in the final lines of the invitation (29–33; the text obeys a metric scheme).

The 28 preceding lines contain a narrative in which it is 'I' who goes to his brother-in-law's house, and the brother-in-law does the inviting. Here is the beginning of the narrative:

I left my brother-in-law's house,
My brother-in-law said: 'Hello',
And I said: 'Hello to you.'
A few moments later, he said:
'Come into the house', etc.

The narrative does not stop there; it brings us to a new episode, in which 'I' asks for someone to join him in his meal; the episode is repeated twice:

I say: 'My brother-in-law,
Call your children,
So they can eat these noodles with me.'
Brother-in-law says: 'Well!
The children have already eaten,
They have already gone to bed.'
I say: 'Well!
So that is the way you are, brother-in-law!
Call your big dog.'
Brother-in-law says: 'Well!
The dog has already eaten,
He has already gone to bed', etc.

Next comes a transition made up of proverbs, and at the end we arrive at a direct invitation, this time addressed by 'I' to his brother-in-law.

Even without going into detail, we can observe that between the verbal act of inviting and the literary genre 'invitation' of which the preceding text is an example, several transformations take place:

1. an *inversion* of the roles of sender and receiver: 'I' invites the brother-in-law, the brother-in-law invites 'I';
2. a *narrativization*, or more precisely, the embedding of the verbal act of inviting in the verbal act of telling; in the place of an invitation, we get the narrative of an invitation;
3. a *specification*: not only is someone invited, but he is invited to eat noodles; not only does someone accept the invitation, but he desires company;
4. a *repetition* of the same narrative situation, but one that includes
5. a *variation* in the actors who take on the same role: once it is the children, another time the dog.

This enumeration is not exhaustive, of course, but it may already suggest the nature of the transformations the speech act undergoes. They are divided into two groups that might be called (a) internal, in which the derivation takes place within the initial speech act itself (this is the case for the transformations 1, 3, 4, and 5); and (b) external, where the first speech act is combined with a second, according to a given hierarchical relationship (this is the case for transformation 2, where 'inviting' is embedded in 'telling').

Taking a second example, still within the same Luba culture, we shall begin with an even more essential speech act, that is, naming, attributing a name. In our culture, the meaning of personal names has generally been forgotten; proper names take on meaning by evoking a context or through association, not by virtue of the morphemes that constitute them. This can be the case for the Lubas; but alongside such meaningless names are found others whose meaning is fully contemporary and whose attribution, moreover, is motivated by the meaning. For example (I have not marked the tones):

Lonif means 'Ferocity'
Mukanza means 'Fairskinned'
Ngenyi means 'Intelligence'

Besides these names, which are essentially official, an individual may also receive more or less stable nicknames, whose function may be praise, or perhaps simply the identification of the individual through characteristic features, for example his profession. The elaboration of these nicknames already brings them close to literary forms. Here are some examples of one of these forms of nicknames, the *makumbu*, or praise names:

Cipanda wa nshindumeenu – beam on which to lean
Dileji dya kwikisha munnuya – shade in which to rest
Kasunyi kaciinyi nkelende – ax that does not fear thorns

Such nicknames may clearly be considered expansions of proper names. In both cases, human beings are described as they are or as they ought to be. From the syntactic viewpoint, we move from the isolated noun (substantive or substantivized adjective) to a syntagma composed of a noun plus a relative clause that modifies it. Semantically, we move from words used in their literal sense to metaphoric expressions. These nicknames, like the names themselves, may also allude to proverbs or popular sayings.

Finally, among the Lubas there exists a well-established – and well-studied[14] – genre called the *kasala*. These are songs of variable dimensions (they may be 800 lines or more), which 'evoke the various people and events of a clan, exalt with high praise its dead and/or living members and proclaim their great deeds'.[15] Once again, then, we find a mixture of characteristics and praises: on the one hand, individual genealogies are indicated, one person being situated with reference to others; on the other hand, remarkable qualities are attributed to these individuals, the attributions often including nicknames like those we have just seen. Moreover, the bard calls upon individuals and instructs them to behave admirably. Each of these devices is repeated countless times. Clearly, the seeds of all the characteristic features of the *kasala* were already present in the proper name and even more so in that intermediate form, the nickname.

Let us now return to the more familiar territory of the genres of Western literature, to try to see whether we can discover transformations similar to the ones that characterise the Luba genres.

My first example is the genre that I myself described in *The Fantastic: A Structural Approach to a Literary Genre*. If my description is correct, this genre is characterized by the hesitation that the reader is invited to experience with regard to the natural or supernatural explanation of the events presented. More precisely, the world described in these texts is indeed our own world, with its natural laws (these stories are not fairy tales), but within that universe an event occurs for which we have difficulty finding a natural explanation. What the genre encodes is thus a pragmatic property of the discursive situation: the reader's attitude, as prescribed by the book (the individual reader is free to adopt it or not). Most of the time the reader's role does not remain implicit but is represented in the text itself through a character who bears witness; the identification of the one with the other is facilitated by the attribution to that character of the narrator's function: the use of the first person pronoun *I* allows the reader to identify with the narrator, and thus also with that witness who hesitates as to the explanation of the events that come to pass.

For simplicity's sake let us leave aside the three-way identification between the implied reader, the narrator, and the character who bears witness; let us acknowledge that we are dealing with an attitude on the part of the represented narrator. A sentence from one of the most representative fantastic novels, Potocki's *The Saragossa Manuscript*, sums up this situation emblematically: 'I almost came to the conclusion that demons had taken possession of the hanged men's bodies in order to trick me.'[16] The ambiguity of the situation is clear. The supernatural event is designated by the subordinate clause; the main clause expresses the narrator's adherence, but an adherence modulated by approximation. The main clause thus implies the intrinsic implausibility of what follows, and constitutes by that very token the 'natural' and 'reasonable' framework in which the narrator seeks to remain (and, of course, to keep the reader).

The speech act underlying the fantastic genre is thus, even if we simplify the situation a little, a complex one. Its formula might be rewritten as follows: *I* (a pronoun whose function has been explained) + verb of attitude (such as *believe, think,* and so on) + modalization of that verb in the direction of uncertainty (a modalization that operates along two principal lines: verb tense, here the past, which contributes to establishing a distance between narrator and character; and adverbs of manner such as *almost, perhaps, doubtless,* and so on) along with a subordinate clause describing a supernatural event.

In this abstract and reduced form, the 'fantastic' speech act may of course be found outside literature: it is the speech act of a person reporting an event that falls outside the framework of natural explanations, when that person still does not want to renounce the framework itself, and thus shares his uncertainty with us (the situation may be less common today but is in any event perfectly genuine). The identity of the genre is entirely determined by that of the speech act, which does not mean that the two are one and the same. This kernel is enriched by a series of amplifications, in the rhetorical sense: (1) a narrativization: a situation must be created in which the narrator ends up formulating our model sentence, or one of its synonyms; (2) a gradation, or at least an irreversibility in the appearance of the supernatural; (3) a thematic proliferation: certain themes, such as sexual perversions or states approaching insanity, are preferred to others; (4) a verbal representation that exploits, for example, the uncertainty one may feel in choosing between the literal and figurative meanings of an expression (I sought to describe these themes and devices in *The Fantastic*).

Thus from the perspective of origins, there is no difference in nature between the fantastic genre and those we encountered in Luba oral literature, although differences of degree – that is, of complexity – may remain. The verbal act expressing 'fantastic' hesitation is less common than the act that names or invites: it is nonetheless a verbal act like the others. The transformations it undergoes to become a literary genre may be more numerous and more varied than those with which we have become acquainted in the Luba literature; they remain of the same nature.

Autobiography is another genre proper to our society that has been described in sufficient detail to allow us to examine it from our current perspective.[17] To put it simply, autobiography is defined by two identifications: the author's identification with the narrator, and the narrator's identification with the chief protagonist. This second identification is obvious: it is the one expressed in the prefix *auto-* and the one that makes it possible to differentiate autobiography from biography or memoirs. The first one is more subtle: it distinguishes autobiography (like biography and memoirs) from the novel, even though a given novel may be full of elements drawn from the author's life. In short, this identification separates all the 'referential' or 'historical' genres from all the 'fictional' genres: the reality of the referent is clearly indicated, because we are dealing with the author of the book himself, an individual who has a civil status in his home town.

Thus we are dealing with a speech act that codifies both semantic properties (this is what is implied by the narrator-character identification; one must speak of oneself) and pragmatic properties (by virtue of the author-narrator identification; one claims to be telling the truth and not a fiction). In this form, the speech act is very widely distributed outside literature: it is practiced every time anyone *tells his or her own story*. It is curious to note that the studies by Lejeune and Bruss on which I am relying here, under the cover of a description of the genre, have in fact established the identity of the speech act that is only its kernel. This shift of object is revealing: the identity of the genre comes from the speech act that is at its root, telling one's own story; however, this initial contact is not prevented from undergoing numerous transformations in order to become a literary genre (I shall leave the task of identifying these transformations to specialists).

What would be the situation with even more complex genres, such as the novel? I do not dare plunge headlong into the series of transformations that presides over its birth; but I shall risk betraying a certain optimism and say that, here too, the process does not seem to be qualitatively different. The difficulty of the study of the 'origin of the novel' understood in this sense arises only from the infinite embedding of speech acts with others. At the very top of the pyramid, there would be the fictional contract (thus the codification of a pragmatic property), which in turn would demand an alternation of descriptive and narrative elements, that is, the description of immobilized states and actions taking place over time (it must be noted that these two speech acts are mutually coordinated and not embedded one within the other as in the preceding cases). To this would be added constraints concerning the verbal aspect of the text (the alternation of the narrator's discourse and that of the characters) and its semantic aspect (private life, preferably with sweeping period frescoes), and so on . . .

The rapid enumeration I have just proposed is in no way different, moreover – except perhaps in its brevity and its schematic nature – from studies that have been devoted to the novel. And yet that is not quite an accurate statement, for such studies have lacked the perspective – a minuscule displacement, an optical illusion perhaps? – that makes it possible to see that there is not an abyss between literature and what is not literature, that the literary genres originate, quite simply, in human discourse.

Notes

1. Maurice Blanchot, *Le Livre à venir* (Paris: Gallimard, 1959), p. 136.

2. Ibid., pp. 243–4.

3. Maurice Blanchot, *The Space of Literature* (Lincoln: University of Nebraska Press, 1982), p. 220; see also Maurice Blanchot, *L'Entretien infini* (Paris: Gallimard, 1969), p. vi.

4. Friedrich von Schlegel, 'Gespräch über die Poesie', in *Kritische Friedrich-Schlegel-Ausgabe*, vol. 2: *Charakteristiken und Kritiken I (1796–1801)*, ed. Hans Eichner (Munich: Schöningh, 1967), p. 306 [Eng. *Dialogue on Poetry and Literary Aphorisms*, trans. Ernst Behler and Roman Struc (University Park: Pennsylvania State University Press, 1968)].

5. We find a similar declaration in Henry James, who as a theoretician belongs to the posterity of Romanticism: ' "Kinds" are the very life of literature, and truth and strength come from the complete recognition of them, from abounding to the utmost in their respective senses and sinking deep into their consistency' (Preface to *The Awkward Age*, in *Henry James: Literary Criticism* (New York: Literary Classics of the United States, 1984), p. 1131).

6. Cited in Robert Godel, *Les Sources manuscrites du Cours de Linguistique générale de F. de Saussure* (Geneva: E. Droz, 1957), p. 270.

7. Wilhelm von Humboldt, *Linguistic Variability and Intellectual Development*, trans. George C. Buck and Frithjof A. Raven (Coral Gables: University of Miami Press, 1971), p. 21.

8. This way of putting the problems is in no way original (the difference between sentence and utterance goes back at least to the distinction between grammatical signification and historical signification made by F.A. Wolf at the beginning of the century); I am only recalling the obvious, though this is sometimes neglected. For more thorough discussions using contemporary terminology, see the writings of Austin, Strawson, and Searle, or my own presentation of this problematics in *L'Enonciation (Langages*, 17 (1970)) and, in collaboration with Oswald Ducrot, in *Encyclopedic Dictionary of the Sciences of Language*, trans. Catherine Porter (Baltimore: Johns Hopkins University Press, 1979). See also Dan Sperber, 'Rudiments de rhétorique cognitive' (*Poétique*, 23 (1975)).

9. This assertion has as its corollary the reduced importance that I am now granting the idea of theoretical genre, or type. I am not at all denying the need to analyze the genres in abstract categories; but the study of the possible types appears to me today to be a reformulation of the general theory of discourse (or of general poetics); the latter fully encompasses the former. The historical genres are theoretical genres; but to the extent that the converse is not necessarily true, the separate notion of theoretical genre seems to me to lose much of its interest, except perhaps within the framework of a heuristic strategy, as in the examples studied by Christine Brooke-Rose.

10. I am ultimately more optimistic than the authors of two recent studies which helped me to clarify my own views (DAN BEN-AMOS, 'Catégories analytiques et genres populaires', *Poétique*, 19 (1974), 265–86, and PHILIPPE LEJEUNE, *Le Pacte autobiographique* (Paris: Seuil, 1975), pp. 311–41, 'Autobiographie et histoire littéraire'). Lejeune and Ben-Amos are prepared to see an unbridgeable gap between the abstract and the concrete, between genres as they have existed historically and the categorical analysis to which they can be subjected today.

11. The idea that the genres can be associated with speech acts is formulated by K. STIERLE, 'L'Histoire comme Exemple, l'Exemple comme Histoire', *Poétique*, 10 (1972), 176–88; LEJEUNE, *Le Pacte autobiographique*, pp. 17–49, 'Le pacte autobiographique'; ELISABETH BRUSS, 'L'autobiographie considérée comme acte littéraire', *Poétique*, 17 (1974), 14–26. P. SMITH examines genres from an ethnological viewpoint in 'Des genres et des hommes', *Poétique*, 19 (1975), 294–312; and LEJEUNE adopts a historical perspective in 'Autobiographie et histoire littéraire', the concluding chapter of the book cited above (it contains further references on the subject). A. KILITO offers a list of genres characteristic of Arab literature, a list that emphasises their relationships with speech acts: 'We have requests that something be accomplished – a promise, for example, reproaches, threats, satire, excuses . . .' ('Le genre "séance": une introduction', *Studia Islamica*, 43 (1976), 27).

12. *Athenaeum*, no. 434, in *Kritische Friedrich-Schlegel-Ausgabe*, 2 (1967), p. 252 [Eng. *Athenaeum Fragments*, in *Friedrich Schlegel's 'Lucinde' and the Fragments*, trans. with intro. by Peter Firchow (Minneapolis: University of Minnesota Press, 1971)].

13. I owe all my information about the literary genres of the Lubas and their verbal context to the generosity of Mme Clémentine Faïk-Nzuji.

14. See PATRICE MUFUTA, *Le chante Kasàlà des Lubà* (Paris: Armand Colin, 1969); CLÉMENTINE FAÏK-NZUJI, *Kasala, chant héroïque luba* (Lubumbashi: Presses Universitaires du Zaïre, 1974). For similar phenomena in Rwanda, see SMITH, 'Des genres et des hommes', esp. 297–8.

15. NZUJI, *Kasala*, p. 21.

16. JAN POTOCKI, *The Saragossa Manuscript: A Collection of Weird Tales*, ed. Roger Caillois, trans. Elisabeth Abbott (New York: The Orion Press, 1960), p. 122.

17. See in particular LEJEUNE, 'Le pacte autobiographique', and BRUSS, 'L'autobiographie considérée comme acte littéraire'.

12   The Architext*

Gérard Genette

In this indispensable essay, the French literary theorist Gérard
Genette sets out to disentangle the 'knot of confusions' that has,
for more than two centuries, surrounded one of the most familiar of generic classifications, the division of literature into three
kinds: lyric, epic and dramatic. Genette shows how this 'all-too-
seductive' triad, which came to dominate Romantic genre theory
(especially in Germany) and has also been the foundation of
many modern genre-systems, conflates two logically dissimilar
categories: 'mode' (an essentially linguistic category, specifying
means of enunciation: e.g. narration, dramatic imitation) and
'genre' (a literary category, defined by thematic as well as formal
criteria, and indicating a historically existent type: e.g. the epic);
and how this tripartite division, habitually but erroneously attributed to Aristotle, has impeded the development of a coherent classification of literature and adequate theory of genre. The critique
is brilliantly sustained and meticulously documented, and has
profound implications not only for our understanding of the history of genre theory, but also for our reckoning of the tasks that
still confront the genre theorist. Yet the tone of the essay is anything but censorious: rarely has so venerable a tradition of intellectual confusion been overturned with such modesty and good
humour – qualities which animate all of Genette's work, even his
most technical. Moreover, as he would be the first to acknowledge, Genette himself is by no means free of the systematising
impulse whose potential dangers he so lucidly analyses, nor of the
'terminological rapture' which Derrida (below, p. 224) sees as the
mark of the true genre theorist ('architext' and 'archigenre' are

* Reprinted from Gérard Genette, *The Architext: An Introduction*, trans. Jane
E. Lewin (Berkeley: University of California Press, 1992), pp. 60–72. An earlier
version was first published as an article entitled 'Genres, "Types", Modes' in
Poétique, 8, no. 32 (1977), 389–421, and subsequently revised as *Introduction à
l'architexte* (Paris: Seuil, 1979).

but two of his many neologisms). The short extract reproduced here formed the original conclusion of the essay; the book version, which runs to 85 pages, carries a postscript in which Genette responds to criticisms of the essay, reviews yet another flawed genre-system, and – very tentatively – sketches his own (three-dimensional) model of the relation between modal, thematic, and formal categories.

The importance of Genette's critique of modern genre theory has been widely acknowledged, even by those who resist some of its conclusions, such as Derrida. For a detailed response, see Schaeffer, 'Du texte au genre', in *Théorie des genres*, ed. Genette and Todorov (1986). Problems of genre and literary classification frequently recur elsewhere in Genette's work: *Palimpsests* (1998) treats genre – or 'architextuality' – as one of five kinds of 'transtextual' relationship, the others being 'intertextuality' (a term which, unlike Kristeva, he confines to allusion, quotation, and plagiarism), 'hypertextuality' (where one text comprehensively reworks another), 'metatextuality' (translation, commentary), and 'paratextuality' (the relation between the body of a text and its titles, epigraphs, notes, etc.). The last of these is also the subject of a separate book, *Paratexts* (1997), which includes a section analysing the history and function of generic labels or what he calls 'genre indications' (pp. 94–103).

I have tried to show how and why theorists reached the point of devising, and then (as a supplementary consideration) of attributing to Plato and Aristotle, a division of the 'literary genres' that the whole 'unconscious poetics' of both philosophers rejects. To get a firmer grip on the historical reality, we should no doubt make clear that the attribution passed through two periods and stemmed from two very distinct motives. At the end of classicism, it stemmed from a still deepseated respect for orthodoxy and a need to treat it with care. In the twentieth century, a better reason for the attribution is retrospective illusion (the vulgate is so well established that imagining a time when it did not exist is very difficult) and also (as is evident in Frye, for example) the legitimate renewal of interest in a modal interpretation of the phenomena of genre – that is, an interpretation based on the enunciating situation. Between the two periods, the romantics and postromantics were not overly concerned about dragging Plato and Aristotle into all these matters. But the present telescoping of these various positions – the fact, for example, that authority is claimed to derive at one and the same time from Aristotle, Batteux, Schlegel (or, as we will see, Goethe), Jakobson, Benveniste, and Anglo-American analytical philosophy – aggravates the theoretical drawbacks of this erroneous attribution, or (to define the error itself in theoretical terms) this confusion between modes and genres.

In Plato, and again in Aristotle, [. . .] the basic division had a clearly defined status, for it bore explicitly on a text's *mode of enunciation*. To the extent that genres in the proper sense of the term were taken into consideration (very little in Plato, more so in Aristotle), they were allocated among modes inasmuch as they came under one enunciating stance or another: dithyramb under pure narration, epic under mixed narration, tragedy and comedy under dramatic imitation. But this inclusive relationship did not prevent the generic and modal criteria from being absolutely dissimilar, as well as radically different in status: each genre was defined essentially by a specification of content that was in no way prescribed by the definition of its mode. The romantic and postromantic division, in contrast, views the lyrical, the epical, and the dramatic no longer simply as modes of enunciation but as real genres, whose definitions already inevitably include thematic elements, however vague. We see this in Hegel, among others: for him there exists an epic *world* defined by a specific type of social aggregate and human relationship; a lyric *content* ('the individual subject'); a dramatic *milieu* 'made up of conflicts and collisions'. We also see it in Hugo, for whom real drama, for example, is inseparable from the Christian message (separation of body and soul). We see it, as well, in Karl Viëtor, for whom the three major genres express three 'basic attitudes': the lyrical expresses feeling; the epical, knowledge; the dramatic, will and action.[1] Viëtor thus resurrects the distribution Hölderlin ventured at the end of the eighteenth century, but modifies it by transposing epic and dramatic.

The transition from one status to the other is clearly, if not intentionally, illustrated by a well-known text of Goethe's, which we [. . .] must now consider on its own account.[2] Here Goethe contrasts the ordinary 'poetic species' (*Dichtarten*) – particular genres, such as the novel, the ballad, or satire – with the 'three genuine natural forms' (*drei echte Naturformen*) of poetry: the epic, defined as pure narration (*klar erzählende*); the lyric, as a burst of rapture (*enthusiastisch aufgeregte*); and the drama, as lifelike representation (*persönlich handelnde*).[3] 'These three poetic modes [*Dichtweisen*]', he adds, 'can function either jointly or separately.' The contrast between *Dichtarten* and *Dichtweisen* clearly encompasses the distinction between genres and modes, and it is reinforced by the purely modal definitions of epic and drama. The definition of lyric, however, is thematic, making the term *Dichtweisen* irrelevant and sending us to the vaguer idea of *Naturform*, which covers all interpretations and is for that reason, no doubt, the term commentators have most frequently used.

But the whole point is, precisely, to know whether the term *natural forms* can still be legitimately applied to the triad *lyrical/epical/dramatic* once that triad has been redefined in generic terms. The modes of enunciation can, in a pinch, be termed 'natural forms', at least in the sense in which we speak of 'natural languages'. Except when using language for literary purposes, the language user is constantly required – even (or especially) if unconsciously – to choose between forms of utterance such as discourse and story (in Benveniste's sense), direct quotation and indirect style, etc. Therein lies the essential difference of status between genres and modes: genres are properly literary categories,[4] whereas modes are categories that belong to linguistics, or (more exactly) to what we now call *pragmatics*. They are 'natural forms', therefore, in this wholly relative sense and only to the extent that language and its use appear as facts of nature vis-à-vis the conscious and deliberate elaboration of aesthetic forms. But the romantic triad and its subsequent derivatives no longer occupy that terrain: lyrical, epical, and dramatic contrast with *Dichtarten* no longer as modes of verbal enunciation that precede and are external to any literary definition but, rather, as kinds of *archigenres*. *Archi-*, because each of them is supposed to overarch and include, ranked by degree of importance, a certain number of empirical genres that – whatever their amplitude, longevity, or potential for recurrence – are apparently phenomena of culture and history; but still (or already) *-genres*, because (as we have seen) their defining criteria always involve a thematic element that eludes purely formal or linguistic description. This dual status is not peculiar to them, for a 'genre' like the novel or comedy may also be subdivided into more specific 'species' – tale of chivalry, picaresque novel, etc.; comedy of humours, farce, vaudeville, etc. – with no limit set a priori to this series of inclusions. We all know, for example, that the species *detective novel* may in turn be divided into several varieties (police procedural, thriller, 'realistic' detective story à la Simenon, etc.), that with a little ingenuity one can always multiply the positions between the species and the individual, and that no one can set a limit on this proliferation of species (the spy story would, I suppose, have been completely unforeseeable to a literary theorist of the eighteenth century, and many species yet to come are still unimaginable to us today). In short, any genre can always contain several genres, and in that respect the archigenres of the romantic triad are distinguished by no natural privilege. At most they can be described as the highest – the most capacious – positions of the classification then in use. But the example of Käte Hamburger shows us that a new reduction is not to be ruled out a priori (and it would not be unreasonable – quite the contrary – to envisage a fusion that would be the reverse of hers, a fusion between the lyrical and the epical that would leave the dramatic as the only form with a rigorously 'objective' enunciation). And the example of W.V. Ruttkowski shows that one can always, and just as reasonably, propose another ultimate position, in this case the *didactic*.[5] And so on. In the classification of literary species as in the classification of genres, no position is essentially more 'natural' or more 'ideal' – unless we abandon the literary criteria themselves, as the ancients did implicitly with the modal position. There is no generic level that can be decreed more 'theoretical', or that can be attained by a more 'deductive' method, than the others: all species and all subgenres, genres, or supergenres are empirical classes, established by observation of the historical facts or, if need be, by extrapolation from those facts – that is, by a deductive activity superimposed on an initial activity that is always inductive and analytical, as we have seen in the charts (whether explicit or implicit) of Aristotle and Frye, where the existence of an empty compartment (comic narrative; extroverted-intellectual) helps one discover a genre ('parody', 'anatomy') otherwise condemned to invisibility. The major ideal 'types' that, since Goethe, have so often been contrasted with the minor forms and intermediate genres[6] are simply more capacious, less precisely defined classes; for that reason they are more likely to have a broader cultural reach, but their principle is neither more ahistorical nor less. The 'epic type' is neither more ideal nor more natural than the genres of novel and epic that it supposedly encompasses – unless we define it as the ensemble of basically *narrative* genres, which immediately brings us back to the division by mode. For narrative, like dramatic dialogue, is a basic stance of enunciation – which cannot be said of the epical or the dramatic or, of course, the lyrical, in the romantic sense of these terms.

In recalling these obvious but often disregarded facts, I by no means intend to deny to literary genres any sort of 'natural' and transhistorical foundation. On the contrary, to me another obvious (albeit vague) fact is the presence of an existential attitude, of an 'anthropological structure' (Durand), of a 'mental disposition' (Jolles), of an 'imaginative design' (Mauron), or (in everyday language) of a 'feeling' that is properly epical, lyrical, dramatic – but also tragic, comic, elegiac, fantastic, romantic, etc. – whose nature, origin, continued existence, and relation to history (among other characteristics) are still to be studied.[7] For as generic concepts, the three terms of the traditional triad deserve no special hierarchical place: *epical*, for example, overarches the *epic*, the *novel*, the *novella*, the *tale*, etc., only if it is meant as mode (= narrative (*narratif*)); if it is meant as genre

(= the epic) and given a specific thematic content (as with Hegel), it no longer *contains* the novelistic, the fantastic, etc., but is instead at their level. Likewise for the *dramatic* with respect to the tragic, the comic, etc., and for the *lyrical* with respect to the elegiac, the satirical, etc.[8] I deny only that a final generic position, and it alone, can be defined in terms that exclude all historicity. For at whatever level of generality one places oneself, the phenomenon of genre inextricably merges the phenomena – among others – of nature and of culture. That the proportions and the type of relationship itself can vary is, again, an observable fact, but no position is totally the product of nature or mind – as none is totally determined by history.

Sometimes a more empirical, and wholly relative, definition of ideal 'types' is proposed (for example, by Lämmert in his *Bauformen des Erzählens*), but those would be only *the most enduring* generic forms. Such differences of degree – for example, between comedy and vaudeville or between the novel in general and the gothic novel – are undeniable, and it stands to reason that the broadest historical range is bound up with the broadest conceptual range. But the argument of duration must be handled carefully: the longevity of the classical forms (epic, tragedy) is not a sure indication of transhistoricity, given the conservatism of the classical tradition and its ability to sustain mummified forms for several centuries. Compared with forms of such durability, the postclassical (or paraclassical) forms suffer a historical erosion that is less their own doing than that of another historical rhythm. A more significant criterion than longevity would be the capacity for dispersion (among diverse cultures) and for spontaneous recurrence (without the stimulus of a tradition, revival, or 'retro' style). One could take as an example the apparently spontaneous return of the epical in the early chansons de geste, in contrast to the labored resurrection of the classical epic in the seventeenth century. But in the presence of such subjects, one quickly sizes up the insufficiency not only of our historical knowledge but also, and more fundamentally, of our theoretical resources. For example: to what extent, in what manner, and in what sense does the species chanson de geste belong to the epical genre? Another example: how can the epical be defined without any reference to the Homeric model and tradition?[9]

Now we are in a position to spell out the theoretical drawback of a fallacious attribution that could at first seem merely an unimportant (if not insignificant) historical mistake. The fallacious attribution projects the privilege of naturalness that inheres *legitimately* in the three modes *pure narration/mixed narration/dramatic imitation* ('there are and there can be only three ways of representing actions in language', etc.) onto the triad of genres, or archigenres, *lyricism/epic/drama* ('there are and there can be only three basic poetic outlooks', etc.). In surreptitiously (and unconsciously) backing both the modal definition and the generic definition,[10] the attribution sets up these archigenres as ideal or natural types, which they are not and cannot be: no archigenre could totally escape historicity *while at the same time retaining a generic definition.*[11] There are modes (for example, the narrative); there are genres (for example, the novel); the relationship between genres and modes is complex and doubtless not, as Aristotle suggests, one of simple inclusion. Genres can cut across modes (Oedipus recounted is still tragic), perhaps the way individual works cut across genres – perhaps differently; but we do know that a novel is not solely a narrative and, therefore, that it is not a species of narrative or even a kind of narrative. In this area, indeed, that is all we know, and undoubtedly even that is too much. Poetics is a very old and very young 'science': the little it 'knows' it would perhaps sometimes be better off forgetting. In a sense, that is all I wanted to say – and that too, of course, is still too much.

Notes

1. Karl Viëtor, 'Die Geschichte literarischer Gattungen' (1931), in vol. 9 of *Deutsche Vierteljahrsschrift für Literaturwissenschaft und Geistesgeschichte* (rpt. in *Geist und Form* (Bern: Francke, 1952), pp. 292–309); French translation in *Poétique* 8, no. 32 (1977), 490–506. We have seen the same term (*Grundhaltung*) in Kayser and the same concept in Bovet, who spoke of 'basic ways of viewing life and the universe'.

2. I am referring to two notes (*Dichtarten* and *Naturformen der Dichtung*) that were made part of the 1819 *Divan*.

3. The list of *Dichtarten*, deliberately put in (German) alphabetical order, is allegory, ballad, cantata, drama, elegy, epigram, epistle, epic, narrative (*Erzählung*) fable, heroic verse, idyll, didactic poem, ode, parody, novel, romance, satire. In Lichtenberger's bilingual edition of the *Divan*, which does not include the German text of the notes, the translations (pp. 377–8) of *klar erzählende* and *persönlich handelnde* ('qui raconte clairement' (who recounts clearly) and 'qui agit personnellement' (who acts in person)) are more cautious or evasive than my translations ('narration pure' (pure narration) and 'représentation vivante' (lifelike representation)). Nevertheless, it seems to me that two other statements in that note confirm the modal interpretation. First, 'In French tragedy, the exposition is epical, the middle part dramatic'; and then, with a strictly Aristotelian criterion, 'The Homeric epic [*Heldengedicht*] is purely epical: the rhapsodist is always in the foreground to recount the events; no one may utter a word unless the rhapsodist first gives him the floor.' In both cases 'epical' clearly means *narrative* (*narratif*).

4. To be more precise, we should say 'properly aesthetic', for, as we know, the fact of genre is common to all the arts. Here, therefore, 'properly literary' means proper to the aesthetic level of literature, the level literature shares

with the other arts, as opposed to the linguistic level, which literature shares with the other types of discourse.

5. WOLFGANG V. RUTTKOWSKI, *Die literarischen Gattungen: Reflexionen über eine modifizierte Fundamentalpoetik* (Bern: Francke, 1968), ch. 6, 'Schlussforderungen: eine modifizierte Gattungspoetik'.

6. *Type* is sometimes one term of the opposition (Lämmert, Todorov in the *Dictionary*); other terminological couples that have been used are *kind/genre* (Wellek and Warren), *mode/genre* (Scholes), *theoretical genre/historical genre* (TODOROV in *The Fantastic: A Structural Approach to a Literary Genre*, trans. Richard Howard (Ithaca: Cornell University Press, 1975)), *basic attitude/genre* (Viëtor), *basic genre* or *basic type/genre* (Petersen), or even, with some slight differences, *simple form/real form* in Jolles. TODOROV's current position is closer to the one I am upholding here:

> In the past, attempts have been made to distinguish 'natural' forms of poetry (for example, lyric, epic, or dramatic poetry) from its conventional forms (sonnets, ballads, odes), or even to oppose [the 'natural' and the conventional]. We need to try to see on what level such an assertion may still have some meaning. One possibility is that lyric poetry, epic poetry, and so on, are universal categories and *thus belong to discourse* . . . The other possibility is that such terms are used with regard to historical phenomena: thus the epic is what Homer's *Iliad* embodies. In the second case, we are indeed dealing with genres, but these are not qualitatively different on the discursive level from a genre like the sonnet (which for its part is based on constraints: thematic, verbal, and so on). ('L'origine des genres' (1976), in *Les Genres du discours* (Paris: Seuil, 1978), p. 50; Eng. *Genres in Discourse*, trans. Catherine Porter (New York: Cambridge University Press, 1990), p. 18. Emphasis mine.) [See p. 199 in this volume.]

7. The problem of the relationship between atemporal archetypes and historical thematics is automatically raised (although not resolved) when one reads works like Gilbert Durand's *Décor mythique*, an anthropological analysis of a novelistic manner that seemingly dates from Ariosto, or Charles Mauron's *Psychocritique du genre comique*, a psychoanalytic reading of a genre that dates from Menander and the New Comedy (Aristophanes and the Old Comedy, for example, do not quite belong to the same 'imaginative design').

8. In this case, terminology reflects and aggravates the theoretical confusion. To set beside *drama* (*drame*) and *epic* (*épopée*) (understood as specific genres) we can offer in (English or) French only the limp *lyric poem* (*poème lyrique*). *Epical* (*épique*) in the modal sense is not really idiomatic, and no one will miss it – it is a Germanism, and we gain nothing by sanctioning it. As for *dramatic* (*dramatique*), it truly, and unfortunately, denotes both concepts, the generic (= characteristic of drama) and the modal (= characteristic of the theater). So at the modal level, (in French) we have nothing to align in paradigm with the adjective *narratif* (the only univocal term) (in English, of course, not even the word *narrative* is univocal): *dramatique* remains ambiguous, and the third term is totally lacking.

9. Cf. DANIEL POIRION, 'Chanson de geste ou épopée? Remarques sur la définition d'un genre', *Travaux de linguistique et de littérature*, 10 (1972), part 2:7–20.

10. To my knowledge, NORTHROP FRYE is the only – or nearly the only – modern literary theorist who maintains (in his own way) the distinction between modes and genres. Even so, he names *modes* what we ordinarily call genres (myth, romance, mimesis, irony), and *genres* what I would like to call modes

(dramatic; narrative (*narratif*)–oral, or *epos*; narrative (*narratif*)–written, or *fiction*; sung to oneself, or *lyric*). In Frye, only the second division is based explicitly on Aristotle and Plato and takes as its criterion the 'radical of presentation', that is, of communication with the public (see *Anatomy of Criticism: Four Essays* (Princeton: Princeton University Press, 1957), pp. 246–51, esp. 247). CLAUDIO GUILLÉN (*Literature as System: Essays Toward the Theory of Literary History* (Princeton: Princeton University Press, 1971), pp. 386–8), for his part, distinguishes three sorts of classes: genres properly so called, metrical forms, and (referring to Frye with a felicitous substitution of terms) 'presentational *modes*, like "*narrative*" and "*dramatic*"'. But he adds, not without reason, that 'unlike Frye, I do not think that these modes constitute the central generic principle of all generic differentiation, and that the specific genres are forms or instances *of* these modes'.

11. The italicised phrase is no doubt the only point on which I part company with PHILIPPE LEJEUNE's criticism of the idea of 'type' (*Le Pacte autobiographique* (Paris: Seuil, 1975), pp. 326–34). Like Lejeune, I believe that type is 'an idealized projection' ('naturalized', I would more readily call it) of genre. Like Todorov, however, I think that there exist a priori forms, let us call them, of literary expression. But in my view these a priori forms are to be found only in modes, which are linguistic and preliterary categories. And then, of course, there is subject matter, which is also largely extraliterary and transhistorical. I say 'largely', not 'wholly': I unhesitatingly concede to Lejeune that autobiography, like all genres, is a historical fact, but I maintain that its thematic commitments are not entirely so and that 'bourgeois consciousness' does not explain everything about them.

13 The Law of Genre*

JACQUES DERRIDA

As a focal point of structuralist endeavours to create a 'science of literature', the concept of genre was an obvious target for deconstruction. In this intricately argued essay, the French philosopher Jacques Derrida duly performs such an analysis, dramatising – in order to subvert – the authoritarian undertones that attach to traditional critical discourse about genre, whilst simultaneously parodying modern structuralism's quest for the 'laws' of literature. Originally delivered as a lecture at an international symposium on genre at the University of Strasbourg in 1979 (contributions to which were published, together with translations, in a special issue of the journal *Glyph*), the discussion falls into two parts. The first examines the logical status of genre classifications, and the nature of 'genericity': that is, the means by which texts belong to, and inscribe themselves within, a genre or genres. Genre logic, Derrida argues, is contradictory, and the 'law of genre' self-defeating, not only because individual texts frequently elude classification, but also because the textual signals which indicate membership of a genre cannot themselves be part of that genre. To illustrate these claims, the second part of the essay (not included here) offers a detailed reading of Maurice Blanchot's *La Folie du jour* (The Madness of the Day), a text which self-consciously enacts the problematic which Derrida's essay addresses, and in so doing invalidates, according to Derrida, the assumptions on which even the most advanced genre theory rests.

As his references indicate, Derrida's discussion is in part a response to Genette's essay on genres and modes (see above, Chapter 12), and to Philippe Lacoue-Labarthe and Jean-Luc Nancy's book *The Literary Absolute* (1988), a post-structuralist study of the literary theory of German Romanticism. Whether Derrida's essay is simply 'a modest annotation on the margins' of these

---

* Reprinted from *Glyph*, 7 (1980), 202–13. Translated by Avital Ronell.

predecessors' work (as he at one points suggests), or a more far-reaching intervention in modern genre theory, is a matter on which opinion is divided. For a positive assessment, see Leitch, '(De)Coding (Generic) Discourse' (1991). The gender issues raised in the second part of the essay are discussed by Mary Jacobus, 'The Law Of/And Gender: Genre Theory and *The Prelude*', *Diacritics*, 14 (1984), 47–57. The full text of Derrida's essay, together with some of his other contributions to literary theory, can be found in Derrida, *Acts of Literature*, ed. Derek Attridge (London: Routledge, 1992). For a selection of critical responses, see *Derrida: A Critical Reader*, ed. David Wood (Oxford: Blackwell, 1992).

Genres are not to be mixed.

I will not mix genres.

I repeat: genres are not to be mixed. I will not mix them.

Now suppose I let these utterances resonate all by themselves.

Suppose: I abandon them to their fate, I set free their random virtualities and turn them over to my audience – or rather, to *your* audience, to your auditory grasp, to whatever mobility they retain and you bestow upon them to engender effects of all kinds without my having to stand behind them.

I merely said, and then repeated: genres are not to be mixed; I will not mix them.

As long as I release these utterances (which others might call speech acts) in a form yet scarcely determined, given the open context out of which I have just let them be grasped from 'my' language – as long as I do this, you may find it difficult to choose among several interpretative options. They are legion, as I could demonstrate. They form an open and essentially unpredictable series. But you may be tempted by *at least* two types of audience, two modes of interpretation, or, if you prefer to give these words more of a chance, then you may be tempted by two different genres of hypothesis. Which ones?

On the one hand, it could be a matter of a fragmentary discourse whose propositions would be of the descriptive, constative, and neutral genre. In such a case, I would have named the operation which consists of 'genres are not to be mixed'. I would have designated this operation in a neutral fashion without evaluating it, without recommending or advizing against it, certainly without binding anyone to it. Without claiming to lay down the law or to make this an act of law, I merely would have summoned up, in a fragmentary utterance, the sense of a practice, an act or event, as you wish: which is what sometimes happens when we revert to 'genres are not to be mixed'. With reference to the same case, and to a hypothesis of the same type, same mode, same genre – or same order: when I said, 'I will not mix genres', you may have discerned a foreshadowing description – I am not saying a prescription – the descriptive designation telling in advance what will transpire, predicting it in the constative mode or genre, i.e. it will happen thus, I will not mix genres. The future tense describes, then, what will surely take place, as you yourselves can judge; but for my part it does not constitute a commitment. I am not making you a promise here, nor am I issuing myself an order or invoking the authority of some law to which I am resolved to submit myself. In this case, the future tense does not set the time of a performative speech act of a promising or ordering type.

But another hypothesis, another type of audience, and another interpretation would have been no less legitimate. 'Genres are not to be mixed' could strike you as a sharp order. You might have heard it resound the elliptical but all the more authoritarian summons to a law of 'do' or 'do not' which, as everyone knows, occupies the concept or constitutes the value of *genre*. As soon as the word 'genre' is sounded, as soon as it is heard, as soon as one attempts to conceive it, a limit is drawn. And when a limit is established, norms and interdictions are not far behind: 'Do', 'Do not' says 'genre', the word 'genre', the figure, the voice, or the law of genre. And this can be said of genre in all genres, be it a question of a generic or a general determination of what one calls 'nature' or *physis* (for example, a biological *genre* in the sense of *gender*, or the human *genre*, a genre of all that is in general), or be it a question of a typology designated as non-natural and depending on laws or orders which were once held to be opposed to *physis* according to those values associated with *technè*, *thesis*, *nomos* (for example, an artistic, poetic or literary genre). But the whole enigma of genre springs perhaps most closely from within this limit between the two genres of genre which, neither separable nor inseparable, form an odd couple of one without the other in which each evenly serves the other a citation to appear in the figure of the other, simultaneously and indiscernibly saying 'I' and 'we', me the genre, we genres, without it being possible to think that the 'I' is a species of the genre 'we'. For who would have us believe that we, we two for example, would form a genre or belong to one? Thus, as soon as genre announces itself, one must respect a norm, one must not cross a line of demarcation, one must not risk impurity, anomaly or monstrosity. And so it goes in all cases, whether or not this law of genre be interpreted as a determination or perhaps even as a destination of *physis*, and regardless of the weight or range imputed to *physis*. If a genre is what it is, or if it is supposed to be what it is destined to be by virtue of its *telos*, then 'genres are not to be mixed'; one should not mix genres, one owes it to oneself not to get mixed up in mixing genres. Or, more rigorously, genres should not intermix. And if it should happen that they do intermix, by accident or through transgression, by mistake or through a lapse, then this should confirm, since, after all, we are speaking of 'mixing', the essential purity of their identity. This purity belongs to the typical axiom: it is a law of the law of genre, whether or not the law is, as one feels justified in saying, 'natural'. This normative position and this evaluation are inscribed and prescribed even at the threshold of the 'thing itself', if something of the genre 'genre' can be so named. And so it follows that you might have taken the second sentence in the first person, 'I will not mix genres', as a vow of obedience, as a docile response to the injunction emanating from the law of genre. In place of a constative description, you would then hear a promise, an oath; you would grasp the following respectful commitment: I promise you that I will not mix genres, and, through this act of pledging utter faithfulness to my commitment, I will be faithful to the law of genre, since, by its very nature, the law invites and commits me in advance not to mix genres. By publishing my response to the imperious call of the law, I would correspondingly commit myself to be responsible.

Unless, of course, I were actually implicated in a wager, a challenge, an impossible bet – in short, a situation that would exceed the matter of merely engaging a commitment from me. And suppose for a moment that it were impossible not to mix genres. What if there were, lodged within the heart of the law itself, a law of impurity or a principle of contamination? And suppose the condition for the possibility of the law were the *a priori* of a counter-law, an axiom of impossibility that would confound its sense, order and reason?

I have just proposed an alternative between two interpretations. I did not do so, as you can imagine, in order to check myself. The line or trait that seemed to separate the two bodies of interpretation is affected *straight away* by an essential disruption that, for the time being, I shall let you name or qualify in any way you care to: as internal division of the trait, impurity, corruption, contamination, decomposition, perversion, deformation, even cancerization, generous proliferation or degenerescence. All these disruptive 'anomalies' are engendered – and this is their common law, the lot or site they share – by *repetition*. One might even say by citation or re-citation (*ré-cit*), provided that the restricted use of these two words is not a call to strict generic order. A citation in the strict sense implies all sorts of contextual conventions, precautions and protocols in the mode of reiteration, of coded signs such as quotation marks or other typographical devices used for writing a citation. The same holds no doubt for the *récit* as a form, mode, or genre of discourse, even – and I shall return to this – as a literary type. And yet the law that protects the usage, in *stricto sensu*, of the words *citation* and *récit*, is threatened intimately and in advance by a counter-law that constitutes this very law, renders it possible, conditions it and thereby renders it impossible – for reasons of edges on which we shall run aground in just a moment – to edge through, to edge away from or to hedge around the counter-law itself. The law and the counter-law serve each other, citations summoning each other to appear, and each re-cites the other in this proceeding (*procès*). There would be no cause for concern if one were rigorously assured of being able to distinguish with rigor between a citation and a non-citation, a *récit* and a non-*récit* or a repetition within the form of one or the other.

I shall not undertake to demonstrate, assuming it is still possible, why you were unable to decide whether the sentences with which I opened this presentation and marked this context were or were not repetitions of a citational type; or whether they were or were not of the performative type; or certainly whether they were, both of them, together – and each time together – the one or the other. For perhaps someone has noticed that, from one repetition to the next, a change had insinuated itself into the relationship between the two initial utterances. The punctuation had been slightly modified, as had the content of the second independent clause. This barely noticeable shift could theoretically have created a mutual independency between the interpretative alternatives that might have tempted you to opt for one or the other, or for one *and* the other of these two sentences. A particularly rich combinatory of possibilities would thus ensue, which, in order not to exceed my time-limit and out of respect for the law of genre and of the audience, I shall abstain from recounting. I am simply going to assume a certain relationship between what has just now happened and the origin of literature, as well as its aborigine or its abortion, to quote Philippe Lacoue-Labarthe.[1]

Provisionally claiming for myself the authority of such an assumption, I shall let our field of vision contract as I limit myself to a sort of species of the genre 'genre'. I shall focus on this genre of genre which is generally supposed, and always a bit too rashly, not to be part of nature, of *physis*, but rather of *technè*, of the arts, still more narrowly of poetry, and most particularly of literature. But at the same time, I take the liberty to think that, while limiting myself thus, I exclude nothing, at least in principle and *de jure* – the relationships here no longer being those of extension, from exemplary individual to species, from species to genre as genus or from the genre of genre to genre in general; rather as we shall see, these relationships are a whole order apart. What is at stake, in effect, is exemplarity and its whole *enigma* – in other words, as the word enigma indicates, exemplarity and the *récit* which works through the logic of the example.

Before going about putting a certain example to the test, I shall attempt to formulate, in a manner as elliptical, economical, and formal as possible, what I shall call the law of the law of genre. It is precisely a principle of contamination, a law of impurity, a parasitical economy. In the code of set theories, if I may use it at least figuratively, I would speak of a sort of participation without belonging – a taking part in without being part of, without having membership in a set. The trait that marks membership inevitably divides, the boundary of the set comes to form, by invagination, an internal pocket larger than the whole; and the outcome of this division and of this abounding remains as singular as it is limitless.

To demonstrate this, I shall hold to the leanest generalities. But I should like to justify this initial indigence or asceticism as well as possible. For example, I shall not enter into the passionate debate brought forth by poetics on the theory and the history of genre-theory, on the critical history of the concept of genre from Plato to the present. My stance is motivated by these considerations: in the first place, we now have at our disposal some remarkable, and, of late, handsomely enriched works dealing either with primary texts or critical analyses. I am thinking especially of the journal *Poétique*, of its issue entitled 'Genres' (32) and of Genette's opening essay, 'Genres, "Types", Modes'. From yet another point of view, *L'Absolu littéraire* (*The Literary Absolute*) has already created quite a stir in this context, and everything that I shall risk here should perhaps resolve itself in a modest annotation on the margins of this magistral work which I assume some of you have already read. I could further justify my abstention or my abstinence here simply by acknowledging the terminological luxury or rapture as well as the taxonomic exuberance which debates of this kind, in a manner by no means fortuitous, have sparked: I feel completely powerless to contain this fertile proliferation – and not only because of time-constraints. I shall put forth, instead, *two* principal *motives*, hoping thereby to justify my keeping to scant preliminary generalities at the edge of this problematic.

To what do these two motives essentially relate? In its most recent phase – and this much is certainly clear in Genette's propositions – the most advanced critical axis has led to a rereading of the entire history of genre-theory. This rereading has been inspired by the perception – and it must be said, despite the initial denial, by the correction – of two types of misconstruing or confusion. On the one hand, and this will be the first motive or ground for my abstention, Plato and Aristotle have been subjected to considerable deformation,

as Genette reminds us, insofar as they have been viewed in terms
alien to their thinking, and even in terms that they themselves would
have rejected; but this deformation has usually taken on the form of
naturalization. Following a classical precedent, one has deemed
natural structures or typical forms whose history is hardly natural,
but rather, quite to the contrary, complex and heterogeneous. These
forms have been treated as natural – and let us bear in mind the
entire semantic scale of this difficult word whose span is so far-
ranging and open-ended that it extends as far as the expression
'natural language', by which term everyone agrees tacitly to oppose
natural language only to a formal or artificial language without
thereby implying that this natural language is a simple physical or
biological production. Genette insists at length on this naturalization
of genres: 'The history of genre-theory is strewn with these fascinating
outlines that *inform and deform reality*, a reality often heterogenous
to the literary field, and that claim to discover a natural "system"
wherein they construct a factitious symmetry heavily reinforced by
fake windows' (italics added, p. 408).[2] In its most efficacious and
legitimate aspect, this critical reading of the history (and) of genre-
theory is based on an opposition between nature and history, and,
more generally – as the allusion to an artificial construct indicates
('. . . wherein they construct a factitious symmetry . . .') – on an
opposition between nature and what can be called the series of all its
others. Such an opposition seems to go without saying; placed within
this critical perspective, it is never questioned. Even if it has been
tucked away discreetly in some passage that has escaped my attention,
this barely visible suspicion clearly had no effect on the general
organization of the problematic. This does not diminish the relevance
or fecundity of a reading such as Genette's. But a place remains open
for some preliminary questions concerning his presuppositions, for
some questions concerning the boundaries where it begins to take
hold or take place. The form of these boundaries will contain me, and
rein me in. These general propositions whose number is always open
and indeterminable for whatever critical interpretation will not be
dealt with here. What however seems to me to require more urgent
attention is the relationship of nature to history, of nature to its
others, *precisely when genre is on the line*.

   Let us consider the most general concept of genre, from the minimal
trait or predicate delineating it permanently through the modulations
of its types and the regimens of its history: it rends and defends itself
by mustering all its energy against a simple opposition that arises
from nature and from history, as from nature and the vast lineage
of its others (*technè, nomos, thesis,* then *spirit, society, freedom, history,*
etc.). Between *physis* and its others, *genos* certainly situates one of the

225

privileged scenes of the process, and, no doubt, sheds the greatest obscurity on it. One need not mobilize etymology to this end and could just as well equate *genos* with birth, and birth in turn with the generous force of engenderment or generation – *physis*, in fact – as with race, familial membership, classificatory genealogy or class, age class (generation) or social class; it comes as no surprise that, in nature and art, genre, a concept that is essentially classificatory and genealogico-taxonomic, itself engenders so many classificatory vertigines when it goes about classifying itself and situating the classificatory principle or instrument within a set. As with the class itself, the principle of genre is unclassifiable, it tolls the knell of the knell (*glas*), in other words of classicum, of what permits one to call out (*calare*) orders and to order the manifold within a nomenclature. *Genos* thus indicates the place, the now or never of the most necessary meditation on the 'fold' which is no more historical than natural in the classical sense of these two words, and which turns *phyein* over to itself across others that perhaps no longer relate to it according to that epoch-making logic which was decisory, critical, oppositional, even dialectical, but rather according to the trait of a contract entirely other. *De jure*, this meditation acts as an absolute prerequisite without which any historical perspectivizing will always be difficult to legitimate. For example, the romantic era – this powerful figure indicted by Genette (since it attempted to reinterpret the system of modes as a system of genres) – is no longer a simple era and can no longer be inscribed as a moment or a stage placeable within the trajectory of a 'history' whose concept we could be certain of. Romanticism, if something of the sort can be thus identified, is also the general repetition of all the folds that in themselves gather, couple, divide *physis* as well as *genos* through the genre, and through all the genres of genre, through the mixing of genre that is 'more than a genre', through the excess of genre in relation to itself, as to its abounding movement and its general assemblage which coincides, too, with its dissolution.[3] Such a 'moment' is no longer a simple moment *in* the history and theory of literary genres. To treat it thus would in effect implicate one as tributary – whence the strange logic – of something that has in itself constituted a certain romantic motif, namely, the teleological ordering of history. Romanticism simultaneously obeys naturalizing and historicizing logic, and it can be shown easily enough that we have not yet been delivered from the romantic heritage – even though we might wish it so and assuming that such a deliverance would be of compelling interest to us – as long as we persist in drawing attention to historical concerns and the truth of historical production in order to militate against abuses or confusions of naturalization. The debate, it could be argued, remains itself a part or effect of romanticism.

A second motive detains me at the threshold or on the edge of a possible problematic of genre (as) history and theory of history and of genre-theory – another genre, in fact. For the moment, I find it impossible to decide – impossible for reasons that I do not take to be accidental, and this, precisely, is what matters to me – I find it impossible to decide whether the possibly exemplary text which I intend to put to the test does or does not lend itself to the distinction drawn between *mode* and *genre*. Now, as you may recall, Genette demonstrates the stringent necessity of this distinction; and he rests his case on 'the confusion of modes and genres' (p. 417). This implies a serious charge against romanticism, even though 'the romantic reinterpretation of the system of modes as a system of genres is neither *de facto* nor *de jure* the epilogue to this long history' (p. 415). This confusion, according to Genette, has aided and abetted the naturalization of genres by projecting onto them the 'privilege of naturalness, which was *legitimately* . . . that of three modes . . .' (p. 421). Suddenly, this naturalization 'makes these arch-genres into ideal or natural types which they neither are nor can be: there are no arch-genres that can totally escape historicity *while preserving a generic definition*. There are modes, for example: the *récit*. There are genres, for example: the novel; the relation of genres to modes is complex and, perhaps not, as Aristotle suggests, one of simple inclusion.'

If I am inclined to poise myself on *this* side of Genette's argument, it is not only because of his ready acceptance of the distinction between nature and history, but also because of its implications with regard to mode and to the distinction between mode and genre. Genette's definition of mode contains this singular and interesting characteristic: it remains, in contradistinction to genre, purely formal. Reference to a content has no pertinence. This is not the case with genre. The generic criterion and the modal criterion, Genette says, are absolutely heterogenous: 'each genre defined itself essentially by a specification of content which was not prescribed by the definition of mode . . .' (p. 417). I do not believe that this recourse to the opposition of form and content, this distinction between mode and genre, need be contested, and my purpose is not to challenge isolated aspects of Genette's argument. One might just question the presuppositions for the legitimacy of such an argument. One might also question the extent to which his argument can help us read a given text when it behaves in a given way with regard to mode and genre, especially when the text does not seem to be written sensibly within their limits, but rather about the very subject of those limits, and with the aim of disrupting their order. The limits, for instance, of that mode which would be, according to Genette, the *récit* ('there are modes, for example: the *récit*'). Of the (possibly) exemplary text

which I shall address shortly, I shall not hasten to add that it is a
'*récit*', and you will soon understand why. In this text, the *récit* is not
only a mode, and a mode put into practice or put to the test because
it is deemed impossible; it is also the name of a theme. It is the
nonthematizable thematic content of something of a textual form that
assumes a point of view with respect to the genre, even though it
perhaps does not come under the heading of any genre – and perhaps
no longer even under the heading of literature, if it indeed wears
itself out around genre-less modalizations, it would confirm one of
Genette's propositions: 'Genres are, properly speaking, literary [or
aesthetic] categories; modes are categories that pertain to linguistics
or, more precisely, to an anthropology of verbal expression' (p. 418).[4]

In a very singular manner, the very short text which I will discuss
presently makes the *récit* and the impossibility of the *récit* its theme,
its impossible theme or content at once inaccessible, indeterminable,
interminable and inexhaustible; and it makes the word '*récit*', under
the aegis of a certain form, its titleless title, the mentionless mention
of its genre. This text, as I shall try to demonstrate, seems to be
made, among other things, *to make light* of all the tranquil categories
of genre-theory and history in order to upset their taxonomic
certainties, the distribution of their classes, and the presumed stability
of their classical nomenclatures. It is a text destined, at the same
time, to summon up these classes by conducting their proceeding,
by proceeding from the proceeding to the law of genre. For if the
juridical code has frequently thrust itself upon me in order to hear
this case, it has done so to call as witness a (possibly) exemplary text,
and because I am convinced copious rights are bound up in all of
this: the law itself is at stake.

These are the two principal reasons why I shall keep to the liminal
edge of (the) history (and) of genre-theory. Here now, very quickly,
is the law of abounding, of *excess*, the law of participation without
membership, of contamination, etc., which I mentioned earlier. It will
seem meager to you, and even of staggering abstractness. It does not
particularly concern either genres, or types, or modes or any form in
the strict sense of its concept. I therefore do not know under what
title the field or object submitted to this law should be placed. It is
perhaps the limitless field of general textuality. I can take each word
of the series (genre, type, mode, form) and decide that it will hold
for all the others (all genres of genres, types, modes, forms; all types
of types, genres, modes, forms; all forms of forms, etc.). The trait
common to these classes of classes is precisely the identifiable
recurrence of a common trait by which one recognises, or should
recognise, a membership in a class. There should be a trait upon
which one could rely in order to decide that a given textual event, a

given 'work', corresponds to a given class (genre, type, mode, form, etc.). And there should be a code enabling one to decide questions of class-membership on the basis of this trait. For example – a very humble axiom, but, by the same token, hardly contestable – if a genre exists (let us say the novel, since no one seems to contest its generic quality), then a code should provide an identifiable trait and one which is identical to itself, authorizing us to determine, to adjudicate whether a given text belongs to this genre or perhaps to that genre. Likewise, outside of literature or art, if one is bent on classifying, one should consult a set of identifiable and codifiable traits to determine whether this or that, such a thing or such an event belongs to this set or that class. This may seem trivial. Such a distinctive trait *qua* mark is however always *a priori* remarkable. It is always possible that a set – I have compelling reasons for calling this a text, whether it be written or oral – re-marks on this distinctive trait within itself. This can occur in texts that do not, at a given moment, assert themselves to be literary or poetic. A defense speech or newspaper editorial can indicate by means of a mark, even if it is not explicitly designated as such, 'Voilà! I belong, as anyone may remark, to the type of text called a defense speech or an article of the genre newspaper-editorial.' The possibility is always there. This does not constitute a text *ipso facto* as 'literature', even though such a possibility, always left open and therefore eternally remarkable, situates perhaps in every text the possibility of its becoming literature. But this does not interest me at the moment. What interests me is that this re-mark – ever possible for every text, for every corpus of traces – is absolutely necessary for and constitutive of what we call art, poetry or literature. It underwrites the eruption of *technè*, which is never long in coming. I submit this axiomatic question for your consideration: can one identify a work of art, of whatever sort, but especially a work of discursive art, if it does not bear the mark of a genre, if it does not signal or mention it or make it remarkable in any way? Let me clarify two points on this subject. First, it is possible to have several genres, an intermixing of genres or a total genre, the genre 'genre' or the poetic or literary genre as genre of genres. Second, this re-mark can take on a great number of forms and can itself pertain to highly diverse types. It need not be a designation or 'mention' of the type found beneath the title of certain books (novel, *récit*, drama). The re-mark of belonging need not pass through the consciousness of the author or the reader, although it often does so. It can also refute this consciousness or render the explicit 'mention' mendacious, false, inadequate or ironic according to all sorts of overdetermined figures. Finally, this re-marking-trait need be neither a theme nor a thematic component of the work – although of course this instance of belonging to one or several genres, not to mention all the traits that mark this belonging, often have been treated as theme, even before the advent of what we call 'modernism'. If I am not mistaken in saying that such a trait is remarkable, that is, noticeable, in every aesthetic, poetic or literary corpus, then consider this paradox, consider the irony (which is irreducible to a consciousness or an attitude): this supplementary and distinctive trait, a mark of belonging or inclusion, does not properly pertain to any genre or class. The re-mark of belonging does not belong. It belongs without belonging, and the 'without' (or the suffix '-less') which relates belonging to non-belonging appears only in the timeless time of the blink of an eye (*Augenblick*). The eyelid closes, but barely, an instant among instants, and what it closes is verily the eye, the view, the light of day. But without such respite, nothing would come to light. To formulate it in the scantiest manner – the simplest but most apodictic – I submit for your consideration the following hypothesis: a text cannot belong to no genre, it cannot be without or less a genre. Every text participates in one or several genres, there is no genreless text; there is always a genre and genres, yet such participation never amounts to belonging. And not because of an abundant overflowing or a free, anarchic and unclassifiable productivity, but because of the *trait* of participation itself, because of the effect of the code and of the generic mark. Making genre its mark, a text demarcates itself. If remarks of belonging belong without belonging, participate without belonging, then genre-designations cannot be simply part of the corpus. Let us take the designation 'novel' as an example. This should be marked in one way or another, even if it does not appear, as it often does in French and German texts, in the explicit form of a subtitled designation, and even if it proves deceptive or ironic. This designation is not novelistic; it does not, in whole or in part, take part in the corpus whose denomination it nonetheless imparts. Nor is it simply extraneous to the corpus. But this singular topos places within and without the work, along its boundary, an inclusion and exclusion with regard to genre in general, as to an identifiable class in general. It gathers together the corpus and, at the same time, in the same blinking of an eye, keeps it from closing, from identifying itself with itself. This axiom of non-closure or non-fulfillment enfolds within itself the condition for the possibility and the impossibility of taxonomy. This inclusion and this exclusion do not remain exterior to one another; they do not exclude each other. But neither are they immanent or identical to each other. They are neither one nor two. They form what I shall call the *genre-clause*, a clause stating at once the juridical utterance, the precedent-making designation and the law-text, but also the closure, the closing that excludes itself from what it includes (one could also speak of a floodgate ('*écluse*') of genre). The clause or floodgate of genre declasses what it allows to be classed. It tolls the knell of genealogy or of genericity, which it however also brings forth to the light of day. Putting to death the very thing that it engenders, it cuts a strange figure; a formless form, it remains nearly invisible, it neither sees the day nor brings itself to light. Without it, neither genre nor literature come to light, but as soon as there is this blinking of an eye, this clause or this floodgate of genre, at the very moment that a genre or a literature is broached, at that very moment, degenerescence has begun, the end begins.

Notes

1. Philippe Lacoue-Labarthe and Jean-Luc Nancy, *L'Absolu littéraire: théorie de la littérature du Romantisme allemand* (Paris, Seuil: 1978) (Eng. *The Literary Absolute: The Theory of Literature in German Romanticism*, trans. Philip Barnard and Cheryl Laster (New York: State University of New York Press, 1988)) [Ed.].

2. Derrida's page references are to Genette's original article, 'Genres, "Types", Mode', *Poétique*, 8:32 (1977), 389–421, not to the later version included in Chapter 12 above [Ed.].

3. In this respect, the second footnote in *L'Absolu littéraire*, p. 271, seems to me, let us say, a bit too equitable in its rigorous and honest prudence [Derrida's note].

4. Compare the revised version of Genette's statement on p. 213 above [Ed.].

14 Transformations of Genre*

ALASTAIR FOWLER

As other parts of this anthology demonstrate, the perception that literary genres are dynamic rather than static entities – that they change or 'evolve' across time – is the single most important factor separating modern from earlier genre theory. In this extract from his book *Kinds of Literature* (1982), a comprehensive introduction to genre theory, the Scottish scholar Alastair Fowler attempts an inventory of the different kinds of transformation that genres can undergo in the course of their evolution. The list does not claim to be exhaustive: the original formation of a genre is distinguished from its subsequent transformations, and discussed elsewhere in the book; and a further chapter is devoted to what Fowler calls 'generic modulation', the process whereby some genres, at a certain point in their history, extend into much broader, 'modal' entities which can combine with and modify other genres (e.g. 'elegy' expands into the 'elegiac', the pastoral form into the pastoral mode). Nor are Fowler's categories mutually exclusive: many changes clearly involve a number of simultaneous transformations, and some – 'inclusionism' and 'generic mixture', for instance – overlap so considerably that the distinction between them may seem questionable. It is, nevertheless, a useful and suggestive typology, characteristic of a book which, although resistant to theoretical genre-systems, aspires throughout to restore order and clarity to what Fowler sees as an unnecessarily chaotic body of knowledge.

Like Rosalie Colie (see Chapter 9), whose work he often cites, Fowler's specialist field is Renaissance literature, to which his own approach to genre is especially attuned. The hermeneutic principles on which his theory rests are partly derived from E.D. Hirsch, to whom the book is dedicated: see Hirsch, *Validity*

---

* Reprinted from Alastair Fowler, *Kinds of Literature: An Introduction to the Theory of Genres and Modes* (Oxford: Oxford University Press, 1982), pp. 170–83.

in Interpretation (1967), especially pp. 68–126. Fowler's other publications include many studies of individual genres, and an ambitious *History of English Literature* (1987) designed to emphasise the role of genres and genre theory in literary history. This project has not been without its critics: for a critique of Fowler's 'ultimately conservative view' of literary history and of genre theory, see Mary Jacobus, 'The Law Of/And Gender: Genre Theory and *The Prelude*', *Diacritics*, 14 (1984), 47–57. For a vigorous reassertion of the value of genre studies, and a refinement of his own definition of genre, see Fowler, 'The Future of Genre Theory: Functions and Constructional Types', in *The Future of Literary Theory*, ed. Cohen (1989). For other accounts of generic transformation (many of which Fowler cites, and seeks to integrate into his own scheme), see the selections elsewhere in this anthology from Tynyanov, Propp, Bakhtin, Frye and Jameson.

The processes by which genres change are the same as those that produce most literary change. To describe them fully – or any one of them – would be far beyond our present scope. It is, after all, a main theme of most literary history and much criticism. However, the processes can at least be categorized. Those that stand out may be identified as: topical invention, combination, aggregation, change of scale, change of function, counterstatement, inclusion, selection, and generic mixture.[1] No doubt there are others; but these would be enough in themselves to cover the main changes known to literary history.

Topical invention

Genres change when new topics are added to their repertoires. Sometimes the topics are entirely novel, as when the photograph was first introduced into the poem about a painting. Cervantes' modern windmill was similarly a *novum repertum* so far as romance was concerned, as Rosalie Colie remarks. More often, as we have seen, it is a matter of specialization: of developing a topic already within the repertoire. Student life was a well-established minor topic of the novel (Thackeray; the *Bildungsroman*) long before the university novel subgenre. Such topical innovations seem to characterise most new literary movements. Perhaps this is because they involve a turning from interest in form to interest in matter. A striking instance is the anti-Petrarchan and anti-Ciceronian movement of the early seventeenth century, which led to prolific invention of new matter – and to pervasive generic change.

'Invented' topics may be transformed from other genres or literatures or even other media. In this way, topics of love and of individual sensibility invaded epic: the English minor ode continued to draw matter from Ronsard and Anacreon and the Greek Anthology, and religious epigrams incorporated sacred iconography and emblem material. In the Middle Ages and the Renaissance, such exchanges between arts were very free, and offered a wealth of resources for generic construction. Thus, the satiric scheme of Seven Deadly Sins owed much to visual art, while Elizabethan comedy made extensive use of matter connected with games and festive rituals, such as the Yuletide customs of *Twelfth Night* or the pageant and masquerade of *Love's Labour's Lost*.[2]

Topical invention may also lie in a fresh approach to existing topics.[3] But this usually amounts to a modal transformation. When Sidney equips Cupid with a gun (*Astrophil and Stella* 20) he does more than add fresh aspects to a Petrarchan topic. He is in effect making a counterstatement, or producing an epigrammatic transformation of the sonnet.

Combination

Combination of repertoires is one of the most obvious means of generic change. As we saw in the last chapter [of *Kinds of Literature*], the repertoire of the river poem may have contributed to the country house poem. But it also combined with other repertoires, such as that of the georgic verse essay, to form the long topographical poem (*Polyolbion* 18; *The Wonders of the Peak* 332–401). And later Marvell combined the local descriptive and estate poems with the retirement poem of Saint-Amant and Sarbiewski, to produce a complex form adumbrating the eighteenth-century poem of retirement. Combination of repertoires plays some part in most new forms of any magnitude. It is most obvious at the assembly stage. So the Elizabethan masque combined mummery, masquerade, pageant, and entertainment: discrete kinds that were to some extent recognised as such and referred to by their separate names. Subsequently, however, a successful combination will come to be regarded as a single repertoire. We are no longer much aware which features of masque derive from which contributory kind.

Aggregation

A different additive process is aggregation, whereby several complete short works are grouped in an ordered collection – as the songs in a song cycle or the ballads in a ballad opera. The composite work may be united by framing and linking passages, sometimes of a very substantial character (*Confessio Amantis; The Canterbury Tales*). Such an aggregate is generically distinct both from its component parts and from unordered collections. Thus, Boccaccio's *Decameron* represents a different genre from that of the tales it orders, as well as from the *Cento Novelle Antiche* or the *Cent Nouvelles Nouvelles*.[4] Aggregation's transforming effect is obvious enough in the epistolary novel or the sequence of sketches.[5] But other aggregate genres also transcend their component repertoires. So the calendars of Spenser, Thomson, and Clare order according to season, and thus create an expectancy of variations and contrasts – which may be fulfilled or finessed. It was certainly a generic transformation when Thomas Watson and Sir Philip Sidney, writing under Continental influence, ordered their love poems in sequences.[6] The Elizabethan sonnet sequence has a complex repertoire of its own, which includes such features as liminal conventions, narrative patterns, literary-critical digressions, mood changes, and numerological structure. In addition to sonnets, it usually includes other metrical forms, either interspersed throughout or (more often) added at or near the end. So *Astrophil and Stella* introduces songs after Sonnet 63; *Amoretti* has Anacreontics and a major ode; and Daniel's and Shakespeare's sequences are followed by complaints.[7] Similarly, any arrangement of lyrics or epigrams *en suite* is liable to change their genre. In Stevens's *Thirteen Ways of Looking at a Blackbird*, for example, thirteen haiku-like momentary lyrics became in aggregate meditative and metaphysical. And sequences by Morgan and by Crichton Smith offer several other striking instances.

Change of scale

During the ages of rhetoric, writers often planned the scale of *dispositio* at a very early stage.[8] In such circumstances, change of scale was a means of generic originality – something that ancient theorists partly recognised when they attempted to describe it.[9] We have to keep it in mind, therefore, in tracing relations between genres. Changes of scale may be by *macrologia* or *brachylogia*. *Macrologia* magnifies, as when the *Divina Commedia* enlarges the epic *nekuia*, or descent into hell, to form a third of the work. Shaw's stage directions exhibit *macrologia*. So do individual letters in epistolary novels, by comparison with nonliterary letters. By contrast, *brachylogia* or *syntomia* diminishes, as when Archibald MacLeish reduces the Horatian epistle to a short poem on poetry, in *Ars Poetica*. Of the two, *brachylogia* is formally more interesting. It is necessarily complex, since in condensing it must find ways to suggest the original features not explicitly present. *Brachylogia* should be considered together with selection, *macrologia* with topical invention.

Macrologia makes room for fuller development, and so for new topics. It may thus have a decisive role in generic change. But it can hardly by itself produce a new kind. John Ashbery's *Self-Portrait in a Convex Mirror* may seem an exception, as *macrologia* of the poem about a painting. But there is also a confessional modulation – to say nothing of combination with the mirror poem, and more broadly with the American long poem. Similarly, Walton's *Complete Angler* not only enlarges eclogue, but also, particularly in the instructive passages, works toward a georgic modulation. And Thomson's *Seasons* offer new topics as well as *macrologia* of georgic description.

In a comparable way, the seventeenth-century vogue for reduction of scale shows again and again that *brachylogia* too is bound up with modal transformation. When Herrick miniaturised form after form in *Hesperides,* or Browne's essays epitomised encyclopedias, or Marvell's *Nymph Complaining* summed up the minor idyll by condensing its main variants, all this was not only an expression of the idea of *multum in parvo*.[10] It was also (or from another point of view) part of the epigrammatic modulation that dominated much of the literature of that period.

Relatively slight changes of scale can have surprisingly wide repercussions. In novels, for example, lengthening the temporal scale beyond a single generation easily shifts the genre toward family chronicle or *roman fleuve*. And how much of the generic character of *Finnegans Wake* springs from the special role accorded to wordplay – or even from the proportions of a single device, the portmanteau word?

Similar to *brachylogia* is the device of omission. This is undoubtedly a source of innovation, as in 'There was a young lady of Crew/Whose limericks stopped at line two'.[11] In a less assertive and more usual form (reminiscent of elision in architecture) it is a regular means of literary change. By disposing of transitions, formulas and the like, it leads to more sophisticated and condensed treatments and so assists the formation of a genre's late stage.

Change of function

In ancient literature, the most minute change of function was enough to alter genre – perhaps no more than varying the speaker or addressee. Horace departed from convention in his First Ode when he addressed a *propemptikon* to a nonhuman addressee, the ship of state.[12] Small as they seem, such variations had a cumulative effect in changing genres and eventually loosening them. In modern periods, change of function has tended to be more drastic. But something very like Horace's addressee-variation can be seen in seventeenth-century religious poetry, in the use of Petrarchist conventions. The human beloved was replaced by the divine lover, the School of Love by the School of the Heart. Even some of the best works in the divine poetry tradition, such as Herbert's *Parody*, altered the functions of a secular genre so directly as to amount to spiritual parodies. However, the features of love elegy could also be reapplied in a subtle and elusive way, as Rosemary Freeman remarks (Herbert's *Dulness* and *Glance*).[13]

Milton shows great audacity in changing the functions of quite fundamental parts of epic. He has a particular penchant for telescoping venerable generic forms in surprising ways. Thus, in *Paradise Lost*, Raphael's visit occasions a conventional flashback to a great work, which takes the unexpected form of creation itself. But simultaneously the episode is an inset and a georgic essay, leading into a dialogue on astronomy. The epic episode is being made to work in a very unusual way. The invocations, similarly, are changed into occasions for autobiographical digression (an innovation that we can almost think of Wordsworth as developing by *macrologia* in *The Prelude*). These instances are obviously deliberate. But function can also change gradually and unintentionally – in response, for example, to changes in the literary model, such as the reduction of the informational value of stanza forms. Gradual change of function is probably perpetual. By contrast, in some periods, notably the seventeenth and nineteenth centuries, there seems to have been an aesthetic preference for altering functions. We can see the same taste in visual art, in the displaced or subverted forms of mannerist and retrospective gothic architecture.

Counterstatement

Claudio Guillén describes the relation of *Don Quixote* to *Lazarillo de Tormes* and especially to Guzmán de Alfarache as that of 'a diametrically opposed masterpiece, which itself was able to serve as seed for a "countergenre"'. Cervantes' work differs from earlier exemplars of the genre in several striking ways: for example, in rejecting fictional autobiography in favor of fictional history.[14] Such antithetic relations within a genre are common enough. But much is gained by extending the idea of counterstatement beyond the limits of a single genre. We may think of certain new genres or 'antigenres' as antitheses to existing genres. Their repertoires are in contrast throughout. In smaller genres, this contrast may take the form of rhetorical inversion, whereby dispraise is modeled on inverted praise, malediction on valediction, and so forth.[15] This has proved a fertile source of generic invention, as many answer poems testify. And on a large scale, something very similar seems to take place. From this point of view, early picaresque is itself an antigenre to romance. It is perhaps particularly antithetic to pastoral romance, whose sensitive hero is fond of contemplating love in retired solitude, and traverses much emotional experience before the final reconciliation. By contrast, picaresque knows no reconciliation of any depth. The *pícaro* is a tough outsider, who learns only the worldly wisdom needed for social adjustment and satiric observation.[16] This contrast of values, motivation, and mimetic 'height' is quite explicit in Cervantes when Don Quixote enacts the exchange of romantic fantasy for down-to-earth reality. There is an element of burlesque in *Don Quixote*, as there is in the antiromance parts of Nashe's *Unfortunate Traveller*. Burlesque exaggerates generic features to absurdity, or juxtaposes them with contraries. However, an antigenre, unlike a burlesque, is not directed against a particular original. Moreover, it has a life of its own that continues collaterally with the contrasting genre. So picaresque and romance proceed in parallel, and may even be interlaced together in the same work, as happens in *Gil Blas*.

Epic has generated several antigenres. One of the oldest is the epic with a recent action (Lucan's *Pharsalia*; Cowley's *Civil War*). The Christian 'brief epic' (*Davideis*; *Paradise Regained*) was supposed to be modeled on the Book of Job, but is obviously an antigenre to classical epic. All the types of biblical epic developed during the Divine Poetry movement answered the pagan epic repertoire feature by feature. To the national or legendary action of Virgilian epic, they opposed the redemptive history revealed in Scripture: to invocation of the pagan Muse, they opposed invocation of Urania, or the Holy Spirit – or prayer to God. Milton takes up all these possibilities with remarkable premeditation, allowing them to confront one another within his own epic. The first two books of *Paradise Lost* use conventions of Christian epic, such as a council of devils; yet they can also be regarded as beginning a pagan epic with Satan as its courageous stoic hero. Later books, less ambiguously, offer a series of Christian epics of various subgenres (hexaemeron in Book 7; Raphael's martial epic in 6; Bartasian epic in 11 and 12).[17] In the Christian parts [. . .] the virtues of Messiah and Adam and the loyal angels directly contrast with those of the pagan hero Satan. Milton, no less than Cervantes, has combined genre and antigenre in a single work.

Among other antigenres, the anti-Petrarchan sonnet should not be omitted. The contrast of sonnet and epigram is somewhat obscured for us by seventeenth-century and Victorian development of the sweet epigram. The Renaissance epigram was predominantly low, spoken, and satiric, whereas the Elizabethan sonnet, being a brief love elegy or small ode, was middle in style, sung, and 'sugared'.[18] Modern readers may therefore miss the bold counterstated character of certain epigramlike sonnets. This applies not only to spiritual sonnets (Constable, Alabaster, Herbert),[19] but to sonnets of unideal love (Sidney, Shakespeare, Barnes). The antigenre comes out particularly clearly where a subgenre such as the *blason* is given a burlesque treatment.[20] [. . .]

So far as pastoral counterstatements are concerned, we have already met the long-standing antithesis between 'native' and 'pure' forms. These are typified by Theocritus, Spenser, Drayton, and Ambrose Philips, on the one hand, and on the other by Virgil and Pope. An antigenre in some ways more radical began with Gay's *Shepherd's Week*. Its near-burlesque treated pastoral topics 'realistically' – just as the delicate *Trivia* did with those of georgic. Later in the century, descriptive realism often took the form of counterstatement to pastoral and georgic.[21] In Crabbe, the opposition is partly explicit:

> Must sleepy bards the flattering dream prolong,
> Mechanic echoes of the Mantuan song?
> From Truth and Nature shall we widely stray,
> Where Virgil, not where Fancy, leads the way?[22]

But if he himself alters the echoes, he by no means silences them. Repeatedly his burden is, in effect, that 'Auburn and Eden can no more be found'.[23] In Hazlitt's words, he checkmates 'Tityrus and Virgil at the game of pastoral cross-purposes'.[24] For his disagreeable landscape is based on a subsoil of conventional topics of eclogue. Even the flower catalogue is there – only replaced with weeds: 'Hardy and high, above the slender sheaf,/The slimy mallow waves her silky leaf' – 'silky' implying the cost of aesthetic values to the poor. Crabbe takes up georgic and pastoral topics, it seems, only to subvert them. So he elegizes the rural sports ('Where are the swains . . . Who struck with matchless force the bounding ball') or diverts them, with changed function, into the inappropriate occupation of a bad priest.[25] Dennis Burden makes an interesting suggestion: 'It is as though the establishing of this sense of contrast . . . was necessary to get Crabbe on the move, but once the poem was in motion then its drive was realism and not contrast.'[26] But from a generic point of view Crabbe's realism is indistinguishable from the 'serious burlesque' of a countergenre.[27] Unfortunately, it was a sort of realism largely pre-empted by the novel. Wordsworth was careful to give it a more subsidiary and muted part.

However that may be, there is no doubt about the novel's thrust for a realism that will look nonliterary. This, as much as any pursuit of 'that advantage which novelty never fails to have with the public',[28] has more than once led novelists to resort to antithetic repertoires. The fictional biography had scarcely been established before a countergenre to it was inaugurated in *Tristram Shandy*.[29] Plot, continuity, scale, authorial intrusion: these and other features of the novelistic repertoire were countered so decisively by Sterne that he achieved a paradigmatic form still being imitated and developed. And the work-in-progress is only one of several antigenres to the novel. So Mitford and Gaskell tried for a form without strong incident or narrative connection – for the impossibility (as Mr Besant might have said) of 'fiction without adventure'. Henry James agreed that 'the story is the thing' ('the story and the novel . . . are the needle and thread'), but counted green spectacles as story, no less than adventures, molding every constituent to the specification of the narrator's reality. And E.M. Forster wished that the novel could be something different and less primitive than a story – wished to belong, in James's figure, to a guild of tailors who recommended the use of the thread without the needle.[30]

With modernism, more extreme antitheses begin. A good example of the consistent antinovel is Joyce's *Ulysses*. A. Walton Litz is surely right to argue that no verisimilar novel can satisfactorily be extracted from it (however brilliantly Goldberg tries), since its fulfilled intention is 'to disintegrate the well-made "novel" into its origins, and then to perform a prodigious act of reintegration'. He also alleges that Joyce 'denies the validity of genres'.[31] Joyce certainly talks about 'the diversity of prose fiction', and attempts to evade the conventions of the novel by comprehensive inclusion, as well as by the use of an extreme digressive *ordo artificialis*. Nevertheless, it remains the verisimilar novel, primarily, that *Ulysses* negates. In spite of Eliot's and Litz's confidence that Joyce has gone beyond the novel ('which will no longer serve'), I feel less sure. Does not he only go beyond (or against) certain recent genres within the novel? 'The novel', after all, continues to develop vigorously. And one of its vigorous genres is precisely the antinovel. *Ulysses*, in fact, raises no special problem for the genre critic, unless he has an unhistorical conception of fixed kinds. Litz's account of how to read *Ulysses* – by attending to the specific generic conventions introduced and negated – is excellent practical advice. The debatable point is the notion of *Ulysses*' unique modernity: 'it resembles many other works of literature, but other works do not resemble it'.[32] From our present standpoint *Ulysses* seems a paradigmatic work, which novels by Beckett, Barth, and Pynchon follow and to some degree resemble. Moreover, *Ulysses* itself may fairly be said to resemble the much earlier antinovel paradigm *Tristram Shandy* – as, for example, in its approach to temporal scale, its narrative discontinuities, and its use of associational transitions.

However, the encyclopedic *Ulysses* is more than an antigenre of the verisimilar novel. Purer embodiments of that genre are Gertrude Stein's *Making of Americans*, or Beckett's later novels, which consistently make antitheses to novelistic forms. Beckett manages this in two ways, principally. First, he progressively eliminates features of the repertoire altogether: event, *mise-en-scène*, dialogue, even paragraphing. Second, he includes forms with a humanistic or religious implication that is effectually 'canceled' (as Kermode puts it). Thus, to quote another critic of Beckett:

> *Watt* . . . is in fact an 'anti-novel' in the tradition of Cervantes, Furetière and of course Sterne, a novel which disdains 'to tell a story about persons recognizable as human beings in recognizable situations,' and which introduces such extraneous matter as digressive anecdotes, snatches of song, exhaustive lists of objects and of logical (and illogical) combinations of possibilities, with an addenda section to contain the rejectamenta from the rest of the book; moreover, it develops minor characters at the expense of major ones, and, finally, fails to show any real action, any progression to a *dénouement*.[33]

It must be said that, in general, counterstatement seems to express a somewhat crude and extreme attitude to literary tradition. The seriousness of a Beckett or the greatness of a Cervantes may make more of it. But even at its best it leads to *tours de force* more often than great works of literature.

So far we have been mainly concerned with single genres. We turn now to transformations where genres are combined or mixed.

Inclusion

By a process as ordinary as embedding in syntax, a literary work may enclose another within it. If the inset form then becomes conventionally linked with the matrix, a generic transformation has taken place. So *The Faerie Queen* contained inset triumphal pageants, tapestry poems, metamorphoses, all of which became features of romantic epic and its descendants.[34] Epic, followed in this by the novel, is particularly capacious: it can contain complete works even of medium size.[35] So *Paradise Lost* achieves an important effect by a transition from Christian epic and hexaemeron to tragedy – 'I now

241

must change/Those notes to tragic'. The Books that follow introduce a remarkable number of the features of tragedy, including *hamartia*, *anangke, peripeteia, stichomythia*, and unity of time.[36] Elsewhere, the same poem has room for a hymn, a sonnet, and various other forms.[37]

Inclusion is found in all literary periods, in a wide variety of genres of all sizes. Eclogues early included inset songs or narratives. And they were themselves inset in the romances of Sannazaro and Sidney. In one type of epithalamium there is recursive inclusion, a nuptial song within a nuptial song (Catullus, *Carmina* 64; Ariosto, *Song for the Third Marriage of Lucrezia Borgia*; Spenser, *Prothalamion*; Gertrude Stein, *Prothalamion for Bobolink and His Louisa a Poem*). Similarly with epitaph: it may have had epigraphic origins, and often reverts to this supposed primitive form, by including an inset inscription. The inscription proposed for Daphnis's tomb, in the epicede (itself inset) in Virgil's Fifth Eclogue, is a paradigmatic instance.[38] Subsequently the device was used to good effect not only for epitaphs, as in *An Epitaph of Sir Thomas Gravener, Knight*,[39] but also for love poems, as in Herrick's *Cruel Maid*, where the lover anticipates his own burial ('And write thereon, *This, Reader, know,/ Love killed this man*. No more but so'). Here, as often, it provides closure for an epigram.[40]

In ancient literature, inclusion seems to have been governed by more restrictive conventions. These might call for a transitional passage introducing the inset. Moreover, the inset and the matrical genres were likely to be closely akin – as when a triumph was included in a genethliacon.[41] Even in Renaissance and later literature, some kinds have been more hospitable to inclusion than others. Loose forms such as satire, dialogue, and anatomy are particularly prone to inclusion, so that they sometimes present a very confusing appearance to the genre critic (Rabelais, Castiglione, Burton).[42] Drama's composite character, too, has tended to encourage inclusion. Fabliaux were included in miracle cycles. Masques were common in Renaissance comedy. And the masque- or play-within-a-play became genre-linked to revenge tragedy, as in *The Spanish Tragedy* – a convention doubled in the *tours de force* of doubly-inset modified entertainments spiked by revengers (*Hamlet*; *Women Beware Women*). Such inclusion may be announced rather explicitly: 'This is some ante-masque belike, my lord' explains Bianca.

The popularity of inclusion in the late Renaissance can perhaps be related to the mannerist vogue for framing devices. Many works were self-embedded, so to speak, in inductions, prologues, epilogues, and the like, with consequent effects of artistic distance. And recognition of genres inset – and sometimes interacting with their setting, like the sonnets in *Love's Labour's Lost* – surely ranks high among the pleasures of Renaissance literature. Think of the complex framing of the play-within-a-play in *Hamlet*, with its own 'prologue', its inset passage inserted by Hamlet, and its three audiences observing one another. Francis Berry has devoted a book to insets in Shakespeare.[43] But we find them everywhere at the time. In poetry, it was a main endeavor of art to achieve novel effects of inclusion. So Cotton inserts among the natural *Wonders of the Peak* (and what a delight to come upon it) an artful description of Chatsworth that is nothing less than a complete country house poem.

Inclusion is a fertile source of generic transformation. Nevertheless, it can hardly in itself provide the basis for a theory of literary change. Often it is a limited phenomenon, without effect on the matrical genre.[44] *Henry VIII* contains an inset masque; it remains a tragical history play. Trollope includes an epigram in *The Prime Minister*; but the novel is not an epigrammatic novel. Inclusion need not effect any generic change. Change is only likely to occur if the inset form is structurally assimilated; or if its proportion to the matrical work is large; or if it is regularly linked to the matrical genre. In any case, a theory based on local inclusion of complete works could not possibly account for the enormous variety of generic mixtures. Many of these can have arisen only from diffuse modulations, in which the transforming agent is an incomplete repertoire. Such modulations are able to color whole works, and eventually to alter genres. With generic mixture, there opens a much wider field of possibility: this is the point at which the theoretical interest of genre abruptly increases. It is like the transition in mathematics from natural to real numbers.

Generic mixture

Cicero, Quintilian, and Horace all advised that the genres should be kept separate – 'Each subject should retain / The place allotted it, with decent thews'[45] – and their English followers repeated the advice. It is a familiar idea, accordingly, that classical and neoclassical theorists have preferred pure unmixed genres, whereas in periods 'inimical to tradition' their fusion has been 'exalted'.[46] However, this contrast seems to be in very incomplete correspondence to the facts. Generic mixture can be found in good classical authors,[47] while in neoclassical English literature, mixed kinds positively thrived (Fieldingesque novel; satiric epic). The mannerist phase of the Renaissance was hardly a period inimical to tradition, yet its theorists pursued ideas of generic mixture with passion, and its writers achieved some of mixture's subtlest effects. Recalling the comparative deficiency of generic theory in the Middle Ages, we may be more inclined to think of proclivity to mixture as passing through a sequence of stages: apparent generic chaos; reassertion of pure genres and revision of labels; and new mixtures, progressively more audacious. The ubiquitous mixtures of the Middle Ages received scarcely any contemporary acknowledgment. Indeed, even the labels – such as 'L'Epitaphe en forme de Ballade' – are often modern. Renaissance Italian criticism offers some sharp resistance to generic mixture (especially in connection with pastoral drama and romantic epic). Pasquier appears to feel the inclusion of documents in a history as a difficult mixture. Later the mannerist and baroque theorists open up the debate on terms more favorable, for a time, to mixed forms. But then the mixtures become chaotic . . .

Minturno emerges as a chief proponent of mixture. His enthusiasm for it shapes the entire *L'Arte Poetica*, which regularly discusses both pure and mixed versions of kinds – so that, for example, 'pure satire' is followed by comic and tragic satire. He is sometimes vague about what constitutes mixture, however. And when he seems to be talking about mixture (being read in this sense by modern critics), he may mean only inclusion, or mixture of verse forms, or of prose and verse.[48] Rosalie Colie represents Sidney as arguing for *genera mixta*, on the strength of a passage in *The Defence*:

> Now in his parts, kind, or species (as you list to term them), it is to be noted that some poesies have coupled together two or three kinds, as the tragical and comical, whereupon is risen the tragi-comical. Some, in the manner, have mingled prose and verse, as Sannazaro and Boethius. Some have mingled matters heroical and pastoral. But that cometh all to one in this question, for, if severed they be good, the conjunction cannot be hurtful.[49]

Sidney cannot have been averse to mixture, since his own *Arcadia* mingled heroical and pastoral. Nevertheless, this passage argues only that mixtures are as morally harmless as their component genres, whereas a later passage attacks 'mongrel tragi-comedy' on aesthetic grounds. Evidence of Elizabethan critics favorable to mixture has to be found in such elusive unexplicit passages as Drayton's comparison of his own odes to Horace's, which were 'of a mixed kind', neither Pindarically high nor amorously Anacreontic. Drayton draws attention particularly to *His Ballad of Agincourt*, which he refers to as an 'Ode . . . or if thou wilt, Ballad'.[50] But the tendency of the evidence, from about 1590, is unambiguous. Labels such as 'hilaro-tragoedia satyropastoralis' and 'tragical-comical-historical-pastoral' show a positive rage for mixture.[51] The archmannerist Nashe can hardly get on with *The Unfortunate Traveller*, for stopping off to notice the latest change of style height or genre. Thus, he follows *Paulo majora canamus* with a string of puns; remembers that 'he must not place a volume in the precincts of a pamphlet'; feels 'more than duncified twixt divinity and poetry'; discusses sermons and slips into one; or warns 'Prepare your ears and your tears, for never till this thrust I any tragical matter upon you'. His satire is mixed with burlesque epic, tragedy, royal entry description, marvel, lyric, 'passion', panegyric, travel literature, *impresa*, proverb, epigram, and other embedded or mingled forms.[52]

In the subsequent period, there was some recoil from the idea of generic mixture to the ideal of pure genre. A neoclassicist such as Rapin repeated Servius's view that only ten of Theocritus's 30 idylls were pure pastorals. He questioned whether pastoral could decently bring in fishermen: piscatory eclogue was for him not a subgenre but an extraneous mixture.[53] But when we move on only a few decades, mixture has gone so far as to call for radical regrouping. Wordsworth's approach to genre is freshly analytic, although when he treats mixture it is with a view to classifying. He lists six modes or 'moulds' or 'classes', then adds: 'Out of the three last [idyllium, didactic, and philosophical satire] has been constructed a composite order, of which Young's Night Thoughts, and Cowper's Task, are excellent examples.'[54] This analytic and classificatory approach to mixture finds its logical conclusion in Northrop Frye's theory of genres. Frye treats fiction as bound together by four chief strands: novel, confession, anatomy, romance. Mixture is simply a matter of combining these, regardless of external structure. 'The six possible combinations of these forms all exist.' And: 'More comprehensive fictional schemes usually employ at least three forms.'[55] The analytic approach will classify and illuminate the most audacious mixture, but has yet to prove itself with the local or microgeneric effects with which, in practice, criticism is concerned.

Notes

1. For different categories see, e.g., FRANCIS CAIRNS, *Generic Composition in Greek and Roman Poetry* (Edinburgh, 1972), p. 99.

2. See C.L. BARBER, *Shakespeare's Festive Comedy* (Princeton, 1959); LESLIE HOTSON, *The First Night of 'Twelfth Night'* (London, 1954).

3. Cf. CAIRNS, *Generic Composition*, p. 123.

4. For many examples of aggregation in round numbers, see ERNST ROBERT CURTIUS, *European Literature and the Latin Middle Ages* (New York and London, 1953), pp. 505–9. On the organisation of Boccaccio's aggregate, see JANET LEVARIE SMARR, 'Symmetry and Balance in the *Decameron*', *Mediaevalia*, 2 (1976).

5. See GODFREY FRANK SINGER, *The Epistolary Novel* (Philadelphia, 1933, rpt. 1963); also *The Novel in Letters*, ed. Natascha Würzbach (Coral Gables, Fla., 1969). For modern examples, see *TLS* (9 Feb. 1973), 153.

6. Petrarch's *Canzoniere* used a calendrical structure that became a paradigm for Spenser and others: see THOMAS P. ROCHE, 'Shakespeare and the Sonnet Sequence', in *English Poetry and Prose, 1540–1674*, ed. Christopher Ricks (London, 1970); idem, 'The Calendrical Structure of Petrarch's *Canzoniere*', *SP*, 71 (1974); and PHILIP BLANK, *Lyric Form in the Sonnet Sequences of Barnabe Barnes* (The Hague, 1974). There were other calendrical models, notably the early fourteenth-century *Sonetti dei Mesi* of Fulgore da San Gemignano.

7. See ALASTAIR FOWLER, *Triumphal Forms* (Cambridge, 1970), ch. 9; ROCHE, 'Sonnet Sequence', pp. 105–6; and ROSALIE L. COLIE, *The Resources of Kind* (Berkeley, 1973), p. 104. By contrast, nineteenth-century sequences tend to be congeries of individual lyric poems. D.G. Rossetti, e.g., 'certainly never professed, nor do I consider that he ever wished his readers to assume, that all items [in *The House of Life*] had been primarily planned to form one connected and indivisible whole'. W.M. ROSSETTI, *Dante Gabriel Rossetti as Designer and Writer* (1888), pp. 181–2.

8. Some of these plans have survived, such as John Philips's for *Cider*, which is particularly interesting in view of the work's generic originality (see JOHN CHALKER, *The English Georgic* (London, 1969), p. 45).

9. See CAIRNS, *Generic Composition*, p. 119.

10. Cf. COLIE, *Resources of Kind*, p. 85; GEOFFREY H. HARTMAN, *Beyond Formalism* (New Haven and London, 1970), pp. 177–80.

11. On the modified limerick, see MARTIN GARDNER, *Scientific American* (April 1977), 134.

12. CAIRNS analyzes many such variations in *Generic Composition*, chs 8–9.

13. ROSEMARY FREEMAN, 'Parody as a Literary Form: George Herbert and Wilfred Owen', *EC*, 13 (1963), 306. See also COLIE, *Resources of Kind*, p. 57; LILY B. CAMPBELL, *Divine Poetry and Drama in Sixteenth-Century England* (Cambridge, 1959); and BARBARA K. LEWALSKI, *Protestant Poetics and the Seventeenth-Century Religious Lyric* (Princeton, 1979).

14. See CLAUDIO GUILLÉN, *Literature as System* (Princeton, 1971), pp. 146–58.

15. See CAIRNS, *Generic Composition*, pp. 129ff. The process was well understood in the Renaissance. See, e.g., Thomas Watson's note to *The . . . Passionate Century of Love* (1582), no. 96: 'In this Passion, the Author is scoffing bitterly at Venus, and her son Cupid, alludeth unto certain verses in Ovid, but inverteth them to an other sense than Ovid used, who wrote them upon the death of Tibullus.'

16. Cf. COLIE, *Resources of Kind*, pp. 93–4.

17. On Milton and Christian epic, see CAMPBELL, *Divine Poetry*; BARBARA K. LEWALSKI, *Milton's Brief Epic* (Providence and London, 1966); and DENNIS H. BURDEN, *The Logical Epic* (London, 1967), pp. 9–13, 63–4, et passim.

18. Those of Bembo, Della Casa, Milton, and others approached the loftier ode. COLIE (*Resources of Kind*, pp. 106–7) quotes Vauquelin de la Fresnaye: 'Si tu fais un Sonnet ou si tu fais un Ode,/Il faut qu'un mesme fil au sujet s'accommode' and 'on peut le Sonnet dire une chanson [canzone] petite'. Cf. Minturno, *L'Arte* 240ff, on the 'Somiglianza tra il sonetto, e la Canzone'.

19. For European practitioners see COLIE, *Resources of Kind*, p. 106. The theorist Minturno himself wrote spiritual sonnets.

20. For a dramatic instance, see George Peele, *Old Wives' Tale* (1595), l. 698; for a fine elegiac version, William Cartwright, *To the Memory of a Shipwrackt Virgin* in *The Plays and Poems of William Cartwright*, ed. G. Blakemore Evans (Madison, Wis., 1951). This particular antigenre has outlived the primary genre: there is an example in *Concrete Poetry: An International Anthology*, ed. Stephen Bann (London, 1967), p. 155.

21. E.g., Johnson related *The Village* to pastoral. For a contrary view, that Crabbe's originality lies outside the pastoral tradition, see Dennis H. Burden, 'Crabbe and the Augustan Tradition', in *Essays and Poems Presented to Lord David Cecil*, ed. W.W. Robson (London, 1970), pp. 77–92.

22. *The Village*, ll. 17–20. On Johnson's contribution to these lines, see Burden, 'Crabbe', pp. 80–1.

23. *The Parish Register*, l. 26. Cf. the allusion in *The Village*, Bk 1: 'He, "passing rich with forty pounds a year?" / Ah! no; a shepherd of a different stock, / And far unlike him, feeds this little flock.'

24. *The Spirit of the Age*, in *Complete Works*, ed. P.P. Howe, vol. 11 (London, 1932), p. 167.

25. *The Village*, Bk 1 ad fin.

26. Burden, 'Crabbe', p. 87.

27. The excellent phrase is Hazlitt's – who did not mean it approvingly. Cf. Burden, 'Crabbe', p. 92.

28. Contemporary review of *Tristram Shandy*; in Ioan Williams, *Novel and Romance, 1700–1800* (London, 1970), p. 239.

29. But contrast the view in Peter Conrad, *Shandyism* (London, 1978).

30. For James and Besant see James, 'The Art of Fiction', in *Selected Literary Criticism*, ed. Morris Shapira (London, 1963), pp. 93f; for Forster's low regard for story, *Aspects of the Novel* (London, 1927), p. 41.

31. A. Walton Litz, 'The Genre of *Ulysses*', in *The Theory of the Novel*, ed. John Halperin (New York and London, 1974), pp. 116, 118.

32. Ibid., pp. 115, 118, 120.

33. J. Fletcher, *The Novels of Samuel Beckett* (London, 1964), pp. 76–7, quoting Christine Brooke-Rose, 'Beckett and the Anti-Novel', *London Magazine*, 5 (1958). John Chalker, 'The Satiric Shape of *Watt*', in *Beckett the Shape Changer*, ed. Katherine Worth (London, 1975), sets Beckett in a satiric context. Antinovel often overlaps with satire, but need not do so. Satire in the ordinary sense may not be the best key to Beckett's work.

34. For the tapestry poem see *The Works of Edmund Spenser: A Variorum Edition*, ed. E. Greenlaw et al. (Oxford and Baltimore, 1932–49), l. 386; for triumphs, Fowler, *Triumphal Forms*; and for many other inclusions, James Nohrnberg, *The Analogy of 'The Faerie Queen'* (Princeton, 1976).

35. On the encyclopedic character of epic, see Northrop Frye, *Anatomy of Criticism* (Princeton, 1957), p. 324. On inclusion, see A. Fowler, *Kinds of Literature: An Introduction to the Theory of Genres and Modes* (Oxford: Oxford University Press, 1982), ch. 12.

36. See John Steadman, *Epic and Tragic Structure in 'Paradise Lost'* (Chicago, 1976); and *The Poems of John Milton*, ed. John Carey and Alastair Fowler (London, 1968), pp. 421–2, 852–3 (n. to 9.6), 966 (n. to 10.773). See also Colie, *Resources of Kind*, p. 119.

37. COLIE lists some of these, enjoying the artificiality with which they are inset; see *Resources of Kind*, pp. 119f; A.K. NARDO, 'The Submerged Sonnet as Lyric Moment in Miltonic Epic', *Genre*, 9.1 (1976), 21–35; *The Poems of John Milton*, ed. Carey and Fowler, p. 683 (n. to 5.153–208).

38. See THOMAS G. ROSENMEYER, *The Green Cabinet* (Berkeley and Los Angeles, 1969), p. 121. Cf. the epitaph to Eurymedon, by Theocritus or Leonidas of Tarentum.

39. Formerly attributed to WYATT; see *Collected Poems*, ed. Kenneth Muir and Patricia Thomson (Liverpool, 1969), p. 439. Cf. S.H.'s *On Cleveland* in *The Poems of John Cleveland*, ed. Brian Morris and Eleanor Withington (Oxford, 1967), pp. xxi–xxii; and Mildmay Fane's epitaph on Ben Jonson, *He Who Began from Brick and Lime*, in *Ben Jonson and the Cavalier Poets*, ed. Hugh Maclean (New York, 1974).

40. The satiric possibility is realised in 'On I.W.A.B. of York', attributed to Cleveland in *Minor Poets of the Caroline Period*, ed. G. Saintsbury, 3 vols (Oxford, 1905–21), 3.71.

41. See, e.g., CAIRNS, *Generic Composition*, pp. 161, 167. George Puttenham treats triumphals, genethliaca, and epithalamies as 'poetical rejoicings': see *The Art of English Poesy*, l. 23, ed. Gladys D. Willcock and Alice Walker (Cambridge, 1936), p. 46.

42. This problem is discussed in COLIE, *Resources of Kind*, pp. 112–14.

43. F. BERRY, *The Shakespearian Inset* (London, 1965). There is a large literature on the play-within-a-play: see, e.g., ROBERT EGAN, *Drama Within Drama* (New York, 1975); and JAMES L. CALDERWOOD, *Shakespearian Metadrama* (Minneapolis, 1971). For the psychology of framing, see ERVING GOFFMAN, *Frame Analysis: An Essay on the Organisation of Experience* (New York, 1974). Many aspects are discussed in *Representation and Understanding*, ed. Daniel Bobrow and Alan Collins (London, 1976).

44. CAIRNS is rightly careful to distinguish inclusion from generic mixture: see, e.g., *Generic Composition*, ch. 7, esp. pp. 158–9.

45. BEN JONSON, *Horace, 'Of the Art of Poetry'*, ll. 124–5, translating 89; *Works*, ed. C.H. Herford, Percy Simpson and Evelyn M. Simpson, 11 vols (Oxford, 1925–52), 8.311. Cf. the classic statement in Cicero, *De Optimo Genere Oratorum* 1: 'In tragedy the comic is a fault, and in comedy the tragic displeases.' *Ancient Literary Criticism*, ed. D.A. Russell and M. Winterbottom (Oxford, 1972), p. 250.

46. ULRICH WEISSTEIN, *Comparative Literature and Literary Theory* (Bloomington and London, 1968), pp. 99–100, instancing the Romantic ideal of *Gesamtkunstwerk*, and citing Behrens and Ehrenpreis.

47. See CAIRNS, *Generic Composition*, pp. 158–9 and ch. 7 passim.

48. E.g., Minturno, *L'Arte* 3–4, which probably underlies COLIE, *Resources of Kind*, p. 21 – a passage not concerned with the problem of distinguishing between inclusion and modulation.

49. SIR PHILIP SIDNEY, *Miscellaneous Prose*, ed. Katherine Duncan-Jones and Jan van Dorsten (Oxford, 1973), p. 94. See COLIE, *Resources of Kind*, p. 28.

50. *The Works of Michael Drayton*, ed. J.W. Hebel et al., 5 vols (Oxford, 1941), 2.346: 'Some [odes] transcendently lofty, and far more high than the Epic (commonly called the Heroic Poem) witness those of the inimitable Pindarus ... Others, among the Greeks, are amorous, soft, and made for Chambers, as others for Theatres; as were Anacreon's, the very Delicacies

of the Grecian Erato.' It is not clear how far Drayton is identifying *ballad* and *balade*: 'the last Ode of this Number, or if thou wilt, Ballad in my Book: for both the great Master of Italian Rhymes, Petrarch, and our Chaucer, and other of the upper House of the Muses, have thought their Canzons honoured in the Title of a Ballad; which, for that I labour to meet truly therein with the old English Garb, I hope as able to justify, as the learned Colin Clout his Roundelay'.

51. The subtitle of *Rubenus*, on which see COLIE, *Resources of Kind*, p. 94. Cf. SHAKESPEARE's criticism of the pedantic classifications that were failing to keep pace with the movement, in Polonius's speech, *Hamlet* 2.2.377ff.

52. *The Works of Thomas Nashe*, ed. McKerrow and F.P. Wilson, vol. 2 (Oxford, 1958), pp. 209, 227, 234f, 241, 320; cf. 292, 'elegiacal history'. In the seventeenth century, the heyday of sophisticated generic mixture, its terminology was even used as metaphor. So in *Philaster*, Bellario entering with a masque says 'I should / Sing you an Epithalamion of these lovers', and the king's response is to promise, in effect, a tragic wedding masque: 'I'll provide a Masque shall make your Hymen / Turn his saffron into a sullen coat, / And sing sad Requiems to your departing souls.'

53. *A Treatise De Carmine Pastorali*, pref. to Thomas Creech's translation of the *Idylliums* of Theocritus (1684), ed. J.E. Congleton, Augustan Rpt. Soc. series 2, no. 3, pub. 8 (Ann Arbor, 1947), pp. 27, 28.

54. W. WORDSWORTH, 'Pref. of 1815'; *The Prose Works*, ed. W.J.B. Owen and Jane W. Smyser, 3 vols (Oxford, 1974), 3.28, or *Wordsworth's Literary Criticism*, ed. W.J.B. Owen (London, 1974), p. 177.

55. Frye, *Anatomy*, pp. 312, 313.

15   Genre and Gender*

MARY EAGLETON

The connections between genre and gender are one of the most fruitful areas of investigation to have emerged from the feminist revolution in literary studies. Although attention was focused initially on the figure of the female author and the cultural conditions of reading and writing, it was inevitable that questions of genre would start to loom large as feminist critics undertook the task of rewriting the history of literature, and rethinking literary theory, from the perspective of women. The etymological connection between the words 'genre' and 'gender' provided further stimulus, if only symbolic, and the pairing of these two terms has occurred frequently in the title of books and articles published in the last two decades. Explaining exactly how these two concepts interrelate, or establishing clear criteria by which a genre might be said to be 'gendered' has, however, proved more difficult. Even where reliable statistical data are available, the numerical predominance of either sex among the practitioners or consumers of a particular genre need not imply any essential affinity, since many other factors may be operative. Other kinds of evidence raise other methodological problems, and one of the current challenges of feminist genre theory is to define these problems and refine its methodology. Mary Eagleton's incisive essay is a helpful contribution to this process. Originally published in an anthology of criticism on the short story, the essay offers a critical survey of previous work in the field, seeking 'to demarcate some of the main areas in feminist analysis of genre', while also proposing future lines of inquiry. Her immediate concern is the short story, but she also discusses a range of other genres, including the one which has received by far the most attention from feminist scholars: the novel.

---

* Reprinted from *Re-reading the Short Story*, ed. Clare Hanson (Basingstoke: Macmillan, 1989), pp. 56–68.

For an excellent selection of feminist work on genre and gender, including extracts from many of the critical texts cited here, see *Feminist Literary Theory: A Reader*, ed. Mary Eagleton, 2nd edn (Oxford: Blackwell, 1996), Section 3. See also Gerhart, *Genre Choices, Gender Questions* (1992); and the interesting discussion of modern genre theory in Lidia Curti, *Female Stories, Female Bodies: Narrative, Identity and Representation* (Basingstoke: Macmillan, 1998), especially Chapter 2: 'D for Difference: Gender, Genre, Writing'. As both Curti and Eagleton indicate, most current theoretical discussion of genre and gender is focused on contemporary fiction, especially popular genres and feminist subversions thereof; for an extension of the debate to earlier periods, see, for instance, Anne Mellor, *Romanticism and Gender* (London: Routledge, 1993), Introduction.

Genre and sexual difference

Feminist criticism's primary response to genre has been to look at it in terms of sexual difference, to try to account for the presence or absence of women in the major genres of the novel, poetry and drama, and to explore further those forms in which women writers are highly represented. As always, a good example to begin with is Virginia Woolf. She noticed in *A Room of One's Own* that women writers have been, predominantly, novelists, that significantly fewer have written poetry – 'the original impulse was to poetry', Virginia Woolf declares, but later admits that 'it is the poetry that is still denied outlet' – and that women who aspire to the theatre, if we are to be guided by Judith Shakespeare's biography, are likely to meet a sorry end.[1] For reasons which I shall consider later, the novel became a possible form for women. Both poetry and drama have been more problematic. We can look to no single determinant, nor even a convenient handful of such, to explain the discrepancy. A myriad of material and ideological factors – the conditions of production, changes in the publishing industry, critical responses, the gender associations of particular forms – interact in complex and shifting ways influenced by history and culture.

For example, nineteenth-century criticism seemed to offer the female *lyric* poet a cautious acceptance. If the woman was duly circumspect in the range of emotions that she expressed in her poetry – no lyrics on lust – then her voice of personal feeling and sensitivity could conform with the dominant sexual ideology. In other contexts, however, the personal female voice could be highly disconcerting. A contemporary review of *Aurora Leigh* firmly warns the reader:

> She tells us her own story in the first person singular, and though
> never woman thought more highly of herself, nor was at more
> pains to describe her supereminent gifts, she is a very ridiculous
> person, and what is worse than ridiculous, she is intolerably
> tedious.[2]

Here the personal voice, because it is declamatory, confident and
questioning, becomes objectionable, becomes unfeminine. The female
voice that is not involved in gentle introspection but is addressing
public issues is intervening in the male arena. In adopting the epic
rather than the lyric Elizabeth Barrett Browning crosses the divide
from the micro to the macro, from private and domestic to public
and social, from feeling to action; in short, her choice of form is a
radical interrogation of sexual difference. But this is not to argue
simplistically that only the epic was contentious and that the lyric
remained an unambiguous and socially sanctioned form for women.
Nineteenth-century criticism continued to quibble at any lyrical
introspection that appeared too self-absorbed. A commitment by
the female lyricist to herself or her art could be interpreted as
dangerously assertive or egotistic; to focus on Nature, God, or a
loved one offered safer material.[3]

In the area of sexual difference, feminist criticism has also
drawn attention to the tendency in literary history to privilege
the male-dominated forms. High tragedy, epic poetry, sermons,
the philosophical treatise, criticism carry more kudos than journals,
letters, diaries, even, for the most part, fiction – forms in which
women have proliferated. The female forms, we have been told,
are less literary, less intellectual, less wide-ranging, less profound.
Feminist criticism has insisted that such prioritising does not happen
by chance, that generic divisions are not neutral and impartial
classifications, and that our aesthetic judgements are ideologically
bound. Feminist criticism has been eager to rediscover the hidden
women, like Dorothy Wordsworth or Alice James, who wrote their
journals and diaries while their male relatives were producing 'great
literature'. Too frequently this has led to an invidious competition: is
Dorothy's journal really as good as *The Prelude*; would not Alice be as
big a name as Henry if only . . . ? But to focus on the women's work
questions the prioritising of genres, the definition of 'literature'; it
rescues the women's work from being secondary source material,
merely an interesting gloss on the primary male text; it raises again
the matter of women's restricted access to literary production, how
they have turned so often to private forms never intended for public
consumption; and it allows the female voice to speak its owner's
own experience.

Genre and subversive forms

The second major way in which feminist criticism has approached the gender/genre debate has been in relating to genre what it sees as the subversive potential of women's writing. There is interest in how women may transform the male-dominated forms and in so doing expose their gender bias. Female appropriations of the *Bildungsroman*, for example, make apparent what was previously unseen – namely, that these books offer an imaginative construct that is almost entirely male-centred. How radical are these appropriations? Feminist criticism tends to be divided between those who see the shift from hero to heroine as an important political move, and those who doubt whether a change of personnel alters fundamentally the aesthetic and social values of the form. Is a tale of female achievement and individualism a significant enough advance on one of male achievement and individualism?[4] What some critics find more subversive is feminism's questioning of realist forms of writing. To query the truth, coherence and resolution of realism is to undermine the symbolic order. Non-realist forms permit the woman writer to express the contradictions, fantasies or desires that the demands of realism silence. It is in this context that we can understand the involvement of feminist criticism in modernist or avant-garde forms of writing which challenge, in Dorothy Richardson's words, 'current masculine realism';[5] we can appreciate the renewed concern with utopian writing, with science fiction, and with what Ellen Moers terms the 'female Gothic'.[6] Above all, we have seen in France the production of a writing that not only disputes realism but which dramatically breaks down all our generic classifications. 'L'écriture féminine' is by turns poetry, philosophy, literary criticism, autobiography, utopian fantasy – and more.

One literary form that has intrigued feminist criticism in recent years, both in terms of sexual difference and in terms of subversive meanings, is popular romantic fiction. The nature of its literary production and consumption, and the analysis of the ideology of romance, are the two areas that critics have most readily related to notions of sexual difference. The form is produced, almost exclusively, by women, for women, and about women, though, significantly, the publishing and marketing industries are predominantly in the hands of men. Feminist readership studies have presented the audience as a kind of female sub-culture, the women constructing in their readings their own range of meanings.[7] The ideology of romance has provided an almost classic case-study of sexual difference. We are all familiar with the quintessential romantic hero, dark, brooding and masterful, and the romantic heroine, tremulous, subordinate and focused with doe-eyed adulation on the male. But it is initially difficult to see how the conservative values of Harlequin or Mills & Boon fiction can offer any subversive potential; for example, the resolution of these works lies always in monogamous marital bliss between two white, upwardly-mobile heterosexuals. It has been the application of psychoanalytical theory to the examination of romantic fiction that has led to new understandings. From this perspective romantic fiction is more a sign of women's dissatisfaction with their social lot, of their unfulfilled desires, than a confirmation of their passive anti-feminism. Feminist psychoanalytical theory finds subversive potential in the compulsive and pleasurable aspects of romantic fiction. As Alison Light comments, these stories are 'fantasies . . . the explorations and productions of desires which may be in excess of the socially possible or acceptable'.[8] The disruptive aspect is in the concept of 'excess', of a female sexuality that cannot be represented or fulfilled, but which, equally, cannot be totally silenced.

Women and fiction

To return to Virginia Woolf in *A Room of One's Own*. Surveying several shelves of works by women she asks, 'But why . . . were they, with very few exceptions, all novels?'[9] Virginia Woolf's response, to look for answers in the social history of women and in the cultural position of the novel, laid the groundwork for future commentaries. The essential pre-condition was the development of capitalism and the move towards industrialisation and urbanisation, which denied middle-class women their traditional occupations. Brewing, baking, spinning, weaving, for instance, which had previously been domestic industries for women, became factory-based industries for men. The aspiration was that the middle-class woman should become a lady of leisure, her inactivity a sign of her own and her husband's status, her idle hours, perhaps, occupied by novel reading. Nancy Armstrong disputes whether in reality middle-class women of the period had either enough time or enough literacy to be the prime novel reading audience.[10] And certainly the majority of eighteenth-century women novelists wrote out of financial need rather than as a means to fill the long days.

The newness of the form, its low status, its relative easiness to read, offered opportunities for the female author. There was no long and intimidating tradition of 'great masters' and, indeed, some of the forms that contributed to the novel were both accessible and familiar to women – letters, diaries, journals. Virginia Woolf refers to the older forms of literature as 'hardened and set', whereas the novel was open and malleable, 'young enough to be soft in [their] hands'.[11]

Moreover, novel writing did not demand a knowledge of the classics, of rhetoric, or of poetic devices – knowledge which was unlikely to be part of female education. George Eliot, lamenting the proliferation of 'silly novels by lady novelists' rather bemoaned the 'absence of rigid requirement' in novel writing; Virginia Woolf, irked that she had never been taught Greek, was probably glad of the fact.[12]

Novel writing, unlike writing for the theatre, is a domestic form of production. Judith Shakespeare, we remember, could not satisfy her theatrical interest by writing plays in Stratford and sending them off by post to the Globe; it was necessary for her to go to London, to be part of the process of production and performance. Michelene Wandor suggests that this has been a continuing problem for women playwrights – and equally, one could add, for women directors. Their visibility, their 'public control of an imaginative world (the action on the stage)' makes them 'a far greater threat than the female novelist to the carefully maintained dominance of men as the custodians of cultural creation'.[13] In patriarchal thinking the public woman, acting outside the confines of proper domesticity, no longer 'the angel in the house', is the whore. Hence Judith Shakespeare's interest in the theatre leads only to seduction and suicide, and generations of mothers have been warned not to put their daughters on the stage. Novels, on the other hand, as the biographies of eighteenth- and nineteenth-century female novelists reveal, were written in the drawing-room or in the kitchen or at a dining-room table. The writing, fitted in between domestic tasks, did not have to disturb the equanimity of the household, and the aspiring female novelist demanded no expensive equipment. As Virginia Woolf tells us with about equal amounts of ironic humour and seriousness:

> The cheapness of writing paper is, of course, the reason why women have succeeded as writers before they have succeeded in the other professions.[14]

Domestic production meant also that the woman novelist could maintain a suitable, feminine reticence; in fact, if she wished to use a pseudonym, she could remain anonymous. A husband or father could act as her agent and link with the public world. If she *had* to involve herself in her work's publishing progress it could be by letter rather than through face-to-face contact.

Some of the most suggestive of recent criticism has looked to what is termed the 'feminisation' of culture to account not only for the rise of the woman novelist, but for the growing emphasis in literature on feminine subject matter – the domestic, the interpersonal, feeling – and a feminine point of view – conciliatory, socially minded rather

255

than ego-centred, healing division and difference. Such a perspective was not confined to the female novelists but was present also in the work of their male colleagues, indicating a general anxiety about the most masculinist aspects of the changing society.[15] The contradictions in this feminising process for the woman author are well attested: she gains status as a writer during a period when women are losing political power; she creates, and yet is constrained by, a certain construction of femininity; she finds a public voice and employs it to extol private virtue.[16] In criticism the problem has been that many commentators have not seen the feminisation of culture in a social and ideological context; rather they have viewed it as some natural consequence of the advent of the woman author. The argument roughly goes: women are very involved in the home and small town life, and in a sensitive engagement with social relations; these elements also constitute, in a large measure, the subject matter of novels; hence women are more predisposed to writing novels than to writing in any other genre. In this thesis culture and biology are conflated and, as it is a view that has particularly dogged the analysis of women writers, it is one that I would like to return to in the final section.

I think links can be made between women as novelists and women as short story writers. If we are talking about new forms and low status then the short story is even newer and lower than the novel. Many critics of the short story have stressed that it is not the primary literary form of our period, that it holds a marginal and ambiguous position in literary culture, and that it is peopled with characters who are in some way at odds with the dominant culture. We can look to Frank O'Connor's oft-quoted comment that the short story deals with 'submerged population groups'; Ian Reid claims that the nineteenth-century French short story tended to be regional rather than metropolitan, portraying characters who were 'aliens'; Declan Kiberd talks of the short story flourishing 'on any cultural frontier'.[17] Although none of these critics actually mentions women – an oversight that speaks volumes – we can see in the image they offer of the short story writer and character – non-hegemonic, peripheral, contradictory – a reflection of the position of women in a patriarchal society.

Of course, the short story is also domestically produced, and there has been the suggestion that short stories, because of their brevity, are easier for women to write. Virginia Woolf, in what seems to me a curious passage, contends that women's fiction would become 'shorter, more concentrated'.[18] This would be prompted by the different 'physical conditions' of women, their inability to enjoy 'long hours of steady and uninterrupted work', and the specific nature of 'the nerves that feed the [female] brain'. All manner of problems are raised by these comments. Woolf seems to believe that shorter forms

are somehow easier and need less labour than the longer forms,
though one would have thought that her own writing career would
have raised doubts in her mind about that. Moreover, considering
the aplomb with which Victorian women novelists turned out three-
decker novels, why should women now feel uncertain about writing
at length? Woolf moves in an unsettling way between a materialist
interpretation – she asks the necessary question: how many available
writing hours has a woman with children and/or domestic
responsibilities – and rank biologism – it's all down to 'nerves'.
The phrase 'physical conditions' is so ambiguous that it is unclear
whether the reference here is to the material world or to the
physiological. Or am I reading this passage too negatively? Perhaps
Woolf's appeal for 'an elaborate study of the psychology of women
by a woman' points us towards recent studies on the construction of
the subject and its relation to literary form and genre. The work that
has already been done, in reference to the novel, to modernist forms,
or to l'écriture féminine, must be only the start of a debate, and
certainly the drift of Woolf's argument asks us to take seriously
the links between gender, genre and the psychic.

Theoretical problems

One of the continuing problems and interests for feminist criticism
is that the concept of sexual difference can be used to promote
both reactionary and radical politics. G.H. Lewes, writing in 1852,
structures his thesis on 'lady novelists' around the concept of sexual
difference. He writes:

> Of all departments of literature, Fiction is the one to which by
> nature and by circumstances, women are best adapted. Exceptional
> women will of course be found competent to the highest success in
> other departments; but speaking generally, novels are their forte.
> The domestic experiences which form the bulk of woman's
> knowledge find an appropriate form in novels; while the very
> nature of fiction calls for that predominance of Sentiment which
> we have already attributed to the feminine mind. Love is the staple
> of fiction, for it 'forms the story of a woman's life.' The joys and
> sorrows of affection, the incidents of domestic life, the aspirations
> and fluctuations of emotional life, assume typical forms in the
> novel. Hence we may be prepared to find women succeeding better
> in *finesse* of detail, in pathos and sentiment, while men generally
> succeed better in the construction of plots and the delineation of
> character. Such a novel as 'Tom Jones' or 'Vanity Fair', we shall

not get from a woman; nor such an effort of imaginative history as 'Ivanhoe' or 'Old Mortality'; but Fielding, Thackeray, and Scott are equally excluded from such perfection in its kind as 'Pride and Prejudice', 'Indiana', or 'Jane Eyre': as an artist, Miss Austen surpasses all the male novelists that ever lived; and for eloquence and depth of feeling, no man approaches George Sand.[19]

Two aspects of this passage are particularly striking. Firstly, Lewes attributes women's involvement in novel writing to both 'nature' and 'circumstance', a combination of historical factors with what he sees as women's innate propensity towards that particular form. The common subject matter of the novel – 'domestic experiences' and 'sentiment' – is to Lewes the 'natural' material for the woman writer; both her social position and her biology lead her in that direction. Secondly, in the allocation of male and female characteristics in writing the pre-eminent position is given to the male. Women show 'finesse of detail', 'pathos and sentiment', 'eloquence and depth of feeling'; the male writer excels in 'construction of plots', 'delineation of character' and 'imaginative history'. Women thus provide emotion and embellishment; the fundamental construction of novels and the conveyance of wide-ranging and significant meaning remains with the male. A hundred years later Ian Watt in *The Rise of the Novel* followed much the same line.[20] There is the obligatory praise for Jane Austen and her ability 'to reveal the intricacies of personal relationships', and reference to 'feminine sensibility' as if this is a generally understood and unproblematic term. Unlike Lewes, Watt does not explain sexual difference in terms of biology; rather in his reference to J.S. Mill he adopts a position which is liberal, sociological and cultural. But the conclusion of his argument returns to the familiar criticism of women writers and readers who have led the novel into a 'characteristic kind of weakness and unreality' and into 'a certain narrowing of the framework of experience and permitted attitude'. Watt's criticism exemplifies that double-bind which places women's writing in restricted categories and then uses that restriction as a sign of women's creative limitations. A similar pattern of argument has been true of the short story. To say that the woman writer would adopt the short story because of the intimacy of the form, the one-to-one relationship between author and reader, or because of the short story's focus on a manageable, single incident is, on the one hand, to recognise women's social experience in our culture and where that experience may take them in their writing; on the other hand, it is to confine women once again in the personal, the closely detailed, the miniature. By implication the short story becomes both a lesser form and about all that women can manage.

Feminism's response to the reactionary concept of sexual difference is varied. One school embraces the notion of feminine values but, rather than seeing these as inferior to the masculine, valorises the difference and locates in the feminine an important oppositional role. Another group stresses that difference is socially constructed and seeks to interrogate and deconstruct our concepts of masculinity and femininity, exposing their fictive nature. Such perspectives encourage a different approach to women and the short story. Perhaps for some women writers their interest in this form has arisen, not from their belief that it is known and safe, but from their hope that the flexible, open-ended qualities of the short story may offer a transforming potential, an ability to ask the unspoken question, to raise new subject matter. Patricia Stubbs suggests such an interpretation concerning the female short story writers at the turn of the century. Hermione Lee also indicates this possibility in her introduction to *The Secret Self*.[21]

I want finally to look a little more closely at Hermione Lee's introduction because it highlights various problems about attempts to define women's writing. Having subtitled the volume 'Short Stories by Women', Lee inevitably has to ask whether there is something distinctive about the female short story writer, some characteristics common to all or most of them, and not to be found in the work of male short story writers. From the start Lee wisely shows a guarded response to essentialist and prescriptive views. Hence she does not accept that the short story by women is necessarily an expression of emancipatory zeal, nor does she believe that there is a female tradition of writing that is independent of a male tradition, and, of course, she rejects any idea that the female short story can be labelled 'better' than the male.

Lee's hesitancy is understandable, for any attempt to locate the specificity of women's writing is fraught with difficulties. We may find a group of women authors whose writings seem in many ways similar. But then we will discover a much larger group of women authors from the same period and culture whose writings are significantly different from the first, and a group of male writers who seem to be writing rather like the women writers. In short it is never possible to produce the definitive evidence to prove that 'x' is the writing of a woman and 'y' the writing of a man. Most studies that attempt such definitions end by offering qualified suggestions and contending that we need more stylistic analysis to really substantiate any proposition.[22] Furthermore, how can we ever know that the similarities between any group of writers are determined by sex, rather than by race, class, literary form, conditions of literary production, or any combination of any number of factors? Indeed, in finding similarities between groups of writers, could we be employing a self-fulfilling prophecy? Given the complexity of writing, the mass of evidential data it offers, it is hardly surprising that similarities are found. Finally, any attempt to define writing as 'male' or 'female' ignores the ambiguity of writing, its bisexuality, its ability to articulate both masculinity and femininity within the same text.

The problem for Lee is, having rejected attempts to characterise a definitive female writing, what theory of gender and genre can she offer in its place; it is at this point that the analysis becomes unsure. The paragraph that begins with a rejection of 'a separatist aesthetic theory of the 20th-century woman's short story' ends with the comment:

> But it could be said that some distinctive angles of vision and ways of expression are apparent in this selection, which would not be found in an anthology of stories by men.[23]

Lee here seems to be reaffirming the claim that there *is* a specifically female way of writing, that there are both perceptions and stylistic modes that are particular to women. Inevitably this has to be modified. Thus when she refers to women's stories about the tension between the child and the adult worlds she adds – 'This subject is not, of course, a female prerogative . . .'. For Lee the problem of finding a concept of gender that she can relate to the short story proves intractable. Progressively, gender as a critical category disappears from the introduction. We end with 'the secret self'. Is this 'secret self' gendered or is it some ungendered human essence? The queries are all still before us. What is the relationship of gender to writing? Should we talk of the female author or of feminine writing? Does the relationship differ with different literary forms and is there, therefore, a particular scope in relating gender to the short story? Can we create a criticism which is non-essentialist, non-reductive but subtly alive to the links between gender and genre?

Notes

1. Virginia Woolf, *A Room of One's Own* (New York: Harcourt Brace Jovanovich, 1963), pp. 69, 80.

2. 'Aurora Leigh', *Tablet* (29 November 1856), 762. Quoted in Elizabeth K. Helsinger, Robin Lauterbach Sheets, William Veeder, *The Woman Question: Literary Issues, 1837–1883* (Manchester University Press, 1983), p. 39.

3. Indeed Sandra Gilbert and Susan Gubar in their introduction to *Shakespeare's Sisters: Feminist Essays on Women Poets* (Bloomington and London: Indiana University Press, 1979) argue that it is the lyric with its 'strong and assertive

"I"' (p. xxii) that is the real problem for women poets, that in a wider sense the form can be seen as dangerous and challenging. All this confirms that there is much interesting work still to be done.

4. For two contrary views on this question see ELLEN MORGAN, 'Human Becoming: Form and Focus in the Neo-Feminist Novel', in *Feminist Criticism: Essays on Theory, Poetry and Prose*, ed. Cheryl L. Brown and Karen Olson (New Jersey and London: The Scarecrow Press Inc., 1978); and ELIZABETH COWIE et al., 'Representation vs. Communication', in ed. Feminist Anthology Collective, *No Turning Back: Writings from the Women's Liberation Movement, 1975–80* (London: The Women's Press, 1981). Of related interest is SUSAN GUBAR's essay, 'The Birth of the Artist as Heroine: (Re)production, the Künstlerroman Tradition, and the Fiction of Katherine Mansfield', in *The Representation of Women in Fiction*, ed. Carolyn G. Heilbrun and Margaret R. Higonnet (Baltimore and London: The Johns Hopkins University Press, 1983).

5. DOROTHY RICHARDSON, *Pilgrimage I* (London: Virago, 1979), p. 9.

6. ELLEN MOERS, *Literary Women* (London: The Women's Press, 1978), p. 90. See also ROSEMARY JACKSON, *Fantasy: The Literature of Subversion* (London: Methuen, 1981); EVA FIGES, *Sex and Subterfuge: Women Writers to 1850* (London: Macmillan, 1982); JANE SPENCER, *The Rise of the Woman Novelist: from Aphra Behn to Jane Austen* (Oxford: Blackwell, 1986); TANIA MODLESKI, *Loving with a Vengeance* (London: Methuen, 1984); JOANNA RUSS, 'Somebody's Trying to Kill Me and I Think It's My Husband: The Modern Gothic', *Journal of Popular Culture*, 6:4 (1973), 666–91.

7. See, for example, JANICE A. RADWAY, 'Women Read the Romance: The Interaction of Text and Context', *Feminist Studies*, 9:1 (1983).

8. ALISON LIGHT, '"Returning to Manderley" – Romance Fiction, Female Sexuality and Class', *Feminist Review*, 16 (1984), 9.

9. WOOLF, *A Room of One's Own*, p. 69.

10. NANCY ARMSTRONG, 'The Rise of Feminine Authority in the Novel', *Novel*, 15:2 (Winter 1982), 128.

11. WOOLF, *A Room of One's Own*, p. 80.

12. GEORGE ELIOT, 'Silly Novels by Lady Novelists' (1856), in *Essays of George Eliot*, ed. Thomas Pinney (London: Routledge & Kegan Paul, 1963), p. 324.

13. MICHELENE WANDOR, 'The Impact of Feminism on the Theatre', *Feminist Review*, 18 (1984), 86.

14. VIRGINIA WOOLF, 'Professions for Women', in *The Death of the Moth and Other Essays* (London: Hogarth, 1981).

15. See TERRY EAGLETON, *The Rape of Clarissa* (Oxford: Basil Blackwell, 1982); SPENCER, *The Rise of the Woman Novelist*; ARMSTRONG, 'Feminine Authority'.

16. JULIET MITCHELL, *Women: The Longest Revolution* (London: Virago, 1984), has valuable comments on how in the novel women 'create themselves as a category: women'.

17. FRANK, O'CONNOR, *The Lonely Voice* (London: Macmillan, 1963), p. 18; IAN REID, *The Short Story* (London: Methuen, 1977), p. 24; DECLAN KIBERD, 'Story Telling: The Gaelic Tradition', in *The Irish Short Story*, ed. Patrick Rafroidi and Terence Brown (Gerrards Cross, Buckinghamshire: Colin Smythe Ltd, 1979), p. 20.

18. WOOLF, *A Room of One's Own*, p. 81. Reference is also for other quotations in this paragraph.

19. G.H. LEWES, 'The Lady Novelists', *Westminster Review*, 11 (1852), 133.

20. IAN WATT, *The Rise of the Novel: Studies in Defoe, Richardson & Fielding* (London: Pelican, 1972), pp. 338–40, from which the following quotations are taken.

21. PATRICIA STUBBS, *Women and Fiction: Feminism and the Novel, 1880–1920* (London: Methuen, 1979); HERMIONE LEE, ed., *The Secret Self: Short Stories by Women* (London: Dent, 1985).

22. See, for example, DEBORAH E. MCDOWELL, 'New Directions for Black Feminist Criticism', *Black American Literature Forum*, 14 (1980); JOSEPHINE DONOVAN, 'Feminist Style Criticism', *Images of Women in Fiction, Feminist Perspectives*, ed. Susan Koppleman Cornillon (Bowling Green, Ohio: Bowling Green University Press, 1972); ANNETTE KOLODNY, 'Some Notes on Defining a "Feminist Literary Criticism"', *Critical Inquiry*, 2:1 (Autumn 1975).

23. LEE, *The Secret Self*, p. ix.

Notes on Authors

MIKHAIL BAKHTIN (1895–1975) studied classics at St Petersburg University, and spent the latter part of his career as Professor of Russian and World Literature at the University of Saransk. His work began to gain serious recognition in the Soviet Union in the 1960s, and has since been widely admired in the West. Although some problems of attribution remain, most of his work is now available in English translation. Books and collections of essays include *The Dialogic Imagination* (1981), *Problems of Dostoevsky's Poetics* (1984), *Rabelais and His World*, trans. Hélène Iswolsky (Bloomington: Indiana University Press, 1984), *The Formal Method in Literary Scholarship* (1985), *Speech Genres and Other Late Essays* (1986), and *Art and Answerability* (1990).

ROSALIE COLIE (1925–72) was, at the time of her death, Nancy Duke Lewis Professor of English and Comparative Literature at Brown University. Her first book was a comparative study of the Cambridge Platonists and Dutch Arminians. Her other distinguished publications include *Paradoxia Epidemica: The Renaissance Tradition of Paradox* (Princeton: Princeton University Press, 1966), *'My Ecchoing Song': Andrew Marvell's Poetry of Criticism* (Princeton: Princeton University Press, 1970), *The Resources of Kind* (1973), and *Shakespeare's Living Art* (Princeton: Princeton University Press, 1974).

BENEDETTO CROCE (1866–1952), philosopher, critic, historian and sometime politician, was a prominent figure in Italian cultural life. In 1904 he founded the influential journal *La critica*, and in 1910 was made a life member of the Italian senate, serving as minister of education in 1920–21. During the Fascist period he withdrew from public life until 1943, when he became a leader of the Liberal party. His best known philosophical work is the *Aesthetic as Science of Expression and General Linguistic* (1902), the first of the four parts of his 'Philosophy of Spirit'. His many other writings include a pioneering study of Giambattista Vico, a commentary on Hegel, and a study of Goethe.

JACQUES DERRIDA (born 1930) is Director of Studies at the École des Hautes Études en Sciences Sociales in Paris, and has been affiliated with several American universities. Much of his prolific output has been translated into English; writings on literary topics are assembled in his *Acts of Literature*, ed. Derek Attridge (1992), and *The Derrida Reader: Writing Performances*, ed. Julian Wolfreys (Edinburgh: Edinburgh University Press, 1998). Other recent books include *Spectres of Marx: The State of the Debt, the Work of Mourning and the New International*, trans. Peggy Kamuf (London: Routledge, 1994), and *The Politics of Friendship*, trans. George Collins (London: Verso, 1997).

MARY EAGLETON (born 1949) is Principal Lecturer in Literature at the University College of Ripon and York St John. She is the author of *Working with Feminist Criticism* (Oxford: Blackwell, 1996), and, with David Pierce, of *Attitudes to Class in the English Novel from Walter Scott to David Storey* (London: Thames and Hudson, 1979). She has also edited a volume of *Feminist Literary Criticism* for the Longman Critical Readers series (1991). A second edition of her influential textbook *Feminist Literary Theory: A Reader* was published by Blackwell in 1996.

ALASTAIR FOWLER (born 1930) is Professor of English at the University of Virginia and Professor Emeritus at the University of Edinburgh. Besides *Kinds of Literature* (1982), his books include *Spenser and the Numbers of Time* (London: Routledge, 1964), *Triumphal Forms: Structural Patterns in Elizabethan Poetry* (Cambridge: Cambridge University Press, 1970), and *Stars and the Afterlife in Renaissance English Literature* (Oxford: Clarendon Press, 1996). He has also edited *Paradise Lost* for the Longman Annotated English Poets series, compiled *The New Oxford Book of Seventeenth-Century Verse* (1991), and written a one-volume *History of English Literature* (1987).

NORTHROP FRYE (1912–91), Canadian critic and theorist, spent most of his career at Victoria College, Toronto. His first book, *Fearful Symmetry: A Study of William Blake* (Princeton: Princeton University Press, 1947), revolutionised Romantic studies, and his *Anatomy of Criticism* (1957) extended further his influence on Anglo-American criticism. His many other books include *The Stubborn Structure: Essays on Criticism and Society* (London: Methuen, 1970), *The Secular Scripture* (1976), *The Great Code: The Bible as Literature* (Toronto: Toronto Academic Press, 1982), and *A Study of English Romanticism* (Brighton: Harvester Press, 1983).

GÉRARD GENETTE (born 1930) is Director of Studies at the École des Hautes Études en Sciences Sociales in Paris, where he conducts a seminar on the history and theory of literary forms. Some of his seminal essays on poetics and narratology were published as *Narrative Discourse: An Essay in Method*, trans. Jane E. Lewin (Ithaca:

Cornell University Press, 1980), and *Figures of Literary Discourse*, trans. Alan Sheridan (New York: Columbia University Press, 1982). His more recent books include *The Architext* (1992), *Fiction and Diction* (1993), *Mimologics*, trans. Thaïs E. Morgan (Lincoln: University of Nebraska Press, 1995), *Paratexts* (1997), and *Palimpsests* (1998).

FREDRIC JAMESON (born 1934) is William Lane Professor of Comparative Literature at Duke University. His work has ranged across many fields, including literary criticism, film studies, cultural studies, philosophy and sociology. Major publications include *Marxism and Form* (1971), *The Prison-House of Language* (1972), *Fables of Aggression: Wyndham Lewis: The Modernist as Fascist* (Berkeley: University of California Press, 1979), *Ideologies of Theory: Essays 1971–1988*, 2 vols (London: Routledge, 1988), *The Political Unconscious* (1981), *Postmodernism; or, The Cultural Logic of Late Capitalism* (1991), and *Signatures of the Visible* (London: Routledge, 1991).

HANS ROBERT JAUSS (1921–97) was, for much of his career, Professor of Romance Philology and Literary Criticism at the University of Konstanz. Together with Wolfgang Iser, he founded the Konstanz school of 'reception aesthetics', whose methodological inquiries have exercised considerable influence in Germany and elsewhere. Two important collections of his essays have been translated into English: *Toward an Aesthetic of Reception* (1982) and *Aesthetic Experience and Literary Hermeneutics* (Minneapolis: University of Minnesota Press, 1982).

IRENEUSZ OPACKI (born 1933) is Director of the Institute for the Study of Polish Literature and Head of the Department of Literary Theory at the University of Silesia, where he has taught since 1973. One of Poland's most respected theorists and literary historians, he has written several books on the history of poetics and of particular literary genres, as well as a number of influential methodological studies. His most recent book is *Król-Duch, Herostrates i codzienność: szkice* (King Spirit, Herostrates and the everyday: sketches) (Katowice: Para, 1997).

VLADIMIR PROPP (1895–1970) studied Slavonic philology at St Petersburg University, and later returned to teach Russian literature and folklore. Influenced by, though not a member of, the Formalist group *Opoyaz*, Propp developed a theory of narrative in the 1920s which later profoundly influenced Continental and Anglo-American literary structuralism, as well as folklore studies. His first book, *The Morphology of the Folktale* (1928), was first translated into English in

1958. Some of his other writings are collected in his *Theory and History of Folklore* (1984).

TZVETAN TODOROV (born 1939) is Director of Research at the Centre National de la Recherche Scientifique in Paris. A native Bulgarian, he studied at the University of Sofia before moving in 1963 to France, where he became one of the pioneers of literary structuralism. Among his many books translated into English are *The Fantastic* (1973), *The Poetics of Prose* (1977), *Introduction to Poetics*, trans. Richard Howard (Brighton: Harvester, 1981), *Theories of the Symbol*, trans. Catherine Porter (Oxford: Blackwell, 1982), *Mikhail Bakhtin* (1984), *Genres in Discourse* (1990), and *The Morals of History*, trans. Alyson Waters (Minneapolis: University of Minnesota Press, 1995).

YURY TYNYANOV (1894–1943) was a leading Russian Formalist critic, and a distinguished literary historian. After graduating from St Petersburg University, he joined the Society for the Study of Poetic Language (*Opoyaz*), working closely with Viktor Shklovsky, Boris Eikhenbaum and later Roman Jakobson. His collection *Arkhaisty i novatory* (Archaists and innovators) (Leningrad, 1929) combined studies of individual authors and genres with essays on the theory and methodology of literary history; parts have been translated into English. Among his other publications are *The Problem of Verse Language* (1981), essays on film theory, studies of Pushkin, and a number of historical novels and film screenplays.

Further Reading

In keeping with the aims of this anthology, the reading list that follows is restricted to works of general theoretical or methodological interest, mostly in English. For studies of individual genres, helpful guidance is offered by the select bibliographies contained in entries to *The New Princeton Encyclopedia of Poetry and Poetics* (1993), and by other volumes in the Longman Critical Readers series. Useful critical introductions to particular genres can also be found in The Critical Idiom series, currently being replaced by The New Critical Idiom series (Methuen). A number of academic journals regularly publish articles on genres and genre theory: these include *Genre, New Literary History, Poetics, Essays in Poetics*, the French journal *Poétique*, and the Polish journal *Zagadnienia Rodzajów Literackich* (Problems of Literary Genre). The four categories adopted below are purely for convenience; many of the works listed span these divisions.

General

DUBROW, HEATHER, *Genre*, Critical Idiom series (London: Methuen, 1982). Lucid introduction, incorporating brief survey of the history of genre theory.

EHRENPREIS, IRVIN, *The 'Types Approach' to Literature* (New York: King's Crown Press, 1945). Traces the development of genre criticism as a pedagogic tool.

FISHELOV, DAVID, *Metaphors of Genre: The Role of Analogies in Genre Theory* (University Park: Pennsylvania State University Press, 1993). Analyses genre theorists' use of four analogies: literary genres as biological species, as families, as social institutions, as speech acts.

FOWLER, ALASTAIR, *Kinds of Literature: An Introduction to the Theory of Genres and Modes* (Oxford: Clarendon Press, 1982).

—— 'The Future of Genre Theory: Functions and Constructional Types', in *The Future of Literary Theory*, ed. Ralph Cohen (New York: Routledge, 1989).

GENETTE, GÉRARD and TODOROV, TZVETAN, eds, *Théorie des genres* (Paris: Seuil, 1986). Collects six key essays by Genette, Jauss, Scholes, Viëtor, Stempel and Schaeffer.

HEMPFER, KLAUS, *Gattungstheorie* (Munich: W. Fink, 1973). Seeks to clarify and synthesise modern theories of genre.

HERNADI, PAUL, *Beyond Genre: New Directions in Literary Classification* (Ithaca: Cornell University Press, 1972). Wide-ranging survey of post-Romantic genre theory across several languages, with excellent bibliography.

PREMINGER, ALEX and BROGAN, T.V.F., eds, *The New Princeton Encyclopedia of Poetry and Poetics* (Princeton: Princeton University Press, 1993). Reference work incorporating substantial entries, with secondary-reading lists, on all major genres.

STRELKA, JOSEPH P., ed., *Theories of Literary Genre*, Yearbook of Comparative Criticism 8 (University Park: Pennsylvania State University Press, 1978). Essays on specific and general topics in genre theory past and present, by an international list of contributors.

VAN TIEGHEM, PAUL, 'La question des genres littéraires', *Hélicon*, 1 (1938), 95–101.

ZUTSHI, MARGOT, *Literary Theory in Germany: A Study of Genre and Evaluation Theories, 1945–1965* (Bern: Peter Lang, 1981).

Formalist and structuralist approaches

BANN, STEPHEN and BOWLT, JOHN E., eds, *Russian Formalism: A Collection of Articles and Texts in Translation* (Edinburgh: Scottish Academic Press, 1973).

BARAN, HENRYK, ed., *Semiotics and Structuralism: Readings from the Soviet Union* (White Plains, New York: International Arts and Sciences Press, 1976). Soviet structuralist essays from the 1960s and 1970s on genre theory and other topics.

BROOKE-ROSE, CHRISTINE, 'Historical Genres/Theoretical Genres: A Discussion of Todorov on the Fantastic', *New Literary History*, 8 (1976), 143–58.

CORTI, MARIA, *An Introduction to Literary Semiotics*, trans. Margherita Bogat and Allen Mandelbaum (Bloomington: Indiana University Press, 1978). Especially Chapter 5 on 'Literary Genres and Codifications'.

CULLER, JONATHAN, *Structuralist Poetics: Structuralism, Linguistics and the Study of Literature* (London: Routledge and Kegan Paul, 1975). Excellent survey of French structuralism; Part 2 includes Culler's own ideas on genre and 'literary competence'.

—— 'Towards a Theory of Non-Genre Literature', in *Surfiction: Fiction Now . . . and Tomorrow*, ed. Raymond Federman (Chicago: Swallow Press, 1975).

EIKHENBAUM, BORIS, 'The Theory of the "Formal Method" ', in *Russian Formalist Criticism*, ed. Lemon and Reis (1965). Lucid summary and defence of Formalist work by a leading exponent.

ERLICH, VICTOR, *Russian Formalism: History-Doctrine,* 3rd edn (New Haven: Yale University Press, 1981). The standard commentary on Russian Formalism.

FRYE, NORTHROP, 'Myth, Fiction, and Displacement', in Frye, *Fables of Identity: Studies in Poetic Mythology* (New York: Harcourt, Brace and World, 1963).

—— *Anatomy of Criticism: Four Essays* (Princeton: Princeton University Press, 1957).

—— *The Secular Scripture: A Study of the Structure of Romance* (Cambridge, Mass.: Harvard University Press, 1976).

GARVIN, PAUL L., ed. and trans., *A Prague School Reader on Esthetics, Literary Structure, and Style* (Washington: Georgetown University Press, 1964).

GENETTE, GÉRARD, *The Architext: An Introduction*, trans. Jane E. Lewin (Berkeley: University of California Press, 1992).

—— *Fiction and Diction*, trans. Catherine Porter (Ithaca: Cornell University Press, 1993). Extends Genette's analysis of genre into a reconsideration of the notion of 'literariness'.

—— *Paratexts: Thresholds of Interpretation*, trans. Jane E. Lewin (Cambridge: Cambridge University Press, 1997).

—— *Palimpsests: Literature in the Second Degree*, trans. Channa Newman and Claude Doubinsky (Lincoln: University of Nebraska Press, 1998).

GREIMAS, A.-J., *Structural Semantics: An Attempt at a Method*, trans. Daniele McDowell, Ronald Schleifer and Alan Velie (Lincoln: University of Nebraska Press, 1983).

HAWKES, TERENCE, *Structuralism and Semiotics* (London: Methuen, 1977). Introductory survey.

JAKOBSON, ROMAN, *Language in Literature*, ed. Krystyna Pomorska and Roman Jakobson (Cambridge, Mass.: Harvard University Press, 1987). Includes two essays of particular relevance to genre theory: 'The Dominant' and 'Linguistics and Poetics'.

JENNY, LAURENT, 'The Strategy of Form', in *French Literary Theory Today: A Reader*, ed. Tzvetan Todorov, trans. R. Carter (Cambridge: Cambridge University Press, 1982). Important essay on intertextuality and genre.

LEJEUNE, PHILIPPE, 'The Autobiographical Contract', in *French Literary Theory Today: A Reader*, ed. Tzvetan Todorov, trans. R. Carter (Cambridge: Cambridge University Press, 1982).

LEMON, LEE T. and REIS, MARION J., eds and trans., *Russian Formalist Criticism: Four Essays* (Lincoln: University of Nebraska Press, 1965). Essays by Shklovsky, Tomashevsky and Eikhenbaum.

LOTMAN, YURY, *The Structure of the Artistic Text*, trans. Ronald Vroon (Ann Arbor: University of Michigan Press, 1977).

—— *Analysis of the Poetic Text*, ed. and trans. D. Barton Johnson (Ann Arbor: Ardis, 1976).

MATEJKA, LADISLAV and POMORSKA, KRYSTYNA, eds, *Readings in Russian Poetics: Formalist and Structuralist Views* (Cambridge, Mass.: Massachusetts Institute of Technology Press, 1971). Major collection of essays by Eikhenbaum, Shklovsky, Tynyanov, Jakobson, Propp, Bakhtin and others.

MOLINO, JEAN, 'Les genres littéraires', *Poétique*, 24: 93 (1993), 3–27.

MUKAŘOVSKÝ, JAN, *Structure, Sign and Function: Selected Essays*, ed. and trans. John Burbank and Peter Steiner (New Haven: Yale University Press, 1978). Wide-ranging theoretical work by a leading Czech structuralist.

ONEGA, SUSAN and LANDA, JOSÉ ANGEL GARCÍA, *Narratology: An Introduction*, Longman Critical Readers (London: Longman, 1996).

O'TOOLE, L.M. and SHUKMAN, A., eds, *Formalist Theory*, vol. 4 of *Russian Poetics in Translation* (Oxford: Holdan, 1977). Includes extremely useful glossary/anthology of Russian Formalist concepts, and a bibliography of translations.

—— eds, *Formalism: History, Comparison, Genre*, vol. 5 of *Russian Poetics in Translation* (Oxford: Holdan, 1978). Includes miscellaneous Formalist writings on genre.

PIKE, CHRISTOPHER, ed., *The Futurists, the Formalists, and the Marxist Critique* (London: Ink Links, 1979). Includes translations of theoretical work by Eikhenbaum, Tynyanov and others.

PROPP, VLADIMIR, *Morphology of the Folktale*, trans. Laurence Scott, 2nd edn (Austin: University of Texas Press, 1968).

—— *Theory and History of Folklore*, ed. Anatoly Liberman (Minneapolis: University of Minnesota Press, 1984).

SCHAEFFER, JEAN-MARIE, 'Literary Genres and Textual Genericity', trans. Alice Otis, in *The Future of Literary Theory*, ed. Ralph Cohen (New York: Routledge, 1989).

—— 'Du texte au genre: notes sur la problématique générique', in *Théorie des genres*, ed. Genette and Todorov (1986).

SCHOLES, ROBERT, *Structuralism in Literature: An Introduction* (New Haven: Yale University Press, 1974).

SHKLOVSKY, VICTOR, 'Art as Technique', in *Russian Formalist Criticism*, ed. Lemon and Reis (1965).

—— *Theory of Prose*, trans. Benjamin Sher (Elmwood Park, Illinois: Dalkey Archive Press, 1990). Includes several essays on genre: 'The Novel as Parody: Sterne's *Tristram Shandy*', 'Dickens and the Mystery Novel' and 'Literature without a Plot: Rozanov'.

STEINER, PETER, *Russian Formalism: A Metapoetics* (Ithaca: Cornell University Press, 1984).

―― ed., *The Prague School: Selected Writings, 1929–1946* (Austin: University of Texas Press, 1982). Essays in literary structuralism from the Prague Linguistic Circle.

STRIEDTER, JURIJ, *Literary Structure, Evolution and Value: Russian Formalism and Czech Structuralism Reconsidered* (Cambridge, Mass.: Harvard University Press, 1989).

TODOROV, TZVETAN, 'Literary Genres', in *Current Trends in Linguistics*, vol. 12: *Linguistics and Adjacent Arts and Sciences*, ed. Thomas A. Sebeok (The Hague: Mouton, 1974).

―― *The Fantastic: A Structural Approach to a Literary Genre*, trans. Richard Howard (London: Case Western Reserve University Press, 1973).

―― *Genres in Discourse*, trans. Catherine Porter (Cambridge: Cambridge University Press, 1990).

―― *The Poetics of Prose*, trans. Richard Howard (Oxford: Blackwell, 1977).

TOMASHEVSKY, BORIS, 'Literary Genres', in *Formalism: History, Comparison, Genre*, ed. O'Toole and Shukman (1978). Extract from Tomashevsky's *Theory of Literature* summarising Russian Formalist theories of genre.

TYNYANOV, YURY, 'Dostoevsky and Gogol. Towards a Theory of Parody', in *Twentieth-Century Russian Criticism*, ed. Victor Erlich (New Haven: Yale University Press, 1975) (partial translation only).

―― *The Problem of Verse Language*, trans. Michael Sosa and Brent Harvey (Ann Arbor: Ardis, 1981). Includes bibliography of Tynyanov's work.

―― 'On Literary Evolution', in *Readings in Russian Poetics*, ed. Matejka and Pomorska (1971).

―― and JAKOBSON, ROMAN, 'Problems in the Study of Literature and Language', in *Readings in Russian Poetics*, ed. Matejka and Pomorska (1971).

WELLEK, RENÉ, 'Concepts of Form and Structure in Twentieth-Century Criticism', in Wellek, *Concepts of Criticism*, ed. Stephen G. Nichols, Jr (New Haven: Yale University Press, 1973).

―― and WARREN, AUSTIN, *Theory of Literature*, 3rd edn (Harmondsworth: Penguin Books, 1968). Influential postwar textbook; Chapter 17 is devoted to 'Literary Genres'.

WINNER, THOMAS G., 'Structural and Semiotic Genre Theory', in *Theories of Literary Genre*, ed. Strelka (1978).

Historical and sociological approaches

BAKHTIN, MIKHAIL, *The Dialogic Imagination: Four Essays by M.M. Bakhtin*, ed. Michael Holquist, trans. Caryl Emerson and Michael Holquist (Austin: University of Texas Press, 1981).

—— *Problems of Doestoevsky's Poetics*, revised edn, ed. and trans. Caryl Emerson (Minneapolis: University of Minneapolis Press, 1984), esp. Chapter 4.

—— *Speech Genres and Other Late Essays*, ed. Caryl Emerson and Michael Holquist, trans. Vern W. McGee (Austin: University of Texas Press, 1986).

—— 'Supplement: The Problem of Content, Material and Form in Verbal Art', in *Art and Answerability: Early Philosophical Essays by M.M. Bakhtin*, ed. Michael Holquist and Vadim Liapunov (Austin: University of Texas Press, 1990).

—— /MEDVEDEV, PAVEL, *The Formal Method in Literary Scholarship: A Critical Introduction to Sociological Poetics*, trans. Albert J. Wehrle (Cambridge, Mass.: Harvard University Press, 1985). Chapter 7 assesses Russian Formalist theories of genre.

BEHRENS, IRENE, *Die Lehre von der Einteilung der Dichtkunst* (Halle: Niemayer, 1940). Valuable study of the history of genre theory from the sixteenth to the nineteenth centuries, with full bibliography.

BENNETT, TONY, *Formalism and Marxism* (London: Methuen, 1979). Part One offers a revaluation of Russian Formalist theories of literary history.

—— *Outside Literature* (London: Routledge, 1990), esp. Chapter 4: 'The Sociology of Genres: A Critique'.

BRUNETIÈRE, FERDINAND, *L'Évolution des genres dans l'histoire de la littérature* (Paris: Librairie Hachette, 1890).

BURKE, KENNETH, *Attitudes Toward History* (Berkeley: University of California Press, 1937, revised edn 1959). Chapter 2 combines Marxism and psychoanalysis in an innovative theory of 'Poetic Categories'.

BUTTERFIELD, ARDIS, 'Medieval Genres and Modern Genre Theory', *Paragraph*, 13:2 (1990), 184–201.

COHEN, RALPH, 'On the Interrelations of Eighteenth-Century Literary Forms', in *New Approaches to Eighteenth-Century Literature*, ed. Phillip Harth (New York: Columbia University Press, 1974). Overturns many misconceptions about Neoclassical genre theory and practice.

—— 'History and Genre', *New Literary History*, 17:2 (1986), 203–18. General methodological statement with case study.

—— 'Genre Theory, Literary History, and Historical Change', in *Theoretical Issues in Literary History*, ed. David Perkins (Cambridge, Mass.: Harvard University Press, 1991).

COLIE, ROSALIE, *The Resources of Kind: Genre-Theory in the Renaissance*, ed. Barbara K. Lewalski (Berkeley: University of California Press, 1973).

CURRAN, STUART, *Poetic Form and British Romanticsm* (Oxford: Oxford University Press, 1986).

DOLOŽEL, LUBOMÍR, *Occidental Poetics: Tradition and Progress* (Lincoln: University of Nebraska Press, 1990). Brilliant study of the quest for a structural poetics from Aristotle to the twentieth century.

DONOHUE, JAMES J., *The Theory of Literary Kinds: Ancient Classifications of Literature* (Dubuque, Iowa: Loras College Press, 1943). First part of two-volume study of classical genre theory.

—— *The Theory of Literary Kinds: The Ancient Classes of Poetry* (Dubuque, Iowa: Loras College Press, 1949). Second part.

FOHRMANN, JÜRGEN, 'Remarks Towards a Theory of Literary Genres', *Poetics*, 17 (1988), 273–85. Analyses shifting historical conceptions of genre and outlines a new 'functionalist' theory.

FOWLER, ALASTAIR, *A History of English Literature: Forms and Kinds from the Middle Ages to the Present* (Oxford: Blackwell, 1987).

FROW, JOHN, *Marxism and Literary History* (Oxford: Blackwell, 1986). Contains insightful critique of Russian Formalist, Marxist, and other modern theories of genre.

GOLDMANN, LUCIEN, *Towards a Sociology of the Novel* (London: Tavistock, 1975).

—— *Method in the Sociology of Literature*, ed. William Q. Boelhower (Oxford: Blackwell, 1980).

GUILLÉN, CLAUDIO, *Literature as System: Essays Toward the Theory of Literary History* (Princeton: Princeton University Press, 1971). Includes key essays 'On the Uses of Literary Genre', 'Genre and Counter-Genre: The Discovery of the Picaresque', and 'Literature as System'.

HAMLIN, CYRUS, 'The Origins of a Philosophical Genre Theory in German Romanticism', *European Romantic Review*, 5:1 (1994), 3–14.

HODGE, ROBERT, *Literature as Discourse: Textual Strategies in English and History* (Oxford: Polity Press, 1990). Methodological inquiry combining discourse analysis and historicism; Chapter 2 is on 'Genre and Domain'.

JAMESON, FREDRIC, *The Prison-House of Language: A Critical Account of Structuralism and Russian Formalism* (Princeton: Princeton University Press, 1972).

—— *Marxism and Form: Twentieth-Century Dialectical Theories of Literature* (Princeton: Princeton University Press, 1971).

—— *The Political Unconscious: Narrative as a Socially Symbolic Act* (1981; rpt. London: Routledge, 1989).

—— *Postmodernism; or, The Cultural Logic of Late Capitalism* (London: Verso, 1991).

JAUSS, HANS ROBERT, *Toward an Aesthetic of Reception*, trans. Timothy Bahti, with intro. by Paul de Man (Minneapolis: University of Minnesota Press, 1982).

—— *Aesthetic Experience and Literary Hermeneutics* (Minneapolis: University of Minnesota Press, 1982).

KRESS, GUNTHER and THREADGOLD, TERRY, 'Towards a Social Theory of Genre', *Southern Review*, 21:3 (1988), 215–43.

LACOUE-LABARTHE, PHILIPPE and NANCY, JEAN-LUC, *The Literary Absolute: The Theory of Literature in German Romanticism*, trans. Philip Barnard and Cheryl Lester (New York: State University of New York Press, 1988).

LEVINE, GEORGE, ed., *Aesthetics and Ideology* (New Brunswick: Rutgers University Press, 1994). Includes several valuable essays on the ideology of literary forms.

LEWALSKI, BARBARA KIEFER, *Paradise Lost and the Rhetoric of Literary Forms* (Princeton: Princeton University Press, 1985). Exemplary study containing much information on Renaissance genre theory.

—— ed., *Renaissance Genres: Essays on Theory, History and Interpretation* (Cambridge, Mass.: Harvard University Press, 1986).

LINDENBERGER, HERBERT, *The History in Literature: On Value, Genre, Institutions* (New York: Columbia University Press, 1990).

LUKÁCS, GEORG, *The Theory of the Novel: A Historico-philosophical Essay on the Forms of Great Epic Literature*, trans. Anna Bostock (London: Merlin Press, 1978).

—— *The Historical Novel*, trans. Hannah and Stanley Mitchell (Harmondsworth: Penguin Books, 1969). Classic Marxist genre study and methodological statement.

—— 'Notes on the Theory of Literary History', trans. Ian Fairley, in *Comparative Criticism*, vol. 13: *Literature and Science*, ed. E.S. Shaffer (Cambridge: Cambridge University Press, 1991). Important but little-known theoretical essay from Lukács's early phase.

MINNIS, A.J., *Medieval Theory of Authorship: Scholastic Literary Attitudes in the later Middle Ages*, 2nd edn (Aldershot: Wildwood House, 1988). Includes much new information on medieval genre theory.

MORETTI, FRANCO, *Signs Taken for Wonders: Essays in the Sociology of Literary Forms*, trans. David Forgacs (London: Verso, 1983). Essays on Renaissance and modern literature and theory, by a leading Italian Marxist critic.

NISBET, H.B. and RAWSON, CLAUDE, eds, *The Cambridge History of Literary Criticism*, 8 vols projected, 3 so far (Cambridge: Cambridge University Press, 1989–). Invaluable resource for exploring the history of genre theory.

ONG, WALTER, *Orality and Literacy: The Technologising of the Word* (New York: Routledge, 1982). Chapter 6 explores the impact on literary genres of the invention of printing.

PERKINS, DAVID, 'Literary Classifications: How Have They Been Made?', in *Theoretical Issues in Literary History*, ed. David Perkins (Cambridge, Mass.: Harvard University Press, 1991).

PREMINGER, ALEX et al., eds, *Classical and Medieval Literary Criticism: Translations and Interpretations* (New York: Ungar, 1974).

RAJAN, TILLOTAMA, 'Theories of Genre in Romanticism', in *The Cambridge History of Literary Criticism*, vol. 5: *Romanticism*, ed. Ernst Behler and Marsall Brown (Cambridge: Cambridge University Press, forthcoming).

ROUSSEAU, G.S., ed., *Organic Form: The Life of an Idea* (London: Routledge and Kegan Paul, 1972).

SIMPSON, DAVID, ed., *The Origins of Modern Critical Thought: German Aesthetic and Literary Criticism from Lessing to Hegel* (Cambridge: Cambridge University Press, 1989). Contains important writings on genre theory; a selection from a three-volume edition of German criticism.

VIËTOR, KARL, 'Probleme der literarischen Gattungsgeschichte', *Deutsche Vierteljahrsschrift für Literaturwissenschaft und Geistesgeschichte*, 9 (1931), 425–47. Important essay on the history of genre concepts; French translation in *Théorie des genres*, ed. Genette and Todorov.

WEINBERG, BERNARD, *A History of Literary Criticism in the Italian Renaissance*, 2 vols (Chicago: Chicago University Press, 1961).

WEISSTEIN, ULRICH, *Comparative Literature and Literary Theory: Survey and Introduction*, trans. William Riggan (Bloomington: Indiana University Press, 1973). Assesses the role of genre in comparative literary studies, and reviews the history of genre theory.

WELLEK, RENÉ, *A History of Modern Criticism, 1750–1950*, 7 vols so far (New Haven: Yale University Press, 1955–).

—— 'Genre Theory, the Lyric, and *Erlebnis*', in Wellek, *Discriminations: Further Concepts of Criticism* (New Haven: Yale University Press, 1970). On German Romantic genre theory and its intellectual legacy.

WILLIAMS, RAYMOND, *Marxism and Literature* (Oxford: Oxford University Press, 1977). Influential methodological statement; includes section on 'Genres'.

—— *Culture* (Glasgow: Fontana, 1981). Chapter 6, on 'Forms', summarises Williams's ideas on the social history of literary forms, especially drama and the novel.

Other approaches and applications

ALLEN, GRAHAM, *Intertextuality*, New Critical Idiom series (London: Methuen, forthcoming).

ALTMAN, RICK, *Film/Genre* (London: British Film Institute, 1999). Reassesses notions of film genre.

BABBITT, IRVING, *The New Laokoon: An Essay on the Confusion of the Arts* (Boston: Houghton Mifflin, 1910).

BEAUJOUR, MICHEL, 'Genus Universum', *Glyph*, 7 (1980), 15–31. Philosophical analysis of post-Romantic genre theory.

BHATIA, VIJAY K., *Analysing Genre: Language Use in Professional Settings* (London: Longman, 1993). Uses genre theory to model a range of non-literary communication acts.

BLANCHOT, MAURICE, *The Blanchot Reader*, ed. Michael Holland (Oxford: Blackwell, 1995). Includes his influential essay on 'The Disappearance of Literature'.

BLOOM, HAROLD, 'The Internalisation of Quest Romance', in Bloom, *The Ringers in the Tower: Studies in Romantic Tradition* (Chicago: University of Chicago Press, 1971). Though focused on romance, Bloom's quasi-Freudian concept of 'internalisation' is applicable to the development of many other genres.

CAWELTI, JOHN G., 'The Question of Popular Genres', *Journal of Popular Film and Television*, 13:2 (1985), 55–61.

CURTI, LIDIA, *Female Stories, Female Bodies: Narrative, Identity and Representation* (Basingstoke: Macmillan, 1998). Chapter 2 theorises gender and genre.

DERRIDA, JACQUES, *Acts of Literature*, ed. Derek Attridge (New York: Routledge, 1992). Includes the full text of 'The Law of Genre'.

DOTY, WILLIAM, 'The Concept of Genre in Literary Analysis', in *The Genre of the Gospels: Studies in Methodology, Comparative Research, and Compositional Analysis* (Missoula, Mont: Society of Biblical Literature, 1972).

FREADMAN, ANNE, 'Untitled: (On Genre)', *Cultural Studies*, 2:1 (1998), 79–99. Playful exercise in applied linguistics.

GEERTZ, CLIFFORD, 'Blurred Genres: The Refiguration of Social Thought', *American Scholar*, 49:1 (1980), 65–79. Influential essay on the organisation of knowledge, by a leading cultural anthropologist.

GERHART, MARY, *Genre Choices, Gender Questions* (Norman: University of Oklahoma Press, 1992). Assesses combined impact of genre theory and feminism on literary and religious studies.

GILBERT, SANDRA M. and GUBAR, SUSAN, *The Madwoman in the Attic: The Woman Writer and the Nineteenth-Century Literary Imagination* (New Haven: Yale University Press, 1979). Pioneering feminist account of nineteenth-century women's writing, partly focused on the gendering of genre.

Glyph, 7 (1980). Special issue containing papers from an interdisciplinary colloquium on genre held in Strasbourg in 1979; with contributions by Derrida, Beaujour and others.

GOMBRICH, E.H., *Art and Illusion: A Study in the Psychology of Pictorial Representation* (London: Phaidon, 1960). Classic study of artistic perception, with important ramifications for literary genre theory.

GRANT, BARRY KEITH, ed., *Film Genre Reader* (Austin: University of Texas Press, 1986). Anthology of criticism and theory on various film genres.

HAMBURGER, KÄTE, *The Logic of Literature*, 2nd edn, trans. Marilynn J. Rose (Bloomington: Indiana University Press, 1973). Uses the concept of genre to explore the 'concealed logical texture of literature'.

HIRSCH, E.D., Jr, *Validity in Interpretation* (New Haven: Yale University Press, 1967). Influential work in modern hermeneutics, partly resting on a theory of genre.

KOHLER, PIERRE, 'Contribution à une philosophie des genres', *Hélicon*, 1 (1938), 233–44, and 2 (1939), 135–42. Explores cultural and psychological function of genres, partly through the notion of the generic 'contract'.

KRISTEVA, JULIA, *Desire in Language: A Semiotic Approach to Literature and Art*, ed. Leon Roudiez, trans. Thomas Gora et al. (Oxford: Blackwell, 1981). Includes Kristeva's foundational essays on intertextuality.

LEITCH, VINCENT B., '(De)coding (Generic) Discourse', *Genre*, 24:1 (1991), 83–98. Surveys modern developments in genre theory and proposes a post-structuralist refinement.

MILLER, CAROLYN R., 'Genre as Social Action', *Quarterly Journal of Speech*, 70 (1984), 151–67. Combines literary theory and applied linguistics to investigate rhetorical aspects of genre.

NEALE, STEVE, 'Questions of Genre', *Screen*, 31:1 (1990), 45–66. Analyses of the role of genre in film studies.

PERLOFF, MARJORIE, ed., *Postmodern Genres* (Norman: University of Oklahoma Press, 1988). Miscellaneous essays using genre theory to investigate postmodern cultural phenomena.

OLSON, ELDER, 'An Outline of Poetic Theory', in *Critics and Criticism: Ancient and Modern*, ed. R.S. Crane et al. (Chicago: University of Chicago Press, 1952). Outlines the neo-Aristotelian methodology of the Chicago school.

REID, IAN, ed., *The Place of Genre in Learning: Current Debates* (Geelong, Victoria: Deakin University Press, 1987). Essays on the uses of genre in curriculum theory.

ROSENBERG, BETTY, *Genreflecting: A Guide to Reading Interests in Genre Fiction* (Littleton, Colo.: Libraries Unlimited, 1982). On the classification of popular fiction.

ROSMARIN, ADENA, *The Power of Genre* (Minneapolis: University of Minnesota Press, 1985). Extends Hirsch's account of the role of genre in literary interpretation with case studies of the 'mask lyric' and dramatic monologue.

RUTLAND, BARRY, ed., *Genre, Trope, Gender: Essays by Northrop Frye, Linda Hutcheon, Shirley Neuman* (Ottawa: Carleton University Press, 1992).

SCHMIDT, S.J., 'Towards a Constructivist Theory of Media Genre', *Poetics*, 16 (1987), 317–95.

STAIGER, EMIL, *Basic Concepts of Poetics*, trans. Janette C. Hudson and Luanne T. Frank (University Park: Pennsylvania State University Press, 1991). Classic theoretical work on the lyric–epic–dramatic triad.

THREADGOLD, TERRY, 'Talking about Genre: Ideologies and Incompatible Discourses', *Cultural Studies*, 3:1 (1989), 102–27.

WORTON, MICHAEL and STILL, JUDITH, eds, *Intertextuality: Theories and Practice* (Manchester: Manchester University Press, 1990). Several essays touch on questions of genre.

Index

acrostic, 41
Adorno, Theodor, 167
Aeschylus, 154
Afanas'ev, 55, 57, 63, 65
Alabaster, William, 239
Alain-Fournier, 173, 190
Aldus Manutius, 150, 156
Alexandria, Library at, 153, 159
Alfarache, Guzmán de, 237
allegory, 137, 138–9, 141, 163,
    216
almanac, 33, 44
Althusser, Louis, 182
Amis, Martin, 1, 16, 18
Anacreon, 234
anecdote, 41, 57, 94, 241
Annensky, Innokenty, 38
aphorism, 41
apocalypse, 106–7, 115–17
Apuleius, Lucius, 108
Arabian Nights, 105
archaism, 8, 87, 144, 186
archetype, x, 13, 98, 174
archigenre, 213, 216, 227
architext, x, 210–18
Ariosto, Ludovico, 108, 115, 149, 158,
    162, 242
Aristophanes, 159, 168
    Lysistrata, 113
Aristotle, xiii, xiv, 1, 3, 4, 17, 71, 73,
    98, 143, 150, 151, 152, 153, 160,
    161, 169, 210, 211–12, 216, 224,
    227
Armstrong, Nancy, 254
Ashbery, John, 236
Auerbach, Erich, 136–7
Augustine, Saint, 137
Austen, Jane, 258
autobiography, 153, 158, 199, 206–7,
    218, 237
automatization, x, xi, 35–6, 38–9, 132,
    141

Bakhtin, Mikhail, x, xiv, xv, xvi,
    8–11, 15, 16, 17, 18, 30, 68–81,
    82–97, 148, 193–4, 233
ballad, xvi, 26, 120, 122, 125, 194, 199,
    212, 216, 217, 235, 244
    opera, 235
Barnes, Barnaby, 239
Barth, John, 240
Batteux, Charles, 211
Batyushkov, Konstantin, 36
Baudelaire, Charles, 196
    Fleurs du mal, 143
Beckett, Samuel, 240
    Watt, 241
Bembo, Pietro, 161
Beneviste, Emile, 211, 213
Benjamin, Walter, 132, 167
Bennett, Tony, 9, 168
Beowulf, 99, 104, 110
Bergson, Henri, 168
Bertrand, Aloysius, 196
Bible, The, 54, 101–10, 115–16, 135,
    136–7, 238
Bildungsroman, xvi, 233, 253
biography, 137, 155
Bion, 156
Blake, William, 106
    Book of Thel, 111
Blanchot, Maurice, 5, 194–6, 219
Blankenburg, Friedrich von, 74–5
Bloch, Ernst, 167
Bloom, Harold, xii, 99
Boccaccio, Giovanni, 155, 159, 160
    Decameron, 114, 155, 235
Bogatyrev, Petr, 50
Boileau-Despréaux, Nicolas, 71
brachylogia, 235–6
Broch, Hermann, 195
Brontë, Emily, 258
    Wuthering Heights, 184–5
Brooke-Rose, Christine, 194, 208
Browne, Thomas, 157, 236

Fowler, Alastair, xv, xvi, 17, 30, 50,
  118, 149, 232–49
Fracastoro, Girolamo, 160
fragment, 32, 41, 157
Frazer, James, 105
Freud, Sigmund, 106, 169, 182, 187
Frow, John, 9, 30, 168
Frye, Northrop, x, xi, 13, 50, 51,
  98–117, 148, 167, 168, 170–8,
  186–7, 193, 211, 214, 217–18, 233,
  245
function, 7, 18, 32, 52, 85–6, 128, 135,
  137, 141, 143, 148–66, 178–80,
  233, 236–7
Futurism, 36, 39

Gaskell, Elizabeth, 240
Gay, John
  Shepherd's Week, 239
  Trivia, 239
Geertz, Clifford, 16
Gellius, Aulus, 157
gender and genre, 16, 168, 220, 221,
  233, 250–62
genericity, xii, 219, 231
genethliacon, 158, 242
Genette, Gérard, x, xiv, 3, 98, 193,
  210–17, 219, 224–8
genology, xiii, 17
genre-consciousness, xiii, 29, 32
genre fiction, 16
  see also popular fiction
genre-system, xii, xiii, xiv, 3, 7, 8, 29,
  32, 39, 50, 133, 140–2, 148–66,
  200, 210–11
genus universum, 159–60, 166
georgic, 133, 152–3, 157, 234, 236,
  237, 239
Goethe, Johann Wolfgang von, xv, 3,
  12, 68, 77, 211, 212–14
  Faust, 110
  Wilhelm Meister, 74, 75
Gogol, Nikolai, 7
Goldmann, Lucien, 9
Gombrich, E.H., 151
gothic, 253
Gower, John
  Confessio Amantis, 235

Gracq, Julien, 190
Greek Anthology, 153, 234
Greene, Robert
  Friar Bacon and Friar Bungay, 106
Greimas, A.-J., 179–84
Guarini, Giovanni Battista, 153, 160, 161
  Pastor Fido, 149, 151, 158
Guillén, Claudio, ix, 148, 149, 151,
  218, 237

habitualization, x, xi, xiv
  see also automatization
Hamburger, Käte, 213
Hardy, Thomas
  Far from the Madding Crowd, 111
Hauptmann, Gerhart, 71
Hawthorne, Nathaniel
  Blithedale Romance, 113
  Scarlet Letter, 108
Hazlitt, William, 239
Hegel, Georg Wilhelm Friedrich, 4,
  68, 74, 75, 188, 212, 215
Heidegger, Martin, 172
Heine, Heinrich, 43, 71
  Buch der Lieder, 39
Heliodorus, 152
Heraclitus, 157
Herbert, George, 237, 239
Herder, Johann Gottfried, 3
Hernadi, Paul, 2, 99
Herodotus, 160
Herrick, Robert, 242
  Hesperides, 162–3, 166, 236
Hesiod, 110, 160
heteroglossia, 72
hierarchy of genres, x, xi, xii, xiii,
  xiv, xvi, 7, 14, 18, 29–49, 70, 79,
  118, 120–1, 123, 127, 140–2,
  152–3, 154
Hirsch, E.D., 15, 148, 149, 151, 160,
  232–3
historical/theoretical genres, xiv, 99,
  193, 198–9, 217
Hölderlin, Friedrich, 212
Homer, 58, 160, 161–2, 166, 199, 215
Hooft, Pieter Cornelisz, 158–9
Horace, 71, 150, 152, 153, 154, 160,
  165, 235, 236, 237, 243, 244